The Politics of Moral Capital

It is often said that politics is an amoral realm of power and interest in which moral judgment is irrelevant. In this book, by contrast, John Kane argues that people's positive moral judgments of political actors and institutions provide leaders with an important resource, which he christens "moral capital." Negative judgments cause a loss of moral capital which jeopardizes legitimacy and political survival. Studies of several historical and contemporary leaders – Lincoln, de Gaulle, Mandela, Aung San Suu Kyi – illustrate the significance of moral capital for political legitimation, mobilizing support, and the creation of strategic opportunities. In the book's final section, Kane applies his arguments to the American presidency from Kennedy to Clinton. He argues that a moral crisis has afflicted the nation at its mythical heart and has been refracted through and enacted within its central institutions, eroding the moral capital of government and people and undermining the nation's morale.

JOHN KANE is the Head of the School of Politics and Public Policy at Griffith University, Queensland. He has published articles in such journals as *Political Theory*, *NOMOS* and *Telos*, and is also co-editor of *Rethinking Australian Citizenship* (2000).

Contemporary Political Theory

Series Editor
Ian Shapiro

Editorial Board
Russell Hardin   Stephen Holmes   Jeffrey Isaac
John Keane   Elizabeth Kiss   Susan Okin
Phillipe Van Parijs   Philip Pettit

As the twenty-first century begins, major new political challenges have arisen at the same time as some of the most enduring dilemmas of political association remain unresolved. The collapse of communism and the end of the Cold War reflect a victory for democratic and liberal values, yet in many of the Western countries that nurtured those values there are severe problems of urban decay, class and racial conflict, and failing political legitimacy. Enduring global injustice and inequality seem compounded by environmental problems, disease, the oppression of women, racial, ethnic and religious minorities, and the relentless growth of the world's population. In such circumstances, the need for creative thinking about the fundamentals of human political association is manifest. This new series in contemporary political theory is needed to foster such systematic normative reflection.

The series proceeds in the belief that the time is ripe for a reassertion of the importance of problem-driven political theory. It is concerned, that is, with works that are motivated by the impulse to understand, think critically about, and address the problems in the world, rather than issues that are thrown up primarily in academic debate. Books in the series may be interdisciplinary in character, ranging over issues conventionally dealt with in philosophy, law, history and the human sciences. The range of materials and the methods of proceeding should be dictated by the problem at hand, not the conventional debates or disciplinary divisions of academia.

Other books in the series

Ian Shapiro and Casiano Hacker-Cordón (eds.)
Democracy's Value

Ian Shapiro and Casiano Hacker-Cordón (eds.)
Democracy's Edges

Brooke A. Ackerly
Political Theory and Feminist Social Criticism

Clarissa Rile Hayward
De-Facing Power

The Politics of Moral Capital

John Kane

CAMBRIDGE UNIVERSITY PRESS

PUBLISHED BY THE PRESS SYNDICATE OF THE UNIVERSITY OF CAMBRIDGE
The Pitt Building, Trumpington Street, Cambridge, United Kingdom

CAMBRIDGE UNIVERSITY PRESS
The Edinburgh Building, Cambridge CB2 2RU, UK
40 West 20th Street, New York NY 10011-4211, USA
10 Stamford Road, Oakleigh, VIC 3166, Australia
Ruiz de Alarcón 13, 28014 Madrid, Spain
Dock House, The Waterfront, Cape Town 8001, South Africa

http://www.cambridge.org

© John Kane 2001

First published 2001

Printed in the United Kingdom at the University Press, Cambridge

Typeface Plantin 10/12pt   *System* Poltype® [VN]

A catalogue record for this book is available from the British Library

Library of Congress Cataloguing in Publication data
Kane, John.
The politics of moral capital / John Kane.
    p.   cm. – (Contemporary political theory)
Includes bibliographical references and index.
ISBN 0 521 66336 9 – ISBN 0 521 66357 1 (pb.)
1. Legitimacy of governments.   2. Political leadership – Moral and ethical
aspects.   3. Political stability.   4. Trust.   I. Title.   II. Series.

JC328.2.K36 2001
320'.01'1 – dc21   00-066693

ISBN 0 521 66336 9 hardback
ISBN 0 521 66357 1 paperback

For Kay

A man has only one death. That death may be as weighty as Mount T'ai or it may be as light as a goose feather. It all depends on the way he uses it.

Ssu-ma Ch'ien, *Han shu*

Contents

Acknowledgments

This book had its genesis in an undergraduate class I convened as Olmsted Visiting Professor to the Department of Political Science, Yale University in 1996–97. The Olmsteds were benefactors who had funded an Ethics, Politics and Economics program in the department as a means of addressing their concern about an apparent decline in the moral sensibility of national leaders. Their hope was that such a program would stimulate serious reflection on ethics and politics among undergraduates who might one day play significant roles on the political stage. Given the task of devising a suitable course, I thought long and hard about how I might approach the topic in a way that took the moral factor in political life seriously while avoiding naivete or fruitless moralizing.

The idea of moral capital was my solution to the problem, and I proposed it to the class as a concept to be collectively explored rather than as an indicator of knowledge to be mastered. All leapt on it with an energy and intelligence that quite overwhelmed me, and in the process provided me with one of the best teaching experiences of my life. It is to the twenty-two members of that class of '96, then, that I owe my first debt of acknowledgment. It was their boundless enthusiasm, more than anything else, that caused me to believe there might be sufficient interest in the topic to make an extended study worthwhile. It would be invidious to name individual names, but I hope that all will remember with as much pleasure as myself the semester in which we first tested the concept of moral capital on a range of political leaders past and present.

I must also thank colleagues and post-graduate students at Yale for many stimulating discussions in which I was first forced to defend and clarify the notion of moral capital. In particular, I would like to mention Leonard Wantchekon, Eric Patashnik, Rogers Smith, Don Green, Steven Smith, Norma Thompson, Casiano Hacker-Cordón and Courtney Jung. Above all, I must thank Ian Shapiro for his unfailing encouragement and always useful commentary. Back home in Australia, I received further valuable critique from a number of colleagues: Elizabeth van Acker, Patrick Bishop, and especially Haig Patapan, whose generous readings of various drafts and long discussions on the nature of the topic have contributed more to the final shape of this book than any other influence. The responses of Carol Bois, both positive and negative, were also a very significant aid in my attempts to clarify the nature of my authorial task. And I must thank two anonymous Cambridge readers whose penetrating comments improved my appreciation of the problems involved. Whatever virtues the book possesses is due in large part to these people. Its shortcomings are, of course, entirely my own.

A further special debt is owed to Geoff Stokes, without whose unstinting, often selfless encouragement and support over many years this book would never have been written. Finally, I must thank wholeheartedly my beloved wife, Kay, whose belief is constantly nourishing and whose patience has been fortunately endless, and my dear children, Matthew and Philippa, who were amazed it could take me so long to write a single book.

Introduction

During the historic first visit by a US head of state to the new South Africa in March 1998, President Bill Clinton listened to President Nelson Mandela boldly defend an idiosyncratic foreign policy that countenanced friendly relations with Cuba, Libya and Iran, states regarded by the Americans as "pariahs." The US president chuckled indulgently and blandly agreed to disagree on such matters. Clinton, according to *Washington Post* correspondent John Harris, was less interested in foreign policy differences than in basking in the "aura of moral authority that had made Mandela so revered." Clinton went so far as to draw lessons from the Mandela myth for his own critics back home. The South African leader's odyssey from political prisoner to president was, he said, a lesson "in how fundamental goodness and courage and largeness of spirit can prevail over power lust, division and obsessive smallness in politics." The clear reference to the sexual scandals in which Clinton was then currently and apparently endlessly embroiled was, remarkably, not followed up by journalists, who declined to raise a subject that they had determinedly pursued for the previous two months. "It was as if," commented Harris, "the luminescent presence of Mandela . . . had briefly chased away the usual appetite for controversy."[1]

It was a curious meeting. On one side stood a president whose exalted moral status lent his country a profile that its size and struggling, marginal economy scarcely warranted; on the other, a president whose morality was something of an international joke but whose position as the executive head of the United States of America commanded necessary respect. If Mandela's moral standing enabled him to relate (as he insisted) on equal terms with Clinton, and to assert a genuine independence, it was nevertheless clearly gratifying to the South African to be so cordially embraced by the chief of the most powerful nation on earth. And if Clinton, for his part, enjoyed the prestige that preponderant power bestowed, he was nevertheless glad to bask for a while in the cleansing light

[1] *Washington Post*, 28 March 1998, p. A01.

of Mandela's moral halo (and on many a later occasion he would re-kindle this glow by referring to the valuable life-lessons he had learned from Mandela). In short, Mandela, despite his saintly status, was not, and could not be, indifferent to the facts of power, while Clinton, for all his power, could not be indifferent to public perceptions of his moral infirmity.

The connections and divergences between temporal power and moral standing so oddly figured in this meeting mark the central theme of this book. The idea it introduces and examines is that moral reputation inevitably represents a *resource* for political agents and institutions, one that in combination with other familiar political resources enables politi-cal processes, supports political contestants and creates political oppor-tunities. Because politics aims always at political ends, everything about political agents and institutions – including their moral reputation – is inevitably tied to the question of political effectiveness. Virtue, though a fine thing in itself, must in the political arena be weighed for its specifi-cally political value. This political value I explore using the concept of moral capital.

To gain an intuitive, preliminary grasp of the idea, consider the case of George Washington. During the American War for Independence Washington acquired a towering reputation as leader of the victorious revolutionary army. A man of notable dignity and integrity, he proved himself capable, brave, enduring and occasionally daring in the danger-ous fight for political liberty. At the war's end he confirmed his devotion to republican values by expressly turning his back on personal ambition and the temptations of tyranny. Exhorted by some to make himself king, he instead voluntarily disbanded his army (then the only cohesive power in the land) and retired from public life with a vow never to return. A few years later, however, Washington re-entered politics to assist in the founding of the United States, first presiding over the constitutional convention and then agreeing to become the new nation's first president. He had not, however, relinquished his solemn public promise without an agonizing inner struggle. Even more than most public figures of his age, Washington was fastidiously obsessed with "reputation," a thing valued for itself and not for the uses to which it might be put. Thus when called by anxious delegates in 1787 to lend his desperately needed moral author-ity to the convention and its products, he hesitated, fearful that going back on his word might fatally undermine his cherished honor and reputation. A confidante, observing his personal Gethsemane, helped him to his final decision by warning of a deeper danger – that of being thought a man too concerned with reputation.[2]

---

[2] See Richard Brookhiser, "A Man on Horseback," *Atlantic Monthly* (January 1996), pp. 51–64.

This story captures much of the essence of what I intend by use of the term moral capital. Washington showed that a high reputation, because it inclines others toward trust, respect, allegiance, loyalty, or perhaps only forebearance, can be politically invested to achieve things otherwise difficult or even impossible. It is significant, too, that Washington's capital was invested to establish first the moral legitimacy of a nation and later of its primary political office, the presidency. It is part of the argument of this book that there exists a dialectical relationship between the moral capital of political institutions and that of individuals. In the case of established regimes that are widely regarded as legitimate, incumbent individuals generally gain more moral capital from the offices they occupy than they bring to them, but the process always works, in principle, both ways. Loss or gain of personal moral capital will have an effect on the institutional moral capital of an office, and *vice versa*.

Washington was mistaken about the effects of breaking his vow, for the public could see it was broken for honorable purposes. His fears were not, however, unreasonable. He ended his second presidential term a deeply disheartened man, having found that a shining reputation is exceedingly hard to maintain in the strenuously partisan, bitterly competitive, end-driven world of politics. If his foundational actions showed the potential force of moral capital as a political resource, his later experiences revealed its vulnerability.

All politicians, even the most cynical, become intensely aware during their careers of both the value *and* vulnerability of moral capital. Vulnerability is a consequence of the fact that moral capital exists only through people's moral judgments and appraisals and is thus dependent on the perceptions available to them. But perceptions may always be wrong or mistaken and judgments therefore unsound. Furthermore, politicians have a vested interest in manipulating public perceptions to their own advantage, which is why, in the modern age, they seek the help of expert political advisers. They know that to survive the political game they must strive constantly to maintain or enhance their stock of moral capital, to reinstate it when it suffers damage, and to undermine their opponents' supply of it whenever they can. Yet the inevitable gamesmanship involved in this has, in the long run, the contrary effect of undermining the credibility of politicians generally, and arousing public cynicism about political processes. This is the central irony in the search for moral capital that raises a question about whether it can actually exist in politics at all, at least long enough to have any real effects. Part of the aim of this book is to show that – and how – it can and does.

Moral criteria form only a single set among the many that people employ in appraisals that take and retake the measure of human beings and institutions whose actions and attitudes impinge on their lives, whether directly or distantly. But it is with the distinctively moral appraisals that give rise to moral capital in politics that this book is concerned. I must point out at the start, however, the kind of questions about morality and politics that such a focus excludes. The book will not, for example, be analyzing and judging particular political decisions to determine their moral justifiability or lack thereof. Whether the wartime allies did enough to assist victims of the Nazi holocaust; whether America should have dropped the atomic bomb on Japan; whether the United Nations did too little to protect Tutsis from genocide in Rwanda – such questions, important as they are, will not be addressed except insofar as they may have some bearing on a question of moral capital. Moral capital is less concerned with the ethical dimensions of decision-making than (to repeat) with the part played in political contests by people's moral perceptions of political actors, causes, institutions and organizations.

PART I

Moral capital

The term "capital" has been extended beyond its traditional economic usages on several occasions in recent years. The idea of human capital, for instance, has been advanced to encompass those natural and acquired skills and abilities individuals may utilize in pursuing a career, or that firms and nations may employ *en masse* for their profit or development.[1] Because of the central role of knowledge and information in modern economies, some writers point to the importance of intellectual capital as the key to the future success of businesses.[2] Then there is the well-known concept of social capital postulated by Robert Putnam to capture theoretically the social networks of trust that individuals form and which allegedly serve quite broad and beneficial functions.[3] Social capital has been argued, for instance, to be an important determinant of a person's ability to progress upward in a job and to obtain higher rates of pay,[4] and been used to hypothesize significant effects that the "social glue" characteristic of particular societies (the relative tightness and robustness of their social institutions) may have on their political and economic health.[5]

---

[1] R. Burt, "The Social Structure of Competition" in N. Nohria and R. G. Eccles (eds.), *Networks and Organizations: Structure, Form and Action* (Boston, Harvard Business School Press, 1992), pp. 57–91. See also G. Becker, *Human Capital* (New York, National Bureau of Economic Research, 1975); and Rita Asplund (ed.), *Human Capital Formation in an Economic Perspective* (Helsinki, Physica-Verlag, 1994).

[2] See Thomas A. Stewart, *Intellectual Capital: The New Wealth of Organizations* (London, Nicholas Brealey, 1997).

[3] Robert D. Putnam (with Robert Leonardi and Raffaella Y. Nanetti), *Making Democracy Work: Civic Traditions in Modern Italy* (Princeton University Press, 1993).

[4] See Burt, "Social Structure," p. 58; P. V. Marsden and N. Lin (eds.), *Social Structure and Network Analysis* (Beverly Hills, Sage, 1982); and M. Higgins and N. Nohria, "The Side-kick Effect: Mentoring Relationships and the Development of Social Capital," *Working Papers* (Boston, The School, 1994).

[5] John F. Helliwell, "Economic Growth and Social Capital in Asia," *Working Papers* (Cambridge, MA, National Bureau of Economic Research, 1996). See also John F. Helliwell and Robert D. Putnam, "Social Capital and Economic Growth in Italy," *Eastern Economic Journal* 21(3) (1995), pp. 295–307; Robert D. Putnam, "Tuning In, Tuning Out: The Strange Disappearance of Social Capital in America," 1995 Ithiel de Sola Pool Lecture to the American Political Science Association, *PS: Political Science and Politics* 28(4) (December 1995), pp. 664–683; Robert E. Rauch, "Trade and Search: Social

Whatever the merits or otherwise of these postulates, the idea is generally the same: things valuable or pleasurable in themselves – people, knowledge, skills, social relationships – can also be resources that enable the achievement of other social, political or economic ends. The presumption is that people, corporations and societies that develop these forms of capital possess investable resources capable of providing tangible returns. Implicit here is the venerable distinction between wealth and capital. Wealth may be loved for itself, used for consumption or display or hoarded against future calamity, but only when it is invested in some productive enterprise for the sake of profitable returns does it become capital. Mere money, then, is not necessarily financial capital, nor skill necessarily human capital, nor knowledge necessarily intellectual capital, nor a network of social relationships necessarily social capital. They become so only when mobilized for the sake of tangible, exterior returns. Capital, in other words, is wealth in action. The same holds for moral capital. Moral capital is moral prestige – whether of an individual, an organization or a cause – in useful service.

Any capital is inevitably put at hazard in its mobilization, and moral capital as much as any other requires both continuous skill and luck in its maintenance and deployment. This is an important, sometimes ignored, consideration for political resources generally. When people speak of power politics they usually think of big bullies pushing little bullies around, outcomes being determined in the end by the sheer size and strength of the protagonists. Political power, on this view, boils down to the extent (observable, in principle) of the organizational, institutional, economic, electoral or military resources at one's command. And it is no doubt natural enough that we should expect power measured quantitatively to be a decisive factor: as a wise gambler once observed, the race may not always be to the swift, nor the battle to the strong, but that is the safe way to bet. Nevertheless, giant and apparently invulnerable corporations are occasionally brought low by the marketing success of tiny rivals; superpowers sometimes suffer humiliating defeat at the hands of rag-tag colonial armies in small and undeveloped, but canny and tenacious, nations. The strategic use of available resources is often more important than their relative abundance.[6]

As with all resources, so with moral capital. It is not enough to be good, or morally irreproachable, or filled with good intentions, or highly and widely respected. It is necessary to have the political ability to turn

Capital, Sogo Shosha, and Spillovers," *Working Papers* (Cambridge, MA, National Bureau of Economic Research, 1996).

[6] See Alan Stam, *Win, Lose or Draw: Domestic Politics and the Crucible of War* (Ann Arbor, University of Michigan Press, 1996).

moral capital to effective use, and to deploy it in strategic conjunction with those other resources at one's disposal that make up one's total stock of political capital. It may be well or foolishly, fortunately or unfortunately invested, it may bring large returns to oneself or one's enterprise or it may be wasted and dissipated – and in politics there are always opponents with a vested interest in doing everything they can to ensure dissipation. If the utility of moral capital explains why politicians scrabble after it with often unseemly enthusiasm and why they desperately try to staunch its hemorrhaging after a moral slip, the fractiousness and contentiousness of politics explain why, as a resource, it is frequently marked by a peculiar vulnerability. The existence of moral capital depends, I have said, on perceptions, but perceptions can be variously manipulated as the spin doctors who have an interest in manipulating them know well enough. Certainly, it is of no great political benefit to politicians if their finer qualities and actions are concealed from the public gaze, and it may be a benign function of the public relations professional to bring these convincingly to light. Sometimes, though, the appearances in which the professionals deal are only tenuously connected, if at all, to realities.

Nor is it just that leaders and their helpers are liable to deceive us, but that we sometimes lend ourselves too readily to deceit. However hard-headed we pride ourselves on being, it is doubtful that any of our assessments of others (or of ourselves) is ever without a tinge of irrational bias. With respect to our political leaders, we are always susceptible to irrationality of judgment, like ever-hopeful lovers liable to be unduly swayed by an attractive face or flattering attention or seductive words of promise. Generally speaking, we want to find them good and estimable, to find them worthy receptacles of our trust, hopes and aspirations, and, if possible, suitable objects of emotional identification. Our modern cynicism often betrays this wish in the negative guise of one too often disappointed. Yet our disappointment serves to remind us of the force and importance of the moral element in political life, just as do the actions of the spin doctors who strive to manipulate it.

Whatever our cynicism, whatever our gullibility, and whatever the real worth of our moral judgments we continue to make them (one is tempted to say we cannot help but make them), and our judgments continue to have political effects. When they are positive they inspire trust, belief and allegiance that may in turn produce willing acquiescence, obedience, loyalty, support, action, even sacrifice. In other words, they give rise to moral capital, an enabling force in politics for both individual politicians and political institutions. When such judgments become consistently negative, on the other hand, moral capital declines and individuals and organizations face severe problems of legitimacy, perhaps of political survival.

The question is, what *kind* of moral judgment counts in the formation of moral capital in politics? The answer to this is closely bound up with the nature of the political field itself, and how it is possible, despite the difficulties of the terrain, for moral capital to gain any traction there at all. This forms the subject matter of Chapter 1, where I argue that moral end-values are integral to any politics, and that in the perceived relationship of political agents and institutions to these we find the basis for attributions of moral capital. Chapter 2 will then discuss the significance of moral capital for political leaders and their constituencies, and also examine the relationship between personal and institutional moral capital. In closing this chapter, I will outline some things that may be learned from case studies of moral capital in action, thus setting the scene for the remainder of the book.

1   Moral capital and politics

> Friendships that are acquired by a price and not by greatness and nobility of spirit are bought but not owned, and at the proper moment they cannot be spent.
>
> Machiavelli, *The Prince*

Politics is about power, and power has attractions and uses independent of its necessity for achieving legitimate social goals. It is not surprising, then, that one often encounters in the political realm acts of selfish ambition, venality, mendacity and betrayal. What is more, even the best-intentioned players are often forced from the straight and true path by the cruel exigencies of politics, so that ordinary standards of decent conduct are oft more honored in the breach than the observance. Yet the Machiavellian game must be seen to be about something larger than gain, ambition and survival. Political agents and institutions must be seen to serve and to stand for *something* apart from themselves, to achieve *something* beyond merely private ends. They must, in other words, establish a moral grounding. This they do by avowing their service to some set of fundamental values, principles and goals that find a resonant response in significant numbers of people. When such people judge the agent or institution to be both faithful and effective in serving those values and goals, they are likely to bestow some quantum of respect and approval that is of great political benefit to the receiver. This quantum is the agent's moral capital.

Since moral capital thus depends on people's specifically moral appraisals and judgments about political agents and institutions, it must be distinguished from mere popularity. Popularity may, indeed, be based in part on moral appraisals but is very often based on quite other sources of attraction. It is possible to be popular while lacking moral capital, or to possess moral capital while not being particularly popular. Moreover popularity, it is usually assumed, may be bought, while moral capital may not. Like popularity, however, moral capital has genuine political effects. It is a resource that can be employed for legitimating some persons, positions and offices and for delegitimating others, for mobilizing support

and for disarming opposition, for creating and exploiting political opportunities that otherwise would not exist.

It is not, of course, the only resource that can be so used. In the
constantly contested arena of politics, political leverage and political
ascendancy can be gained by a variety of means – an efficient electoral
machine, a surety of numbers in the party or legislature, the support of
key players, occupation of a political office and consequent access to
institutionalized levers of power, the possession of timely intelligence, a
superior organization capable of coherent action, powers of patronage, an
incompetent or divided opposition, a record of success, a booming economy. Such factors make up the stock of what we usually call an agent's
political capital. They are the things to which we ordinarily look when we
seek to understand political processes and outcomes. Moral capital dis-
places none of them but is usually entangled with each of them, for it
generally undergirds all the systems, processes and negotiations of political life. Often, its crucial supportive role is not clearly seen until it is lost
and individuals or institutions face consequent crises of legitimacy and
political survival.

This book, then, uses the concept of moral capital to investigate one
aspect of the real force and movement of moral judgment in political life.
Its theoretical premise is (to reiterate) that politics seeks a necessary
grounding in values and ends, and that people's moral judgments of
political agents and institutions with respect to such values and ends have
important political effects. It thus rejects overly cynical views, both popular and academic, that typically suppose politics to be an inherently
amoral realm. In such views, moral judgments in politics are thought to
be at best naïve and irrelevant, at worst hypocritical and pernicious. Or if
moral judgments are relevant at all, they are understood to be formed
beyond the realm of politics itself and applied to it – forced on it, as it were
– from the outside. The action of politics is conceived to be, in this
respect, akin to the action of markets, whose sole internal principle is the
amoral law of supply and demand. If effective demand exists for slaves,
drugs or child pornography, suppliers will invariably arise to meet it.
When people judge such forms of trafficking immoral or evil, they adopt
an ethical vantage point outside of the market itself; to prevent the trade
they must impose external controls on market forces. But politics, I
argue, is not like the market in this respect. Moral judgment is neither
exterior to nor irrelevant to politics, but intrinsic to it and in principle
inescapable.

Even so, it can scarcely be denied that what might be termed "realist"
or Machiavellian views of politics have considerable force, for they seem
so often to provide convincing descriptions of the way politics actually

works. For it is true that the political environment, even at its mildest, is tough and unforgiving of weakness or excessive scrupulousness. Acknowledging this, I must begin my essay by describing more fully how the field of politics can be understood in such a way as to allow the concept of moral capital genuine purchase.

Politics and legitimacy

Politics is the pursuit of ends. It is about what is to be done, how it is to be done, by whom it is to be done, and with what means it is to be done. It is, in other words, about *policy* – the making of socially directive decisions and the allocation of the resources and instruments necessary to carry them out. The ultimate aim of political competition – inter-personal, inter-party or inter-national – is therefore the control of policy. Political power is the power to determine policy and thus to dispose of social and material resources (including human beings) in certain ways and for certain ends rather than in others. It is also the power to distribute political resources – honors, offices, authority – in particular ways rather than in others. The first end of politically engaged people is therefore to gain command of (or access to) political power in order to control (or influence) the decisions that are made. This involves, on one level, a struggle for personal position among allies and rivals sharing essential aims, and, on another, a contest for political advantage among people with opposed objectives. These political objectives may be either narrowly specific or broadly general. At their broadest, they may aim at the preservation of existing social, political and distributive arrangements, or at their reform and restructuring, or even at their complete dismantlement and replacement (to cover the traditional spectrum from conservatism to revolutionism).

While politics aims at ends, the political process is endless, for life is endless and the possibility of change and challenge always present. Change may be exceedingly slow, permitting islands of historical stability, or it may be very rapid, throwing even long-prevailing social and political relations into flux. Though political action generally strives for stable ends, it necessarily occupies uncertain ground between the existently real and the conceivably possible. Its aim may be preservation of the already existent or, alternatively, its alteration. Thus political ends may embody present interests or may envisage the annihilation of such interests and the creation of altogether new ones (and there is nothing to stop a nihilistic politics from pursuing the extermination of all human interests whatsoever).

Political ends and interests are seldom uncontested, and champions of opposing ends and interests must be either accommodated, neutralized or defeated. Though compromise is possible – and indeed sometimes lauded as a central political virtue – the game is generally played to be won, particular outcomes being determined by the fluctuating balance of political power and the relative exercise of political skill. Compromise – the settling for less than all one wanted – marks an acceptance that opposing forces are too strong to be utterly defeated and too weak to be utterly victorious. Politics is contestation, and contests are about winning and losing, even if wins and losses may often be only partial. This emphasis on competitive action toward ends makes *effectiveness* a key political value. As the good hammer is the one that efficiently drives in nails, the good politician is the one that achieves some reasonable proportion of the ends that he or she intends, promises or deems necessary. But if winning is all, or almost all, in politics then those who are excessively squeamish about means surely do not belong in the game. Losers may cry "foul" when rough means are employed, but once the final whistle has sounded the result will generally stand, leaving outright losers nowhere. In vicious forms of politics, they may be physically annihilated and thus not even live to fight another day. Even in liberal democracies, where consensually accepted, institutionalized limits on political practice usually prevent such vicious outcomes, the principles of end-driven politics remain constant within these constraints.

The basically vulgar emphasis on winning and losing inevitably has a somewhat vulgarizing effect on anything touched by politics. If effectiveness is key, then it follows that everything will tend to be assessed in terms of its value as political capital (capital being, by definition, a resource for the achievement of further ends). Thus moral standing, because it can be as useful a resource as any other, invariably assumes the form of moral capital in politics. In any human enterprise where sound character and dedication are deemed necessary for the effective achievement of common goals, it is natural that moral standing will tend to take the form of moral capital. Problems arise, however, if moral standing starts to be treated as *primarily* a means to further ends. In ordinary life we presume that moral character is a value-in-itself, something that governs both the ends we choose and the means we think it proper to adopt in pursuit of them. Moral character equates with self-respect, and moral standing with public respect, either of which are put at risk when treated mainly as a currency for acquiring other things. We devalue character by commodifying it, and generally deem it a cause for shame and regret to attain some desired end at the expense of our good name. "What profiteth it a man if he gain the whole world and lose his own soul?"

Yet the political version of Jesus' question is surely "What profiteth it a politician if he keep his purity and lose his advantage?" Everything in politics – including moral reputation – is liable to be assessed for its potential as a means for securing political advantage. Political practice, that is, tends to invert the usual order, causing moral characteristics to be judged for their utility rather than for their intrinsic significance. Extreme forms of politics, in which the political realm attempts to swallow up social and private spheres, go even further and deny any intrinsic significance to moral character independently of political action and commitment.

The "all's fair" tendency of competitive political life often evokes cynicism that creates difficulties for any politician seeking moral capital. The politician who attempts to establish a moral reputation *for the sake of* its capital value faces a difficulty akin to that of the salesman. Salesmen seek our trust in order to sell us something, but their need to sell us something undermines trust; politicians seek our respect in order to further their political ends, but their need to further their political ends provokes suspicion and forestalls respect. The honor of politicians having so often proved as hollow as their promises, their reputation as a class has frequently tended to fall, like the salesman's, to the level of the scoundrel or the hypocrite. "Get thee glass eyes," cries Lear, "and like a scurvy politician, seem to see the things thou dost not." The suspicion arises that the entire realm of political action is one where honeyed words and high-sounding phrases cloak raw self-interest, its real driving force.

Raw self-interest may be conceived in terms of power understood as an end-in-itself, as though all politicians were, covertly, megalomaniacal Dr. Dooms bent ludicrously on world domination – and indeed, given the centrality of power to politics this is a possible pathology into which it may fall.[1] Alternatively, the notorious tendency of power to corrupt may lead to the presumption that all who seek power are interested only in feathering their own nests – and certainly cases of institutionalized corruption, occasionally on a spectacular scale, are easy enough to find. More generally, a dominant strand of Western political thought (often labelled "realism" or, latterly, "rational choice theory") is characterized by what might be termed *methodological* cynicism, for it purports to explain all political phenomena by reducing them to the amoral, quasi-mechanical clash and adjustment of rationally pursued, but essentially selfish interests – and who would deny that interests, both individual and collective, are often selfishly asserted and defended in politics?

Were any of these forms of cynicism universally and sincerely adopted,

[1] See Hannah Arendt, *The Origins of Totalitarianism* (London, André Deutsch, 1986), pp. 124–133.

it would be impossible that moral capital could play any genuine role in political life. Yet it does, and not because people are too weak-minded to be constant in either their cynicism or their rational self-interest, or so liable to be misguided by passion that they foolishly fall into indulging hope, trust and a desire for justice. It is merely because no human action and set of human arrangements can ever be placed *in principle* beyond the reach of the moral question – beyond, that is, the demand for justification in general terms. Political action always presumes such justification.

Every claim and counterclaim, charge and countercharge of political debate attests the inescapability of the moral question in politics. The language of political argument is always and inevitably highly moralized (though not necessarily "moralizing"). This is not because politicians are hypocrites, but because the ends of politics must always present themselves as morally justified according to some set of standards or other. Even where politics becomes pathological or corrupt, those seeking power face an urgent political need to justify themselves in general terms. "The strongest man," wrote Rousseau, "is never strong enough to be master all the time, unless he transforms force into right and obedience into duty."[2] Political power can never merely assert itself, but must establish its moral legitimacy and thus, at the same time, the non-legitimacy of actual or potential challengers. The same necessity confronts all interests that assert themselves in the political arena: they must first constitute themselves, at the very least in the eyes of their supporters, as *legitimate* interests, arguing not just the contingent existence of their desires but the rightness and justness of their claims and demands.

This is not a morality that is either prior to or external to an amoral political realm and imposed upon it from without. It is a morality intrinsic to the very idea of politics, for politics must always deal with questions of legitimacy.[3] If politics is the eternal pursuit of ends, it is also the eternal pursuit of legitimacy. When a regime proclaims its legitimacy, it argues that existing structures of society and government, their manner of distributing power, the general ends and interests they encompass, are morally and practically justified. The more generally these claims are accepted (or at least acquiesced in) by the governed, the more stable is the regime.

Yet in the end-driven processes of politics, there is a perpetual tension between the implicit demand for justificatory reasons and the permanent temptation to use any means at hand, including coercive power, to

[2] Jean-Jacques Rousseau, *The Social Contract* (Harmondsworth, Penguin, 1968), Book I, chapter 3, p. 52.
[3] This is the essential point made by Bernard Williams in "Realism and Moralism in Political Theory," paper delivered to Law Society, Yale University, May 1997.

achieve designated ends. Power's ideal is no doubt to have its existing form accepted as unchangeably given by God and Nature, to have legitimacy built in, so to speak, to the very fabric of social and political relations. This has hardly been possible in the West since early modern times, when religious and political dissent, economic expansion and the forces of the Enlightenment cracked the medieval citadel of unified faith. Indeed, as Pratap Mehta has pointed out, it is now hardly possible anywhere, since dissent and demands for reasonable justifications are no longer peculiar to the West but ubiquitous around the world.[4]

Faced with this necessity, power has seldom felt confident enough to rely solely on the strength of rational argument and unforced consent. Indeed, one can offer a generalization that reliance on moral persuasion declines in proportion as a political order succeeds in accruing power and has, consequently, more and different means available for consolidating itself. Power has many traditional ways of maintaining and enlarging itself that do not depend on moral reason but rather on the arousal of motives such as fear, suspicion, envy or greed – for example, military subjection, rigid organization, techniques of divide and rule, the judicious employment of terror, the use of patronage or pork-barreling bribery. Regimes and movements may also try to bind subjects by emotional rather than rational means, for example by fostering love or awe for nation, monarch or party leader.

As for reasonable justification, power frequently acknowledges the need for that in a negative manner, by attempting to control the processes of consent formation and by constraining the ability of the governed to question and criticize. Bureaucratic rule by decree (of the kind anatomized by Kafka), for example, evades justification by creating an atmosphere of absurdity in which people feel themselves the helpless playthings of an arbitrary fate that robs reason of meaning and therefore of political purchase. Totalitarian governments combine ruthless suppression of opposing opinion with indoctrination and the use of terror while building isolating walls round the community to prevent contamination from outside. And even in "open," liberal democratic regimes where "the people" are expected freely to consent to policy and to help choose their governors, and where critical opinion and debate is not just tolerated but in principle encouraged – even here the resources of power are frequently used to monitor, manipulate and channel public opinion so as to manufacture consent.[5]

---

[4] Pratap B. Mehta, "Pluralism after Liberalism?," *Critical Review* 11 (1997), pp. 503–518.
[5] See, for example, an interesting analysis of the manipulation of "public opinion" in Amy Fried, *Muffled Echoes: Oliver North and the Politics of Public Opinion* (New York, Columbia University Press, 1997).

Yet all the crude or ingenious techniques and strategies that attempt to elude or manipulate consent and foster acquiescence attest to the central significance of legitimacy in political life. The problem of legitimacy may be met by offering rationalized justifications or by the manipulative use of power or (usually) some combination of these, but it must be met.

Ideology and moral choice

As well as the perennial tension between justification and coercion, we must note a further significant tension within the notion of political justification itself. This is a tension between the demand for moral certainty and the existence of pervasive rational doubt. The end-driven practice of politics demands conviction and commitment, at least among an activist core, but moral reason cannot, according to modern thinking, provide the level of certainty that such conviction demands. In a world no longer squarely anchored in universally recognized ultimate foundations, any attempted legitimation is always potentially vulnerable to someone else's delegitimation, one's own certainties are always challenged by the incompatible certainties of others. The temptation is to claim that one's political commitments are somehow uniquely, objectively grounded in reality, therefore undeniable, not a matter of moral choice at all but of mere rationality. This stratagem lends a certain repressive, totalitarian air to even "moderate" political discourse.

It is a tendency that can be most clearly seen in the *ideologies* which, in self-conscious modern times, have been the principal vehicles for political end-values. Ideologies can be described as structures of argument and explanation that assert a set of political values, principles, programs and strategies allegedly deduced from arguments about religion, metaphysics, history, sociology, humanity, economics or justice. Though ideologies thus typically offer responses to philosophical, theological and social-scientific questions, ideological thought does not constitute a form of pure rational inquiry. Its descriptive claims are never disinterested. However elaborately ideologies may be supported by rational argument, they generally present their prescriptions as dogmas, political articles of faith, rather than invitations to further examination. This is precisely because political practice requires not dispassionate inquiry but sincere, usually passionate commitment. Ideology is, in other words, a vehicle of value more than of knowledge, geared not to contemplation but to an effective practice that must feel itself sufficiently assured of its own rightness. It must provide the moral force of legitimation without which political practice founders in a puzzlement of will. It demands a finality and certainty that is foreign to the kind of inquiry in which questions of fact and value may always be reopened for rational scrutiny (where, indeed, certainty about both, or about the possibility of deriving unquestionable values from facts, is taken to be intrinsically problematical). It is not endless doubt and openness that an ideology needs in order to be effective, but conviction and closure.

Liberal ideologies might seem to be the exception here, for they tend to emphasize principles that are congruent with those of pure intellectual inquiry – toleration of variety of opinion, freedom of speech, and suspension of judgement in value matters. Yet the "ifs," "buts" and "on the other hands" of intellectual debate simply will not serve to get the vote out in a liberal democracy. Such a form of government can be seen as institutionalizing a consensually agreed principle superior to all ideologies and intended to tame and civilize the conflict between them. Democratic governance and the rule of law put constraints on the contestants and set limits to acceptable political behavior. The liberal democratic regime acts, so to speak, as the moral character of the polity, governing the political means that may be employed and also determining, to some extent, what may be regarded as acceptable ends (forbidding, for example, the destruction of democracy and the rule of law). Within this principled consensus, however, political action still requires certainty of purpose and commitment. There is always much at stake in a political contest, and constantly to defer or withhold judgment is to condemn oneself to political sterility.

Omnipresent doubt combined with the need for certainty causes ideologies to present their normative prescriptions not as choices to be made in the light of reasonable argument about values and goals, but as matters of *necessity*. The message tends to be that opposition is less a matter of reasonable disagreement than of downright irrationality. In fact, there is a strong tendency for political positions making the necessity argument to claim that they are not ideological at all, the label "ideology" being reserved for opposing views that somehow fail to see the objective necessity indicated. Here the term ideology, in addition to implying a politically ordered program, is freighted with the pejorative meaning of "false consciousness" given it by Marx. Opposing arguments are refuted by relativizing them, that is, by alleging that they are not a product of reason but of deterministic social and historical forces – thus conservative values express the social conditioning of an aristocratic class, liberal values the particular interests of a mercantile order, and so on. The contrasting objective "necessity" of one's own position may be founded on any of several bases – "scientific" rationality, an inexorable historical progress, the irresistible force of nature, inevitable economic development, or plain "common sense." Such arguments may come, what is more, from the economistic Right, the technocratic Center or the revolutionary Left. Marxism may, for example, spring most immediately to mind when historical necessity is mentioned, but the doctrine is equally evident in neo-liberal responses to the globalizing market. It was Margaret Thatcher, after all, who coined the acronym TINA ("there is no alternative") as the motto of her reforming New Right government. It was a dogma that received theoretical expression in the liberal triumphalism of Francis Fukuyama when he proclaimed that the fall of communism marked the "end of history." Fukuyama argued that the market was the most "natural" form of economic organization and that "the logic of modern natural science would seem to dictate a universal evolution in the direction of capitalism." The only opposition he could conceive to a univerally triumphant, "rational" capitalist order was the *irrational* opposition of history's "last men" (a concept borrowed from Nietzsche) who, bored with material plenty and peace, would want to drag the world back into history, warfare and squabbling.[6]

Such rhetorical tactics, as well as a means of disarming opposition, are an attempt to evade modern doubts about the possibility of deriving any certain moral position from any set of asserted "facts" – that is to say, of getting an objectively prescriptive "ought" out of an objectively descriptive "is." The tendency has been to collapse the two categories together and regard imperatives for action as somehow inscribed in the very fabric of descriptive reality.[7] If "is" and "ought" are indistinguishable, then action will follow automatically from a correct understanding of reality and obviate the need for moral deliberation and choice. This was the idea at the heart of Marx's famous unity of theory and practice,[8] but it can also be found in the conservative philosophy of Michael Oakeshott who argued that, in intelligent, unselfconscious practice within a living political tradition, "there is, strictly speaking, no such experience as moral choice."[9]

Mutually contradictory necessities tend, of course, to cancel each other out and raise suspicion about all such assertions. Claims that political consent and commitment follow automatically and unproblematically from "correct" understandings of reality beg too many questions to be taken seriously. Since I assume that the possibility of moral capital is

---

[6] Francis Fukuyama, *The End of History and the Last Man* (London, Hamish Hamilton, 1992), pp. xv and 312.
[7] For an excellent analysis on these lines, see Bernard Susser, *The Grammar of Modern Ideology* (London, Routledge, 1988).
[8] See my "The End of Morality? Theory, Practice, and the 'Realistic Outlook' of Karl Marx," *NOMOS XXXVII: Theory and Practice* (New York University Press, 1995), pp. 403–439.
[9] Michael Oakeshott, *On Human Conduct* (Oxford, Clarendon Press, 1975), p. 79.

based on the reality of moral judgment and moral commitment and therefore the possibility of moral choice, it is important to stress the falsity of all necessitarian arguments. The real nature of political commitment is always moral – a moral commitment to particular ends believed legitimate or valuable and inevitably also to other people with whom one shares such beliefs. The free moral character of political-ideological commitment is evident from the behavior even of determined ideologues who deny altogether the authenticity of moral language and thought, and also from their treatment of colleagues who have strayed from their allegiances. Consider the typically contrasting consequences of a change in pure intellectual belief, say in science, and of a corresponding shift in political allegiance. It is no doubt painful for a researcher if a long-cherished scientific theory is authoritatively overturned by new evidence, for it may have been at the core of a whole structure of belief, not to mention of a career. But the morally culpable course here would be to resist, for exterior motives, the adjustment of one's beliefs. A corresponding shift in political allegiance following a sincere alteration of belief, on the other hand, inevitably courts accusations of treachery.

The frequency of charges of betrayal and "selling out" reminds us that the point in politics is not just to bind oneself to beliefs about values and ends, but to bind oneself *faithfully*. I take this notion of faithful service to be the main hook to which moral capital attaches. Morality presumes moral choice, an identification of values argued to be worth defending or pursuing and directions held to be worth taking. Moral capital is credited to political agents on the basis of the perceived merits of the values and ends they serve and of their practical fidelity in pursuing them. It is only thus that the breed of "scurvy politicians" is redeemed if it is redeemed at all. Embarked on an ever-treacherous sea, politicians are forced to tack and trim and alter course, sometimes to lighten a leaky craft by abandoning a precious cargo of solemn promises, even to deal with the devil himself if that is the only way to make headway. But if they can keep their enterprise afloat and hold some sense of true direction toward the destination which alone justified the risky voyage, they will sometimes be rewarded with a reputation that enhances their political influence and effect.

Moral capital and moral ends

The end-driven nature of politics means that fidelity to professed values and goals must always be tied to effectiveness or, to put it another way, that character must be tied to political skill and *vice versa*.[10] Being a saint

[10] See Erwin C. Hargrove, *The President as Leader: Appealing to the Better Angels of Our Nature* (Lawrence, University Press of Kansas, 1998), p. 180.

in politics is meaningless unless goodness is combined with the skill to achieve goals that others judge valuable. Even personal integrity, however fine in itself, is seldom enough in politics. A reputation for integrity, absent skill or ungirded by some larger principled commitment, can be easily destroyed amid the inevitable maneuvers, bargains and discarded promises of politics. Deviations and compromises are forgivable, even acceptable, however, where the compromiser is visibly, ably and consist-ently committed to particular goals and principles. Tactical retreats and digressions are legitimate if they are clearly for the sake of such larger ends. Because politics is end-driven practice, it is only in faithful commit-ment and effective practice over the long term that political players can expect to gain the moral credit that will sustain them among their col-leagues, their followers and even their opponents, and thus solve that plaguing dilemma of the salesman mentioned above. But what must be the nature of the ends that thus give rise to moral capital?

"Politics is the pursuit of ends; decent politics is the pursuit of decent ends," wrote Leo Strauss, adding that "The responsible and clear dis-tinction between ends which are decent and ends which are not is in a way presupposed by politics. It surely transcends politics."[11] Strauss claimed that the task of identifying eternally valid "decent" ends belonged to a small class of classically oriented, great-souled philosophers whose purity of purpose, largeness of mind and contemplative training placed them above the conflicting ideological opinions generated by opposed interests and allowed them to discern deep and enduring philosophical "truths." Whether such a condescending class exists, and whether it could effec-tively influence the denizens of the political realm even if it did, are debatable points. Strauss, at any rate, points to an important question for a study of moral capital in politics, namely: must the investigator express or imply a view of what constitutes a properly moral (or "decent") political end if he or she is to identify genuine instances of the phenom-enon? It goes without saying that in all political contests each side argues the rightness of its own position and wins support on this differential basis. The ends to which politics may be put are very numerous and often incompatible even within a single culture, never mind from culture to culture.

For one species of ends – the venal – this is scarcely a problem. Though the rhetoric of politicians generally centers on values and principles, their practice may descend to the level of selfish competition and grubby deals that have nothing to do with the wider goals that found their political legitimacy. It hardly matters what values are proclaimed and betrayed;

[11] Leo Strauss, *Liberalism Ancient and Modern* (New York, Basic Books, 1968), p. 13.

hypocrisy is always vulnerable to immanent critique which, by revealing the disparity between word and action, morally undermines the hypocrite. Regimes given over to such hypocritical practices forfeit moral capital and soon begin to lose their legitimacy in the eyes of their own constituents. Much more serious for the current project than the sometime ascendancy of selfishness and hypocrisy, however, is the extreme diversity of political ends that may be asserted and pursued with perfect moral sincerity. Since moral capital comes into being only through the judgments of people persuaded that a cause or party or person is morally right or morally inspired, it will exist wherever people may be so persuaded, whatever the content of the moral views. In a world unmoored from certain, divinely ordained foundations, the greatest danger is therefore less the exercise of an amoral, irresponsible freedom than the freedom to conceive of any end at all as moral and any means toward it as right.

The totalitarian movements of the twentieth century constituted a limiting case that proved conclusively there is no inherent restriction on what might be adopted as a political end and no necessary limit to the ruthless means that might be employed in achieving it. They showed that it was possible to conceive and carry out the destruction not just of a particular legal and political system, but of the nation state itself, of laws as such, of whole bureaucratic structures, of whole social classes and entire categories of people defined by race, nationality or state of health, and to eliminate any activity pursued independently for its own sake (even chess!) that might undermine an individual's total subjection to totalizing power.[12] And for the most part, the initiators of totalitarian rule pursued their aims in the name of some grand moral imperative – the Aryan domination of the sub-human races of the world or the final establishment of pure socialist equality. There is no doubt that Hitler regarded the goal of racial domination which produced his murderous policies towards Jews and other groups as a moral imperative; indeed, he thought himself a moral hero for undertaking a dirty but necessary task that few others could stomach.[13] A core of Nazi functionaries certainly regarded the programs of euthanasia, deportation and extermination, even when these progressed at the expense of the war effort, as "ethical" necessities.[14] There is no doubt, either, that millions of Germans were responsive to such claims.[15] Even the doctrine of destruction which was

[12] Arendt, *The Origins of Totalitarianism*, p. 322.
[13] See Adolf Hitler, *Mein Kampf* (London, Hutchinson, 1969), p. 46.
[14] Arendt, *The Origins of Totalitarianism*, p. 429.
[15] This appears to be an implication of the controversial book by Daniel Jonah Goldhagen, *Hitler's Willing Executioners: Ordinary Germans and the Holocaust* (New York, Knopf, 1996).

such a feature of Nazi ideology had moral appeal for people in 1930s Germany, who desired nothing more than the destruction of a social-political regime characterized by hypocrisy and ineffectuality, whose last shred of legitimacy had been stripped in the crises of the 1920s.

It may thus have been a savage morality that Hitler embodied but it was formally a morality nonetheless, and insofar as he won approval and devotion partly on the strength of it he must be taken as showing, in his terrible way, the potential power of moral capital in politics. Certainly, no one could fault his fanatical commitment nor his political effectiveness. It is also true, of course, that it is impossible, when one is not under the thralldom either of bitter despair or of totalitarian power, to find Nazi morality rationally intelligible. Such moralities are able to persuade deeply disgruntled people of the good of evil policies, or rather that doing good for oneself and one's kind requires doing great evil to one's enemies, however arbitrarily defined. This is only to make the point that the quality of our moral judgments about leaders, parties and policies implies at the same time a judgment on ourselves and the manner in which our own moral capacities may be affected by our fears, anxieties, prejudices and desires. A sometime tendency (notably in America) to distinguish a populace that is by definition virtuous from a political elite that is invariably corrupt, radically falsifies the reality of the interrelationship between governors and governed, leaders and led. As Machiavelli noted, it is not just princes that may be "corrupt" and "corruptible," but whole populations.[16] The possibility of the demagoguery that shadows democratic politics attests to the ubiquitous existence of baser impulses that, rather than what Lincoln called "the better angels of our nature," may be tapped by unscrupulous politicians capable of gracing sordid desires with a mask of seeming virtue. They provide the opportunity for what in contemporary parlance is called wedge politics, the technique of dividing electorates by creating scapegoats and hate objects on the basis of categories such as race, receipt of welfare, religion and so on – human caricatures that, as Joseph McCarthy (a master of wedge politics) said, dramatize the difference between Them and Us.

It is also true that all political movements of a totalitarian tendency end up subverting the capacity for free moral judgment that is the essential condition for the formation of moral capital. Whatever reliance the famous totalitarian leaders placed on moral appeals on their way to power, once power was achieved their aim was to paralyze the ability of their populations to think in properly moral ways at all. This they achieved through ruthless indoctrination, terror and the consolidation of a social-

---

[16] Machiavelli, *The Discourses* (Harmondsworth, Pelican, 1970), Book I, Discourses 16–18, pp. 153–164.

political organization that determined people's effective reality. The role of the absolutely obedient individual was neither to understand nor to judge, but blindly and selflessly to do. All manifestations of individual initiative or independent thought and action had to be ruthlessly expunged. Even sincere commitment to the regime and its goals became suspect insofar as it denoted an independent will. The basis of all social trust between individual and individual was destroyed as each person (merely by virtue of having a capacity to think and therefore to change his or her mind) was turned into a potential suspect, every neighbor into a perpetual spy. The result was the production of morally incapacitated human beings who would accept the commission of huge evils and even help to operate the engines of extermination provided evil was routinized as a duty attached to an ordinary job.

The suffocating leader worship characteristic of totalitarian masses, intentionally fostered by the "cult of personality," is a manifestation and function of this curtailment of moral freedom and moral sensibility. It cannot be identified with the free grant of moral capital which it is the intention of this book to analyze. For moral capital to be a political phenomenon worthy of study, we must assume that people are capable of making relatively unforced judgments about the worth and rightness of political values and goals, as well as of the fidelity, sincerity and effectiveness of political actors and organizations who embody and pursue these goals; and, further, these judgments must be deemed capable of political effect insofar as they underpin allegiance, loyalty and service to persons, causes and parties. One might say, indeed, that moral capital operates in a political system in inverse proportion to that system's use of extrinsic power to engineer submission, loyalty and belief.

No hard and fast line can be drawn here, however, and one may rather assume a spectrum of possibilities. On the one end, even totalitarian regimes (which can be cultural-religious as well as political) preserve some overarching moral ideal that serves to legitimate the domination they practice; on the other, even the most open and democratic systems use power, as we have noted, to influence belief in more or less subtle ways. Many contemporary writers rely on such a principle to argue that power produces its own reality in our liberal democracies just as surely as in totalitarian regimes, so that the apparently free assent of individuals to their own domination is explicable in terms of social coercion.[17] (Bernard

---

[17] For example, Michel Foucault's claim that "truth" is an effect of systems of power: "Truth and Power," in Paul Rabinow (ed.), *The Foucault Reader* (Harmondsworth, Penguin, 1984), pp. 51–75. See also Catharine A. MacKinnon, *Toward a Feminist Theory of the State* (Cambridge, MA, Harvard University Press, 1989), p. 237: "The force underpins the legitimacy as the legitimacy conceals the force." This is a form of critique traceable to Marx, of course, but beyond him to Jean-Jacques Rousseau who, in the *Social*

Williams has formulated the general type of this argument as a "critical theory principle," which states that "the acceptance of a justification does not count if the acceptance itself is produced by the coercive power which is supposedly being justified.")[18] It is also true, on a more mundane level, that all political systems need to instill their values in the populace, and what we in Western countries call "civics" or "political education" can seldom be wholly distinguished from indoctrination. Moreover, the legions of propagandists, spin doctors and vested interests reveal the power of money and technique to manipulate the opinion of a populace who often tend anyway to "like not with their judgment, but their eyes." We need not assume, therefore, that we can always simply differentiate in practice values irrationally inculcated and values rationally adopted.

Despite this, it would be foolish to deny the reality and importance of choice. In non-totalitarian environments there is generally a fairly wide range of moral positions actively competing for attention and allegiance as well as a permanent battle engaged for the enlargement of the sphere of genuine deliberation. We must take seriously the existence of leaders and would-be leaders, parties, causes and movements who cannot simply command obedience but must win and maintain support, at least in part on the strength of their expression of and service to principled goals and commitments. If moral capital is a genuine political resource then it is one based more on an attractive than on a compulsive power. Therefore, though it is impossible to put a limit on what people may be persuaded are moral ends worth struggling for, I intend to limit my inquiry here to values and ends that can be broadly characterized as "decent." By this I mean ends capable in principle of dispassionate assessment and affirmation (even if one does not in fact affirm them), whose general acceptance is explicable in terms of intrinsic moral appeal rather than dependent on a sociological-psychological analysis of the acceptor.

Having introduced this element of "bias" into my study, it does not follow that it is either possible or necessary to provide a definitive list of decent ends and values that alone may form a proper basis for moral capital. That would be absurd, since even decent ends non-coercively chosen are infinitely contestable and liable to conflict. Think, for example, of the inherent tension between the values of freedom and order which different people try, in good faith, and sometimes in quite different circumstances, to resolve in quite different ways. More than that, moral argument in politics is very often about the proper *means* to ends rather than about "decent ends" as such, and evil can be done as readily in the

---

Contract (Harmondsworth, Penguin, 1986), pp. 51–52, explains the slave's acceptance of the rightness of slavery in such terms.
[18] Bernard Williams, "Realism and Moralism in Political Theory," p. 10.

name of genuine good as in the name of a perverted goal. Indeed, the tragedy is more poignant when zealotry subverts decent aims. "The ardour of undisciplined benevolence seduces us into malignity," as Coleridge said, writing of Robespierre, leading us into "the dangerous and gigantic error of making certain evil the means to contingent good."[19] Yet there can often be genuine doubt in this matter that is not easily settled. Malcolm X and Martin Luther King both sought the liberation of black Americans, but one argued the necessity of violent resistance and separation, the other of peaceful protest and integration. Both attracted adherents who believed the superior argument lay with their own movement.

As Max Weber put it, "the ultimately possible attitudes toward life are irreconcilable, and hence their struggle can never be brought to a final conclusion. Thus it is necessary to make a decisive choice."[20] The play of moral capital in politics is most clearly seen in the contest between alternative and conflicting choices.

[19] Samuel Taylor Coleridge, *Introductory Address, Addresses to the People* (London, no publisher named, 1938), p. 32.
[20] Max Weber, "Science as a Vocation," in H. H. Gerth and C. Wright Mills (eds.), *From Max Weber* (London, Routledge, 1970), p. 152.

2   Moral capital and leadership

> He was more concerned to be a good man than to be thought one; and so the less he courted fame, the more did it attend his steps unsought.
>
> Sallust (on Cato), *Conspiracy of Catiline*

In the following chapters I will be looking at the politics of moral capital largely through the prism of leadership. Leaders generally form a significant repository of trust for those whose interests they try to advance, or whose causes they actively and symbolically represent, or in whom they have inspired some ideal to be realized. It is in studies of leadership, or in political biographies, that students of politics most commonly address the subject that I here label moral capital, usually under the banner "moral authority" or "moral character." (During electoral campaigns, it arises as "the character issue.") It is often clear from leadership studies that the perceived character of a person along with assessment of their general leadership competence is a significant factor in the way they are appraised and dealt with, not only by supporters and followers, but even by political opponents.[1] Genuine respect facilitates the achievement of political goals, while its absence or loss may make it impossibly difficult to gain even trivial ends.

My purpose is not, however, that of most leadership studies which try to define kinds or qualities of leadership and the conditions under which they are likely to emerge. I am not interested – except incidentally as it may touch on the moral factor in leadership – in whether leadership is best understood as a matter of the possession of certain physical and psychological traits, or as an expression of different behavioral styles, or the result of the contingent situational contexts in which leadership emerges, or as a causative process through which "charismatic" individuals influence followers and subordinates.[2] I study certain leaders in

---

[1] See, e.g., Martin Benjamin, *Splitting the Difference: Compromise and Integrity in Ethics and Politics* (Lawrence, University Press of Kansas, 1990), chapter 6.

[2] On trait theory, see, e.g., R. Stogdill, *Handbook of Leadership* (New York, Free Press, 1974); and J. Conger, *Learning to Lead* (San Francisco, Jossey-Bass, 1992); on behavioral theory, see R. White and R. Lippitt, *Autocracy and Democracy: An Experimental Inquiry*

order to understand the workings of moral capital in politics, not to investigate the nature of leadership as such. Nevertheless, some general points relevant to my enterprise may be derived from the leadership literature.

Leadership: the moral dimension

The first is the general recognition of the noncoercive, reciprocal nature of the relationship between leaders and followers, or between leaders and (to use a less loaded term) constituents. Leadership may involve the use of power but cannot be reduced to an exercise of power, for it relies crucially on persuasion. Though political leaders may occupy positions of official authority, acts of leadership are not authoritative commands since constituents are not subordinates. Leaders are inevitably symbols, with the top leader of a community or nation symbolizing the group's collective identity and continuity. Leadership is thus generally distinguished from management, partly on account of this symbolic role and partly on the grounds that the leaders are less tightly linked to an organization than are managers – and indeed some leaders may not be attached to any organization at all.[3]

The relative freedom of both political leaders and constituents means that the relationship between them must generally be one of confidence and trust and not of coercion. I have stated that for moral capital to exist it must have attractive and not compulsive power, that people must be relatively free to judge for themselves and to exhibit uncoerced moral consent. This is congruent with James MacGregor Burns' definition: "Leadership over human beings is exercised when persons with certain motives and purposes mobilize, in competition or conflict with others, institutional, political, psychological, and other resources so as to arouse, engage, and satisfy the motives of followers."[4] Moral capital may be conveniently thought to be included among the "other resources" noted here.

It was in fact Burns among modern leadership theorists who drew specific attention to the moral dimensions of leadership. He distinguished two forms of political leadership apt for different conditions, the *transactional* and the *transforming*. Transactional leaders are effective horse-

---

(New York, Harper, 1960); and R. Likert, *Human Organization* (New York, McGraw-Hill, 1967); on contingency theory, see F. Fiedler, *A Theory of Leadership Effectiveness* (New York, McGraw-Hill, 1967); on charismatic or transformational theory, see B. Bass, *Performance Beyond Expectations* (New York, Free Press, 1985); and A. Bryman, *Charisma and Leadership in Organizations* (London, Sage, 1992).

[3] John W. Gardner, *On Leadership* (New York, The Free Press, 1990), pp. 2–3 and 18.
[4] James MacGregor Burns, *Leadership* (New York, Harper Colophon, 1978), p. 18.

traders, brokering deals between various interests represented by groups, factions or parties. Typical of transactional leaders are those who dominate the processes of complex legislatures like the American Congress. They are means-dominated, *status quo* politicians who operate as insiders within a pluralistic political environment, and for their leadership to work they must observe what Burns calls *modal values* – honesty, responsibility, fairness and the honoring of commitments. Transformational leaders, on the other hand, attempt to alter the *status quo* and create a new political culture. To do this they must be teachers who can elevate the motives, values and goals of followers, uniting their particular interests in the pursuit of "higher" goals. The values of transformational leaders are *end-values*, like liberty, justice and equality.[5]

Burns' distinction recalls an earlier one made by Max Weber, who was also concerned with the moral dimensions (and indeed the moral dilemmas) of political leadership. Weber observed a dichotomy in politics between what he called an ethic of responsibility and an ethic of ultimate ends, the former characterizing what can be broadly termed pragmatic politics and the latter a "politics of conviction." These were Weberian "ideal-types" of political action, as performed, on the one hand, by the responsible leader who takes a relativistic view of a complex world and prudentially weighs action, goals, means and foreseeable consequences with cautious care; and, on the other, by the leader of conviction who is so blinded by the absolute value of ultimate ends as to be largely indifferent to the actual present consequences of action. Burns, without noting the parallel of Weber's dualistic categorization to his own, argues that the danger of the politics of responsibility is that it can lead to values so hopelessly fragmented and relativized as to be able to justify anything, thus cloaking hypocrisy and opportunism in undeserved moral raiment. Conviction politicians, by contrast, are dangerous because of their fanatical devotion to a single millenarian end-value that is both indifferent to and destructive of other values. Burns observes (again without noting the applicability of the argument to his own dichotomization) that this dualism is oversimplified, and that most leaders and followers in fact shift back and forth from specific, self-involved values to broader, public-involved ones. He argues that the ethic of responsibility is really the considered, day-to-day application of the "ethic of ultimate ends" to complex circumstance.[6]

This view is in fact identical to that which Weber himself defended. He argued that the ethic of ultimate ends and the ethic of responsibility are not absolute contrasts, but supplements, which only in unison can

---

[5] Burns, *Leadership*, p. 426.   [6] *Ibid.*, p. 46.

constitute a man with a genuine "calling for politics."[7] The potential barrenness of pragmatic, instrumental politics is redeemed by a passionate, vitalizing attachment to valued ends; the irresponsibility of a passionate conviction that dispenses with scruples in its drive to power is defeated by a constant concern to appraise and reappraise both means and consequences. This difficult synthesis of realism and idealism is necessary for Weber because of the tragic element he discerns in all politics. Politicians, he argues, operate within a world that is ethically irrational, where the consequences of action even for "good" ends are inherently unpredictable. Moreover, it is impossible to dodge the fact, he says, that all political action is ultimately sanctioned by the use of force, and consequently that attaining good political ends requires a willingness to pay the price of using morally dubious means. "From no ethics in the world," he wrote, "can it be concluded when and to what extent the ethically good purpose 'justifies' the ethically dangerous means and ramifications."[8] The responsible politician therefore takes on the burden of using sometimes dubious and dangerous means for ends that cannot be wholly guaranteed, striving for political success while trying to keep some proportionality between the means employed and the ends desired, between political action and actual consequences. The instrumentally rational ethic of responsibility thus avoids the sin of ruthless monism while the passionate ethic of conviction gives meaning to the compromises and casualties of pragmatic maneuver. Weber argues that the politician to whom politics is a true vocation must stand for *something*. "To take a stand to be passionate – *ira et studium* – is the politician's element, and above all the element of the political leader."[9]

Weber's (and Burns') ideal-types are better interpreted as the extreme ends of a spectrum of possibilities of political practice and political leadership. At the pragmatic extreme, politicians become so absorbed in wheeling-dealing, number-counting and horse-trading – so involved in the political game as given – that they forget (or cease to believe in) any larger goals the game is supposed to serve. In these circumstances power may be cynically used for frankly self-serving and client-serving ends, dispensing even with a shield of hypocrisy to conceal its moral nakedness. At the other extreme, power is placed at the service of an absolute value which consumes all other values and interests and may annihilate all human interests whatsoever. Particular political practices and particular leaders will occupy positions somewhere along this spectrum, leaning either more toward the pragmatic, or more toward the politics of conviction.

---

[7] Max Weber, "Politics as a Vocation," in H. H. Gerth and C. Wright Mills (eds.), *From Max Weber* (London, Routledge, 1970), p. 127.

[8] *Ibid.*, p. 121.   [9] *Ibid.*, p. 95.

Weber was engaged in a normative exercise for the serious political leader who, he believed, should occupy the difficult middle ground between the extremes. (Gandhi, who called himself a "practical-idealist," also preached and tried in his own way to occupy this middle ground, though unlike Weber he believed that ethically "pure" practical decisions were both possible and necessary.)[10] A study of moral capital, however, is more concerned with the relational aspects of leadership than with leadership *per se* and must therefore consider the above-mentioned spectrum from its own perspective. One may conclude that moral capital is unlikely to be an important factor at either extreme. Cynically pragmatic politics do not tend to inspire favorable moral judgments while the totalitarian propensities of fanatical monomaniacs are, in the end, likely to prove destructive of the capacity even for making such judgments. Short of these extremes, the nature and force of political leadership, and of the moral capital it inspires, must vary according to circumstances. In a stable political environment with accepted institutions that are presumed to be legitimate and to serve legitimate interests, the leaders that Burns calls "transactional" will gain moral capital by their effectiveness and trustworthiness in brokering deals among plural interests. But challenges, whole or partial, to the legitimacy of the *status quo* cannot be effectively carried or repulsed by such transactional leadership. These require an emphasis on end-values typical of conviction politics or of transformational leadership, and moral capital will accrue to leaders who effectively articulate, defend and symbolize these values. In circumstances where bitter contestation and conflict occur over questions of legitimacy and justice, moral capital will play a particularly conspicuous role. (It is for this reason that I have chosen such circumstances for investigation in the studies that follow.)

Weber did in fact deal with the relational aspects of leadership in a discussion of the different forms of authority and the different styles of leadership associated with them. He famously discerned three ideal-types of these: the charismatic, the rational-legal, and the traditional or customary. I mention this Weberian ideal-typology because I mean to be clear that when I speak of the moral capital of leaders I am *not* implicitly talking about charismatic leadership. It is true that several of the leaders treated in this book – Mandela, Aung San Suu Kyi, Kennedy – have often been described as charismatic in the popular sense equally applicable to film stars, but none were charismatic leaders in Weberian terms. The criteria he enumerated for charismatic leadership were: the demand that followers put absolute trust in the leader personally as an ultimate authority

---

[10] Still the best book on Gandhi's thought is R. N. Iyer, *The Moral and Political Thought of Mahatma Gandhi* (New York, Oxford University Press, 1973).

and obey his or her will without question; the corresponding dissolution of the authority of all ordinary rational-legal rules and norms; the formation of a fluid, nonhierarchical community of followers bound together by common devotion and submission to the leader; and proof in action of the leader's special, magical powers.[11]

Charles de Gaulle comes closest to fulfilling these criteria, and it is true that his career also lends itself peculiarly well to analysis in terms of moral capital (a concept, indeed, he applied to himself). It is also true that I will often be dealing with critical political situations of the kind in which charismatic leaders have been observed typically to emerge. Yet crises and large-scale conflicts over legitimacy do not *necessarily* produce Weberian charismatic leadership. They do tend to produce leaders in the heroic mold, but such leaders do not necessarily, or even usually, have the messianically personal character attributed to charismatic leaders. Some crisis-emergent leaders are in fact of distinctly unheroic mien, charismatic in neither popular nor Weberian senses (think, for example, of Cory Aquino of the Philippines). Their cases show clearly how the possession of moral capital may elevate even quite ordinary persons into positions of leadership. The dissident leaders, indeed, cannot be properly or wholly understood in terms of *any* of Weber's categories, which suggests the incompleteness of the latter. My claim is that the concept of moral capital reveals another dimension of authority that is important in the understanding of politics generally and of leadership in particular. If I tend to dwell on crises and conflicts of legitimacy it is, to repeat, because the political generation and operation of moral capital, and the dependency of politicians on this as a resource, is most clearly and dramatically revealed under such conditions. They are conditions which demand, and therefore tend to produce, "transformational" leadership even among leaders (like the American presidents I examine) whose authority derives mainly from the rational-legal structure of political institutions in which they hold office. The "teaching" function of such leaders lies in their effective deployment of rhetoric and symbolism to maintain the morale of constituents, to inspire devotion and instil a sense of the rightness and nobility of a cause, and to mobilize support for specific policy directions.

Moral capital and constituencies

The fact that leaders cannot exist without someone to lead raises a general question about the relationship of moral capital to constituencies. Moral capital subsists in the general judgment of people, but people's judgments

[11] Max Weber, *Economy and Society* (New York, Bedminster Press, 1968, originally published 1922), pp. 242–245.

differ, as we have seen, very dramatically. But if moral capital lies, so to speak, in the eye of the beholder, then it would seem to follow that it must be bound to specific constituencies that make up particular sets of beholders defined by things like class, culture, interest, nationality and so on. Moral capital, in other words, would appear to be bound to particular constituencies, defined by particular end-values and goals, within which it is formed and maintained. Thus the Irish Republican Army appears morally heroic to Republican sympathizers but hardly to Ulster loyalists; a Ben-Gurion is honored by Israelis but despised by Palestinians. But this obvious point has to be qualified in several ways that make the tie between moral capital and constituency less tight than it might initially seem.

First, maverick loners do, by virtue of moral capital, occasionally attain to positions of power in exceptional and critical circumstances. One might point to the sudden ascent of Winston Churchill in the wartime crisis of 1940 despite a patchy and controversial political career up to that point and despite his lack of either a significant electoral constituency or of a power base among fellow parliamentarians. Churchill was appointed because he had stood in long, vocal and rather lonely opposition to the rise of Nazi Germany in the 1930s, and had called repeatedly for Britain to arm against the threat of it. This singular stance, dismissed as an irritant in a Britain desperate to avoid another debilitating conflict, turned suddenly into a substantial fund of moral capital once Hitler had propelled Europe into war. It lent huge authority to Churchill's remarkable oratorical efforts to rouse a dispirited nation to action and defense, creating a single united constituency out of the whole nation at a critical time. By contrast, Churchill's favorite *bête noire* and fellow maverick, Charles de Gaulle, tried to stand for all of France all the time, basing his career, as we shall see in Chapter 4, on a general appeal across particular constituencies and classes to an ideal that transcended them all.

Secondly, though politicians and parties may have their prime constituencies, they must often appeal beyond these to wider national or international audiences if they are to hope to achieve their political aims. This may create dissonance and tension if the values and expectations of the wider constituency differ significantly from those of the narrower. Witness, for example, the difficult and dangerous balancing act of Sinn Fein leader Gerry Adams as he tried to maintain the necessary trust and acquiescence of the "hard men" of the Provisional IRA while presenting himself internationally as a man of peace and reason in order to negotiate a settlement in Northern Ireland. On the other hand, if values are congruent, wider moral entreaties can have the effect of strengthening a political position without threatening rebellion in one's own back yard; the international moral appeal of Aung San Suu Kyi, for example, allowed external political pressure to be brought to bear on her political oppressors without great risk of conflict within her own Burmese constituency.

The need to appeal across constituencies is a particularly pressing challenge for political leaders in democratic regimes. Being tied to a constituency, though usually essential to the achievement of power, can also be a decided obstacle to the acquisition and maintenance of necessary moral capital. It is one of the perennial conundrums of electoral politics that victory often requires winning votes from a number of distinct constituencies with varying, often contradictory views and values. The need to capture votes militates against taking the sort of strong stands on positions that generate moral credibility. Political candidates need to offer strong leadership and firm policy yet campaigns are often dominated by the need not to offend anyone either of their own party or among the floating voters between or across parties. Instead of exuding moral authority, the candidates often begin to appear morally vacuous or slippery. Constituency concerns, in other words, often pose an impediment to the formation of moral capital in electoral circumstances that would-be leaders must strive to overcome.

A third point to note with regard to the tie between moral capital and constituencies is that, in a political system widely regarded as legitimate, anyone who attains office generally receives a large, gratuitous dollop of moral capital which has effect across all constituencies. Further, parties and persons that win democratic office, whatever their particular constituencies, are supposed to govern for the good of the whole population (at least they must appear to), and their job will be easier if they win respect across party and sectional lines. In fact this expectation generates another familiar problem for moral capital in democratic government, namely whether the governor should give effect to the contingent *will* of the people (expressed in their "mandate") or alternatively to his or her own responsible estimation of their general interest. Either or both of these may be deemed morally imperative, leading to a recurring dilemma. To attend too closely to an electorate's desires courts accusations of pandering and populism and gives rise to the suspicion of unscrupulous ambition or lack of personal moral fiber; to take the line enunciated by Edmund Burke, on the other hand, and heed only one's own responsibly considered judgments, is to court condemnation for high-handedly ignoring the people's expressed will, the presumed source of democratic legitimacy. Negotiating this dilemma while trying to maintain moral capital among particular constituencies and across the whole electorate is a perpetual problem for democratic governors, and one that plays an important part of the story of Lincoln in the next chapter.

Finally, we must note that politics can sometimes produce strange bedfellows, and political necessities can drive leaders and parties to make common cause with supposedly mortal enemies. Respect for an opponent makes for greater ease of negotiation than does mutual contempt and may even create political opportunities that would not otherwise exist. It is not particularly unusual for leaders to have more respect for able and dedicated opponents than for some of their own colleagues and rivals.

Despite the general salience of constituencies, therefore, the concept of moral capital should not be thought to be logically or inherently tied to them. Moral capital may accrue in many ways and be effective across constituency lines in unexpected ways.

Personal and institutional moral capital

Leaders as individuals strive to acquire personal moral capital on the strength and quality of their commitment and service to end-values, goals and justified interests shared by large numbers of people. But the essential connection between leaders and end-values is usually (even if not invariably) mediated by organizations or institutions themselves dedicated to these values. Indeed for most individuals, whether leaders or not, such moral capital as they enjoy in political life is largely a function of their membership of larger collective entities – parties, movements, governments, even nations. These entities are themselves the bearers of moral capital insofar as they are perceived to embody principles, purposes and interests believed noble, just, legitimate or morally necessary.

The relationship between *personal moral capital* and what I shall call, for the sake of convenience, *institutional moral capital* is generally dialectical. Where, for example, stable institutions exist within a stable regime, and where stability is in part a function of wide acceptance of the regime's legitimacy, political offices will form significant repositories of the regime's moral capital and be available to incumbents more or less independently of their character or ability. It is also true, nevertheless, that incumbents' actions are liable either to degrade or confirm the reputation of the institution. Revelations of behavior inconsistent with institutional aims and values will tarnish the whole, while honorable service will serve to confirm and enhance the reputation of both individual and institution. The actions, statements and conduct of leaders, because of their representative role, naturally carry especial significance. Evidence of irregularity at the top may cause a loss of moral capital that constitutes a veritable body blow to an institution, severely impairing its effectiveness and even calling into question its legitimacy.

Such crises of legitimacy can be more or less severe. For example, the existing political structure may retain its legitimacy while current power holders lose credibility by virtue of, say, misgovernment or corruption. This describes what David Easton called the loss of "specific support" for incumbents and their policies.[12] Such situations are potentially remediable by actions to oust the scoundrels or incompetents and replace them with a better lot, whether by democratic or other means (say a "palace revolution" in which the personnel change while the structures of government remain essentially the same). Secondly, and more seriously, there is what Easton termed a failure of "diffuse support," where there is an erosion of belief in the legitimacy of the legal-political structure itself. In such cases, challengers will typically argue either for the reform of present arrangements or their replacement by a more legitimate set – for example, the need to replace a despotic government with a democratic one, or a corrupt and inefficient democracy with an honest and efficient military dictatorship, or a bourgeois regime with a socialist/communist government. The causes of such general loss of legitimacy are always historically complex and involve far more than problems in the leadership. Nevertheless, the quality of the leadership will generally be an important factor in whether the erosion is accelerated or halted. Though incumbents in such circumstances must struggle without the benefit of the institutional moral capital normally attaching to legitimate office, an exceptionally able leader may build personal capital that can, in a contra-movement, be transferred to the office or institution thus refounding its legitimacy.

As well as the possibility of mutual reinforcement or mutual attrition of personal and institutional moral capital, there exists the possibility of a partial separation of the two. Sometimes outstanding leadership service in a securely legitimized office is rewarded with such a mass of personal moral capital that it becomes virtually an independent political force that may produce tensions within the institutional context. The extent of such tensions will depend partly on the nature of the organization itself, in particular on the values emphasized and the role accorded to leadership within it. Where the institutional moral capital of an organization is largely a function of the personal moral capital of the leader – for example in cases of charismatic leadership – tensions are unlikely to be severe. In an anarchist organization, on the other hand, the moral elevation of a particular individual is likely to create powerful institutional stress. In organizations that lie between these extremes, where both leadership and subordination to institutional values are expected, the dialectical relationship between personal and institutional moral capital is likely to be highly dynamic and unpredictable. As noted above, leadership must imply some

---

[12] David Easton, *A Systems Analysis of Political Life* (New York, Wiley, 1965).

measure of discretionary freedom or it can hardly be said to exist. This relative freedom even of highly constitutionally constrained leaders produces the permanent potential for moral capital to become somewhat detached from institutions and more firmly affixed to leaders themselves.

This phenomenon is particularly marked in contexts where political values and purposes take the form of a *cause*, something either to be bravely achieved or to be staunchly defended against bitter foes. Political conflict in these circumstances tends to be painted in the broad strokes of good versus evil, and the symbolical significance of leaders often becomes hugely exaggerated. Individuals may become something more than, and something different from, the sum of their perceived virtues. Their status may rise to the level of the mythic. However useful the myth may be as a potent symbol in the struggle, it can also present practical difficulties. A leader's personal moral capital may indeed become a two-edged weapon, cutting both ways for themselves (when mundane politics reveal the all-too-fallible humanity beneath the hallowing glow) and for their organization (whose independent strength may decline under the huge shadow cast by the leader). Nevertheless, the acquisition of so much moral capital can provide significant political opportunities that would not otherwise exist, though realizing them usually demands great skill and care (as we shall see in the case of Mandela).

On the other hand, the separation between personal and institutional moral capital can work the other way. There are occasions (as we shall see in our study of Lincoln) where leaders serve a great cause conscientiously and effectively – even subsuming their whole being to it – without that service being unproblematically rewarded with personal moral capital. This is to be reminded that moral capital depends on people's judgments and perceptions and that these can be sound or mistaken, accurate or inaccurate. The personal moral capital of leaders may thus be only very imperfectly related to their actual contributions and characters.

Studying moral capital

All these questions (concerning leaders in relation to ends-values, leaders in relation to constituencies, and leaders in relation to organizations and institutions) can be usefully illuminated, I argue, using the concept of moral capital. I will try to illuminate them in Parts II and III of this book by focusing on the careers of four individual leaders from different periods and different countries. In Part IV my focus will be less on individuals than on a particular political office, the American presidency, and the loss of institutional moral capital that that office suffered in recent historical times.

The leadership studies will be organized around four principal sources typically available to a leader to build moral capital, to maintain it, and to mobilize it politically. These, extracted from the arguments above, I summarize briefly as *cause*, *action*, *example*, and *rhetoric/symbolism*.

Cause

I use "cause" to denote the end-values and goals that leaders claim to serve and by virtue of which they expect to maintain and expand their constituencies. It establishes their *ground of right* and is typically a framework of ideological, moral and political values that both orders existing realities and provides a strategic response to them. The more forcefully, cogently and effectively a leader enunciates such values and goals, the stronger a base he or she has for the creation of a store of moral capital. Sometimes leaders feel that altered circumstances require them to convince their constituencies to accompany them along paths of ideological change, but maintaining trust while altering value direction requires extraordinary skill and care. To succeed in any such enterprise, leaders must be seen to remain constant to *something*, if only to the genuine (if reinterpreted) good of their following.

Action

Leaders, whatever the general end-values and principles for which they stand, must make difficult particular choices for which they will be judged responsible (and often they must take responsibility for any decision made under their aegis). Their moral capital will be partly a function of their policy- and decision-making performance judged with respect to whether they have advanced or retarded desired goals. I use the term "action" as shorthand for leadership performance as measured by such acts, policies and decisions. Once the established ground of political right has set the bounds of right political action, the need is then to act diligently and ably to secure the objectives that flow from occupation of such a ground. In the dynamically shifting world of politics, this will demand an ability to maneuver and manipulate (an art described by William Riker as "heresthenics")[13] without seeming to betray core values. In the end-driven world of politics, success or the expectation of success is inevitably an important source of moral capital.

[13] William H. Riker, *The Art of Political Manipulation* (New Haven, Yale University Press, 1986).

Example

As well as taking useful action to achieve desired goals, leaders must behave as effective moral exemplars for the values they represent and not appear to transgress them. This may raise difficult questions about means and ends since action in the uncertain field of politics frequently requires taking curiously twisted paths. Nevertheless, a champion of democracy should not, for example, behave as a tyrant. Furthermore, leaders must do more than simply *not betray* proclaimed values; they must show exemplary *commitment* to them, a stalwart and if necessary sacrificing commitment. Exemplary courage in defending core values is usually rewarded with a flood of moral capital, while half-heartedness, inconstancy or cowardice invites its immediate loss.

Rhetoric/symbolism

Leaders generally try to employ effective rhetoric, exhortation and appropriate symbolism to strengthen constituency morale and resolve, and to maintain commitment through setbacks, disappointments or defeats. Those who are gifted in this respect can hugely enlarge their own and their cause's moral capital, but even those who are not cannot be indifferent to the symbolic aspects of their leadership. Political leaders are usually expected to be more than merely devoted functionaries of organizational values; they are generally required to represent the latter symbolically in their own person.

Mention of the symbolical aspect of leadership should serve as a warning that the four sources of moral capital I have distinguished here for analytical purposes are in practice closely bound together. The extent to which leaders are deemed worthy to carry a symbolically representative function depends precisely on public assessments of their capacity to articulate the cause convincingly, their actions in serving it, their manifest devotion to it and their exemplary behavior with respect to it (for living symbols that behave inappropriately endanger not only their personal moral capital but that of their entire cause).

The reader might wonder why I have not included "character" as a separate category in this list, given that judgments of the character of individuals must play a crucial role in the formation of personal moral capital. It is obvious, of course, that the question of character is comprehended in, and comprehended by, all the four sources noted above, but there are several points that need to be made here. First, the actual character of a leader, however important it may be politically, is not inevitably the foundation of their moral capital. The *perceptions* and *judgments* of that character are what count, and these can be based only on the publicly revealed persona, actions, reactions, statements and conduct of a leader. The four categories above all imply matter that is in principle publicly observable. While it might be hoped, and may often be the case, that the true character of a leader will eventually shine through (or be dispiritingly revealed), the fact is that this can be misjudged, either to their advantage or disadvantage, and for long periods. Leaders who (like Lincoln) are unfairly calumnied or despised will undoubtedly need a strong character if they are to survive, and such a character should always be seen as a valuable political resource. This is not, however, the resource I intend to identify in the idea of moral capital.

Second is the question as to what *kind* of character we are talking about. Moral character as commonly conceived, even when justly judged, is not necessarily a prime source of moral capital. It is true that communities generally want their leaders to uphold and exemplify the moral values they hold dear, values that are not always specifically political, and a serious slip on a leader's part can have grim consequences. What is thought important in this respect varies, of course, among communities and within a single community over time; divorce was once considered a bar to political office in many Western countries but is so no longer, and attitudes to the sexual morality of leaders have been famously changeable in recent times. If a candidate today adopts a political stance centered on preserving or restoring "family values," then his or her own sexual conduct will be politically very relevant, but it may be much less so otherwise. Generally speaking, however, the visible observance of public-ly approved moral values is, at best, a necessary but insufficient condition for acquiring any moral capital at all. It establishes what might be termed a minimum baseline below which a representative may not fall without grave risk. It is a baseline that is to some extent renegotiable over time as community standards and expectations alter. It also sometimes happens (as we will see in the case of Bill Clinton) that constituents will overlook, however they may disapprove, transgressions of what we may call private morality if a leader is judged committed to central political values and effective on their behalf.

This brings me to the third point. I have argued that the nature of politics makes even peerless character and integrity of limited political relevance unless clearly harnessed to values and goals commanding the allegiance and devotion of significant numbers of people. In view of this, the four categories above are intended to emphasize the qualities of perceived character that are most vital for the acquisition of moral capital.

These are the qualities of fidelity, commitment and able action in the service of publicly valued goals. Moral capital is always vulnerable to perceptions of serious betrayal of, or incapacity to pursue, valued goals and principles, but character and integrity alone, absent some publicly tested commitment, are more intensely vulnerable to the mere, often unsavory processes of politics itself.

In the following four chapters I will undertake interpretive case studies of different leaders in an attempt to illustrate these themes and to show something of the nature of moral capital as a specifically political resource. I have chosen leaders in circumstances of dramatic contest over legitimacy where the force and consequence of moral capital can be most clearly seen. I have also chosen in order to allow significant comparisons and contrasts, so that not only the general importance of moral capital in politics can be judged, but also its relative importance in different circumstances. I seek to explore the different opportunities it provides and the different vulnerabilities to which it is subject, as well as its relation to other political resources at the disposal of leaders.

In Part II I look at two men, Abraham Lincoln and Charles de Gaulle, each of whom came to political leadership at a time when war and political fragmentation raised critical questions about moral, political and legal legitimacy. Each man saw his task or mission as the preservation of an ideal threatened by forces from both within and without, and each was unwaveringly devoted to this ideal. In Lincoln's case personal moral capital of any large weight accrued to him only after his assassination. While he lived, the important contest over moral capital, in which he was such a prominent participant, took place largely at the level of the causes represented by each part of the divided nation. Lincoln's part in securing the North's moral capital was crucial, but his achievement was not directly or immediately recognized in his personal capital. He was able to govern in difficult circumstances and to survive to win a second term because he legitimately occupied (at least in Northern eyes) the office of the presidency with all the institutional moral and political capital that implied, and also because he had the ability and determination to make effective use of these resources to impose his political will. Lincoln's story reveals both the importance and sometimes perversity of the contest over moral capital in politics. De Gaulle's case was quite different. Rejecting the legitimacy of existing regimes and institutions, and despising also the game of political parties, de Gaulle seldom had significant institutional or organizational capital to support himself and his political goals. His entire career was therefore based on the self-conscious accumulation of a personal moral capital that allowed him to gain the leadership of France not once, but twice in his lifetime, and eventually to secure institutional arrangements more congenial to his own style of leadership. De Gaulle shows what a remarkable force moral capital can be in critical political circumstances, but also how vulnerable a resource it is when ungirded by more familiar political resources.

In Part III I deal with two modern political heroes, Nelson Mandela and Aung San Suu Kyi, whose rise to leadership occurred in circumstances of democratic dissidence to severely oppressive regimes. In such circumstances the possession of moral capital is inevitably a central consideration. The moral capital of each leader was significantly enhanced by their long-suffering endurance on behalf of the cause of the democratization of their countries – in the one case by the dismantlement of apartheid and in the other by the replacement of an authoritarian Burmese military junta by a democratically elected civil government. Mandela, indeed, became a living symbol largely as a result of a long incarceration that made him the exemplary and representative prisoner of a wicked system. Suu Kyi, on the other hand, *began* her career as a living symbol by virtue of her inheritance – and her conscious acceptance of this inheritance – from her hero father. In both Mandela's and Suu Kyi's cases, a burden of moral capital attributed largely independently of their own actions, characters or abilities had to be effectively proved and consolidated in political action. In Mandela's case the proving had to be done against serious resistance not just from the South African government but from within his own organization and the coalition of forces it led. Mandela's remarkable burden of personal moral capital became seriously divorced from the institutional moral capital of the organization to which he was allegedly subservient even while it advanced the latter, and though it gave him the opportunity of leadership it also made him an object of suspicion and resentment. Suu Kyi's party, on the other hand, was created precisely as a vehicle for the political mobilization of her own personal moral capital amidst the maelstrom of Burmese revolt in the 1980s, so that such tensions between personal and institutional capital were much less evident.

De Gaulle, Mandela and Suu Kyi all reveal the importance of a concentration of moral capital in a single individual in revolutionary circumstances. Such an individual, appealing across divisions and even across enmities, can act as a stable center around which the wildly disparate array of competing forces, interests and opinions that have been unleashed can congeal, achieving political coherence and allowing movement toward a common goal. By contrast, a severe loss of moral capital from a stable institution in which it has long been concentrated can create political divisions that may be very difficult to heal. This was the case, as I will argue in Part IV, with the American presidency in the last part of the twentieth century. My study of the presidency will be less concerned with the way in which moral capital attaches to notable individuals fighting for high causes than with the way it institutionally resides in a respected political office.

Though I deal with all American presidents from Kennedy to Clinton, my interest is less in the men themselves than in their relationship with the institution of the presidency and the alleged "crisis" that this inter-relationship produced in recent historical times. The four chapters in this part will not, therefore, be so directly organized around the themes of cause, action, example and rhetoric/symbolism. Rather they focus on what I take to be one of the central myths of American government and the American nation upon which its national and institutional moral capital was partially founded. I will argue that the fracturing of this myth caused a serious drain in that capital that has been very difficult to stem. The presidency, because of its unique position within the American political system, and because of the mythology that attaches to that system (and by extension to the whole American people), represents a peculiarly significant repository of the nation's moral capital. Whatever the man brings to the office, the office generally brings a great deal more to the man. The course of the presidency after Kennedy's assassination shows to some extent the dialectical relationship that exists between the moral capital of an incumbent and that of the office, as the acts of the former impact negatively or positively on the latter. From a wider per-spective, however, I argue that it shows how a moral crisis afflicting the nation at its ideological heart can be refracted through and largely enact-ed within its central institutions, eroding the moral capital not just of particular presidents or governments, or even the particular office, but of the nation itself, thus undermining the national morale.

PART II

Moral capital in times of crisis

In this section I will look at two leaders who, despite great differences of character, circumstance and time, have some interesting things in common (in addition to unusual height). Both Abraham Lincoln and Charles de Gaulle were highly ambitious and intellectually dominating men with early intimations of individual greatness, each believing himself, though in very different ways, a chosen instrument of fate. For both, too, personal ambition was subsumed within and put at the service of an ideal which gave it expression and meaning while simultaneously placing restraints upon it. In each case the ideal was connected to the historical destiny of a particular nation, for Lincoln to the United States as the testing ground of democratic government on earth, and for de Gaulle to a semi-mystical notion of France as the exemplary nation among nations, the nation *par excellence*. Because of this, the main thrust of the politics of each was similarly aimed at preserving the ideal they believed their nation embodied. Despite their political restraint, both men were at times suspected of dictatorial tendencies and tyrannical intentions. Both were consummate political operators, skilled at the kind of maneuvers and obfuscations that wrong-foot or neutralize opponents. Each came to understand the political possibilities of burgeoning media outlets – the press in Lincoln's time, radio and television in de Gaulle's – and each proved highly adept in their use. Both were (or became) deeply interested in military strategy and appeared to have a gift for it. Each loved writing and language and showed some skill in their own literary productions: de Gaulle with his memoirs and a book on leadership; Lincoln mainly in highly crafted public pronouncements. Each, too, left a decided constitutional mark on his country: Lincoln with the (posthumously accomplished) thirteenth amendment that abolished slavery and arguably put equality on a constitutional par with liberty; de Gaulle more thoroughly by fashioning in his own image a new constitution for the Fifth Republic that has endured with only minor modification.

The differences, however, are at least as marked as the similarities. Lincoln's advent to power precipitated a civil war, de Gaulle's return to power (his second coming) was orchestrated in order to prevent one. De Gaulle was by career choice a military man, whereas Lincoln always treated his brief sojourn in the militia during the Black Hawk war as a tragi-comic episode. Lincoln, risen from mid-Western rural poverty and obscurity, famously retained and utilized "the common touch"; de Gaulle, from an old, respectable Catholic family of the *haut bourgeois* French Right, based his leadership style on the cultivation of a haughty aloofness. Partly from this difference but also for deeper reasons of character, Lincoln was wholly without the absurd pomposity of manner that occasionally infuriated even some of de Gaulle's most devoted followers. Lincoln with his jocularly self-deprecating manner appeared lacking in common vanity and never responded to even gross and blatant personal insults with any show of injured pride. People who gained an audience were invariably impressed by his apparently genuine sympathy and kindly interest in their stories. By contrast, de Gaulle's narcissistic self-absorption was legendary, and his attitude to colleagues and strangers alike often very harsh (though he was perfectly capable of turning on the charm to get his political way). One difference above all: Lincoln was an unsentimental but convinced democrat and lifelong party man, whereas de Gaulle despised the "regime of parties" that had ill-served and weakened France through most of the first half of the twentieth century. De Gaulle wanted to destroy this regime by any means he could in order to provide strong, effective government. His desire for a constitution that sidelined the parties and allowed a direct, plebiscitary link between leader and people aroused suspicion of fascist tendencies. Lincoln, on the other hand, was a firm constitutionalist who admired the achievements of America's founding fathers and believed that needed alterations to their document should be achieved only by properly constitutional means.

From the perspective of this study, however, the most interesting difference – which reflects in part some of the differences already noted – relates to the role and significance of moral capital in the career of each. Lincoln was certainly not – could not be – indifferent to the esteem in which he and his administration were held by the public, but his efforts were always geared toward maintaining the moral advantage of the Northern cause even at the expense of his personal moral capital. De Gaulle, on the other hand, was always concerned first and foremost with creating and perpetuating the myth of "de Gaulle," single-handed savior of the French nation. De Gaulle's self-identification with the semi-mystical entity he called the "real France" produced a concentration on his own person and personality as a basis of political authority.

The manner of de Gaulle's rise was in sharp contrast to that of Lincoln. Lincoln had been nominated and elected through normal American democratic processes. Though well-known and admired as a lawyer and politician in his native Illinois, he was relatively unknown nationally and his success was largely due to the divisions racking the parties in the United States in 1860. Nevertheless, his election gave him an automatic legitimacy which, though denied by the South, was hardly questioned by Northerners even when they felt most dissatisfied with him. De Gaulle, however, was not even a politician in 1940 when opportunity (or destiny, as he saw it) descended upon him. He was merely an obscure, dissenting officer who refused to accept either the defeat of France by Hitler or the legitimacy of the ensuing Vichy French government, and decided to oppose them with little more than his own will, audacity and cunning. The creation of "de Gaulle," the self-proclaimed embodiment of a free and never-to-be-conquered France, was no doubt congenial to de Gaulle's temperament but it also provided a convenient focus for rallying the disparate forces of opposition that emerged and grew as the war went on and as German and Vichy fortunes receded. De Gaulle, from very slim beginnings, would build alliances and allegiances that would make him the leader of post-war France, but his legitimacy would remain fundamentally extra-organizational. It always rested ultimately on the personal moral capital he claimed for himself as the genuine representative and deliverer of Free France.

This peculiar identification of man and ideal meant that de Gaulle's personal moral capital was never really separable from the moral capital of his cause, so that the fortunes of each were radically conjoined. What I have described as a dialectical relationship between leader and cause was in his case rather one of fusion. De Gaulle's unideological vision of a France elevated above the common fray of partisan politics, though it resonated sometimes in the nationalistic French soul, was too idiosyncratic to carry much weight independently of himself (at least in its pure form). Moreover, the fact that the identification had, for practical purposes, been forged in response to a national crisis meant that the cashable value of de Gaulle's moral capital was – as he himself freely acknowledged – always greatest at times of similar crisis.

Lincoln's leadership also occurred at a critical hour, and for all the historical emphasis on his centrality to the struggle that ensued, there was no such presumed indissoluble link between himself and the national cause. Though he was probably the most coherent and effective articulator and developer of the Northern position (or at least the Republican version of it), his views were in no way idiosyncratic. In fact they were widely and strongly shared throughout the course of the war. Lincoln, despite his presidential legitimacy, was never seen by contemporaries as indispensable to the cause he so stoutly championed, and in fact many thought him guilty of damaging it by his actions and inactions and believed it would be better served by a different president. General opinion on this changed only gradually, and changed significantly only after his re-election and then assassination. While Lincoln's personal moral capital and that of his cause were ultimately strongly linked, the extraordinarily difficult political situation he faced meant that genuine service to the cause was not necessarily, and in fact not often, rewarded by an increase in his personal moral capital. Though his contribution was vital, it was in fact only very belatedly acknowledged. When it was – on the eve of victory, with the prospective difficulties of Reconstruction looming, and in the shock of his assassination – his moral capital soared to heights he himself could scarcely have foreseen, with effects that rippled through subsequent ages.

The following chapter is a retelling of the Lincoln story organized around these themes.

3   Abraham Lincoln: the long-purposed man

> If I were to try to read, much less answer, all the attacks on me, this shop might as well be closed for any other business . . . If the end brings me out all right, what is said against me won't amount to anything. If the end brings me out wrong, 10 angels swearing I was right would make no difference.
>
> Lincoln

For the greater part of his presidency, Abraham Lincoln was widely regarded as a weak leader, a mere figurehead controlled by more powerful men in his cabinet. He was generally granted, except by the bitterest foes of Union, to be well intentioned and honest – a welcome change after a Democratic administration tainted by corruption – but much more was needed at a desperate hour. It seemed to observers that Lincoln lacked the caliber of a statesman, that he "did nothing – neither harm nor good."[1] Eventually there would be doubt whether he was an advance even on his despised predecessor, James Buchanan, whose failure of nerve in the political storm over Kansas in 1857–58 had practically guaranteed secession and war, causing him to be reviled in the North as a traitor.[2] Twelve months into Lincoln's first term, a British journalist was predicting that when Mr. Lincoln left office "he will be no more regretted, though more respected, than Mr. Buchanan."[3] A year later and a member of his own party was calling him a vacillating, weak, fearful and ignorant man who would stand even worse in posterity than Buchanan.[4]

Newspapers, even those of Republican sympathies, were often savagely scornful of his capacities and character, and regarded his entire administration as a shambles. The foreign press, much of it sympathetic to the Southern cause, was equally disparaging.[5] At home and abroad Lincoln was portrayed as an ineffectual clown, a man too fond of common jokes

---

[1] Anthony Trollope, *North America* (New York, Alfred A. Knopf, 1951), p. 326.
[2] See Allan Nevins, "Douglas, Buchanan and the Coming of War," in *The Statesmanship of the Civil War* (New York, Collier, 1962), p. 38.
[3] Edward Dicey, cited in David Herbert Donald, *Lincoln* (London, Pimlico, 1996), p. 352.
[4] Asa Mahan, cited in Donald, *Lincoln*, p. 425.
[5] Generally, see Robert S. Harper, *Lincoln and the Press* (New York, McGraw-Hill, 1951).

who was himself something of a joke. According to fellow Republicans in Congress he "lacked will, purpose and power to command." His sometime top general, George McLellan, called him an "idiot" and a "well-meaning baboon." He was, according to others, lacking in "moral heroism," a "tow-string of a president," "weak, irresolute and wanting in moral courage," "shattered, dazed and utterly foolish," a "half-witted usurper," a "damn fool," an "awful, woeful ass" . . . the list could be continued indefinitely. Lincoln himself described his usual treatment, and his habitual reaction to it, in a letter to an actor who had inadvertently exposed him to yet another round of press derision late in 1863. He reassured the man that he had "not been much shocked" by what the newspapers had written, adding: "those comments constitute a fair specimen of what has occurred to me through life. I have endured a great deal of ridicule without much malice; and have received a great deal of kindness, not quite free of ridicule. I am used to it."[6]

Part of the cause of the persistent underestimation of Lincoln was simple prejudice. He was a mid-Westerner whose appearance, accents and manners were, to both Easterners and foreigners, outlandish. He was also relatively unknown, such fame as he had won beyond Illinois being of very recent origin. Though familiar in his home State as a successful lawyer and politician, it was only during an 1858 Senate contest that he had come to national attention through a series of celebrated debates with Democratic arch-rival, Stephen A. Douglas. The reputation thus acquired put him in demand as an effective exponent of the Republican cause, but he won the party's nomination in 1860 not because he was the favorite but because he had offended fewer important interests than better known rivals.[7] Nor was he swept into presidential office, subsequently, on the strength of public esteem for his political leadership. A Republican victory was assured whoever was nominated because the Democratic Party, the last remaining national institution linking North and South, split along sectional lines into slavery and anti-slavery factions. In a four-cornered contest, Lincoln was bound to win in the electoral college even on a minority of the popular vote. Significantly, too, Lincoln had conducted a populist campaign as the "Rail Splitter" candidate, forging an enduring image of himself as the sturdy, self-reliant "frontiersman," ideal representative of free labor and free soil. It was pure hokey in the American manner, and hugely popular, but it

[6] Letter to James A. Hackett, 2 November 1863, in Roy P. Basler, Marion D. Pratt and Lloyd A. Dunlap (eds.), *The Collected Works of Abraham Lincoln*, 8 vols. plus index (New Brunswick, NJ, Rutgers University Press, 1953–55) (hereinafter *CW*), vol. 6, pp. 558–559.
[7] See Mark E. Neely, Jr., *The Last Best Hope of Earth: Abraham Lincoln and the Promise of America* (Cambridge, MA, Harvard University Press, 1995), p. 56.

suppressed his legal and political experience and ignored his intellectual and oratorical strengths.

For elite opinion-formers, therefore, Lincoln was simply not the stuff from which great statesmen were made. After his death, the *New York Herald*, which had often bitterly denounced him in life, accurately observed that people were educated to a different, antique image of the great founders of nations – noble figures, toga-clad and laurel-crowned. Rhetorically it asked: "How can men so educated . . . ever be brought to comprehend the genius of a character so externally uncouth, so pathetically simple, so unfathomably penetrating, so irresolute and yet so irresistible, so bizarre, grotesque, droll, wise and perfectly beneficent?"[8]

There were other factors too. Lack of success in bringing the war to a swift and satisfactory conclusion was fundamental, but Lincoln's real weakness, as he himself was acutely aware, was less personal than political. He was a minority president lacking a secure political base, a Washington outsider with a cabinet full of men better known and more experienced in office than himself. Four of these had been his rivals for the Republican nomination, and at least two of them – Secretary of State William S. Seward and Treasurer Salmon P. Chase – considered themselves of superior presidential timbre to a greenhorn, hayseed president over whom they had expected easily to gain the whip-hand. Republican control of Congress was hardly an unalloyed blessing either, since many Republicans refused to accept Lincoln's view that the prosecution of the war was the task of the executive, not the legislature. They had, in any case, little respect and no loyalty for a man they regarded as a probable one-termer, an accidental president of doubtful political relevance.

Contemporary attitudes toward Lincoln thus pose something of a puzzle for a study that examines him in terms of moral capital. In the deadly context of civil war, with each combatant claiming the better hold on right, the possession of moral capital was naturally an important issue. As in all such struggles, its mobilization to sustain political, industrial and military power was of crucial concern to both sides. In historical retrospect, it is tempting to assume that the North possessed the superior ordnance, here as elsewhere, and that Lincoln played a crucial role in its mobilization. Why, otherwise, would the world enshrine him in its memory as a semi-legendary statesman and heroic martyr to his triumphant cause? Certainly, later generations of historical observers treated Lincoln with a respect bordering on reverence. James Bryce would say he possessed all three of the essential qualities of a great statesman – a powerful and broad-ranging intellect, strength of will and nobility of cause – and that

[8] *New York Herald*, 17 April 1865, in Herbert Mitgang (ed.), *Lincoln as They Saw Him* (New York, Collier Books, 1962), p. 452.

he needed all three to pilot the republic through the worst storm that had ever broken upon it.[9] Yet few among Lincoln's political contemporaries would readily have conceded that he possessed any of them. Reading their dismissive, often malignant views, one wonders how Lincoln managed to lead the North through a difficult war, end slavery and become the first president in thirty-two years to be re-elected to a second term.

Lincoln and moral capital

The bluntest answer to this question was given some years ago by David Herbert Donald, who argued that, though Lincoln failed to win either press, parties or people, he was nevertheless a successful politician – for a simple reason: "he was an astute and dextrous operator of the political machine."[10] Donald has devoted a good part of his life to pursuing "Lincoln the canny politician" rather than "Lincoln the great man," and his work has dispelled any doubts there may have been about the sixteenth president's mastery of the game. Lincoln was an old political hand, a dedicated party strategist, an able judge of opportunity who well understood the utility of the vast powers of patronage that came with presidential office. True, he lacked executive experience, and in a cabinet of seasoned and powerful men he seemed to some observers like a lamb thrown among wolves; but Lincoln was too tough, too shrewd and too self-confident to be anyone's easy meal.[11] Robert Ingersoll wrote that he had "as much shrewdness as is consistent with honesty," honesty being a point of honor for a man who, in Illinois, had been tagged "Honest Abe, the lawyer who never lies." Honesty, however, was a useful selling point in both law and politics, and refusing to tell lies was perfectly consistent with a sly use of indirection, secretiveness and obfuscating humor. Lincoln's honesty and seeming mid-Western simplicity had the added advantage of causing people to underestimate his sagacity and guile, often to their eventual bafflement. As one commentator noted after Lincoln's re-election in 1864: "He may seem to be the most credulous, docile and pliable of backwoodsmen, and yet . . . he has proved himself, in his quiet way, the keenest of politicians, and more than a match for his wiliest antagonists in the arts of diplomacy."[12]

Was canny politics then the whole story of Lincoln's success? Donald's own later, highly researched biography scarcely upholds this radical

[9] James Bryce, Introduction to *Speeches and Letters of Abraham Lincoln, 1832–1865* (London, J. M. Dent & Sons, 1917), p. xvi.
[10] David Herbert Donald, *Lincoln Reconsidered* (New York, Knopf, 1959), p. 65.
[11] See Neely, *The Last Best Hope of Earth*, p. 166.
[12] Editorial, *New York Herald*, 6 March 1865, in Mitgang, *Lincoln as They Saw Him*, pp. 424–425.

earlier claim.[13] On balance it gives some credence to the more familiar, posthumous image of Lincoln as a leader steeling a nation's heart to an arduous task and consecrating its soul to a great cause. It is quite true, however, that Lincoln had very severe problems in building the moral capital he needed to sustain the Northern cause. Lincoln would always seem to contemporaries either too slow or too fast, too indecisive or too peremptory, too weak or too powerful, depending on who was judging him. It is important to note, however, that the confusion *about* Lincoln in no way reflected confusion *within* Lincoln about his values and purposes. Few political leaders have been as firmly settled as he on their view of the right political course, and few have held to their course so steadfastly in trying times. Lincoln once joked that he was sure he would turn tail and run at the first sound of battle, but added seriously, "Moral cowardice is something which I think I never had."[14] Once set, his moral-political compass seldom wavered. It was no vacillation of soul that eventually shifted his policies and aims, but the weight of momentous events.

Of the four principal, interrelated means by which leaders create moral capital – cause, action, example and rhetoric/symbolism – Lincoln neglected none. With regard to *cause*, he had very early and very clearly marked out the ground of right on which he and his Republican Party would stand. As regards *action*, he faithfully used all the power at his command as president and all his political skill to pursue the policies and secure the objectives that he believed flowed from occupation of this ground. Likewise, for example, he was careful to act, even under great duress, so as not to betray, but rather morally to exemplify, the values for which he was struggling. Lastly, he deployed highly effective *rhetoric* and *symbolism* to ennoble the Northern cause and to convince people of the soundness of his administration's aims and policies. Yet Lincoln's conscientious leadership produced quandaries that frequently caused him, his administration and the whole Northern cause to seem seriously deficient in moral capital.

Lincoln's case shows how complex and conflicted political circumstances can make moral capital the object of strenuous contest while at the same time making it extremely difficult to secure. It was, ironically, Lincoln's very fidelity to his avowed principles and purposes that caused problems in short and medium terms. Over the long run, however – and

---

[13] Donald does not repeat this argument in his 1996 biography, *Lincoln*, either to uphold or disclaim it. It is tempting to think, indeed, that the curious noncommittal tenor of this book – its alleged treatment of all materials solely from Lincoln's viewpoint without ranging further to make wider judgments – reflects uncertainty on Donald's part on whether to affirm or disaffirm this earlier strong claim.

[14] Noah Brooks, "Personal Recollections of Abraham Lincoln," *Harper's Monthly*, May 1865, in Mitgang, *Lincoln as They Saw Him*, p. 479.

here there was an undoubted element of fortune at play – it paid large dividends that continued to have effects long after his death. Lincoln's story can thus be used to demonstrate several things about moral capital: one, that it is in general extremely difficult to gain and maintain when forced to bestride radically discordant constituencies for the sake of a fragile alliance; two, that it is quite possible to win moral capital for one's cause without this being reflected in one's personal stock; three, that personal moral capital may be very imperfectly related to actual moral character and conduct; and, four, that whatever the calumnies and mis-representations one suffers, firm character and fidelity can, given an element of good fortune and sufficient time, transcend the cacophonous dissonance of immediate politics and receive its proper due.

I begin, then, with Lincoln's closely reasoned ground of right, and the historical dilemma to which it was meant to provide the moral and political solution.

Cause: Lincoln's ground of right

"Let us have faith," Lincoln said in a speech that helped launch his bid for the presidency, "THAT RIGHT MAKES MIGHT, and in that faith, let us, to the end, dare to do our duty as we understand it."[15] That phrase, "right makes might," can be taken as his acknowledgment of the power and importance of moral capital in politics. As a man with a powerful, logical mind and an almost religious belief in the efficacy of reason, Lincoln was extremely difficult to shift once he had labored mentally to discern a position that seemed to him right. As early as 1845, in the context of the annexation of Texas, he had enunciated his ground of right on the question of the expansion of Southern slavery into Western territories. A decade later it would form the creed of the new Republican Party. He wrote:

I hold it to be a paramount duty of us in the free states, due to the Union of the states, and perhaps to liberty itself (paradox though it may seem) to let the slavery of the other states alone; while, on the other hand, I hold it to be equally clear, that we should never knowingly lend ourselves directly or indirectly, to prevent that slavery from dying a natural death – to find new places for it to live in, when it can no longer exist in the old.[16]

Lincoln believed his paradoxical stance, grounded as it was in a combination of principle, constitutionality and political realism, was the only one

---

[15] "Address to the Cooper Institute," New York, 27 February 1860, *CW*, vol. 3, p. 550. The whole of the last sentence is in capitals in the original transcript.
[16] Letter to Williamson Durley, 3 October 1845, *CW*, vol. 2, p. 348.

that would answer both morally and politically. Though it did not palter with slavery, it quite consciously temporized with it. Lincoln argued vehemently that slavery was evil, and he staunchly defended his right, as a citizen, to proclaim it evil as clearly and as often as he wished; but moral certainty implied no legal right to interfere with an institution implicitly tolerated by the Constitution. Any attempt to abolish slavery by extra-legal force, on the other hand, risked the integrity of the Union itself. Lincoln made an analogy with cancer: removing it surgically from the body politic put the patient's life at risk, but leaving it to flourish condemned the patient to a painful, protracted death. The safest course for the Union was not to try to abolish slavery but to contain it, *quarantine* it within the South and let it wither.

Lincoln's doctrine had respectable antecedents in the views of men that Lincoln revered, national founders like Jefferson and Madison, as well as his political idol, Henry Clay of Kentucky, co-founder of the Whig Party to which Lincoln long adhered.[17] Like these men, Lincoln was painfully conscious of the moral contradiction at the national heart. As a devotee of the Declaration of Independence, he believed its principles held the promise of equality and liberty for all humankind, independently of race or color.[18] It was significant that the date he would indicate at the opening of his famous Gettysburg Address – "Four score and seven years ago our fathers brought forth upon this continent a new nation . . ." – was 1776, the year of the Declaration of Independence, not of the Constitution. The constitutional founders had, on political and economic grounds, tacitly condoned slavery, leaving the decision on its continuance as a matter for the States with an implication of no federal authority to interfere. They were themselves, many of them, reluctant slave-owners who trusted that the problem would be self-abolishing in time, for even in the South slavery was generally regarded as a necessary evil that would inevitably decline and disappear with national development.

But slavery persisted in the aristocratic, plantation economy of the South and the nation became effectively divided into free Northern and Southern slave sections along the line of the Ohio River and the southern boundary of Pennsylvania. Legal abolition could not be accomplished except by a constitutional amendment, impossible so long as the South maintained a voting balance in the Senate by ensuring the number of slave States continued to match the number of free. There was therefore

---

[17] The Whigs had been founded by Clay and Daniel Webster to oppose Andrew Jackson's Democrats. They advocated a nationalistic economic policy comprising tariff protection, federally funded communications projects (internal improvements) and a national bank, the so-called "American System."

[18] See "Fragment on the Constitution and Union," *CW*, vol. 1, p. 169.

recurring controversy over whether new States carved out of western territories would be slave or free, and whether Congress had the constitutional authority to forbid slavery in them. A crisis over Missouri in 1820 was defused by a compromise Bill guided through Congress by Clay which admitted Missouri as a slave State balanced by the admission of Maine as a free State and excluding slavery from the rest of the Louisiana territory north of 36°30' (Missouri's southern border). The "Missouri Compromise" held for three decades but came under increasing strain as the doctrine of "manifest destiny" drove more and more people west. Sectional conflict loomed between Southern "friends of slavery" and Northern "Free-Soilers,"[19] and in 1850 another legislative compromise was required to deal with a fresh crisis over the status of the new State of California.

The increasing politicization of slavery reflected a hardening of moral attitudes as North and South grew economically and technologically apart while being brought into greater contact through improved communications. After 1830 the South came under closer moral scrutiny from educated, evangelical Northerners self-consciously embarking upon an "age of reform." White Southerners were particularly alarmed by a small but vocal Northern abolitionist movement,[20] and began to produce defensive arguments, on Biblical and Aristotelian grounds, for slavery as a positive good (a view that Lincoln took as representative of Southern opinion). They also became more aggressively determined to secure their "civilization" by expanding it westward. This inevitably put strain on the paradoxical Lincolnian position. The strategy of tolerance was feasible only on the assumption of slavery's inevitable demise; the idea that the South's "peculiar institution" might instead gain strength and territory rendered it impossible. It was a risk made vividly real in 1854 by Lincoln's old rival, Senator Douglas, who bullied and bluffed through Congress an Act aimed at opening up the Kansas–Nebraska territory to settlement and a transcontinental railroad. To appease Southern opposition, Douglas divided the region into two territories, Kansas and Nebraska, then repealed the anti-slavery rule above the 36°30' line, leaving the question of whether a State would be free or slave to be decided by "popular sovereignty" ("squatter sovereignty"). In an unpolitic moment, Douglas declared that he cared not whether a territory voted slavery up or voted it down, so long as the advancement of white civilization was secured.

---

[19] In 1846, during the Mexican war, Representative David Wilmot of Pennsylvania sponsored a legislative proviso that would prohibit slavery in any territory won from Mexico. Though it failed in the Senate, the Wilmot Proviso aroused enormous Southern bitterness and politicized the slavery issue once and for all.

[20] William Lloyd Garrison of Boston with his anti-slavery newspaper, *The Liberator*, was the movement's most vocal prophet.

But Northerners were "thunderstruck" (to use Lincoln's word) by the passage of the Act.

Lincoln, whose own political ambitions had been all-but-blighted in 1849, found himself propelled back into the political arena to pit the "Spirit of '76" against squatter sovereignty.[21] Kansas–Nebraska, by challenging values Lincoln had always held, harnessed his personal aspirations to a larger cause, one that humbled ambition even as it provided the opportunity for its fulfillment. (He would express this late in his presidency when he wrote that "the public interest and my private interest have been perfectly parallel, because in no other way could I serve myself so well, as by truly serving the Union.")[22] Kansas–Nebraska also caused the final collapse of a Whig Party torn between pro- and anti-slavery factions, making room for a Republican Party whose leading figure in Illinois would be Lincoln. If the nascent party were to successfully oppose the extension of slavery, however, it would have to be a very broad church. Lincoln, a political realist, knew this and welcomed even anti-slavery Know-Nothings,[23] members of the "nativist" American Party whose anti-immigrant principles he despised. He had no objection, he said, to "fusing" with anybody "provided I can fuse on ground which I think is right."[24] This was the crux: to attract the necessary support across a range of diverse opinion and feeling without compromising on essential matters of principle, in particular on the containment of slavery and the maintenance of the Union.

There were hard political reasons why the emancipation of slaves could *not* be one of these essential matters. The need to reassure an agitated South was one, but Republican realism also meant recognizing that the feeling against slavery in the North implied little sympathy for "the negro" as such. Moral enlightenment and confirmed prejudice went hand in hand, and the problem of what to do with a large black population should slaves be emancipated greatly troubled whites everywhere. As a British agent in the North derisively reported, freedom was acceptable in America as long as blacks were kept at a distance.[25] Lincoln's own State had voted overwhelmingly for a constitutional amendment that would exclude blacks from Illinois, so he had direct knowledge of these

---

[21] See the speech at Peoria, IL, 16 October 1854, *CW*, vol. 2, p. 283.

[22] Draft of a letter to Isaac M. Schermerhorn, 12 September 1864, in Don E. Fehrenbacher (ed.), *Abraham Lincoln: A Documentary Portrait Through His Speeches and Writings* (Stanford University Press, 1964), p. 263.

[23] For Lincoln's attitude to the nativists, see Letter to Joshua Speed, 24 August 1855, *CW*, vol. 2, p. 320.

[24] Letter to Owen Lovejoy, 11 August 1855, *CW*, vol. 2, p. 316.

[25] Cited in Howard Jones, *Union in Peril: The Crisis over British Intervention in the Civil War* (Chapel Hill, University of North Carolina Press, 1992), p. 193.

ingrained attitudes. (The belief they induced in him that peaceful black and white coexistence was impossible helped explain his constant advocacy of recolonization for ex-slaves until the events of war convinced him of its impossibility.)[26] Republicanism thus had to be anti-slavery without being abolitionist. Only a "moderate" platform which took a firm stand against the Douglasite expansionists without exciting the prejudices of anti-expansionists could provide the principled ground on which Abolitionists might cohabit with anti-Abolitionists, German Republicans with nativist Know-Nothings, Western farmers with Eastern businessmen, Radicals with Conservatives, former anti-slavery Whigs with former free-soil Democrats. The Lincolnian-Republican ground of right, then, was a blend of the *moral* (anti-slavery and opposed to slavery's expansion), the *constitutional* (toleration of Southern slavery) and the *politically realistic* (conciliating the South, appeasing Northern negrophobia). Lincoln would be its most effective exponent.

After the Kansas–Nebraska Act, an increasingly polarized nation stumbled through a series of crises[27] that culminated in the October 1859 raid of fanatical abolitionist John Brown on the federal arsenal at Harper's Ferry, Virginia. This futile attempt to ignite a slave insurrection wildly inflamed Southerners' paranoia about the North's perfidious intentions. Though Brown's action was roundly repudiated by prominent Republicans, including Lincoln, Southern leaders were in no mood to distinguish between people opposed to slavery's expansion and those who would abolish it altogether, by violence if necessary. They began to strengthen their militias and to mobilize for the defense (as they saw it) of their civilization, threatening to leave the Union if a "Black Republican"[28] won the forthcoming presidential race. Lincoln's victory was taken as a signal, and with South Carolina leading the way, the Southern States began to secede.

The South thus cracked its shins on the hard rock embedded in the

[26] An American Colonization Society, supported by Southerners like James Madison and Henry Clay, had been founded in 1817 to colonize free blacks in Africa. It was to this society's colonization philosophy that Lincoln so long adhered, despite the dubious results of its only real achievement, the foundation of Liberia.

[27] First, of "bleeding Kansas" where the harm of Douglas' popular sovereignty doctrine was exposed; then of the 1856 presidential race, won by Democratic friend-of-the-South James Buchanan but in which John C. Frémont swept the most northerly states under the slogan "Free soil, free speech and Frémont"; then of the Supreme Court's *Dred Scott* decision which outraged Republicans by implying the unconstitutionality of prohibiting slavery in the territories; then of the pro-slavery Lecompton Constitution produced for Kansas by a rigged convention, an affair that left both North and South feeling profoundly cheated and aggrieved.

[28] A term of abuse coined by Douglas suggesting that the Republican Party was really a Northern abolitionist party. See John S. Wright, *Lincoln and the Politics of Slavery* (Reno, University of Nevada Press, 1970), pp. 190–191.

"moderate" Lincolnian ground of right – the insistence on Union. Lincoln's Republican position had about it the nature of a bargain with the South: the North would guarantee not to interfere with slavery where it already existed – was even prepared to embed this guarantee in the Constitution – if the South would desist from trying to transplant it elsewhere. But if the evil of slavery was to be tolerated for the sake of the Union, it followed that what could *not* be tolerated was destruction of the Union. This was the point where no moderation, no compromise, was possible. Therefore if Southerners, distrusting the North's sincerity, attempted to secede, the North would try forcefully to prevent them. Lincoln presented the legal-constitutional case in his First Inaugural Address when he said that the United States was a contract among parties that might be *unlawfully* broken by one or more of them, but could not be "peacefully unmade" (rescinded) except by the agreement of all. South Carolina and the other States *could* not secede, therefore, though people within them may be in a state of insurrection or revolution. The Union, once made, had constitutionally to defend and maintain itself, from which Lincoln deduced the "simple duty" placed on himself as chief executive to do whatever was necessary to that end.[29] The larger case underlying the legalistic arguments, however, concerned the specific nature of the American Union which Lincoln, like many before him, regarded as a great and noble "experiment" in democratic government.

This idea formed the moral clasp that tied all of Lincoln's political thought together and gave historic resonance to many of his greatest speeches. It carried profound implications for the preservation of Northern moral capital through democratic example, as we shall see. Here I will merely recall some of Lincoln's characteristic utterances on the matter: America was a "nation conceived in Liberty, dedicated to the proposition that all men are created equal." The central question was whether a democratic government so dedicated could long exist on the earth. "Must a government, of necessity," he asked, "be too *strong* for the liberties of its own people, or too *weak* to maintain its own existence?" It had been shown that popular government could be established and administered, but the war was the great test as to whether it could be maintained against a formidable internal attempt to overthrow it, a question of profound importance not just to Americans but to all humanity. It had to be demonstrated to the world that "those who can fairly carry an election, can also suppress a rebellion – that ballots are the rightful, and peaceful, successor of bullets."[30]

The idea of the American experiment, or mission, explained why

---

[29] *CW*, vol. 4, pp. 264–265.
[30] Message to Congress in Special Session, 4 July 1861, *CW*, vol. 4, p. 427.

preservation of the Union was fundamental. It also resolved the apparent paradox that Lincoln had pointed to in 1845, namely that tolerating slavery could be a duty imposed by devotion to liberty. It justified at once the Republican policy of non-interference with existing slavery, the stern resistance to slavery's expansion, and the determination to conduct and endure a civil war rather than accept disunion. Here was a foundation for moral capital, a ground of right on which, Lincoln believed, the North could firmly stand, an ideal for which it was worth fighting, sacrificing and dying. The question was whether others would share his view or find it adequate to the circumstances of secession and civil war.

Action: Lincoln's policies

Lincoln was adamant about the strength and confidence imparted by the feeling of *being* in the right, but he also understood the political importance of being *seen* to be in the right. His acute sense of it was demonstrated in the first important decision of his presidency, the relief of Fort Sumter. Sumter, a beleaguered offshore federal fort in South Carolina, any reinforcement of which that seceded State had promised to resist, became (along with Fort Pickens in Florida) an important symbol of national authority in the South. The five-week drama over Sumter was Lincoln's Gethsemane, a period of acute anxiety and strain in which the threat of a war that he did not want but could not refuse hung heavy upon him. Since he had promised in his Inaugural Address to "hold, occupy and possess" the places and property of the national government, evacuating Sumter would have been "politically ruinous" though militarily sensible. It would, he later explained, have discouraged the Union's friends and emboldened its enemies, and perhaps have led to foreign recognition of the Confederacy. An anxious Lincoln took his time to canvass options and consider his course, holding one overriding thought in mind: it would not be *him*, or the North, that began the war if war there must be. The seceding States had to be seen to be the aggressors in any conflict and to be kept "constantly and palpably in the wrong." Any attempt to resupply or reinforce Sumter would provoke Confederate aggression and the government "would stand justified, before the entire country, in repelling the aggression."[31]

On 12 April 1861 a Union fleet arrived with supplies, Confederate guns opened fire on Fort Sumter, and the war began. The reaction in the North was an instantaneous outpouring of public sentiment, even among Democrats, for defense of the Union. Lincoln's call for 70,000 volunteers

---

[31] The words of Lincoln's friend, Orville Browning, who had laid out the plan Lincoln followed prior to his Inauguration. Cited in Donald, *Lincoln*, p. 293.

was immediately overfilled and could have been met eight times over. "The plan succeeded," he wrote. "They attacked Sumter – it fell, and thus, did more service than it otherwise could."[32] His opinion was ironically mirrored in the South. "He chose to draw the sword," one Southern newspaper was still bitterly arguing at the war's end, "but by a dirty trick succeeded in throwing upon the South the *seeming* blame of firing 'the first gun'."[33] Yet it was an irony typical of Lincoln's tenure that, though he had successfully maneuvered the North into a position that justified the use of force to resist force, the moral capital thus gained failed utterly to redound to his personal credit. His slow deliberation over the crisis had looked like procrastination to his cabinet and to the press, who accused him of lacking a firm policy. The impression of dilatoriness, indecision and drift set a pattern of misapprehension that was to dog him over the ensuing years, reinforced by his difficulty in finding a general who would give him the decisive victory he sorely needed.[34]

His problems were exacerbated by the firmness with which he adhered to his original ground of right. Although the South, by seceding, had repudiated the Republican bargain, Lincoln stuck grimly to one of its essential terms, the promise to leave slavery alone. The war would be fought to restore the Union, not to free the slaves. In the context of civil war this incurred serious moral capital costs, both at home and abroad.

Lincoln always emphasized his lack of constitutional authority to act on slavery, but there were also domestic political reasons for insisting on Union at the expense of emancipation. One was the necessity of building, from a weak position, the fragile coalition needed to make the Union cause possible. Lincoln had to maintain the allegiance, or at least neutrality, of the slave-owning border States – Maryland, Kentucky, Missouri and Delaware – which had not seceded but were torn between attachment to the Union and sympathy for their rebellious Southern brethren.

---

[32] Cited in *ibid.* p. 293.

[33] *Daily Express*, Petersburg, VA, 9 March 1865, in Mitgang, *Lincoln as They Saw Him*, p. 429.

[34] An impression that seems to linger still in the historical judgment of David Donald who frequently refers to Lincoln's "passive personality" and his general "passivity" in the face of events. See *Lincoln Reconsidered*, chapter 4, and *Lincoln*, pp. 14–15 and 415. Donald perhaps owes it originally to Harriet Beecher Stowe's description of 1864, in which she describes Lincoln's strength as of a peculiar kind, "not aggressive so much as passive, and among passive things, it is like not so much the strength of a stone buttress but of a wire cable. It is strength swaying to every influence, yielding on this side and on that to popular needs, yet tenaciously and inflexibly bound to carry its great ends." *The Watchman and Reflector*, reprinted in Mitgang, *Lincoln as They Saw Him*, p. 370. But see Fehrenbacher's acute discussion on Lincoln as event-maker in his introduction to *Abraham Lincoln: A Documentary Portrait*, pp. xxv–xxvii; also James M. McPherson's review of Donald's book, "A Passive President?" in *Atlantic Monthly* (November 1995), www.theatlantic.com/issues/95nov/lincoln/lincoln.htm.

Any move toward abolition automatically tested their loyalty and jeopardized the entire enterprise. He also needed to reach beyond his own Republicans for support among the Democrats. There was little he could do about the Peace Democrats (Copperheads, so-called, after the venomous snake of that name) whose sympathies were with the South, but he was always concerned to keep on side the War Democrats, some of whom he promoted to high military office. He even favored a political realignment that would have the Republicans fuse with War Democrats on a Union ticket. To one Republican unhappy with such bipartisan policies he wrote:

The administration came into power, very largely in a minority of the popular vote. Notwithstanding this, it distributed to its party friends as nearly all the civil patronage as any administration ever did. The war came. The administration could not even start in this, without assistance outside of its party. It was mere nonsense to suppose a minority could put down a majority in rebellion.[35]

Most War Democrats, however, were as committed as border State politicians to restricting the war's aims solely to restoration of the Union.

Lincoln's own Republican Party was hardly at one on this issue, or indeed any other, having been assembled from disparate groups united only by the impulse to halt slavery's expansion. Some of its more powerful figures were in fact former Democrats. Lincoln's two most prominent cabinet members, Seward and Chase, were not merely personal rivals, but opposed on the war aims, Chase taking an abolitionist stance and Seward a "moderate" one. The same division was evident in Congress, where Radical Republicans advocated emancipating Southern slaves and confiscating Southern property while others wished to leave Southern society intact, fearing that emancipation would lead to the horrors of a "servile insurrection." Leading Radicals became highly active opponents of Lincoln's policy, bemoaning his folly in attempting to preserve slavery while prosecuting a war against slave owners. They were unhappy about what they saw as his neglect of the moral anti-slavery arguments that were the party's foundation, and urged him to make the contest one between freedom and slavery. Lincoln rejected this course as too far in advance of public opinion, whose pulse he was ever intent on sounding. The Radicals, however, thought him too subservient to Northern negrophobic opinion, whose sway was allegedly diminishing. It was true that the war had to some extent galvanized and altered public feeling on the subject,[36] and Lincoln observed this encouraging shift hopefully but was less convinced than others about its extent, especially in the West.

[35] Letter to Carl Schurz, 10 November 1862, *CW*, vol. 5, p. 494.
[36] See Trollope, *North America*, p. 358.

To one set of clamorous opinion, therefore, any move toward making slavery an object of the war was a betrayal or a mistake; to another, *not* making it so was tragic and dangerous folly. The only thing upon which all the conflicting elements in Lincoln's fragile coalition agreed was Union, a fact which underpinned the constitutional propriety of maintaining Union as the sole war aim. The difficulty of maintaining it thus, however, was demonstrated by the Frémont affair in late 1861. John C. Frémont was a former Western explorer and now a commanding general fighting Confederate guerrillas in Missouri, where he issued a martial law proclamation declaring, among other things, that slaves of anyone aiding the rebellion would be freed. Lincoln repudiated this as a political decision only the president was authorized to take. In the North there was furious indignation and savage criticism from friends as well as political enemies at Lincoln's overruling of the popular Frémont's emancipation proclamation. But among the border States the response was completely the opposite. There Frémont's action provoked Kentucky into a threat to go over to the rebels. Lincoln explained that if he had not quashed Frémont's emancipation plans Kentucky would have been lost, if Kentucky then Missouri, then Maryland. "These all against us, and the job on our hands is too large for us. We would as well consent to separation at once, including the surrender of this capitol."[37]

In the international arena, the consequences of Lincoln's war policy were perhaps even more serious, for there the contest over moral capital had the potential to be politically decisive. The perceptions that mattered were those of the powerful nations of Europe, particularly Britain and France, whose actions in the American war had the power to determine events. The North's greatest fear and the South's greatest hope was that the European nations would recognize the Confederacy as a legal entity. Though fearful of being drawn into the war themselves, most of the Europeans were inclined to extend recognition should the South prove to their satisfaction that it had "made a nation." The main strategic goal of Robert E. Lee's armies in their thrusts into Maryland and Pennsylvania was precisely to convince Europe of this fact.[38] It was a delicate diplomatic matter, for even a statement of neutrality by a power like Britain was seen by an angry North as a tacit form of "recognition."[39] Slavery, however, formed a great stumbling block to full recognition because, as Prime Minister Palmerston observed, the South (especially after Lincoln's

---

[37] Letter to Carl Schurz, 10 November 1862, *CW*, vol. 5, p. 494.
[38] Only Russia (somewhat paradoxically) wholeheartedly supported the Northern cause. The French government of Louis Napoleon unabashedly favoured the South, while Lord Palmerston's government in Britain, though officially neutral, believed that separation of the South was inevitable.
[39] Jones, *Union in Peril*, p. 230.

Emancipation Proclamation of 1862) would surely insist on the North's sanctioning slavery and undertaking to return runaways.[40] Nevertheless, there was constant plotting among European leaders, horrified by the savagery and scale of the American war, either to intervene or to force mediation. The result would have been, as Lincoln knew, a *de facto* acceptance of separation.

Lincoln's policy of expressly keeping slavery out of Northern war aims undoubtedly exacerbated this danger, and in fact played to the moral advantage of the South. Slavery might be, as Lincoln later said, "somehow, the cause of the war," but the issue over which it was fought was Union versus States' rights (or more correctly State sovereignty).[41] Lincoln prosecuted the war on the grounds of suppressing a rebellion of misguided Southern individuals attempting illegally to destroy the Union; the South, for its part, fought it on the grounds of a right of States to withdraw from a voluntary Union in order to found an independent nation. The rights and wrongs of this issue formed a technical legal question over which nineteenth-century views could and did vary as they did not over slavery. By mid-century most enlightened and popular European opinion was opposed to slavery and the slave trade. The wonderful irony was that Lincoln's exclusive insistence on Union relinquished the flag of liberty to the slave-owning South. Europeans, the British in particular, often confessed themselves bewildered by the Northern attachment to Union, and never properly understood the moral conjunction of Union and the democratic experiment on which Northerners insisted. They could easily appreciate, however, the plea of Southerners for the liberty to depart in peace from an association that had become intolerable to them. European ruling elites also felt some sympathetic kinship for the Southern aristocracy, and were deeply impressed by the valiant achievements of its armies against Northern might in the war. The London *Times* expressed the prevailing ambivalence when it editorialized:

To slavery we have ever held the most rooted aversion. Not all the valour, not all the success of the South, has ever blinded us to this black spot on their fair escutcheon. But even tainted as they are with this foul stain, they have commanded our admiration and our sympathy from the gallantry with which they have maintained their cause, and from the obvious truth that the struggle was for the separation on the one part and compulsory retention on the other.[42]

European commentators often expressed the opinion that, anyway,

---

[40] *Ibid.*, pp. 167 and 191.
[41] See Phillip S. Paludan, *A Covenant with Death: The Constitution, Law, and Equality in the Civil War Era* (Urbana, University of Illinois Press, 1975), pp. 30–35.
[42] *The Times* (London), 15 January 1863, in Mitgang, *Lincoln as They Saw Him*, p. 331.

whether the South won or lost, slavery had been doomed by the war.[43] On such an assumption the "foul stain" could perhaps be ignored when considering which cause to support. But if the North had made emancipation a war aim from the start, the South remaining adamantly pro-slavery, it would have been very difficult if not impossible for Europe to justify recognizing the latter.

Lincoln was fortunate that the South's dilemma here was even more acute than the North's. Enlightened Southerners, including many in the leadership, accepted that slavery was bound for extinction, and if their views had determined policy the outcome of the civil war might have been very different. An announcement of plans to end slavery, legalize slave marriages and educate slave children would not only have brought the Europeans firmly on side, but would also have preempted the North and increased divisions there between peace and war factions, aiding the Copperheads and swelling the chance of a Democratic victory in the presidential election of 1864.[44] But Jefferson Davis could not make such a declaration for he knew the Confederacy would immediately fly asunder. To the minds of many Southerners, particularly in the deeper South, it had been created precisely to *maintain* and *strengthen* slavery. Davis' vice-president, Alexander Stephens, expressed this attitude in a popular speech that declared the cornerstone of the Confederacy to be the exact opposite of that in the Declaration of Independence, resting on "the great truth that the negro is not equal to the white man, that slavery . . . is his natural and normal condition." The Davis administration felt it had no option but to maintain a stony silence on the matter until the last desperate days of the war when it was too late (and even in those terminal circumstances, an announcement of an intention to enlist 40,000 slaves on a promise of liberty created a storm of Southern protest).

The moral capital the South gained as the champion of freedom and self-determination was thus constantly undermined by its addiction to black servitude. Southern leaders had, it is true, banked on rather more material factors to counteract this weakness, specifically on *realpolitik* calculations about the power of "King Cotton." The linen factories of Britain and France were being starved of raw materials by Lincoln's blockade of Southern ports, and Southerners gambled that, if slavery were kept out of Northern war aims, and if Southern armies could match the North long enough to make the cotton famine bite, France and Britain would eventually be forced to break the blockade and thus destroy the Union cause. For as long, then, as the war was defined in terms of States' rights versus Union – for as long, that is, as Lincoln kept slavery

[43] See *The Times*, 7 October 1862, in Mitgang, *Lincoln as They Saw Him*, p. 321.
[44] See Nevins, "The Southern Dilemma," in *The Statesmanship of the Civil War*, p. 92.

out of it – the Confederacy could continue to hope for *de facto* or *de jure* recognition.[45]

The South's gamble failed. Lincoln would say that he had always been aware that "favor or disfavor of foreign nations might have a material influence in enlarging and prolonging the struggle," but that he had "reckoned on the forebearance of nations." His reckoning, interestingly, was based on his estimate of the accumulated moral capital of his nation, "whose history has seemed to authorize a belief that the past action and influence of the United States were generally regarded as having been beneficent towards mankind."[46] Yet an early declaration making emancipation an object of the war (a course that several Republicans urged with great vigor) would have made forbearance more certain, authorizing the North to proclaim itself the real champion of liberty in the affair. When Lincoln eventually decided to play this card, it was indeed partly to forestall British and French recognition.

But if Lincoln had anticipated an immediate access of international moral capital after his Preliminary Emancipation Proclamation of September 1862, he was disappointed. Many Europeans interpreted the proclamation as a belated, cynical and desperate move forced by military failure. Worse, since emancipation was limited to slaves in rebel-held territory and justified as a war measure, it was taken as an attempt to stir up bloody slave insurrection in the South, a horrifying thought to white people everywhere. *The Times* declared that "the emancipation or continued slavery of the negro [is] used only as means to forward the ends of the North."[47] The *Courier des Etats-Unis*, a French-American paper, commented:

If Mr. Lincoln wished to act on principle, he should repudiate the institution of slavery wherever it exists; if he wished to act with policy, he should abstain from menacing it at all. In trying to steer between these two inflexible alternatives he has committed an act which is neither that of a man of solid conviction nor a statesman.[48]

The irony of this comment lies in the fact that Lincoln never regarded these as "inflexible alternatives." His statesmanship was based on the perpetual attempt to justify policies and actions with arguments that, like his grounding position, contrived to combine right principle, constitutional propriety and political necessity. Despite the bad initial

---

[45] Howard Jones, *Union in Peril*, p. 16, notes that Lincoln's laying aside of the slavery issue "relieved the British from having to make a decision between their moral commitment to anti-slavery and their economic interests in Southern cotton . . . The focus on commercial issues . . . increased the possibility of recognition of Southern independence."

[46] "Reply to the Workingmen of Manchester," 19 January 1863, *CW*, vol. 5, p. 64.

[47] Mitgang, *Lincoln as They Saw Him*, p. 321.

[48] Reprinted in *National Intelligencer*, Washington, 8 October 1862, in Mitgang, *Lincoln as They Saw Him*, p. 319.

reaction, he would be justified in this instance. By the time of the issuing of the Final Emancipation Proclamation on 1 January 1863, Europeans had realized that the long-range effect would be the end of slavery. In England there were mass rallies of workers, a flood of petitions and resolutions to the government in support of Lincoln, and with this the possibility of foreign intervention disappeared completely. Expanding the war aims to Union *and* liberty thus ended the danger once and for all.

Example: the democratic imperative

Moral capital by example was of peculiar importance in a civil war that many, including Lincoln, regarded as a test of the sustainability of consti-tutional, democratic government. Lincoln combined what Margaret Canovan has called the pragmatic and redemptive faces of democracy – that is, democracy as merely a particular form of government, on the one hand, as a form of salvation through politics on the other.[49] He had no illusions about the processes of democratic politics in which he was himself an adept, but he nevertheless emphasized the redemptive promise of a free people governing itself. Democratic government was govern-ment by, of and for the people under the rule of law, especially the foundational law of the Constitution. For Lincoln, the Constitution embodied the pragmatic, institutional forms without which democratic government could scarcely be imagined as functioning. The redemptive promise of democracy, however, was embodied in the Declaration of Independence. Lincoln maintained that the connections between democ-racy and the values of liberty and equality enshrined in the Declaration were very intimate: "As I would not be *slave*, so I would not be *master*. This expresses my idea of democracy. Whatever differs from this, to the extent of the difference, is no democracy."[50]

The people could alter the Constitution, if they collectively chose, to bring it more into accord with the redemptive ideal, but such a choice must be the product of political struggle within constitutionally available institutions and processes. The Southern States by unilaterally breaking the Union had repudiated this principle, and upholding it required that they not be permitted to succeed. On the other hand, the North, in forcefully resisting their attempt, must be careful not to destroy the thing

[49] Margaret Canovan, "Trust the People! Populism and the Two Faces of Democracy," *Political Studies* 47 (1999), pp. 2–16, at p. 16. Her distinction is an adaptation of Michael Oakeshott's between the "politics of faith" and the "politics of scepticism": M. Oakeshott, *The Politics of Faith and the Politics of Scepticism* (New Haven, Yale University Press, 1996).

[50] *CW*, vol. 2, p. 532.

for which it was fighting. The Union was to be preserved, but not at *all* costs, specifically not at the cost of sacrificing the very ideals that made it worth preserving – the forms of popular, constitutional government and the rights and liberties of its citizenry guaranteed by the Constitution. But even free people are, as Lincoln observed, good and bad, silly and wise, weak and strong, and the outcome of a struggle between them cannot be certain.[51] This was why the war was interpreted as a "fiery trial" for popular government itself. It was "a People's contest," and the people themselves would "nobly save or meanly lose the last best hope of earth."

Lincoln's government must then maintain its own moral capital, and that of the Union cause, by the practical example it set. It would permit free speech, criticism, elections as usual, even putting its own administration to the electoral test with the task of war yet incomplete. But permitting fierce dissent in extraordinary times carried peculiar risks for an untried minority president in the emotionally charged circumstances of a civil war. As we have seen, Lincoln came under increasing fire from radicals and citizens who wanted finally to abolish the divisive evil of Southern slavery once and for all. He put his constitutional argument for his "hands-off" policy as follows:

I am naturally anti-slavery. If slavery is not wrong, then nothing is wrong. I can not remember when I did not so think, and feel. And yet I have never understood that the Presidency conferred upon me an unrestricted right to act officially upon this judgment and feeling. It was in the oath I took that would, to the best of my ability, preserve, protect, and defend the Constitution of the United States. I could not take the office without taking the oath . . . I understood, too, that in ordinary civil administration this oath even forbade me to practically indulge my primary abstract judgment on the moral question of slavery. I did understand, however, that my oath to preserve the constitution to the best of my ability, imposed on me the duty of preserving, by every indispensable means, that government – that nation – of which that constitution was the organic law.[52]

Though Lincoln declared himself ready to bend or break parts of the Constitution in order to save the whole thing in an emergency – to cut off a limb to save the body, as he put it – he continued to regard constitutional justification of his actions as fundamental. Politically, he probably had little other choice given what Phillip Paludan called the "pervasive constitutionalism" of the country.[53] But Lincoln sincerely shared this constitutionalism. After listing the dire political consequences – loss of the border States – that would have followed had he not overridden

[51] See *CW*, vol. 8, p. 101.
[52] Letter to Albert A. Hodges, 4 April 1864, *CW*, vol. 7, pp. 281–282.
[53] Paludan, *A Covenant with Death*, p. 46.

Frémont's emancipation proclamation, he went on to warn that he must not be understood to have acted *for the sake of* Kentucky. Frequently accused by the Democratic press of dictatorship and tyranny, Lincoln argued that it would be tyranny indeed if he seized the legislative function of government to interfere with the property of loyal as well as disloyal citizens. "Can it be pretended," he asked a friend, "that it is any longer the government of the US – any government of Constitution and laws – wherein a General, or a President, may make permanent rules of property by proclamation?"[54]

Lincoln tried to maintain this careful constitutionality even when at last compelled to shift policy. By summer of 1862, a war expected to be short, sharp and victorious was in its second year, with Union armies and generals unable to deal a decisive blow against a numerically inferior foe. Northern costs in both men and materials were mounting, recruitment was falling sharply, paper currency had had to be issued, and economic hardship was increasing, particularly in the North-West where traditional access to the Mississippi had been curtailed. After the failure of a compensated gradual emancipation scheme for the border States, Lincoln decided at last to lay an executive hand upon slavery. He argued that the only place such power might constitutionally exist, and even then only as a military necessity, was within the war powers that the president had assumed "as Commander-in-Chief of the Army and Navy" in time of rebellion. In his First Inaugural Address he had argued that "when an end is lawful and obligatory, the indispensable means to it are also lawful and obligatory." Freeing rebel slaves appeared to have become an indispensable means to weaken the South and strengthen the North by mid-1862, and could thus be militarily justified. The Preliminary Emancipation Proclamation that Lincoln promulgated on 22 September 1862, and the Final Proclamation that followed it 100 days later, were therefore purposely limited.[55] Emancipation did not extend to the loyal States because, as Lincoln argued, no military necessity justified that.

Though the dry, legalistic tone of the documents emphasized their impliedly lawful purpose, Lincoln's careful constitutionalism seemed to please nobody. To the Radicals his measure was too limited, while to anti-abolitionists it was too radical. But Lincoln well knew, even as he signed the Final Proclamation, that the *effects* of his action could not be limited to its legal range. The inevitable "friction and abrasion" of the

---

[54] Letter to Orville H. Browning, 22 September 1861, *CW*, vol. 4, p. 532.
[55] Preliminary Emancipation Proclamation, 22 September 1862, *CW*, vol. 5, pp. 433–436; Final Emancipation Proclamation, 1 January 1863, *CW*, vol. 6, pp. 23–26. One hundred days were granted between the warning of the Preliminary Proclamation and the final decree, partly in order to let Northern opinion adjust but also to give the rebellious States one last chance to return to pre-war "normality."

war itself had eroded the citadel of slavery. Lincoln knew there could be no going back, and was determined there *would* be no going back despite the storm of Democratic and negrophobic hostility that the Proclamation stirred up in the North and North-West. Concerned, notwithstanding his constitutional arguments, that a future legal challenge might find his Proclamation invalid, he began to work for a constitutional amendment that would foreclose on this possibility. (January 1865 would find a re-elected Lincoln doing some political log-rolling to ensure a two-thirds congressional majority for the Thirteenth Amendment prohibiting slavery in the United States forever.)

The mid-term elections of 1862 clearly revealed the costs of maintaining democratic processes while adopting perhaps necessary but inevitably unpopular policies. Further disaffection was caused by the introduction in August of conscription, undoubtedly the most unpopular policy of the war.[56] The Democrats, seeing their opportunity for a comeback, effectively attacked emancipation and the administration's sweeping use of arrests under the suspension of *habeas corpus* to suppress protests at the draft. Radical Republicans, meanwhile, unhappy at the limited nature of Lincoln's emancipation, campaigned half-heartedly. The Democrats made huge gains at both State and federal levels (though, importantly, failed to win a majority in Congress). Lincoln's own analysis of Democratic success included the observation that "Our newspapers, by vilifying and disparaging the administration, furnished them all the weapons to do it with."[57] For despite the accusations of despotism and tyranny, the press was left mostly free to attack the government at will, and to denounce Lincoln himself "as a perjurer, a usurper, a tyrant, a subverter of the Constitution, a destroyer of the liberties of his country, a reckless desperado, a heartless trifler over the last agonies of an expiring nation" – among other things.[58]

By 1864, Lincoln was convinced that the whole cause, after three years of trial, was at risk in the forthcoming presidential election. The main problem, he knew, was still "the ill-success of the war," for in spite of the win at Gettysburg in 1863 final victory remained elusive, and Lincoln had had to announce repeated drafts (which occasionally provoked bloody riots) for hundreds of thousands of men. Maintaining bipartisan support for the war was virtually impossible when the prize of the presidency was at stake, and the Democrats opted to run with a "peace plank." On 23 August 1864 Lincoln wrote a secret note:

---

[56] See Neely, *The Last Best Hope of Earth*, pp. 126–127.
[57] Letter to Carl Schurz, *CW*, vol. 5, p. 494.
[58] Henry Raymond's editorial, *New York Times*, 28 May 1864, in Mitgang, *Lincoln as They Saw Him*, p. 386.

This morning, as for some days past, it seems exceedingly probable that this administration will not be re-elected. Then it will be my duty to so cooperate with the president-elect, as to save the Union between the election and the inauguration: as he will have secured his election on such ground that he cannot possibly save it afterward.[59]

Lincoln had to face a leadership challenge from his own Radical Republicans, still complaining of his slowness, timidity and incompetence. Their attempts foundered and Lincoln stood (under the banner of the National Union Party)[60] against his former commanding general, George McLellan, now running for the Democrats.

It was a rancorous, overheated campaign in which the Lincoln camp emphasized Union at the expense of emancipation. Aided by timely victories by Admiral Farragut and General Sherman, Lincoln won with a substantial increase in the popular vote, the first president to obtain a second term since Andrew Jackson in 1832. The Democrats had failed to unite Lincoln's opponents, divided among those wanting a negotiated peace and those wanting the war more vigorously prosecuted. Lincoln thus entered his second term with his political base secured, certain for the first time in the triumph of the Union cause and with his eyes now firmly set on the difficult business of Reconstruction.

Rhetoric/symbolism: Lincoln's lasting capital

If maintaining moral capital by democratic example had been an enormous gamble, it had eventually paid off. The election was widely regarded as a victory not just for Lincoln, but for democracy itself. As Lincoln put it, "if the rebellion could force us to forego, or postpone the national election, it might fairly be claimed to have already conquered and ruined us."[61] Lincoln himself, moreover, seemed at last to be emerging as a *bona fide* symbol of the Northern cause. His democratic commitment, by providing a free field for attack and vilification, had not appeared to play much to his personal advantage during that agonizing first term, but by the time of the election his apparent popularity was a cause of debate and concern among Republicans trying to oust him in favour of a new candidate. Their agents reported strong support for him from Maine to California – though some hoped it was only "on the surface."[62] There was some suggestion among Lincoln supporters of a populist

---

[59] *CW*, vol. 7, p. 514.
[60] On the logic and legacy of this name change (disastrous for Democrats), see Neely, *The Last Best Hope of Earth*, pp. 176–177.
[61] Response to a Serenade, 10 November 1864, *CW*, vol. 8, p. 101.
[62] See Donald, *Lincoln*, pp. 493–494.

division between untrustworthy political elites and "Honest Abe," man of the people, and indeed there seems always to have been a positive image in mass circulation running in competition with the negative ones in the press. This was the lovable figure of a wise, presiding elder ("Father Abraham"), a kindly soul who had the common person's interest at heart, who pardoned more deserters than the generals thought good for discipline, who was accessible to anyone that came seeking help or favor.[63] Henry Raymond noted that the popular sentiment for Lincoln "is the more extraordinary in view of the unexampled abuse which has been poured on the administration for the last two years. No living man was ever charged with political crimes of such multiplicity and such enormity as ABRAHAM LINCOLN."[64]

By 1864 Lincoln had won over most of the initially skeptical Northern intelligentsia, and their authoritative voices rang clearly through the fog of abuse. James Russell Lowell published an influential series in the *North American Review* on the eve of the election, calling Lincoln "a long-headed and long-purposed man," who "had shown from the first the considerate wisdom of a practical statesman." *Harper's Weekly*, in interpreting the lesson of the election for the North, noted that Lincoln had acquired an important symbolic role:

In himself, notwithstanding his unwearied patience, perfect fidelity, and remarkable sagacity, he is unimportant; but as a representative of the feeling and purpose of the American people he is the most important fact in the world.[65]

Phillip Paludan, noting Lincoln's vital role in strengthening faith in the political system, concluded that "Example as well as rhetoric persuaded Northerners that their system was worth fighting for."[66] Yet rhetoric was important too, though Lincoln was slow to employ it.

In a long, frustrating war, the problem for either side was one of sustaining unity, will and morale by fostering a continuing conviction of the righteousness, necessity, even sacredness, of the cause. Though the North had the preponderance of power and population, it had to maintain its will through the deep ebbs in morale that inevitably accompanied calamitous defeats and grievous loss of young manhood. It had to be constantly reassured that the cause was worth the candle, for there were

[63] Ralph Waldo Emerson, responding with enthusiasm to the Preliminary Emancipation Proclamation, noted in passing that "great as the popularity of this President has been, we are beginning to think that we have underestimated [his] capacity and virtue." "The President's Proclamation," *Atlantic Monthly* (November 1862), in Mitgang, *Lincoln as They Saw Him*, p. 325.

[64] *New York Times*, 28 May 1864, in Mitgang, *Lincoln as They Saw Him*, p. 286.

[65] 19 November 1864, in Mitgang, *Lincoln as They Saw Him*, p. 405.

[66] Phillip Shaw Paludan, *"A People's Contest": The Union and Civil War 1861–1865* (New York, Harper & Row, 1988), p. 378.

those in their midst, even among the Republicans, who were for negotiating a truce that would recognize a permanent division.

The North was richly blessed in comparison with the South in the numbers of people of talent it could command to stir and gird the national spirit – in effect, to create it.[67] Lincoln was but one among many, but he was in a crucial position of leadership, and therefore with a potentially unique role in heartening and uniting the masses and in strengthening their resolve and belief. Lincoln's role was in fact more pivotal than had been that of most previous presidents who had operated under a tradition of a minimal executive, for he had both accepted the war and then personally assumed control of it as a presidential responsibility and prerogative. Moreover, Lincoln's idea that *right would make might*, provided that one held faithfully to course, depended on persuading and reassuring people that the administration's course was indeed right and its actions on track. And Lincoln had the rhetorical gift to cope with such a task. He had an unusual ability to present a case by arguing with seemingly inexorable logic, from moral first principles to irrefutable political conclusions, in a manner so sincerely impassioned and so laced with pointed humor that audiences were persuaded, inspired and delighted. Even the erratic Republican editor of the *New York Tribune*, Horace Greeley, always half-hearted about Lincoln, grudgingly admitted that "his *forte* was in debate, or rather in the illumination of profound truths, so that they can hardly evade the dullest apprehension."[68] Lincoln's plain man's language – sometimes belittled by people fond of the florid and orotund excesses of the age – was clear and efficient but capable of rising to the heights of a sinewy political poetry.

An article of 1863, noting the efforts of the press to cut Lincoln down on account of his appearance, intellect and cultivation, argued that: "The very fact that Mr. Lincoln's thoughts come to us in such English that pleases Heaven, bears witness to his courage and honesty. We have . . . long enough worshiped mere intellect without purpose or adroitness without high purpose."[69] This accurately reflected Lincoln's own ideal of political speech, which he had described in 1852 in a eulogy on Henry Clay. Clay was a man of "surpassing eloquence," he said, though his

---

[67] For example, poets like Emerson, Lowell, Henry Longfellow and Walt Whitman; editors like Samuel Bowles, Henry J. Raymond and William Cullen Bryant; eloquent clergymen like Henry Ward Beecher and T. Starr King; orators like Edward Everett; pamphleteers like David A. Wells and Charles J. Stillé; songwriters like Julia Ward Howe who penned "Battle Hymn of the Republic"; and writers like Harriet Beecher Stowe whose sentimental epic, *Uncle Tom's Cabin*, had worked deeply upon the conscience of the whole reading world.

[68] *New York Tribune*, 19 April 1865, in Mitgang, *Lincoln as They Saw Him*, p. 406.

[69] *Galesville Transcript*, Wisconsin, 3 November 1863, quoting from *Home Journal*, in Mitgang, *Lincoln as They Saw Him*, pp. 353–354.

eloquence "did not consist of types and figures and elegant arrangements of words, but rather of that deeply earnest and impassioned tone, and manner, which can proceed only from great sincerity and thorough conviction in the speaker of the justice and importance of his cause. This is what truly touches the chords of human sympathy . . . All his efforts were made for practical effect. He never spoke merely to be heard."[70] Lincoln always spoke publicly for "practical effect" – to convince by the strength of reason, to persuade by the force of right, to arouse to action, commitment and allegiance by the power of a noble cause.

There are many testimonies to Lincoln's power to move an audience. Typical was the reaction of the New Yorkers who gathered to hear him at the Cooper Union on 27 February 1860. Initially disconcerted by Lincoln's long, ungainly figure, his ill-fitting clothes, his unkempt hair, his high, piercing tone and his mid-Western twang, these big city folk were soon enthralled by his careful dissection of popular sovereignty and his humorous, scathing attack on Southern reactions to the Republican platform. They applauded frequently and, at the close, stood and cheered, waving hats and handkerchiefs. Four New York newspapers enthused and printed the speech in full.[71] Yet this inestimable gift for a politician was used sparingly by Lincoln during his hardest years, largely due to a republican tradition, that he continued to observe, of executive reticence and statesmanlike dignity. Being seen to remain above the fray meant no press conferences and no official press releases. Though profoundly aware of the pernicious effect of a hostile press on public opinion, he only occasionally intervened to limit the damage or to put his own point of view. His Inaugural Addresses and messages to Congress (the latter not delivered personally) were widely spaced and hardly substituted for public addresses or regular communiqués on governmental thinking. Lincoln had no spin doctors, no propaganda unit, none of the instruments that modern politicians take for granted. The limited interventions Lincoln did make were often ridiculed according to the prejudice of the times. The *New York World* commented on the absurdity of a chief magistrate of a great nation writing "a labored letter to Horace Greeley in response to a newspaper criticism." Lincoln, it wrote, does "quaint things which show nature and naivete, but not a high and studied official bearing."[72]

Maintaining aloofness meant that even staunch supporters were often genuinely uncertain about the administration's aims and direction of the war, and there was little opportunity to provide executive succor to people bewildered by repeated military disasters. It was not until the

[70] "Eulogy on Henry Clay," 6 July 1852, in Fehrenbacher, *Abraham Lincoln*, p. 67.
[71] See Donald, *Lincoln*, p. 239.
[72] *New York World*, 5 February 1865, in Mitgang, *Lincoln as They Saw Him*, pp. 415–416.

middle of 1863, two and a half years into his term and following six months of Proclamation strife and a calamitous defeat at Chancellorsville, that Lincoln finally moved to take positive control of public opinion. He had already in January of that year sent a letter to the workingmen of Manchester in England, praising them for the heroism of their support of the cause of human liberty despite personal losses caused by the war. According to David Donald, speaking out over the heads of foreign leaders to the common people "daringly broadened the powers of the presidency," and gave Lincoln a taste for trying the same thing at home.[73]

His first domestic occasion was provided by the political upheaval over the arrest under the suspension of *habeas corpus* of prominent Copperhead Clement Vallandigham. Lincoln, having been accused by New York Democrats of overriding the civil rights of Americans and subverting the rule of law, drafted a public letter to Erastus Corning in the *New York Tribune* defending his policy. In it he asked rhetorically whether he was supposed to "shoot a simple-minded soldier boy who deserts, while I must not touch a hair of the wily agitator who induces him to desert?" He denied that emergency measures necessary to a war situation set precedents for peacetime, saying that this was equivalent to the argument "that a man could contract so strong an appetite for emetics during temporary illness, as to persist in feeding on them through the remainder of his healthful life."[74] The Corning letter, to Lincoln's gratification, received great public acclaim, reassuring people who had feared the use of "despotic power." It was reissued as a pamphlet and widely read.

Lincoln began to seek other suitable occasions for public letters that might influence public opinion. When Union army successes at Gettysburg and Vicksburg had the paradoxical effect of encouraging the desire for peace negotiations, Lincoln decided he must explain the need to stand firm for complete rebel capitulation. He took an opportunity to have a letter addressed to James Conkling read out to 50,000 cheering Unionists at a rally in Springfield. In this he declared his belief that it was impossible since the Emancipation Proclamation to have "any compromise, embracing the maintenance of the Union." He had given the slave-owners every chance for two years to return to the *status quo ante* with their "property" untouched, but now it was too late. Centrally at issue was the fate of "the negro" who had been armed and had fought valiantly for the Union cause. "You say you will not fight to free negroes," Lincoln addressed the

---

[73] Another surprising innovation, perhaps, for a "passive" president? Donald, *Lincoln*, p. 416.
[74] "Letter to Erastus Corning and others," 12 June 1863, *CW*, vol. 6, pp. 260–269. See Donald, *Lincoln*, pp. 441–443; Neely, *The Last Best Hope of Earth*, pp. 132–134.

peace party. "Some of them seem willing to fight for you." They had staked their life on the promise of freedom, and "the promise being made, must be kept." The Lincolnian rhetoric stepped up a gear at the close. He noted that a peace that would prove there was no appeal from the ballot to the bullet seemed not so far away, and when it came "there will be some black men who can remember that, with silent tongue, and clenched teeth, and steady eye, and well-poised bayonet, they have helped mankind on to this great consummation; while, I fear, there will be some white ones, unable to forget that, with malignant heart, and deceitful speech, they strove to hinder it."[75]

The Conkling letter, reprinted in every major newspaper and re-read to a mass meeting in New York City, was euphorically received by Union supporters. Press reports called it a "remarkably clear and forceful" document, a "true and noble letter," and Lincoln a leader "peculiarly adapted to the needs of the time . . . clear-headed, dispassionate, discreet, steadfast, honest."[76] This and other presidential letters were given much of the credit by Republicans for a string of convincing party victories in the ensuing State elections. They were regarded as so effective that they were collected for wider circulation as *The Letters of President Lincoln on Questions of National Policy.*[77] There followed in November 1863 the now-famous Gettysburg address, framed to commemorate the battlefield but effectively elevating the meaning of the war to a moment in humanity's progress toward liberty, and asserting that the promise of equality embodied in the Declaration of Independence lay at the nation's constitutional heart. Its reception was, as usual, divided on partisan lines, but appreciation for its strength, meaning and beauty steadily grew in the days that followed. His annual message to Congress in December (a "specimen of political dexterity" that trimmed between radical and conservative factions, as a Democratic paper sourly acknowledged) defended his recent Proclamation offering amnesty to rebels provided they accept emancipation as an essential condition of Reconstruction. It was so well received publicly that even former critics began to declare that Lincoln may be unbeatable in the 1864 election.

The question of Lincoln's rhetorical mobilization of moral capital comes down to how deeply his words penetrated the nation's conscience and how effectively they moved or strengthened them. His intention was to interpret and ennoble the war for Northerners, establishing continuity with the ideals of America's founders by confirming and reinvesting the nation in its self-conceived historical mission. By making sense of the

---

[75] "Letter to James C. Conkling," 26 August 1863, *CW*, vol. 6, pp. 406–410.
[76] Cited in Donald, *Lincoln*, p. 457.   [77] *Ibid.*, p. 458.

horror and sacrifice Lincoln tried to firm the moral tendons that bound people together. The country was divided of course, and he could not expect to win the defenders of separation (though at the end of the war even Southern voices that had vilified him for years began to see in his justice and moderation their best hope for an unvindictive Reconstruction). As for the mass of people sincerely devoted to Union but alternately cast between hope and despondency, resolve and defeatism, the question of Lincoln's moral effect cannot be answered with any degree of exactness.

Yet such evidence as exists argues that it was substantial. Even at our distance in time, his best words have the power to move with their passionate logic and to conjure into immediacy a mind forceful, authoritative and just. More than those of most politicians, Lincoln's speeches seem to reveal the character of the man, a character not in the least weak nor vacillating (as even his enemies had sometimes to admit). Herbert Mitgang's opinion is that "In his own time, his truths came through, with the help of the opinion makers and in spite of them."[78] And perhaps the best evidence of it was the profound shock that his assassination caused, and the strength of the instant outpouring of public grief that greeted the news, taking press and politicians (including the Radical Republicans) by surprise. The *Daily Alta California* expressed well the instantaneous Northern reaction:

Never did a nation mourn more deeply for its dead Chief than does the American Union to-day for Abraham Lincoln. The flags at half-mast, the drapery in black, the tolling bells, stoppage of business, are not the mere demonstrations of ceremonious respect for a dead President; the sad faces, the sad hearts, the general expression of sorrow show the popular love for, and trust in, the man who had led his country through the great trials of the last four years, and who, having been crowned with success, was about to achieve a second triumph in healing the wounds that remain after the victory.[79]

The whole world rushed to reappraise a figure it had so often castigated, astonished in retrospect at what he had achieved and at their own failure to notice it. An apologetic poem of Tom Taylor, who had endlessly and mercilessly lampooned him in *Punch*, summed it up best:

Yes, he had lived to shame me from my sneer
To lame my pencil and confute my pen—[80]

[78] Mitgang, *Lincoln as They Saw Him*, p. 447.
[79] *Daily Alta California* (San Francisco), 16 April 1865, in Mitgang, *Lincoln as They Saw Him*, p. 464. See also Harper, *Lincoln and the Press*, chapter 40.
[80] *Punch*, 6 May 1875, in Mitgang, *Lincoln as They Saw Him*, p. 470.

Conclusion

If moral capital in politics depends on public acknowledgment of faithful and effective service to worthy principles, goals or constituencies, then the best politicians (in the sense of those most likely to gain moral capital) will be those who manage to combine firm, clear commitments with sufficient political realism and skill to make their efforts count. No politician has ever been clearer about the need to integrate firm foundational commitments and political realism than Lincoln, yet his experience shows how difficult it can be in a complex political environment – particularly a democratic environment – to attract the moral capital needed to perform essential tasks. The very virtue of Lincoln's grounding doctrine – its carefully realistic adaptation to historical and political circumstances – became its greatest problem as war altered the political landscape. "Moderate" in its refusal to countenance abolition but adamant on maintenance of the Union, it made for a prudent political platform in a North strong on Union feeling but antipathetic to abolition. In the context of political fragmentation, it was enough to win the presidency.

In the life and death struggle that ensued, however, the policy Lincoln pursued consonant with that doctrine proved problematic. Restoration of the *status quo ante* was maintained as the only aim of the war, eschewing emancipation, and this appeared to increasing numbers of "friendly" critics to fall short of the moral high ground they instinctively sought to justify the sacrifices demanded. On the other hand, and paradoxically, the harsher aspect of his doctrine – the absolute insistence on preserving the Union – seemed to hostile critics a recipe for tyranny. While his allies were accusing him of vacillation and weakness, his political enemies were calling him a fearsome, bloodthirsty tyrant, virtually a Russian despot, heedlessly sacrificing lives to bring a reluctant South to heel, usurping the functions of Congress under a supposed War Power, trampling on civil liberties and suppressing dissent by frequent suspension of the writ of *habeas corpus*. The most critical problem with Lincoln's policy, however, was that it failed to resonate with foreign audiences whose action or restraint had the potential to determine the conflict's outcome. Indeed, in the international arena it gave the moral advantage to a Confederacy desperate for foreign recognition. As long as Lincoln kept "the negro" out of it, slave-owning Southerners were able incongruously to pose as champions of liberty trying to escape the wrath of a subjugating power.

Foreign observers never clearly appreciated the moral significance of Union for Northerners (and *a fortiori* for Lincoln) which made the struggle appear to them a trial of democratic government on earth. But for the North, this view of the Union set the conditions under which moral capital was to be accrued by example: the leadership had to strive to maintain democratic and constitutional forms and processes even in the midst of a desperate civil war. But permitting party competition and regular elections meant putting one's leadership record to the test of the ballot and inevitably encouraged partisan politics at a time when, as Lincoln thought, a degree of bipartisanship was necessary for national unity and survival. The dangerous anomaly was that sustaining the ideal risked putting into power a party or person imperfectly committed to Union or without the strength to see the job through, thus throwing the game away.

Lincoln met and passed all these severe tests, sustained by a hardy character and a sense of duty that met misunderstanding, resistance, calumny, personal tragedies and political vicissitudes with remarkable patience and fortitude. If these qualities did not translate immediately into personal moral capital, they emerged the more remarkably once time and success had permitted a clearer view. By the end of 1864 perceptions of his leadership and endurance had begun to shift, owing partly to military victory but also in important part to his own written and spoken words, the famous Lincolnian rhetoric. Here were words that, whatever their immediate effect, could be returned to again and again, that could form an important heritage, their meaning plumbed to enlarge the nation's understanding of itself. Lincoln spoke to make sense of the horror and sacrifice, reinterpreting and ennobling the war for Northerners, establishing continuity with the ideals of America's founders and reinvesting the country in its self-conceived historical mission. It was the feat of nation-building that Jefferson Davis, his counterpart in the South, failed so signally to perform for the Confederacy. If Lincoln emerged as the only great statesman of the Civil War it was not just because the North was ultimately victorious, but because he managed at length to stamp his own vision of the significance and meaning of the conflict, and of America itself, on the national psyche.

In the immediate aftermath of his assassination, Lincoln's moral capital expanded to immense proportions. The sudden growth of this stock and the uses to which it was put form the matter for another story altogether, one that stretches to the present day. Lincoln's posthumous moral capital generated an unseemly struggle between rival political parties and factions over its ownership – "a ghoulish tugging at Lincoln's shroud," as David Donald put it.[81] It was a struggle won by the Republicans, some of whom discovered that they could win the black vote in Southern constitu-

[81] David Donald, "Getting Right with Lincoln," *Atlantic Unbound* (1956) (www. theatlantic.com/issues/99sep/9909lincoln2.htm).

encies by printing the face of Lincoln on their voting cards. For a long
time the Republicans retained Lincoln as their exclusive property, a
resource that could be endlessly recycled to ensure clement fortune for
the party even through a series of corrupt and incompetent administrations. The corollary of this victory was destroyed hopes for Democrats,
now tarred (unjustly) as a party of "traitors" or even complicit assassins.
They would not gain a share of the Lincoln legacy until the 1930s, when
Franklin Roosevelt succeeded in wresting it from the Republican grasp
and pressing it into the service of his New Deal. After that it would be
claimed by communists, socialists, vegetarians and just about anyone
with a cause that might gain substance by association with the revered
martyr.

It is an intriguing question whether Lincoln himself would have been
surprised at all this. He had pursued a course he thought right and
necessary with peculiar fidelity, and was often castigated for his pains,
bereft, it must sometimes have seemed, of any moral capital at all. And
then the triumph with which posterity most credited him was one he had
not intended. Lincoln became The Great Emancipator despite himself.
Indeed, he regarded it as deeply ironic that the South's rebellion had
accomplished the demise of that thing it sought most to preserve, and
which he would have allowed it to preserve had it not chosen war. In a
frank justificatory letter to Albert Hodges, Lincoln explained in detail
how his firm policy had been displaced by the pressure of circumstance
and necessity. He concluded this extraordinary letter with a disclaimer as
to his own sagacity in this chain of events, and with an observation that
was to form the central theme of his Second Inaugural Address:

I claim not to have controlled events, but confess plainly that they have controlled
me. Now, at the end of three years struggle the nation's condition is not what
either party, or any man devised, or expected. God alone can claim it. Whither it is
tending seems plain. If God now wills the removal of a great wrong, and wills also
that we of the North as well as you of the South, shall pay fairly for our complicity
in that wrong, impartial history will find therein new cause to attest and revere the
justice and goodness of God.[82]

With the war all but won and Reconstruction looming, Lincoln shifted
his moral emphasis dramatically. The need was no longer to bolster
Northern will and determination but rather to prepare it for the difficult
and murkier task of rebuilding a shattered nation. Lincoln moved his
stance to that of Old Testament Prophet, teaching a different lesson from
the one with which he had begun, that "right makes might" – for even in
their best, most honest efforts at discerning the right, people remain

[82] CW, vol. 7, pp. 281–282.

fallible. That the war had become a fiery trial of unforeseen proportions, that the outcome was not that which Lincoln's "right course" had anticipated, was evidence, he thought, of divine intervention. God's purpose differed from that of either protagonist, each of whom had "looked for an easier triumph, and a result less fundamental and astounding."

The biblical cadences of the Second Inaugural Address painted an unflattering and unpopular (or so Lincoln alleged) description of events, but one, he believed, that people needed to hear.[83] The national compromise with the sin of slavery, for which the North was as responsible as the South, meant there was an inevitable limit to how "in-the-right" anyone could be until the sin was redeemed by the blood of all. Shared guilt also gave a reason for nonvindictiveness and nonjudgmentalism in victory, and for being forgivingly flexible in Reconstruction.[84]

"With malice toward none; with charity for all; with firmness in the right, as God gives us to see the right, let us strive on to finish the work we are in." How the tragic process of Reconstruction might have gone had Lincoln lived to guide it in the spirit counselled in his last great message to his people remains one of the great "what ifs" of history.

[83] Letter to Thurlow Weed, 15 March 1865, *CW*, vol. 8, p. 356.
[84] Garry Wills says of Lincoln's Second Inaugural Address, his last great speech, that it advanced the daring principle of not acting on principle: "Lincoln's Greatest Speech?", *Atlantic Monthly* (September 1999) (www.theatlantic.com/cgi-bin/o/issues/99sep/9909lincoln.htm); see also William Lee Miller, "Lincoln's Second Inaugural: The Zenith of Statecraft," *Center Magazine* 13 (1980), pp. 53–64.

4   Charles de Gaulle: the man of storms

> In the midst of dangers, the troops were ready to obey him implicitly and would choose no other to command them; for they said that at such times his gloominess appeared to be brightness, and his severity seemed to be resolution against the enemy, so that it appeared to betoken safety and to be no longer severity. But when they had got past the danger and could go off to serve under another commander, many would desert him; for there was no attractiveness about him, but he was always severe and rough, so that the soldiers had the same feeling toward him that boys have toward a schoolmaster.   Xenophon, *The Anabasis*

General Charles de Gaulle had been in political retirement for some years when, in May 1958, a military rebellion in Algeria plunged France's Fourth Republic into crisis. De Gaulle was neither surprised nor displeased. He had forecast disastrous failure for the faction-ridden Republic at its birth, twelve years previously. It had been a source of irritation to him that the "regime of parties," as he contemptuously called it, had survived so long, though the truth was that the republic had, with the help of American aid, served the country moderately well during the post-war period. But increasingly short-term governments, already shaken by a series of international crises,[1] proved unequal to the problem of Algeria.

France had been trying since 1954 to retain its North African colony in the face of armed resistance from the Algerian Liberation Front (FLN).[2] The presence in Algeria of nearly a million *colons* of French descent – the so-called *pieds-noirs* – made the conflict a peculiarly bitter affair that threatened to sunder French politics and society. Though by 1958 a war-weary French public was ready to accept a resolution even at the cost of withdrawal, successive governments proved unable to grasp the nettle and move toward Algerian independence. It was a policy precluded by the

---

[1] There was defeat in Indochina; violent controversies over a proposed European Defense Community and German rearmament; the phenomenon of Poujadism, a mass movement of the lower middle class that displayed all the more unpleasant characteristics of the extreme right – anti-Semitism, xenophobia and imperialism.
[2] *Front de Libération Nationale.*

stalemating balance of the numerous parties within the National Assembly, and also by the fact that Algeria divided not only parties from one another, but parties within themselves. There were politicians of the left as profoundly committed to an *Algérie Française* – an Algeria integrated into the body politic of Metropolitan France – as were the "*ultras*" from the extreme right. Most of de Gaulle's own supporters in parliament were themselves "Algerians."

The most dangerous feature of the situation was that the issue had severed the political leadership of the nation from the leadership of the armed forces conducting the increasingly dirty war in North Africa. The Algerian generals were overwhelmingly integrationist, and in May 1958 they grew alarmed at a rumor that a new coalition government under Christian Democratic leader Pierre Pflimlin,[3] a "liberal" on the Algerian question, meant to surrender Algeria. On 13 May 1958 some of them took part in a military *putsch* in Algiers and set up a Committee of Public Safety under General Massu. Massu wired the President of the Fourth Republic, M. René Coty, arguing that the action had been necessary to maintain order. He demanded "the creation in Paris of a Government of National Safety, alone capable of keeping Algeria as an integral part of Metropolitan France."[4]

The announcement caused confusion in the National Assembly in Paris. Pflimlin's new government, though it had just won an impressive parliamentary vote of confidence, was immediately assailed by right-wing representatives with strong links to the Algerian generals. Pflimlin's[5] leadership was desperately incoherent, mixing tough talk with lenient actions toward the Algerian rebels, and he was threatened with a coup in his own parliament. Influential newspapers began proclaiming that only de Gaulle could provide a solution that would save the country from either civil war or fascist dictatorship. The Algerian generals, meanwhile, hearing of Pflimlin's unusually large confidence vote, feared they had overstepped and began to think that only de Gaulle could save their skins. On 15 May 1958, General Salan, the commander-in-chief of the army in Algeria – and the man supposedly directly responsible to the government in Paris – concluded an address to a crowd in Algiers with a cry of "*Vive la France! Vive l'Algérie Française! Vive de Gaulle!*" That afternoon, de

---

[3] See J.-R. Tournoux, *Secrets d'Etat* (Paris, Plon, 1960), pp. 243–244.

[4] Cited in Alexander Werth, *De Gaulle, A Political Biography* (New York, Simon and Schuster, 1965), p. 29. See also Werth, *The de Gaulle Revolution* (London, Robert Hale, 1960).

[5] "Pflimlin" reveals the moral capital latent in a name. In the Alsatian dialect it means "Little Plum," and it was under this belittling appellation ("*Petite Prune*") that Pflimlin was commonly referred to in the press and among colleagues. No one, in the end, was prepared to die for Little Plum.

Gaulle responded with a letter to the press, making an offer to return from the political wilderness to save his country once again.

Four days later, at his first press conference in three years, de Gaulle reiterated his readiness to lead if requested to do so. It was a time, he said, when events in Metropolitan France and in North Africa threatened a grave new national crisis, a time, therefore, in which he might prove directly useful. He had, he said, proved useful to France once before at a critical moment in its history and neither the French people nor the world had ever forgotten it. He reflected:

Perhaps this sort of moral capital, in the face of the difficulties that assail us, the misfortunes that threaten us – perhaps this capital might have a certain weight in political life at a time of serious confusion.[6]

So it was to prove. Though the majority of French people felt deeply ambivalent about de Gaulle, they could not overlook the weight of moral capital that his towering figure embodied. They were inclined to hope that this weight, thrown into the political balance, might enable "the General" to achieve what the politicians of the Fourth Republic had been unable to achieve – a conclusion to the Algerian crisis and a removal of the threat of civil war.

De Gaulle's dependency on moral capital

The Algerian revolt offered de Gaulle something more than the challenge of an unusual public responsibility – it offered a long-awaited opportunity. In 1958 he was already sixty-seven years of age, had been out of government for twelve years and retired altogether from public life for three. Yet his prestige remained such that he was able to use this opportunity both to settle the Algerian question and, more importantly, to reshape the French political system in his own image, once and for all. It was an extraordinary achievement, and it rested entirely on an earlier extraordinary achievement – his "salvation" of France during World War II.

The peculiar interest of de Gaulle's story for this study lies not just in the fact that he applied the concept of moral capital to himself in exactly the way I use it here, but in the central importance of moral capital to his whole career. A comparison with Lincoln is instructive. The American,

[6] "Press Conference of General de Gaulle Held in Paris at the Palais d'Orsay on the Conditions of His Return to Power on May 19, 1958," *Major Addresses, Statements and Press Conferences of General Charles de Gaulle, May 19, 1958–January 31, 1964* (New York, French Embassy Press and Information Division, 1965), p. 1. De Gaulle had previously used the term "moral capital" in his little book on military leadership, *Le Fil de l'Epée* (The Edge of the Sword) (London, Faber and Faber, 1960), p. 73.

too, gained national leadership by virtue of a national crisis, but his election, though it took place in unusual circumstances, was perfectly regular and his authority therefore politically and legally legitimate. Despite being a rather unknown quantity, Lincoln could govern and govern reasonably effectively provided only that he won his internal encounters with cabinet and Congress. The larger national and sectional contest over moral capital was, as I have tried to show, extremely important, but Lincoln's personal moral capital was not absolutely central to his political effectiveness. De Gaulle's ascent to power was, by contrast, highly irregular and singularly dependent on the moral capital to which he laid claim.

Unlike Lincoln, who was a solid party man, de Gaulle was not a regular politician at all. Though a highly skilled political operator, he was, in his own mind and aspiration, never a "mere" politician. He was a maverick who distrusted parties and organizations, who therefore lacked the ordinary political machinery on which most successful politicians depend. In fact he had linked a large part of his moral appeal precisely to his "independence" from such regular processes and organizations, regarding them as hopelessly corrupt and futile. It was therefore inevitable that his own brand of moral capital, at least until such time as he had created his Fifth Republic (and even thereafter), should be his primary political resource. He was himself acutely conscious of this fact, and always concerned to create, foster and deploy this capital to maximum advantage. He became, indeed, something of a master in the art of its use.

But if de Gaulle's personal moral capital was his main source of strength it was also his main weakness. His peculiar dependency on it was an advantage only when there existed a crisis in political legitimacy, when stable "structures of political opportunity" (as James MacGregor Burns called them)[7] broke down. As soon as crisis faded and regular processes restabilized, de Gaulle's stance of moral elevation above the party fray became largely irrelevant. He then had little in the way of more mundane political resources to fall back upon, even had he wanted them which he manifestly did not. Worse still, dreaming of leading a resurgent France but bitterly excluded from a governmental system he despised, de Gaulle fell prey to the temptation to mobilize his one resource by *engineering* the crisis conditions under which it became most effective. In so doing he almost forfeited the moral capital he had striven so hard to build. Had it not been for fortune in the shape of the Algerian crisis (a fortune admittedly somewhat assisted by his own followers), he would hardly be remembered today. Algeria gave him the chance to play his single political

[7] James MacGregor Burns, *Leadership* (New York, Harper Colophon Books, 1978), pp. 119–129.

De Gaulle's cause: "France"

Sometime during the war, the writer André Malraux, de Gaulle's chief intellectual cheerleader and later Minister for Cultural Affairs, coined the expression "Gaullism." When, many years later, de Gaulle asked him what he had meant by it, Malraux replied: "During the Resistance, something like political passions in the service of France, as opposed to France in the service of the passions of the Right or the Left. Afterwards a feeling . . . and above all, after 1958, the feeling that your motives, good or bad, *weren't the motives of the politicians.*"[8] It was a description that chimed perfectly with de Gaulle's idea of himself. He felt himself elevated (a favorite word) above the ranks of the politicians by his devotion to his ideal conception of France, whose greatness[9] was evidenced in its historical and cultural achievements. "The General," wrote Malraux, "was haunted by France as Lenin was by the proletariat."[10]

His identification with an ideal France had begun early, under the influence of parents devoted both to France and to Catholicism. Charles' father, who could trace his ancestry back through a line of nobility to the thirteenth century, transmitted to his son a passionate devotion to French history. The family was monarchist, Catholic and patriotic, firmly of the French right yet repelled by the anti-republican hatreds, xenophobia and anti-Semitism typical of the right at the beginning of the century. The attitude of all the de Gaulles has been called one of "intense moderation," denoting a deep attachment to values combined with an aversion to excess.[11] The values imparted were, moreover, eminently public ones, affirming devotion to the service of the nation, its history and culture as the highest good, and stressing the honor of the military as their defender.

Charles could not help, therefore, but be deeply affected by France's acute contemporary distress: *revanchisme,* an unsatisfied desire for revenge against Germany for its defeat of France in 1870, was still strong during de Gaulle's youth (and an obsession with his parents);[12] the turmoil of the Dreyfus affair had split the nation, tarnished the army, and (in the opinion of the elder de Gaulle) brought honor to no one; church had been separated from state and the Jesuit schools (including that in

---

[8] André Malraux, *Fallen Oaks: Conversations with de Gaulle* (London, Hamish Hamilton, 1972), p. 68 (emphasis in the original).

[9] A translation of the French *grandeur*, which often recurred in de Gaulle's prose and speech.

[10] Malraux, *Fallen Oaks*, p. 3.

[11] The description comes from Stanley Hoffman and Inge Hoffman, "The Will to Grandeur: de Gaulle as Political Artist," in Dankwort A. Rustow (ed.), *Philosophers and Kings: Studies in Leadership* (New York, George Braziller, 1970), p. 251. I draw heavily on the Hoffmans' psychological portrait of de Gaulle here.

[12] See Brian Crozier, *De Gaulle* (New York, Charles Scribner's Sons, 1973), p. 18.

card one last time. He played it well, and in the process put his ov
stamp on the modern French polity.

It is no simple task, in de Gaulle's case, to disentangle the four
sources of moral capital that I have distinguished: cause, action,
and rhetoric/symbolism. The difficulty lies in the manner in
Gaulle fused his cause with his own personality. With respe
rhetorical dimension, for example, it is true that de Gaulle c
ployed a rather ponderous and occasionally overblown rhetoric f
cal effect, but the more important fact was that his public pers
more than for most leaders, itself a kind of conscious rhetorical
glum and towering symbol of French grandeur and of the F
hoped to recreate through his leadership. It could act as such be
Gaulle had identified himself *personally* with his ideal ground of
vision of "France" as a transcendent nation symbolizing and en
the very essence of grand and virtuous nationhood. The absolute
ity of moral capital to de Gaulle's career was largely a fun
this identification, which as well as being idiosyncratic seeme
anachronistic, an apparent attempt to play Louis XIV in the co
twentieth-century politics. Yet no one could deny that de Gaulle'
cal dedication, his tireless and often astute action in the servio
vision, bore significant political fruit that founded the moral ca
which his whole career was based.

His self-identification with his ideal gave peculiar importanc
role of moral exemplification, and also made him peculiarly vulne
perceived mis-steps. Though his colorlessly respectable private
vided no material for scandal, his public persona as the embodi
French legitimacy meant that any perceivedly illegitimate
threatened immediately to undermine his sole political resource
than that, illegitimate action threatened to blow apart the very
Gaulle represented. Ordinarily, political betrayal destroys the cr
of the betrayer without necessarily threatening the standing of th
betrayed. De Gaulle's cause, however, though it had historical a
ents and undoubtedly touched chords in many French hearts,
firmly attached to and so peculiarly the product of his own eg
exploding de Gaulle was virtually equivalent to exploding hi
revealing it as the hollow sham that his opponents often claimed it

De Gaulle courted this danger and indeed fell victim of it, but
resurrect himself and his dream by a combination of fortune and p
skill. Despite some difficulties in disentangling the analytical ele
then, I will try to organize the story of his eventual triumph arou
themes of cause, action, example and rhetoric/symbolism. I begin v
Gaulle's cause, his own, idiosyncratic ground of right and legitima

which his father taught) closed; socialism, unionism and strikes were on the rise; the confusing multiparty politics of the Third Republic offered neither hope nor direction.[13] The young de Gaulle, a romantic boy of rambunctious energy and martial disposition, saw a France with its ancient grandeur tragically assailed, a France that needed rescuing through heroic leadership. He thus commenced a semi-religious love affair with his country that persisted, undiminished, throughout his life. If the France of his imagination was often betrayed by deeds of "mediocrity," this was an "absurd anomaly" he would habitually impute to the faults of Frenchmen, not to the genius of the land.[14]

Despite an attraction to politics, Charles chose a military career because it provided an honorable way of serving France without serving the despised Third Republic. He fought in the Great War, was wounded and captured during the Battle of Verdun, and emerged convinced that Pétain, the hero of Verdun, was France's greatest general. Pétain was in turn impressed by his young admirer, calling him one of France's most brilliant officers. Whatever advancement de Gaulle achieved in the army during the 1920s and 1930s he owed to Pétain's patronage. If this advancement was unspectacular it was largely because of de Gaulle's uncompromising attitude that did not endear him to his fellows or superiors. It was an attitude consciously adopted in accordance with the theory of leadership that he argued in his first book, *The Edge of the Sword*, in 1932.[15]

Apart from prophesying the inevitability of future war, the book was notable for the similarity between the ideal leader it delineated and de Gaulle himself. This leader had three essential elements: a doctrine, character and prestige. He was always sure of himself, ever ready to act alone even against the commands of superiors. He was never motivated by the desire to please but only by what he knew to be right and necessary in accord with his chosen doctrine. He would often, therefore, be rough with subordinates while inevitably acquiring a reputation for arrogance and indiscipline among "mediocre" superiors. He would also be regarded as distant, for it was necessary to remain aloof in order to maintain the mystery and prestige necessary for real authority. Above all else, the leader must have an irresistible urge to act when danger pressed and a readiness to accept the responsibility for his actions whether these brought triumph or disaster. This last requirement was the essence of

---

[13] See Charles de Gaulle, *The Complete War Memoirs of Charles de Gaulle* (Jonathon Griffin trans., New York, Simon & Schuster, 1967), p. 4.

[14] De Gaulle, *Complete War Memoirs*, p. 3.

[15] See Malraux's comments on this in Claude Mauriac, *The Other de Gaulle: Diaries 1944–1954* (Moura Budberg trans., London, Angus & Robertson, 1973), p. 137.

what de Gaulle meant by "character," essential for effective leadership in a world where social rank no longer guaranteed authority, in which the individual himself must command authority by his own actions and achievements. It was an "uncomfortable virtue," to be sure, to which ordinary people would pay lip service in times of peace and otherwise ignore. But, however repellent an individual of "character" might ordinarily appear, at the onset of danger he would surely be swept to the forefront as on a tidal wave.

There was a necessary egoism in this, de Gaulle asserted, and also a need for determination and guile: "Every man of action has a strong dose of egoism, pride, hardness and cunning."[16] But egoism and cunning were elevated above pure power-seeking by being made the means to "great ends," by being put to the service of "high ideals." A telling recollection from de Gaulle's war memoirs illustrates his adherence to this doctrine. Late in 1944 he was summoned to the United States to converse with President Roosevelt (who had hitherto resolutely snubbed him), and at a meeting in Washington the two discussed America's post-war vision for the world, in which Europe did not figure among the great powers. Since "Europe" for de Gaulle meant "France," he profoundly demurred. After the visit, a letter was leaked to him in which Roosevelt noted that de Gaulle was "very touchy in matters concerning the honor of France or of himself. But I suspect that he is essentially an egoist." To which de Gaulle, in his memoirs, appends the comment that he was never to know "if Franklin Roosevelt thought in affairs concerning France Charles de Gaulle was an egoist for France or for himself."[17] The point was an important one. De Gaulle's notorious obstinacy and arrogant exigency, whatever roots they may have had in his nature, were always deployed to a political purpose, and the purpose was always the same – the maintenance and strengthening of an independent, free France.

De Gaulle had in fact subsumed his own ego – and his narcissism – within a consciously created persona that embodied not only his conception of leadership but his conception of the whole French nation. His habit of referring to himself in the third person – "De Gaulle demands . . ." – revealed how far the public historical personage, "the General," transcended Charles himself. Stanley and Inge Hoffman argued that this transcendence provided de Gaulle both with a means of personal fulfillment and with the limits he needed as a leader: "The vocation is all-consuming, yet a restraint . . . It is a restraint, because of the constant need not to do anything that would, by sullying his own public personage, spoil the chances and soil the honor of the nation."[18]

---

[16] De Gaulle, *The Edge of the Sword*, pp. 45–56 and 61.
[17] De Gaulle, *Complete War Memoirs*, p. 576.
[18] Hoffman and Hoffman, "The Will to Grandeur: de Gaulle as Political Artist," p. 267.

De Gaulle was an inheritor of a nationalistic tradition of "eternal France" to which he gave a Kantian twist, regarding the nation-State, as Kant did, as "a trunk with its own roots," a "moral person" among similar moral persons in an international society.[19] Each nation had a right to pursue its unique destiny in its own way, and possessed an independence that no other State had a right to destroy. But France was more, for de Gaulle, than simply one nation-State among others; it was *the* nation-State. Here, he was a modern representative of a tradition traceable at least to Auguste Comte – France as exemplar, inspiration and servant of the cause of freedom of all mankind. To serve France and its grandeur was, by implication, to serve the whole of humanity. Sentiment as much as reason, de Gaulle admitted, caused him to believe that:

France is not really herself unless in the front rank; that only vast enterprises are capable of counterbalancing the ferments of dispersal which are inherent in her people; that our country, as it is, surrounded by the others, as they are, must aim high and hold itself straight, on pain of mortal danger. In short, to my mind, France cannot be France without greatness.[20]

De Gaulle attempted to appeal to this conception of a greater France to rise above party and ideology, to represent Frenchmen simply *as* Frenchmen. Again, this was in a tradition of French nationalism that demanded the abandonment of personal and party interests in favor of enthusiastic loyalty to the national interest. De Gaulle's doctrines and policies would sometimes be more leftist than rightist – it did not matter, so long as the "real France" was served by them. But France, to be France, must be independent. This was the fundamental tenet of faith that would motivate what many regarded as the absurdities of his "independent" foreign policy during his last days of power; but de Gaulle would not have been de Gaulle had he relinquished it. He refused to be tied by either ideology or party; everything was subservient to French independence, an independence inevitably manifest in the sometimes bafflingly independent actions of the man who in his person claimed to represent France.

Action: De Gaulle establishes his moral capital

This identification with "France" might have seemed merely absurd had not Adolf Hitler provided the desperate opportunity that made it relevant. De Gaulle was a junior officer who had spent the 1930s pushing the view that only a small, modern, mechanized army was capable of

---

[19] Kant, *Perpetual Peace: A Philosophical Essay* (M. Campbell Smith trans., London, Dent, 1915).
[20] De Gaulle, *Complete War Memoirs*, p. 3.

defending France against a German attack across its north-eastern plains.[21] The "Great Army" of France, however, had invested its faith in an outworn, static, defensive strategy concretized (literally) in the massive fortifications of the Maginot Line. Only one political leader, Paul Reynaud, had tried, unsuccessfully, to promote de Gaulle's position in parliament.

By the time of the Battle of France in June 1940, however, Reynaud was prime minister and de Gaulle had been promoted from colonel to brigadier-general for his effective command of an armored division near Lâon. As the shattered British and French armies awaited evacuation at Dunkirk, Reynaud appointed de Gaulle Under-Secretary of Defense. The mood in cabinet was decidedly defeatist, but de Gaulle argued that the fight should continue as long as possible to give the political leadership and the remainder of the army time to remove to North Africa, from there to carry on the war with British assistance and the aid of the French Empire. Reynaud dispatched him to London to plead with Winston Churchill to support this plan, the first of a series of desperate and ultimately futile exchanges. Reynaud resigned and the ageing Marshal Pétain (with whom de Gaulle had by now fallen out) formed a new government that quickly capitulated to the Germans. It was a humiliation made inevitable in de Gaulle's eyes by the war-averse mentality of the army and by years of disunited, incompetent, often paralyzed government by the multiparty Third Republic.

Terms were negotiated with Hitler under which the German army would occupy northern France while allowing a "neutral" French State under Pétain's authoritarian government in the south. Given Hitler's vow in *Mein Kampf* to destroy France utterly, this was a significant concession that was accepted with relief by many French people. Pétain had apparently saved what he could of France, and his Vichy French regime (as it came to be called once the government had removed to the town of Vichy) was undoubtedly legally continuous with the now dissolved Third Republic. De Gaulle, however, citing a favorite distinction between "the legal country" and "the real country," denied Vichy's legitimacy. He hastened to London, and on 18 June 1940 broadcast a radio appeal to French people everywhere via the BBC (which Churchill had obligingly placed at his disposal). Pleading for assistance so that the war could go on, he declared: "The flame of French resistance must not and shall not die." He then contacted the senior commanders of the French army and navy in Metropolitan France and in North Africa, pleading with them to refuse the armistice, offering to put himself under their command. Rebuffed by

---

[21] De Gaulle had written a book on the subject in 1933, *Vers L'Armée de Métier*, in English translation, *The Army of the Future* (London, Hutchinson, 1940).

all, de Gaulle came to a fateful decision that he later recalled in his memoirs:

no responsible man anywhere acted as if he still believed in [France's] indepen-dence, pride, and greatness. That she was bound to be henceforth enslaved, disgraced, and flouted was taken for granted by all who counted in the world. In face of the frightening void of the general renunciation, my mission seemed to me, all of a sudden, clear and terrible. At this moment, the worst in her history, it was for me to assume the burden of France.[22]

It was a momentous decision by an obscure officer hardly known to France never mind to the rest of the world. In making it, de Gaulle laid the first foundation of his own myth. He then began the slow process of building the moral capital that would allow him, by the war's end, to command his country.

This meant persuading sufficient numbers of people to accept as fac-tual his claim that he had become the legitimate representative of the "real," undefeated France. De Gaulle reasoned that, whatever the even-tual outcome of the war, an effective denial of his proposition that France had never capitulated would mean that France's "self-disgust and the disgust it would inspire in others would poison its soul and its life for many generations." His main aim was not, consequently, to help win the war, and certainly not to put French fighters at the disposal of Britain's forces as other defeated European states had done. "For the effort to be worthwhile," he wrote, "it was essential to bring back into the war not merely some Frenchmen, but France."[23] De Gaulle's main battle would be less with the Germans than with his own allies, to convince them that he represented a genuinely independent force recognized as a legitimate authority by a majority of French citizens.[24] De Gaulle would "save France" by inventing and maintaining in existence, however minimally, a Free French State.

His first step was to set up a "French National Committee" through which to direct his war effort. His next was to persuade Churchill and his war cabinet of the usefulness of recognizing it and of recognizing de Gaulle as "the leader of the Free French." He also extracted a commit-ment from the British government to "the integral restoration of the independence and greatness of France," and in the meantime was guaranteed financial assistance and given a headquarters at Carlton Gar-dens in London. Carlton Gardens at first attracted too few French figures of any note, and too many adventurers, Pétainist spies and extreme

[22] De Gaulle, *Complete War Memoirs*, pp. 84 and 87–88.
[23] *Ibid.*, p. 81.
[24] For a good account of de Gaulle versus his Allies, see Crozier, *De Gaulle*, chapters 5 and 6.

right-wing thugs; but from this inauspicious acorn de Gaulle would grow the oak to support his leadership of France.

Despite his utter dependency on the generosity of the hard-pressed British, de Gaulle never hesitated to bite the hand that fed him, demanding the respect due to an independent sovereign nation, however notional its power. He was an infuriating ally ("my Cross of Lorraine," as Churchill famously quipped) – proud, intransigent, eternally demanding. De Gaulle's real problems, however, would always be with the Americans in whose eyes he possessed no moral capital whatsoever. It annoyed him that the Roosevelt administration believed the best means of countering Nazi influence in France was to maintain good relations with Vichy, but it was worse that the Americans thought of de Gaulle himself as an upstart Fascist with dictatorial ambitions.[25] It was a perception that would haunt de Gaulle for two decades.

To understand the American reaction, it must be noted that de Gaulle's alienation from the corrupt and ineffectual multiparty regime of the Third Republic was typical of a pattern of political alienation across an economically depressed pre-war Europe. The common solution had been to look to a strong leader "above the parties," one who could form direct connections with the disenchanted populace while expressing some overriding national interest. Most European States, not just Italy and Germany, had moved before the war from discredited multiparty systems to fascist or authoritarian forms of government. De Gaulle conformed with this pattern of leadership closely enough to fall under justified suspicion, and during the war he would have to assert himself repeatedly against the American prejudice.

Throughout the war de Gaulle dedicatedly pursued two interconnected tasks: to give increasing substance to Free France by creating the semblance of a government in exile and by providing it with a territorial base and an armed force; and to win support for his organization from whatever sources he could. Once the fiction of Free France had been turned into an organizational reality, its *de facto* existence would stimulate further support and commitment. De Gaulle turned to the governors of French colonial dependencies and won large parts of French Equatorial Africa to his cause (Arab North Africa remaining determinedly Pétainist). He thus gained a territorial base (the official headquarters of Free France was now removed to Brazzaville in the Congo) and substantial numbers of colonial troops. The latter were of small military but large symbolic value (though the Free French would eventually field effective and psy-

[25] *Ibid.*, pp. 170–171.

chologically important forces under Generals Larminat and Leclerc in North Africa).

After Hitler had attacked Russia in 1941, de Gaulle successfully wooed Josef Stalin.[26] Stalin's support was to have important consequences for one of his most vital aims, to become the acknowledged leader of the Home Resistance. This movement was tiny after the French collapse in 1940, and even when a serious Resistance began to emerge in 1942, it was as a congeries of disconnected, mutually mistrustful groups of widely variant political allegiances.[27] Weekly BBC broadcasts had, however, made the name de Gaulle, if not the man, widely known in France, and the General now dispatched an emissary to try to unite the Resistance under his Free French banner. This difficult task was immensely aided by the Russians after de Gaulle, in July 1942, renamed his movement "Fighting France." The Soviet government immediately recognized Fighting France as "the totality of French citizens and territories not recognizing the capitulation and contributing anywhere and by every means to the liberation of France." It simultaneously recognized de Gaulle's National Committee as "the only body with a right to organize the participation in the war of French citizens and territories" and with whom the USSR would deal.[28] This implied Soviet recognition of de Gaulle's authority even over the Communists, the most dynamic element within the Resistance. More and more Resistance leaders began to come over to de Gaulle, and an important moral victory was achieved in May 1943 when all the movements were finally united in a Gaullist National Resistance Council (CNR).

The Allies were, in the meantime, trying to find a "third solution" for France that was neither Pétainist nor Gaullist. De Gaulle defeated their plans in a convoluted political drama following the Allied invasion of North Africa. He wanted a regular French government in Algiers immediately, with himself at the head, and proceeded to play, very skillfully, every significant card he held: his Free French forces fighting in Africa; the support of the Soviet Union which he now further courted by taking up a radically left-wing, "revolutionary" stance (thus also bolstering his image as an anti-Vichyite hero in occupied France); and his command of the Home Resistance newly united in the CNR (which demanded a provisional government in Algiers with de Gaulle as president). De

---

[26] See *ibid.*, pp. 181–182.
[27] For a good overview of the development and significance of the French Resistance and of the Communists' role within it, see Alexander Werth, *France: 1940–1955* (New York, Henry Holt, 1956), chapters 8 and 9.
[28] Cited in Werth, *De Gaulle*, p. 180.

Gaulle easily outwitted the politically naïve General Giraud, whom the Anglo-Americans had installed as governor,[29] but even Churchill and Roosevelt proved no match for the determined General.[30] They had miscalculated in believing de Gaulle's primary commitment to be, like theirs, winning the war.[31]

The outcome was de Gaulle at the head of a French National Liberation Committee which, to the annoyance of the Americans, he did not scruple to describe as a provisional French government awaiting the liberation of Paris. He now proceeded, through patriotic rhetoric and an assertion of France's great power status among the Allies, to gain the allegiance of the Vichyites of North Africa who had initially hated him. Such softening did not extend, however, to the Vichy regime itself, whose thorough extinguishment was an essential precondition of de Gaulle's aim to be at the head of the only legitimate governing authority directly upon the liberation of France. To his fury, the Free French were permitted only a minor role on D-Day, though he himself managed a brief visit to the Normandy beachhead a week after the landings. He was received with a popular enthusiasm that proved, he said, that France had accepted him as its legitimate leader. His fear was that the Allies would take over the administration of France, as they had of Italy, and then use the remnants of Vichy to set up a government. The Americans were indeed plotting to foil him in this manner on the very eve of the liberation of Paris, but their plans failed. General Eisenhower, the Allied commander, allowed Leclerc's Free French Armored Division the honor of first entry into Paris and encouraged de Gaulle to follow quickly, "as the symbol of French Resistance."[32]

The subsequent procession across Paris was de Gaulle's "apotheosis." He was hailed by some two million delirious citizens – "*a peculiar kind of referendum to which de Gaulle – then as later – attached the greatest importance.*"[33] It was the moment in which he definitively established himself, in the eyes of the world and to his own satisfaction, as the "savior" of France. He had saved it by saving the French Republic, a republic which (he declared that day) had never ceased to exist, for it was embodied in his Free French Committee, in Fighting France and in the provisional government that he now quickly established. By a combination of absolute determination and political skill he had, remarkably, achieved everything

---

[29] Giraud was also, according to Werth, a "remarkably stupid" man: Werth, *De Gaulle*, p. 152.

[30] See Crozier, *De Gaulle*, p. 216.

[31] Crozier, *De Gaulle*, p. 216. Chapters 9 and 10 of Crozier's biography give a clear account of de Gaulle's complex path to political victory in North Africa.

[32] Dwight D. Eisenhower, *Crusade in Europe* (Garden City, NY, Doubleday, 1948), p. 325.

[33] Werth, *De Gaulle*, p. 169 (emphasis in the original).

he had intended in the dark days of 1940. He had staked an heroic personal claim to moral and political legitimacy superior to claims of mere legal legitimacy and then, through political skill and determination, had proceeded to establish it in reality.

The foundation of de Gaulle's leadership would always be the moral capital he had created in this wartime endeavor, and when circumstances permitted, he would mobilize it with remarkable effectiveness. When circumstances did not permit, he would find himself politically sidelined and left like some huge, solitary monument, respected but irrelevant. In such an event, de Gaulle was inclined to become dangerously impatient.

Moral capital by example: De Gaulle stumbles

As the tide turned against the Germans, a great deal of opportunistic side-changing occurred in France. Millions suddenly sought to associate themselves with the Resistance, and would claim after the liberation (to the cynical sneers of hardcore resisters) to have been part of it. It is doubtful whether many of this legion of opportunists, or of French people generally, profoundly shared de Gaulle's particular ideal of France, nor was it necessary that they did. De Gaulle himself believed it, and in acting in its service he had, in the eyes of many French people, kept alive a spark of French pride and independence during a time of deep humiliation. In the bleak post-war period, with the country in ruins and near to anarchy, his moral capital formed a central legitimating point around which a shattered nation could once again begin to congeal.

For several months de Gaulle headed the provisional government, ruling as a sort of "monarch by consent," dampening revolutionary expectations that he had himself helped to arouse, managing the Communists, and bringing the country back under central political control. He engaged in complex foreign negotiations to ensure France's place at the councils of power in the post-war world, and at home initiated a progressive, even radical, policy of reconstruction. In October 1945, elections were held for a constituent Assembly that would draft a constitution for the Fourth Republic, and de Gaulle was elected prime minister. He could not, however, exert effective control over the constitutional deliberations of deputies who appeared set on reproducing the pattern of the Third Republic – a figurehead president and a parliament in theory all-powerful but in fact given over to the ill-concerted "regime of parties." Appalled at the prospect, de Gaulle briefly considered prolonging his own rule indefinitely, but in the end rejected, as he later wrote, his own despotism. He had always promised to submit his record to the people's electoral will, and to break that promise now would court disruption and violence. The Resistance coalition that had supported him in wartime had broken up into rival parties, so he would have had to rely on the backing of the army to create a military dictatorship which, he argued, could not be justified by circumstances.

De Gaulle thus paid the price for basing his political fortunes solely on his unique moral capital while remaining aloof from parties and interests. It meant that he had no organized political machine through which to work his will in parliament. In his own mind, his capital was inextricably tied to a vision of France that comprehended *all* French people and dedicated them to something beyond their own petty and sectional interests. He saw himself, with his own extra-parliamentary "legitimacy," as a sort of embodiment of a Rousseauian "general will" that included all. To descend into the bear pit and align himself with one or another partisan group was to forsake this lofty function along with the moral capital that attached to it. Yet without this capital he would be just another party leader with no clear ideology and perhaps no very large following, therefore with little ability to influence the factional quarrels of multiparty government. His solution – his hope – was to order the Fourth Republic so that the presidency would embody the nationally representative role he craved, sitting powerfully above and commanding the fractious Assembly. But this, paradoxically, could only have been achieved had he led a party strong and numerous enough to dominate the parliamentary deliberations. As it was, all he could do was to pit his moral authority and his political wits against the determinedly centrifugal parties – who listened with respect and then proceeded to ignore him.

He stuck it out until 20 January 1946, when in anguished mood he called his ministers together and stated: "The exclusive regime of the parties has come back. I disapprove of it. But, short of establishing by force a dictatorship which I don't want and which would probably turn out badly, I lack the means to prevent this experiment. I must therefore retire."[34] Privately he looked forward to the speedy descent of the Fourth Republic into chaos and crisis and a popular outcry for his own return, in which circumstances he could reorder the polity to his own liking. His departure, however, caused less public dismay than he expected, and the call failed to come. From the sidelines he watched as the new Constitution was given lukewarm approval at its second referendum in October 1946, setting up a responsible, bicameral parliamentary system with a president whose powers were largely ceremonial – a virtual replica of the Third Republic.

The Fourth Republic was born in circumstances of economic hardship,

[34] Cited in Crozier, *De Gaulle*, p. 394.

political strife and rising international tension. The sovietization of Eastern Europe had begun, an "iron curtain" was descending across the continent. Malraux and other ardent Gaullists soon began to argue that only the return of "the General" from his self-imposed retirement could halt the process of "national decadence" and avert disaster. De Gaulle thereupon embarked on a misconceived course that, though it brought short-term gains, almost destroyed his whole remaining stock of moral capital and thus his career.

By 1947 the impatient General had seen that the new republic would not fall without a shake or two. In April, therefore, he inaugurated a "mass movement" (never to be known by the despised name of "party") to do the necessary shaking. He called it the Rally of the French People (RPF).[35] In the memoirs of Gaullists and of the General himself the RPF period tends to get passed over hastily, or dismissed as a "mistake," for it revived the suspicion of fascist tendencies that had shadowed him in wartime. Though he wanted the RPF to include elements of the left (like Malraux) so as to appear truly representative of the whole people, it was in fact dominated by the right. Moreover, the style of the movement, with its grand flag-waving rallies, its inflated rhetoric and its bully-boy tactics on the fringes, recalled pre-war fascist "movements" and the fanatical displays of Munich. De Gaulle, for his part, mercilessly employed a demagoguery of fear, harping incessantly on the Soviet menace from which he alone could save France. Nor did it seem that the RPF intended to abide by democratic tactics in its bid for power. Years later, Malraux, who had worked hard to give the movement an "epic dimension," admitted without hesitation that, as far as he was concerned, "the RPF was an insurrectionary movement."[36] But insurrection was a dangerous game in the atmosphere of incipient civil war that hung over France in 1947, with strikes and street demonstrations erupting everywhere, and with extra *gendarmes* and steel-helmeted *gardes mobiles* being rushed to Paris to reinforce its hard-pressed police force.

Around this time, de Gaulle became fond of referring to himself as "*l'homme des tempêtes*" ("the man of storms"). He perfectly understood that his moral capital was indissolubly linked with the idea of national salvation, and that it therefore became most politically salient at times of national crisis when the State was under serious threat. But he seemed now to be invoking the furies for his own ends rather than quelling them for the sake of the general safety. With the ruthless sovietization of Eastern Europe proceeding and the Cold War looming, however, de Gaulle's fiercely anti-Communist tactics met with success; the RPF

---

[35] *Rassemblement du Peuple Français.*
[36] Curtis Cate, *André Malraux* (London, Hutchinson, 1995), pp. 365–366.

gained a membership of over 800,000. At the municipal elections in October, RPF candidates, to the surprise of everyone, gained control of France's thirteen largest cities. The movement that was not a party had moved overnight ahead of every party in the country.

Yet what seemed to be the first stage in a triumphant return to power proved to be the zenith of the RPF's political achievement. The composition of the National Assembly, elected in 1946 for five years, remained unchanged and the Gaullists had only a slight foothold there. Worse, the unexpected municipal triumph caused the General to overestimate his hand and consequently to overplay it. He declared that the people had condemned the "regime of division and confusion" and called for a general election and a drastic reform of the Constitution – the domestic and international situation, he said, demanded immediate action. But his ultimatum backfired, arousing suspicion among the populace and a renewed spirit of republicanism in the Assembly. People were alarmed at de Gaulle's arrogance and began to question the realism of his war hysteria. It was a profound miscalculation that started the rot in the RPF at the very moment of its victory.

The Fourth Republic, with its endless round of governments made up of the same familiar faces in different combinations, carried on. Though burdened with two sets of representatives who were implacable foes of the regime – the Communists on the left and the Gaullist RPF on the right – it proved surprisingly resilient.[37] As the Cold War congealed into a nuclear stand-off between two powerful blocs and economic prosperity began to revive, the tide turned against the Gaullists, and the RPF became virtually spent as a political force. Worse, from de Gaulle's point of view, many Gaullist deputies began to play the parliamentary game and compete for government posts. The movement had become a party after all, and in 1953 de Gaulle dissociated himself from it in disgust and retired once more from public life, retreating to his home at Colombey-les-Deux-Eglises to write his memoirs.

De Gaulle enjoyed lingering respect and suffered lingering suspicion, but by and large he became simply irrelevant, an historical curiosity. By 1957 he was virtually a "forgotten man" – and would have remained one but for Algeria. And when that genuine crisis came, de Gaulle showed he had learnt an important lesson from his RPF blunder: he would not force himself upon the French people, for they would resist him if he tried. Instead he would simply call attention to the moral capital he had won

---

[37] There was a total of twenty-five governments between 1947 and 1958. Communist and Gaullist hostility meant governments could only be formed out of weak "Third Force" coalitions of Socialists, Radicals and members of the *Mouvement Républicain Populaire* (the MRP, who tried but failed to act as a bridge to the Communists).

during the war and declare himself "available," awaiting the summons of the nation. The French, in other words, must *choose* de Gaulle, inviting him to step into the breach and save the nation. Even so, he had repeatedly to defend himself in the days of May 1958 against the suspicion of dictatorial ambition. In the press interview of 19 May he was asked whether he would respect public freedoms if asked to form a government, to which he gave what was to be his customary reply: "It was I who reestablished these public freedoms. Do you believe that, at sixty-seven, I shall start a dictator's career?" If called, he promised to give the French people strong government that would help them realize France's economic possibilities, and concluded: "Now I shall return to my village and remain there at the country's disposal."[38]

The days that followed were filled with new alarms and rumors. A second military *putsch*, in Corsica, and stories of the imminent arrival in Paris of rebel paratroopers, revealed that Pflimlin's government had no control over the army either abroad or in France. In parliament, *ultras*, Gaullists and representatives of embittered Vichyite generals and *pieds-noirs* sought to destroy the Republic they hated.[39] No significant group apart from the Gaullists wanted de Gaulle, but no grouping was solid enough to create an authoritative government of its own. The "Algerian" deputies could bring down governments but were not strong enough to form their own. The Communists, alarmed, offered an alliance with the Socialists, but Socialist leader Guy Mollet recalled the bitter experience of Popular Front government in the 1930s and preferred what had become known as the "de Gaulle compromise." The idea of de Gaulle as the lesser evil steadily made headway among the Socialists, and even among the Communists who decided they feared the fascist intentions of the military more than they feared the General. Meanwhile, in Algiers, General Salan's cry of "*Vive de Gaulle!*" (prompted, it must be said, by one of de Gaulle's men on the spot) seemed to bespeak his acceptability to the military. And in fact de Gaulle's refusal explicitly to condemn the rebellion had convinced the rebels that they had the General's backing.

In these uncertain and dangerous times, with the air filled with plots and counterplots, de Gaulle himself oscillated between hope and pessimism. He resolutely refused, however, any impulse or advice to act hastily or to commit himself unequivocally to any party. In his "moral capital" speech he had noted, significantly, that he could be useful to France in its crisis because he was "a man who belongs to nobody, and who belongs to

---

[38] De Gaulle, *Major Addresses*, p. 6.
[39] See Crozier, *De Gaulle*, pp. 455–458. Crozier draws his account from Pierre Viansson-Ponté, *Histoire de la République Gaullienne* (Paris, Fayard, 1970), vol. I, pp. 23 *et seq.* See also M. Bromberger and S. Bromberger, *Les 13 Complots du 13 Mai* (Paris, Fayard, 1969).

everybody."[40] This aloofness from particular parties, even from parties of his own supporters, was of course a traditional part of his mystique, but at this hour it was also a political necessity. De Gaulle could not afford to condemn the rebellion as many demanded he should, partly because it had provided him with the chance for power, but also because of the fear that condemnation would alienate the generals and thus precipitate the army's move on Paris. If he could not condemn, however, neither could he afford to condone or appear to support the rebellion. He had no wish to acquire the taint of coming illegally to power as leader of a military *putsch*, even one he had had no hand in organizing. It was not, of course, that legality was especially important to de Gaulle; legitimacy was the more basic value, and he regarded the government as illegitimate because it could no longer ensure the defense of its territories.[41] But his own moral legitimacy rested on his power to embody in his person the "real" France, to rise above its partisan divisions and to represent all French people, thus providing the center that could hold against the centrifugal forces that threatened to tear the nation apart. He could not risk compromising his moral capital by an act that most French people would condemn, and he could hardly claim to represent the whole nation while blatantly taking one side in the conflict.

So while parliament dithered, de Gaulle played his careful game, moving positively only when he received news that the "conquest of France," begun with the Corsican coup, was about to be completed on 27 and 28 May 1958. Knowing that continued parliamentary stubbornness would lead to civil bloodshed (and to the end of his own hopes), he decided on a strategic intervention to "hasten the march forward." On the afternoon of 27 May he published a statement of "masterly ambiguity"[42] that claimed he had "embarked on the regular process necessary for establishing a republican government" capable of maintaining the unity and independence of France, disapproving of disturbances to public order and demanding the loyalty of the military. The trick worked. The military plotters abandoned their plans. Alexander Werth described this ploy as "perhaps the greatest piece of statesmanship in the whole of de Gaulle's career; while now making his return to power practically certain, it at the same time averted the establishment of a military dictatorship in France or, more likely still, the outbreak of civil war."[43]

On 29 May 1958, President Coty declared to parliament his intention of asking "the most illustrious Frenchman" to set up a government

---

[40] De Gaulle, *Major Addresses*, p. 1.   [41] Tournoux, *Secrets*, p. 228.
[42] Crozier, *De Gaulle*, pp. 473–474; see also Werth, *De Gaulle*, pp. 43–44, whose translation of the text I use here.
[43] Werth, *De Gaulle*, p. 44.

"within the framework of republican legality." A few days later de Gaulle was in the Assembly he had so long despised, offering in a stiff and haughty manner "to lead the country, the State and the Republic along the road of salvation once again," requesting plenary powers for six months and the necessary legal machinery to draw up a new Constitution to be submitted to referendum. The "Man of Destiny" was back, and would soon have the powers he needed to reshape the republic in his own image.

Gaullist rhetoric, de Gaulle as symbol

Suspicious deputies of the left and center had to be repeatedly reassured that a man "imposed" on parliament by the threat of civil war would observe "republican legality" and bring Algiers and Corsica to order while preserving civic freedoms. Rightists and *ultras*, for their part, hoped they could *use* the General to destroy the Republic and set up a military-fascist government that would save Algeria for the *colons* and for France, though they never wholly trusted him because of his anti-Vichy past and his uncertain commitment to *l'Algérie Française*.[44] Meanwhile, for the majority of French citizens who cared nothing about Algeria except to end the war, de Gaulle was accepted as a plausible defense *against* fascist dictatorship.[45] De Gaulle was thus, at best, a compromise solution accepted in confused and dangerous circumstances for contradictory reasons, and partly as the "devil we know."

Nevertheless, his self-proclaimed personification of a singular and "essential" France now proved a rhetorical device of the first importance. There were probably few (outside of worshipful Gaullists) who wholly accepted de Gaulle's valuation of himself, but many still granted, if only grudgingly, his status as wartime savior and were willing to hope he might repeat the miracle. The link he had forged between his moral capital and his political aloofness, which in other circumstances had made him irrelevant, in the dangerously divided France of 1958 made him a reassuring symbol of the maintenance of national unity – a very fragile one, to be sure, but the only plausible one available. De Gaulle, aware of this fragility, was for a long time deeply concerned to ensure that his provisional acceptability not be compromised by any false move or gesture that would rekindle the suspicions aroused by his RPF days or reveal him to be a partisan of one side or another. His stance as the symbolical embodiment of a transcendent, undivided France had become politically central

---

[44] The generals had already had intimations of de Gaulle's real attitude in 1957. See Pierre Galante, *The General* (London, Leslie Frewin, 1969), pp. 132–133.
[45] See Werth, *De Gaulle*, pp. 45–46.

and must not be jeopardized by speech or action. His rhetoric, in these circumstances, had to be carefully and studiedly ambiguous in order to reassure different sections without committing clearly to any.

Fortunately, the General was adept at ambiguity. On 4 June 1958, immediately after his parliamentary investiture, he flew to Algiers and addressed a huge, enthusiastic crowd with a V-sign and the words "*Je vous ai compris!*" ("I have understood you"), a reference to the perennial complaint of the *pieds-noirs* that they were *not* understood by the metropolis; yet de Gaulle's understanding would prove to imply no attachment to their cause. At home, his first major achievement was to reassure domestic opinion concerning his leadership. France relaxed as it witnessed a radically mellowed de Gaulle who had become a master of informal communication on the largely state-owned radio and television, and who appeared deeply sensible of the French people's antipathy toward any authoritarian regime. He further appeased domestic sentiment by publicly condemning the torture widely used by the *paras* on Algerian prisoners. Since this, however, risked alienating the *ultras* and the generals, he traveled immediately to Algeria to appease and mollify them with carefully chosen words. At the same time, he began to deal with the "problem of the army" by quietly transferring to France large numbers of officers who had been involved in the May events.

By the end of August 1958, de Gaulle had his new Constitution for the Fifth Republic, one with greatly expanded presidential powers and severely reduced legislative powers for the Assembly. The president, elected for seven years, would appoint the prime minister and other ministers and had the absolute right to dissolve parliament. Machinery was put in place for holding referenda, providing means for the president to by-pass parliament altogether and go directly to the people, while the controversial Article 16 allowed him to resort to emergency powers when he himself deemed it necessary. The Constitution was put to a referendum in September 1958 and received a yes vote of almost 80 percent.[46] In December 1958, the presidential election took place with de Gaulle standing for office for the first time in his life and receiving 78.5 percent of the electoral college votes, whereupon he appointed a faithful acolyte, Michel Debré, his first prime minister.

Yet the legal authority granted by a Constitution modeled so closely on de Gaulle himself remained crucially dependent on his own personal legitimacy and on his political survival. He had to convert constitutional dominance of a rebellious Assembly into political reality, while in the country he must subdue an army that would be his most dangerous

[46] On the Constitution generally, see Dorothy Pickles, *The Fifth French Republic* (London, Methuen, 1962).

opponent over the next four years. The test of survival became increasingly severe as he started to move steadily, if deviously, toward Algerian independence, thus betraying the hopes of *ultras*, army and *pieds-noirs* (not to mention some Gaullists). He would twice be confronted by military rebellion, and would deal with it by abandoning ambiguity and mobilizing his moral capital in dramatic rhetorical fashion.

The first serious challenge occurred after he suddenly abandoned a gradualist policy toward Algeria and announced, in September 1959, an offer of "self-determination" for the colony. The hostile reaction in Algeria led within a few months to the so-called "week of the barricades" of January 1960. In Algiers, a group of *ultra* thugs massacred fourteen *gendarmes* and wounded 123 more before barricading themselves in buildings and calling on de Gaulle to renounce "self-determination" and commit to French Algeria. They were treated as heroes by the white settlers who thronged to support them. Commander-in-Chief General Challe rushed troops to the city ostensibly to deal with the situation, but no one was sure they would not fraternize with the revolutionaries and precipitate another *putsch*. Prime Minister Debré, dashing to Algiers to confer with the generals, became convinced of this and returned in a state of panic.

De Gaulle, by contrast, responded with cool determination and a show of personal authority. He ordered Massu's paratroopers withdrawn from Algiers and replaced them with presumptively loyal troops from the interior. Then he went on television, pointedly dressed in his brigadier-general's uniform, to call the insurgents liars and conspirators, to condemn the complacency of certain military men and to demand from the army its strictest discipline. He indicated (to the alarm of colleagues and ministers) his willingness "in the last resort" to order troops to fire upon the rebels. He concluded with a sentimental appeal to his own moral legitimacy.

Finally, I want to say a few words to France. Well, my dear old country, here we are, together again, facing a heavy ordeal. In virtue of the mandate given me by the people and in the name of that legitimacy I have incarnated for the last twenty years, I ask all my countrymen and countrywomen to support me, whatever happens.[47]

The firmness of de Gaulle's response made a huge impression on French opinion. Even the Communists and trade unions took part in supportive demonstrations. So great was the reaction that settler support for the rebels in Algiers wavered and faded. The insurgents meekly surrendered and de Gaulle took the opportunity to purge the centers of resistance of the *pieds-noirs*.

---

[47] Cited in Werth, *De Gaulle*, pp. 260–261.

Dangers remained, however. The rebel General Salan had now organized a terrorist group, the OAS (*Organisation de l'Armée Secrète*), that would cause great bloodshed in France and Algeria and make several attempts on de Gaulle's life. The principal threat, however, was still the professional soldiery who, though dazed and insecure, were not defeated. De Gaulle decided to meet their challenge head on with a referendum on Algerian self-determination (the implication of which was the need to negotiate with the FLN). The result was a 76 percent yes vote, a resounding vindication of his negotiating policy. Before talks with the FLN could get properly started, however, de Gaulle had to face his most serious challenge yet, a military *putsch* by four generals and five colonels.

On 21 April 1960, Foreign Legion paratroopers occupied the main buildings of Algiers, arresting one of de Gaulle's ministers (who happened to be visiting) and the new commander-in-chief of the army. Next morning, General Zeller, broadcasting on Radio Algiers, announced a state of siege and appealed for the rest of the army in Algeria to join them. The government feared that the army in France would also respond to the call, and once again Debré and several ministers panicked. De Gaulle told them to "stop whining," and, relishing the challenge, ordered the detention of "doubtful" members of the army in France and an economic and financial blockade of Algeria. He then declared a state of emergency and assumed dictatorial powers under Article 16. As more officers in Algeria joined the insurrection, de Gaulle remained calm, confident in his ability to face down the generals using what had now become his favorite weapon – the projection of his own moral authority via radio and television.[48]

His confidence was not misplaced. As Brian Crozier notes, when it was announced the General would go on air at 8 p.m. on 23 April 1960, "the announcement alone was a blow in the war of nerves, for on one side of the Mediterranean anticipation strengthened the faint of heart, while on the other it weakened resolve."[49] At 8 p.m., appearing again in military uniform to remind those he addressed of their traditions of obedience to authority,[50] he sharply condemned the group of officers "who are leading us straight into national disaster." He demanded in the name of France that every means to be used to stop "these men" until they were brought down, and ordered all soldiers to disregard the orders of the mutineers, promising they would be crushed with the full rigor of the law. Again, he finished with his by now familiar appeal, invoking the "French and

---

[48] See Aidan Crawley, *De Gaulle: A Biography* (London, Collins, 1969), pp. 400–401.
[49] Crozier, *De Gaulle*, p. 513.
[50] De Gaulle, who never made it above Brigadier-General, was of course outranked by the rebel generals, but the point was effective nevertheless.

republican legitimacy which the nation has conferred on me, which I shall maintain, whatever happens, until the term of my mandate or until I lose my strength or my life . . . *Françaises, Français, aidez-moi!* [French-women, Frenchmen, help me!]"[51]

This broadcast produced what became known as the "transistor victory" because of its effect on the hundreds of thousands of Algerian conscript soldiers listening on transistor radios. Most of them, unlike the professional soldiery, believed in de Gaulle and were now determined to resist "the foursome of generals." Wavering officers suddenly decided it would be wiser not to join the rebellion. Meanwhile, in France, the public reaction was even more powerful than in January 1960, with virtually the whole nation (apart from extreme right-wingers) lining up behind de Gaulle. A one-hour general strike was called, and unions demanded arms for the workers to resist a military-fascist *putsch*. But by 25 April 1960 the rebellion had plainly collapsed. One general surrendered and the other three went into hiding. Hundreds of officers were arrested, guilty regiments disbanded and thousands of loyal police flown into Algeria.

With the army now finally broken, de Gaulle moved determinedly on the Algerian question. The OAS, however, remained destructively active, and in September 1961 the terrorist organization ordered his "physical elimination." Over the next eleven months, as Algeria sank into chaos on its bloody final path to independence, there were four attempts on de Gaulle's life. The last and most serious provided a coda to the Algerian crisis that demonstrated once again de Gaulle's unfailing ability to turn a moral capital windfall to his political advantage, this time to assert his dominance over the Assembly. On 22 August 1962, as his car passed through the Paris suburb of Petit-Clamart, OAS assassins fired an estimated 150 bullets at it, one of which missed de Gaulle's head by inches. After being driven to safety, the unflappable General stepped out and coolly remarked that they had had "a close shave" this time.[52] The incident created a sensation, with even opponents declaring admiration for the General's courage. The nation wondered aloud what would have happened to France had the assassins succeeded. De Gaulle, riding high on a wave of heroism and sympathy, declared his intention to hold a referendum on a plan to have the president elected by universal suffrage.

By 1962, de Gaulle had decided that the Constitution of 1958 needed amendment in order to provide for the strong State that France, in his opinion, desperately needed. He believed his successor would have more authority if chosen by the whole people rather than by an electoral college. But the anti-plebiscitary sentiment of parliament was strong, and

[51] Crozier, *De Gaulle*, p. 513; Werth, *De Gaulle*, p. 269.
[52] Werth, *De Gaulle*, pp. 293–294.

the parties, now that the General had served his purpose in Algeria, thought his regime should be "liberalized" rather than strengthened. Resistance was so solid that de Gaulle had hesitated to push the issue. The assassination attempt of August 1962, however, provided an opportunity that he immediately seized, precipitating one last showdown. All parties save the Gaullist UNR attacked the unconstitutionality of the move, for no procedure for such a fundamental change was provided by the 1958 Constitution. De Gaulle again went on radio and television to appeal directly to the people, arguing that democracy would be promoted by the reform. A censure motion tabled in parliament succeeded and the government was overthrown, whereupon de Gaulle dissolved the Assembly and called a referendum for 28 October 1962. He then gave another broadcast that made the issue one of his own political survival, vowing to leave if the no vote was even large, never mind victorious. It was a classic piece of de Gaulle theater. Acting outside the legality of his own constitution, he stood tall on his personal authority, on his unique legitimacy, on his own mountain of moral capital in order to face down the assembled hordes of "mere politicians."

The majority yes vote was not, as it turned out, the overwhelming acclamation de Gaulle had wanted, but he welcomed it as a great victory over the huge array of political forces aligned against him. It was a victory greatly magnified in the ensuing parliamentary elections when the Gaullist parties won a near absolute majority in the new Assembly. The Fourth Republic had received its final quietus. De Gaulle now had the parliament he needed to pursue his real purpose, the assertion and defense of France's "greatness."

Conclusion

De Gaulle would rule for a further six years as elected monarch over an increasingly prosperous France,[53] though his ambition to be a world leader would be hampered by the fact that France could not be a great power in the post-war world.[54] Of course, he understood the relative weakness of a France – indeed of Western Europe – sandwiched between two great, mutually hostile blocs with their arsenals of nuclear weapons, but he refused to become the satellite of one or the other. He would remain true to his vision of France. He believed the "age of the big blocs" would come to an end and that France's highest interests would be served by preserving room for maneuver between them. France, by remaining ideologically independent, could still maintain its historical preeminence

---

[53] He narrowly won re-election in 1965.
[54] See David Schoenbrun, *The Three Lives of De Gaulle* (London, Hamish Hamilton, 1966), p. 317.

and universal significance by showing the way to a future, polyvalent world in which all nations, rich and poor, worked out their own destinies free from the thrall of overawing powers. The key to all his national strategies – from insistence on an unaligned nuclear deterrent through a whole series of independent (many would say eccentric) policy initiatives toward Russia, the United States, Germany, Europe, Africa and Asia – was always the maintenance of French independence in a binary world, and thus of French leadership of a potential "third force" carving its way between the two blocs.

With de Gaulle at its head, France still seemed to cut a figure in the world. The French people, their enduring nationalism flattered by policy stances that often baffled or infuriated both allies and enemies, for the most part went along with him – at least until a new generation arose moved by a *Weltgeist* with which the ageing General was wholly out of touch. The "events of May" 1968 created in France once again a state of revolt, even revolution, and found the General for the first time disoriented and bewildered, his legendary nerve momentarily paralyzed. He was able to recover his wits sufficiently to pull off another characteristic *coup de théâtre* that quelled the rebellion and produced a landslide victory for the Gaullists in new parliamentary elections. But though he had helped save the Fifth Republic from radical factions that sought to destroy it, he had lost his certainty about the faith of the French people in de Gaulle and de Gaulle's vision of France.[55] With the economy failing in the aftermath of the disruption, he was forced to impose financial austerity, and seems to have begun to doubt his own leadership. Feeling a need to test his legitimacy, that mystical legitimacy upon which he had so long relied, he placed all his remaining moral capital on the table for one final throw of the dice – a referendum over constitutional amendments of minor importance – and lost. Sorrowfully accepting the rebuff, he quietly left office to round out his days working on his memoirs.

His republic lived on, however, confounding the expectations of many who thought it too dependent on de Gaulle's persona and prestige to stand without him. As to the rest of his legacy, commentators have not been altogether kind. Aidan Crawley argued that the upheavals of 1968 exposed "the fantasies of Gaullism" even to Gaullists, that de Gaulle's "third force" leadership had proved chimerical,[56] that his stance as an unideological statesman of the civilized world and patron of the underdeveloped one was a mere mask for a "pathological" anti-Americanism.[57]

[55] See Crawley, *De Gaulle*, chapter XXV, p. 434; also Crozier, *De Gaulle*, Part VI, chapters 5–7.
[56] Crawley, *De Gaulle*, p. 471.
[57] Crawley, *De Gaulle*, p. 432. Crozier agrees, noting that de Gaulle's famous veto of British entry into the European Economic Community resulted from his conviction that Britain was America's "Trojan Horse"; *De Gaulle*, p. 683.

Brian Crozier, too, argued that de Gaulle's fame far outstripped his achievements. Much of Crozier's critique relates to the General's foreign policy after 1962 and need not concern us here, but he also discusses the "myth," or "mystique," of Gaullism on which his whole career rested. This was comprised, he says, of four propositions: that de Gaulle saved both the honor of France and France itself; that the Vichy government was illegal because of its capitulation to the Nazis; that de Gaulle's BBC appeal of June 1940 had conferred national "legitimacy" on him which he never lost; and that it was de Gaulle who restored to France its republic and its greatness. While accepting that the myth was "enormously useful" to the Gaullists and to de Gaulle himself at certain points, Crozier is concerned to puncture it by a cold-eyed examination of realities: Pétain's Vichy regime could in no way be considered illegal; de Gaulle's incarnation of national "legitimacy" was nothing more than a fantasy of his own not shared by most French people, and one that if accepted would have made the entire Fourth Republic illegitimate; and his claim to have restored French greatness could hardly be sustained since France in the modern world could never be more than a second-rank power. Moreover, Crozier argues that de Gaulle's creation of a "legitimate" state of Free France condemned all who supported or went along with Vichy as collaborators or traitors, and proved socially divisive after the war. De Gaulle in 1940 represented "nobody but himself," he says, and was distinctly unrepresentative of the defeated French people who mostly turned with relief to Pétain, a much better known leader than de Gaulle.

Yet, for all that, Crozier discerns elements of truth in the myth. He notes the emotional and symbolic significance of de Gaulle's presence to the British, standing alone against Hitler after the fall of France. He notes too that, as the war went on, more and more French people were drawn into the Resistance under de Gaulle's acknowledged leadership, and were inclined to look on his lonely stand as symbolic of French honor. And though his contribution to the war effort was negligible, there was no doubt that he did "restore the republic" by his preemptive actions against Allied occupation in 1944. Then, when the Germans were gone, the image of his "purity" and intransigence in defense of France "provided millions of Frenchmen and women with a model of patriotism to look to after the humiliation of defeat and occupation." Crozier writes that the fact that de Gaulle's mythical claims were unfounded actually adds to, rather than detracts from, his great achievement in having "pulled off" his great adventure, something that would probably not have been possible without a myth of some sort.[58]

[58] Crozier, *De Gaulle*, pp. 672 and 677.

But on Crozier's own account it is more accurate to say that there was enough truth in the myth to give it genuine hold on the French psyche, however overblown it frequently became in Gaullist rhetoric. The important point is that it was de Gaulle's belief in his own vision of France, his own identification with it, that allowed him to act so as to pull off the adventure. Whether many wholly shared his views is probably irrelevant. Sufficient numbers of people were inclined to grant him credit for his accomplishments regardless of whether they found his ideal convincing or absurd, and himself captivating or infuriating. Under the right conditions, de Gaulle was able consciously to turn that credit into moral capital that brought remarkable political returns. It was not that he inspired absolute trust – he could stumble badly, as we have seen, and was often deeply distrusted – but the wartime odyssey was always there like a moral nugget that could not be ignored. At a critical time, when all other options seemed too dangerous or too unreliable, this moral capital tipped the balance toward hope and belief, or at least the benefit of the doubt, giving him the foothold he needed to build a late-life political reign and to establish a new republic.

PART III

Moral capital and dissident politics

A story related by Vaclav Havel, leader of the "velvet revolution" in Czechoslovakia in the 1970s and 1980s, illustrates the importance of moral capital in dissident politics. Under interrogation during his first period of imprisonment, Havel foolishly mentioned his intention to re-sign as spokesman of the Czechoslovakian freedom movement known as Charter 77. His reason was personal disagreement with other leaders, but news of Havel's "betrayal" was immediately broadcast by the communist government in order to discredit him and his cause. Havel described his shame and humiliation on his release, and how, in an attempt to restore his credibility, he flung himself "almost hysterically" into the movement. After two years he was, to his great delight, reimprisoned for six weeks – good weeks indeed, he wrote, each one "another small step toward my 'rehabilitation'."[1] A later four-year term of imprisonment put the final seal on his dissident credentials.

The central importance of moral capital to dissidents has, in a sense, already been demonstrated in the case of de Gaulle, who could be described as an eternal political dissident. His whole career was charac-terized by dissident stances – first against the Third Republic, then against the Vichy regime, then against the Fourth Republic. Even as head of his own Fifth Republic, he acted on the world stage as a kind of international dissident at large. Of course, de Gaulle's dissidence was a response to the incompetence of regimes to maintain the greatness of his beloved France, not to the oppression of a wicked regime seeking to deny him voice or liberty. His was not a struggle for the political rights of a persecuted people, as was that of the modern dissidents treated in the next chapters. Nevertheless, the claims to leadership of both Nelson Mandela and Aung San Suu Kyi were founded just as surely in personal moral capital as was that of de Gaulle, though in their cases the capital was not wholly self-created.

Part of the reason for the exaggerated role of personal moral capital in

[1] Vaclav Havel, *Disturbing the Peace* (New York, Knopf, 1990), p. 143.

dissident politics is that dissidence inevitably implies a rejection of the legitimacy of established regimes, so that dissident politicians must necessarily lean on moral grounds other than those which support the existing rational-legal authority. The cause, it is true, is usually held to be larger than any particular person, and frequently finds embodiment in an organization created to give it political force. Nevertheless, the dramatic nature of dissident politics, in which vulnerable good is conceived as in conflict with oppressively powerful evil, tends to encourage the emergence of individual heroes who can effectively symbolize and personalize the cause. One of their main political functions becomes then to centralize and bring coherence to the disparate forces of opposition in circumstances of revolutionary upheaval. In the midst of a political maelstrom, when a multitude of voices compete for attention, and when dramatic, often traumatic, incidents follow hard one upon the other, the advent of one who can command loyalty and respect across a wide spectrum of political interests, and who can focus in his or her own person the forces and energies released, can have a profound effect.

The individual in such circumstances must be able to acquire and mobilize moral capital that crosses a great many constituencies that may have in common only their opposition to the existing order. When this fails to happen, as for example was for long the case with the anti-Milosevic parties in Yugoslavia, the weaknesses of division can be easily exploited by the wielders of institutionalized power. In Burma, the democratic opposition consciously sought such a figure, and courted Suu Kyi as a potential candidate; in South Africa by contrast, the anti-apartheid movement with its predominantly socialistic and egalitarian ideology was deeply ambivalent about the unexpected rise to prominence of one of its imprisoned members. The remarkable volume of extra-organizational moral capital that Mandela acquired in fact brought him into serious conflict with the internal rational-legal structures of the African National Congress, though the party could not but admit his usefulness as a political symbol.

The manner of Mandela's rise points (as does Havel's story above) to a common and important means for the accumulation of moral capital in dissident causes – a period of persecution. Such causes are undertaken to right great wrongs perpetrated by regimes whose preponderant power makes dissidence very dangerous. More is required than an ordinary conscientious attachment and service to values and goals. Courage and even heroism are necessary. Nothing attests better to one's true devotion than facing the risk and enduring the reality of persecution at the hands of the oppressor. Indeed, as the incarcerations of Suu Kyi and Mandela show, leaders may sometimes do as much for their cause through periods of exemplary suffering as in the active political battle outside the prison walls. Conscious of the dangers, they are even liable to view possible assassination as a political opportunity to be grasped by their followers.

Not surprisingly, perhaps, Suu Kyi and Mandela have many things in common apart from long imprisonment. Each had (as is not uncommon in political leaders) premonitions of their personal destiny: Suu Kyi foreseeing her inheritance of her father's mantle, Mandela reportedly claiming at age twenty-four that: "One day, I'm going to be prime minister of South Africa."[2] Each fought for democracy and justice against oppressive regimes that had become international pariahs, and each was (though to different degrees) significantly influenced by the inheritance of Gandhi. Each displayed gifts of leadership and political ability, and each had the capacity to be a teacher to their following. Each sacrificed family love and the common pleasures of ordinary life to their cause, and each proved tough, devoted and long-suffering on its behalf. Most importantly, as noted, the possession of moral capital (albeit from very different sources) was for each the foundation of their claim to leadership.

Just as interesting as these obvious points of similarity, however, are the points of difference. Mandela, convinced by 1960 that the fight against apartheid could not proceed peacefully, inaugurated an armed organization, a decision that had far-reaching consequences. Suu Kyi, on the other hand, always remained adamantly against the use of violence by her following. She had, apart from moral objections, a political reason – the fear of precipitating civil war by splitting the Burmese army, part of which was sympathetic to her. Her following in the military showed that Suu Kyi, though a dissident, was deeply connected to the regime against which she fought. Had it not been for this connection, a consequence of her famous father's heritage, she would never have been the leader she became. Suu Kyi's familial identity was the first source of her moral capital, just as it has been for those other female political leaders in the region whose chance at power arose through inheritance from assassinated husbands or fathers. It is a phenomenon that reveals the potential transmissibility of moral capital to suitable recipients should they wish to claim their heritage. No doubt there is an element of magic or symbolism in this transmission, but it is quite common. The essential connection is the one that passes through the inheritor to the values and goals championed by the esteemed forebear. The latter's moral legacy provides a political opportunity whose fulfillment depends on how well the inheritor serves that same cause.

[2] Cited in Martin Meredith, *Nelson Mandela: A Biography* (London, Hamish Hamilton, 1997), p. 39.

The Burmese struggle was thus, in a real sense, a political struggle between people who, despite their enmity, were deeply interrelated.[3] This fact made it possible for Suu Kyi (or rather her party) to participate in and win an election that (once the results had been denied by a regime regretting its moment of foolish liberality) formed an important continuing source of her moral capital. This was an unimaginable option for the black movement in South Africa. Apartheid policy effectively denied any intrinsic, communal or political connections between white and colored populations. Colored organizations represented groups both subjugated by and excluded from the legal and political nation, and were outlaw practically from the beginning. The few white organizations who were actively sympathetic to their cause were, like the communists, mostly themselves regarded as outlaw. Neither Mandela nor his colleagues had the option of realistically appealing to any large section within the white tribes or their armed forces. They faced a unified and ruthless apparatus of oppression that appeared utterly impervious to peaceful protest.

The bedrock of Mandela's moral capital was not familial inheritance but rather his incarceration at the hands of the apartheid regime. Mandela was an important black leader by the end of the 1950s, an eloquent articulator and defender of the values his organization represented. But it was his long imprisonment that gave birth to the extraordinary mushrooming of moral capital that propelled him, even from within prison, to the leadership of his movement and eventually to the head of his country. There was an important element of unforeseeable contingency in Mandela's rise that allows us to say that the moral capital created the man as much as *vice versa*. This capital opened up peculiar opportunities and also presented peculiar problems.

De Gaulle, as we saw, intentionally founded his moral capital on devotion and service to a cause above and therefore independent of particular parties, and had to face the difficulties inevitably produced by lack of a coherent political organization. Mandela did not choose, but found himself in possession of, moral capital that was equally radically disjoined from parties and organizations. Being a committed party man, however, and convinced that only through the party could the South African transition be accomplished, he faced the problem of reconciling his unwonted status with ordinary party membership and discipline in order to realize his chance at leadership. In the following chapter, we shall investigate how his opportunity arose and how he managed it.

---

[3] I exclude here the important exception and problem of the numerous tribal peoples of which Burma is composed.

5   Nelson Mandela: the moral phenomenon

> Under a government which imprisons any unjustly, the true place for a
> just man is also in prison.   Henry David Thoreau

In July 1997, Nelson Rohlilahla Mandela (commonly known among his
own people by the African name, Madiba) spoke to the Oxford Centre for
Islamic Studies on two themes that lay at the heart of his efforts to
construct the foundations for a new South Africa – reconciliation and
renaissance. The Director, Farhan Nizami, thanked Mandela for the
"extraordinary honour" and "extraordinary favour" he had bestowed,
declaring that "Your willingness to lend your moral authority to the aim
of the centre surely will inspire others to recognise the necessity of
tolerance and mutual respect between different cultural traditions in the
world."[1] Mandela replied that he had been eager to accept the invitation,
conscious of a debt owed to religious leaders and missionaries who had
educated black people in the days of their malign neglect by white rulers.
Though he did not mention it, he was no doubt also conscious of the debt
that he owed to the friendship and financial aid of the Saudi royal family,
who had also donated the money to construct a new building for the
center in the heart of Oxford. Bearing a large dome and a 33-meter
minaret, this building had been vigorously opposed by members of the
Oxford establishment. Since there was a suspicion abroad that opposition
was founded on cultural prejudice, there was a political point to be won
by Mandela's show of support.

It was a small but typical instance of the kind of intervention beyond
the shores of South Africa that Mandela frequently made after his inauguration as president of the post-apartheid republic in 1994. It was typical
in that it aimed at three interconnected purposes: repaying debts of
loyalty and support acquired during the years of apartheid by Africans
generally and by his party (the African National Congress) in particular;
tackling a moral-political problem with roots in the ideological clash

[1] Cited in Marion Edmunds, "Mandela's Discreet Nod to Islam," *Electronic Mail &
Guardian*, 22 July 1997, p. 3.

between Western and "third world" cultures; and furthering the interests, broadly conceived, of a regenerated, multiracial South Africa. To these purposes (and with variable effect) Mandela consistently lent the considerable weight of his own moral capital abroad.

No modern leader possessed this resource in such bounty as Mandela, and few were as explicit in their attempt to use it for considered ends. The purpose of this chapter is to explain how Mandela acquired this unusual burden of moral capital, and how he employed it to gain leadership of a South Africa undergoing a traumatic transition. Though each of the four sources of moral capital – cause, action, example, rhetoric/symbolism – was important to his case, the real key to the Mandela phenomenon lay in a combination of the last two.

Mandela's *cause* was that of the African National Congress (ANC), which sought the establishment of a multiracial democracy in South Africa under some form of socialist government. This implied a rejection of an idea that had appealed to Mandela in his youth – an "Africa for black Africans" – and that continued to be represented by the ANC's chief rival for black allegiance, the Pan Africanist Congress (PAC). As important as the goal itself was the question of the means used to reach it. The ANC long held to a Gandhian program of nonviolence but shifted, under Mandela's urging, to an armed struggle that had profound and rather mixed consequences for the movement at home and abroad, as well as for Mandela himself.

Mandela's *action* in the service of ANC goals must be separated into two sections, one before his imprisonment and one after his release. His activities before his arrest in 1962 were energetic and colorful (if not always wise), though his training as a lawyer stood the movement in good stead and assisted his rise to a leadership position. His imprisonment (along with most of the black leaders of the first wave of anti-apartheid movement) led after many years to his becoming the "best known prisoner in the world." Here was the element of *example*, for Mandela became the exemplary martyr to his cause. More than an example, Mandela became the prime *symbol* of the entire movement, and the cry "Free Mandela!" a universal shorthand for the demand that the apartheid system be dismantled. This had occurred in part as a result of Mandela's own rhetorical ability – his "defense" statements at his trials remained key documents of the movement. The most interesting thing about Mandela's "mythification," however, was that it was as much a product of adventitious historical circumstances as of his own qualities. Nevertheless, the moral capital amassed enabled him to enter a second period of active service beginning in 1986, when he initiated independent talks with the white government.

Yet moral capital did not lead to leadership authority in any simple or easy manner. To realize his opportunity, Mandela had to manage two difficult relationships, one with President de Klerk, the other with his own party among whose ranks he suffered something of a moral deficit. Mandela's story is always the story of Mandela *and* the African National Congress, for his moral rise coincided with, and was intricately and causally tied to, the modern resurgence of the party. As the ANC maneuvered to assert leadership over a renascent anti-apartheid movement, so "Comrade Mandela," the obedient party man, had to move carefully to translate the moral capital won in extra-party fashion into effective leadership. He encountered suspicion and opposition from colleagues who realized the political value of his symbolic elevation but remained deeply ambivalent about it. Mandela's moral capital thus proved not only his main chance but also one of his main difficulties as he tried to negotiate the transition to a fully democratic, multiracial South Africa. Balancing independent maneuver with party appeasement was a delicate and difficult task that he was forced to perform over a number of years filled with drama, violent incident, hope and frustration.

The political cause

The main choice of goals presented to opponents of the white regime (aside from black liberation) was that between a multiracial, democratic South Africa and a black nationalist South Africa. The principal choice of means was between nonviolent action and armed resistance. The cause eventually championed by the ANC – Mandela's cause – was that of a multiracial, socialist democracy to be achieved by means of armed resistance. In terms of moral capital, this combination played differently and dissonantly in different constituencies, presenting serious leadership problems for Mandela after 1988 as he tried to steer negotiations toward a peaceful transition.

Mandela's connection with the ANC began when, as a young law student in Johannesburg in 1943, he fell in with a group of activists that included two people, Walter Sisulu and Oliver Tambo, who would be lifelong friends, influences and fellow leaders. This group had come under the intellectual leadership of Anton Lembede. Lembede's philosophy ("Africa belongs to black Africans") was an early version of black consciousness. It insisted on the need for black people to have pride in their culture, to forget tribal difference and to unite to achieve their own liberation. Mandela, deeply impressed, remained for some years a determined Africanist, suspicious of any organization that might wrest leadership from the black community.

Mandela, Sisulu and Tambo together established a Youth League as a vehicle for taking over the ANC, a venerable but small and moribund party, which they then committed to a strategy of mass mobilization. In June 1952 they launched a "defiance campaign" conceived by Sisulu to protest against the restrictive laws of the National government. The campaign, in which Mandela acted as an energetic and effective organizer, was conducted in association with the Indian Congress. It employed Gandhian nonviolent civil disobedience tactics and was a dramatic popular success, attracting international attention to the African cause for the first time and transforming the ANC into a mass party. The campaign fully converted Mandela to the idea of a multiracial alliance. It also elicited a massively repressive response from the government, which declared a state of emergency that rendered further protest next to impossible.

In 1955 the party moved to establish its multiracial, democratic ideals as the dominant commitment of the entire protest movement. It promulgated a Freedom Charter, written and adopted by a so-called Congress Alliance at ANC instigation. The three other organizations involved were the Indian Congress, the Coloured People's Organisation, and the Congress of Democrats, the last of which was dominated by white members of the banned South African Communist Party (SACP). It was one of their number, Rusty Bernstein, who was largely responsible for drafting the Charter which, not surprisingly, also committed the movement to socialistic goals. The ANC officially adopted the Charter in 1956 at a meeting disrupted by noisily protesting Africanists.

The multiracial ideal had been established, but nonviolent action was proving ineffectual against a hardening regime. The thunder of international denunciation after the Sharpeville massacre in 1960 (when sixty-seven protesters were killed by police) momentarily shook white confidence, but President Hendrik Verwoerd, grand architect of apartheid, proved implacable. He responded to ANC-organized mass action with a savage crackdown, a state of emergency and new legislation under which organizations like the ANC and the PAC were banned. Tambo fled across the border to establish an ANC-in-exile, while 18,000 other activists were arrested (including Mandela who spent five months in prison). The home ANC regrouped as a covert organization and Mandela went underground.

During this period, he organized a three-day strike to protest the government's declaration of an independent republic of South Africa on 31 May 1961. The strike failed due to an unprecedented government mobilization to suppress it, and Mandela concluded that the ANC had to abandon nonviolent mass action and move to armed resistance. It was a shift much discussed after Sharpeville but resisted by the ANC's then president, Chief Albert Luthuli, who believed in nonviolence for moral reasons. Mandela, however, had never committed to nonviolence as a Gandhian moral-spiritual imperative but merely as a prudent tactic in the face of a powerful foe. He now became instrumental in establishing a guerrilla organization, *Umkhonto we Sizwe* (Spear of the Nation, commonly known as the MK), separate from the ANC but controlled by its leadership and committed to a narrowly defined sabotage campaign aimed at harming state installations, not people. At his 1962 trial, Mandela would defend the MK on the grounds that it was necessary to satisfy an increasingly militant constituency. By pursuing a strictly limited violent campaign, he said, the party hoped to maintain control and prevent a descent into bloody civil war – a doubtful judgment, perhaps, given the success of the State in suppressing all protest during the next decade and a half.

The move to violence played differently to different constituencies. However justified, however limited, it had negative repercussions among potential foreign friends. The party's strong association with communists both inside and outside its organization, and its control of a "terrorist" group which came to be largely financed and trained by communist countries, made it the object of suspicion in the West and even among African sympathizers. It dealt a useful card to a South African government desperate for any scrap of moral capital it could deploy among nations liable to treat it as a pariah. National Party presidents, so long as the Cold War lasted, could harp ceaselessly and fruitfully on the "communist menace," and were prone to describe, in tones of ludicrous martyrdom, white South Africa as the last bastion of liberty on the continent, tragically forsaken by its friends. The tactic had particular success in the 1980s among conservative governments in the United States, the United Kingdom and West Germany, who were inclined to accept Pretoria's view that all black radicals were revolutionaries controlled by Moscow and thus to lend *de facto* support to the regime. In an ideologically divided world, the ANC's communist links and its proclaimed socialistic goals allowed the government to equate "communist menace" with armed black opposition, thus justifying even its strongest counter-insurgency measures. They also encouraged National Party governments to provide overt and covert support to black rivals of the ANC who spouted suitably right-wing rhetoric, most notably Zulu chief Mangosuthu Buthelezi whose Inkatha movement would fight what became a bloody civil war with ANC supporters during the period of transition.

On the other hand, for large sections of the ANC's black constituency, communism was never the bogey it was for Western governments. If friends are judged by their actions, then blacks could feel justified in regarding communists of whatever color as loyal friends and allies given the latter's long and active commitment to ending white supremacy in South Africa. Often the only white people that blacks like Mandela knew personally as friends, and in whose homes they were welcome, were communists. Mandela himself had many such friends, but was nevertheless for a long while fiercely opposed to ANC–communist links, fearing that an alliance would result in a communist takeover of the leadership of the black movement. As time went on, however, he became convinced that the communists were indispensable allies, though he, like other ANC leaders, never ceased to insist that the ANC was not, and must not be seen as, a communist-dominated organization.

Nor would (or could) he easily retreat from the MK's path of violence once taken, though it became a crucial sticking point in the run up to negotiations. The white government constantly demanded that the ANC renounce its "terrorism." Mandela always argued that, dislike it though he may, the ANC had been forced onto this road by the violence and repression of the government that made any other means of resistance impossible.[2] The fact was, though, that it was impossible simply to drop a policy approved by so many black people happy to see someone striking back (even if ineffectually) at the white oppressor. The MK had particular significance for the recruitment of radical youths who would hardly have been absorbed into the ANC organization in later years if no show of armed struggle had been on offer. It would be one of Mandela's chief political challenges after his release from prison to convince ANC cadres that negotiations with the government were not a form of surrender or an admission of military defeat. When the negotiating policy produced only slow returns, he would argue that "negotiations themselves are a theater of struggle, subject to advances and reverses as any other form of struggle."[3]

If the communist alliance and the choice of violent resistance thus had more positive than negative effects in Mandela's core constituency, they were nevertheless things he was obliged to defend time and again to fearful white South Africans, to international investors and to otherwise sympathetic Western critics. Even Amnesty International would not campaign on behalf of ANC leaders during their imprisonment because of the party's commitment to armed struggle. (So conscious was Mandela of this opprobrium, that he was surprised in 1993 to be awarded the Nobel Peace

[2] On Mandela's reasoning, see Nelson Mandela, *Long Walk to Freedom* (Boston, Little, Brown & Co., 1994), pp. 453–454.
[3] *Ibid.*, p. 516.

Prize along with de Klerk, having presumed that the founder of *Umkhonto* would be automatically disqualified.) When Mandela, still in prison, began weekly meetings with government representatives after May 1988, the talks centered on just three issues: the armed struggle, the link with communists, and the fate of whites under majority rule. The demise of the Soviet empire, when it came, was thus enormously fortunate for Mandela. It took much of the sting from the communist threat and made his continuing loyalties to old comrades more tolerable. It was greeted joyfully by then President de Klerk who had determined that the days of apartheid were numbered. The collapse of the socialist countries of Eastern Europe who had been the ANC's principal means of support, and the announced withdrawal of the Soviet Union from regional conflicts, represented, he said, a "God-given opportunity" for his new government.[4]

Mandela's difficult task was to convince his own party to grasp this opportunity. He saw that the Afrikaner State had lost confidence in apartheid but was terrified at the prospect of annihilation at the hands of the black majority. Yet it remained too powerful militarily for the weak and inefficient MK ever to hurt badly, never mind defeat. Mandela therefore concluded that negotiation was the only way forward. At Harare, in August 1989, the ANC's National Executive Committee issued a declaration listing five preconditions for negotiations in exchange for which it would suspend all armed violence. The decision produced deep division between a small group favoring negotiation and a fiercely opposed majority psychologically wedded to the concept of armed struggle, partly as a matter of pride and training, partly through deep distrust of a government that had been so long the brutal enemy. To Mandela, the internal controversy over the Harare Declaration revealed the extent to which the party was unprepared for the new era breaking upon it, and defined the challenge he must meet if he were to make his leadership real.

If the resistance strategy thus proved problematical across constituencies, the ANC's central goal of a multiracial polity, to which Mandela staunchly held, proved to be more advantageous than otherwise. The National government was forced, very reluctantly, to deal with Mandela because of his status in the world's eyes and because the ANC gained the backing of most of the people of color in South Africa. Yet the ANC's multiracial commitment made negotiation possible despite the "terrorist" impediment, a course that would have been scarcely conceivable had, for example, the PAC commanded the majority.

[4] Martin Meredith, *Nelson Mandela: A Biography* (London, Hamish Hamilton, 1997), p. 397.

Political action: first period

Mandela's moral capital before his imprisonment was gained wholly through his service to the ANC. He was in some ways a natural leader, identified from the start by colleagues as bright, idealistic, energetic, magnetically attractive. He was also in youth physically imposing and good at boxing (a sport much admired among Africans), and never allowed himself to be treated as a mere "kaffir."[5] His enduring consciousness of his own dignity as a descendant of the royal line of the Thembu, a branch of the Xhosa peoples, often produced public behavior that colleagues thought too aristocratically imperious, aloof and arrogant.[6] In the early days, however, he was the self-admitted "gadfly" of the movement, lacking the real seriousness or moral authority of a man like Sisulu. He could also be prickly, argumentative and hot-headed, with a romantic, self-promoting spirit that sometimes served him ill. Yet he was perceived by colleagues to mature significantly over the years, and several actions during the 1950s and early 1960s brought him prominence within the party.

The first was his invention of a cellular, semi-clandestine organizational structure to avoid police harassment known as the "M" Plan ("M" for Mandela), that was never effectively implemented. The second was his performance at a ludicrously protracted trial that arose out of arrests following the promulgation of the Freedom Charter – the so-called Treason Trial for fomenting "communist revolution." In the course of it Mandela demonstrated lawyerly skills and resolution, emerging for the first time as a genuine leader in his own right.[7] A more colorful chapter was added during his life on the run following the failed strike of 1961. He evaded capture for sixteen months by moving constantly and adopting various disguises and personas, occasionally surfacing to give highly publicized press conferences. For these exploits the media dubbed him "the Black Pimpernel," an image that would continue to resonate with disaffected black youths down through the years.

With the foundation of *Umkhonto*, Mandela indulged himself as the romantic revolutionary, wearing military fatigues and carrying a pistol. His Pimpernel role became devoted to raising support and funds abroad to train and equip the MK. Slipping out of the country, he traveled to ten African nations then on to London. Back in South Africa, he took some foolish risks and was captured on 5 August 1962. For his part in the

---

[5] See, for example, Allister Sparks, *Tomorrow is Another Country* (Cape Town, Struik, 1994), pp. 24, 34, 46, 121 and 183.
[6] But see Albertina Sisulu's comment cited in Meredith, *Nelson Mandela*, p. 107.
[7] See *ibid.*, p. 187.

three-day strike, he was sentenced to a total of five years' imprisonment. He had served only a year, however, when police raided a farm near Rivonia, outside Johannesburg, which Mandela's inept and security-lax co-conspirators used as a headquarters. They netted eight of the aspiring revolutionaries (including Sisulu) and found documents outlining a grandiose guerrilla war project as well as several others in Mandela's hand. Thus implicated in a conspiracy, he was again brought to trial, found guilty and sentenced along with his fellows to life imprisonment.

Mandela's skilled, dignified and powerfully theatrical performances at his two trials constituted his finest hours in this first period of service and left a lingering mark. Mandela contrived in effect to put the white State and its whole legal system on trial rather than himself, and used the proceedings to deliver a powerful indictment of apartheid from within its legal heart. He also bequeathed the movement an articulate exposition of the philosophy of a multiracial democracy for South Africa. At the Rivonia trial, convinced that he and his colleagues would receive the death penalty, he concluded with the words:

During my lifetime I have dedicated myself to this struggle of the African people. I have fought against white domination, and I have fought against black domination. I have cherished the ideal of a democratic and free society in which all persons live together in harmony and with equal opportunities. It is an ideal which I hope to live for and to achieve. But if needs be, it is an ideal for which I am prepared to die.[8]

Though locally unheeded at the time because of reporting restrictions, his statements were noted internationally, and later became crucial documents of the movement within South Africa. They helped to keep alive the nonvindictive, multiracial and transtribal ideal at a time when more vengeful forces threatened to swamp it.

The practical outcome of this period of activity, nevertheless, was disaster for the movement. Most of its leadership was either in prison or in exile. The MK, amateurishly optimistic about its ability to combat the power of the white State, had fatally underestimated its foe. The liberation forces had been crushed, and it would be more than a decade before voices of effective protest were once again raised in the land. The longest part of Mandela's "long walk to freedom" had begun.

Example: the representative prisoner

During his long incarceration, Mandela acquired the moral capital that allowed him to assume the leadership of a new South Africa. It would not

[8] Nelson Mandela, "Second Court Statement 1964," in *The Struggle is My Life* (South Africa, Mayibuye Books, 1994), p. 181.

have been possible, of course, had he not established a leadership role in this first period, but the phenomenon of Nelson Mandela cannot be wholly explained by his early reputation. Mandela became more than just another martyr to the cause; he became in time its most representative and exemplary martyr, a fate that seemed impossible during most of the endless days of captivity.

By the mid-1970s, Zulu leader Chief Buthelezi, despite his partnership with the white government over its homelands policy, seemed to many black South Africans a more pertinent symbol of black struggle than did an impotent, ageing Nelson Mandela. Mandela and the other leaders from the 1950s had by then been moldering on far-off Robben Island for fourteen years, and there was little in the political situation to encourage hope of an imminent release. With the black population intimidated by the heavy hand of the State, the edifice of apartheid had proved stubbornly strong. The banned ANC survived in exile and continued to prosecute a desultory and ineffectual guerrilla campaign within South Africa, but it had collapsed as an effective force of popular internal mobilization.

Nor did it augur well for Mandela and his colleagues that, when protest did at last revive, it was inspired not by the multiracial ideals of their own organization, but by the angrier sentiments of the black consciousness movement. To the generation of militant youngsters led by the likes of Steve Biko, the leaders of the 1950s were names from the past, of scant relevance to their own contemporary struggles. Their attitude was often one of contempt toward elders who seemed to have bequeathed them little but political quietism and racial subjection.[9] Yet it was through the actions of such youths, in the first instance, that Nelson Mandela became once again a name to be reckoned with in South African politics. In 1976 thousands of them showed astonishing bravery by standing up to the armed might of the security forces in Soweto[10] to protest compulsory teaching in Afrikaans. The shock waves emitted by the six-month long clash reverberated round the world and made the white establishment tremble. As the violence escalated, the students widened their initial protest and began to conceive of the possibility of destroying the entire "Bantu" education system (geared to the permanent inferiority of blacks), or even of bringing down the government itself. Yet by December the revolt had petered out, and it was clear that the regime would not to be toppled by schoolchildren, however courageous, especially when their actions failed to transcend protest and become a definite political program. The concrete gains made within South Africa had been minimal,

[9] See Allister Sparks, *The Mind of South Africa* (New York, Ballantine Books, 1990), p. 301.
[10] Soweto is an abbreviation of South Western Township, a crowded black residential area on the outskirts of Johannesburg.

while the costs – in terms of injuries, loss of life and intensified police suppression – had been inordinately high.

Nevertheless, the apartheid regime had been put squarely back onto the international agenda. Television pictures of policemen shooting unarmed schoolchildren (and later stories of the manner of Biko's death) provoked outrage that found expression in new demands for economic sanctions against South Africa. Foreign multinationals with operations there came under increasing pressure from anti-apartheid groups to withdraw. International business generally began to review the security of South African investments, fanning winds of change already stirring within the local business community. But the two most significant results of the Soweto revolt for our story were the acclamation of Nelson Mandela as national leader, and the revival of the fortunes of the ANC.

The cry most frequently heard in Soweto prior to the uprising was "Viva Samora!" (Samora Machel, the radical president of newly independent Mozambique). Why Mandela's name should have been particularly invoked during the struggle is a matter for conjecture. It is true there was an important local connection. Orlando, a district of Soweto, had been Mandela's home since the time of his first marriage in 1947, and his second wife, Winnie, still lived there in 1976 with their children. But Sisulu was also a long-time resident of Orlando, though according to Eleanor Sisulu, his niece, Mandela's former image as Pimpernel and revolutionary gave him greater appeal for the young rebels.[11] Most important, perhaps, was the role of Winnie Mandela, though she herself expressed surprise that 20,000 schoolchildren who ought to think of Mandela as a myth from the past should chant and sing of him and other leaders on Robben Island, demanding their release.[12] As a political activist and constant victim of official harassment, Winnie had kept the Mandela name locally alive through the years. When Soweto erupted, Winnie flung herself with customary vehemence into the fray, playing a central role in a Black Parents Association (BPA) set up to act (ineffectually) as an intermediary between students and authorities. It was indicative of her local reputation that, when she went to the police to try to halt the shooting, they accused *her* of having organized the riots. Frustrated, Winnie demonstrated at the police station with reckless violence, was targeted afresh by security police and detained for five months in August 1976.

Winnie was thus a very public figure, and the brazen fearlessness of her

[11] Personal communication, May 1998.
[12] Winnie Mandela, *Part of My Soul* (edited by Anne Benjamin and adapted by Mary Benson, Harmondsworth, Penguin, 1985), p. 113.

advocacy had undoubted appeal for the rebellious young. Dr. Nthatho Motlana, commenting on her role in the BPA, noted:

For a long time there has been this awful schism between the PAC, the Black Consciousness Movement and the ANC. When we founded the Black Parents Association we needed to form an organization that could bridge the gap. The youth, many of whom came under the influence of Black Consciousness, related very well to Winnie Mandela; they never had any problems accepting Winnie's leadership, she transcends these differences. They go to her from all over. So in the BPA we needed the kind of role Winnie can play, her ability to bridge the gap between youth and the adults and the different ideological factions.[13]

It would be ironic in view of the problems that Winnie later caused Mandela and the ANC if she should have played such a causal role, but it was very possibly so. At any rate, in the years that followed, both Nelson and Winnie were to become increasingly identified, both at home and abroad, as *the* representative heroes of the struggle against apartheid. By 1978, it was possible for a UN Special Committee and the Anti-Apartheid Movement successfully to stage a worldwide observance of Nelson's sixtieth birthday as an effective protest. The British Prime Minister, James Callaghan, paid tribute to Mandela in the House of Commons, and tens of thousands of letters of protest from governments, organizations and individuals poured into Robben Island, and into the humble cottage in Brandfort to which Winnie had by then been banished. The stage had been set for the mushrooming of the Mandela myth, whose more radical growth commenced in March 1980.

According to Mandela's own testimony, this was deliberately engineered by his old friend and former law partner Oliver Tambo.[14] Tambo and the ANC-in-exile, at their headquarters in Lusaka, had decided to "personalize" the quest for the release of prisoners by focusing on Mandela. Tambo noted that it was easier for masses of people to grasp a momentous moral conflict when it is personified in the cruel fate of a particular individual. Mandela recalls in his autobiography that some of his fellow prisoners regarded this as a betrayal of the collectivist principles of the ANC but that most saw it as a useful way of rousing people. But the campaign had already become highly personalized. Mandela's name was by now the one most frequently chanted on the township streets and the one most spoken abroad. Tambo's move was intended to capitalize further on an already accomplished fact, and its results would hardly have been so spectacularly successful had it not been so. On 9 March 1980, Percy Qoboza, editor of the Soweto *Sunday Post*, published (presumably at ANC instigation) the headline "Free Mandela!" and a petition for

[13] *Ibid.*, p. 115.   [14] Mandela, *Long Walk to Freedom*, p. 440.

people to sign demanding the release of political prisoners. Over 86,000 signatures were received in response. Qoboza had written (with reference to Robert Mugabe's recent victory over Ian Smith in the Zimbabwe elections):

One of the realities we must face up to is that Nelson Mandela commands a following that is unheard of in this land. To embark on any solution or discussion without his wise input would only be following the blind politics of Ian Smith and Muzorewa in Zimbabwe and the outcome would be just as disastrous.[15]

Given the huge national and international reaction it eventually evoked, this was something of a self-fulfilling prophecy. Whatever had been the case beforehand, it was certainly true afterwards that the white regime, if ever it wished to negotiate a fundamental restructuring of the South African polity with its black noncitizens, could scarcely afford to ignore Nelson Mandela. And, as a corollary, the regime's shifting attitude toward Mandela inevitably became a reliable weathervane indicating its intentions with respect to radical reform.

The call for Mandela's release was soon augmented by a multitude of voices, including those of all notable black leaders and of several white ones, of the South African Council for Churches, of the Organization of African Unity, of leaders of the Commonwealth and of Europe, and of the UN Special Committee against Apartheid. Significantly, the Security Council and the General Assembly of the United Nations, which had been demanding the release of political prisoners in South Africa since 1963, specifically mentioned Nelson Mandela by name for the first time.[16] He had become a lightning rod for world opinion, and the demand for his release was synonymous with the demand for an end to apartheid – for an end, too, unmarked by blood and vengeance. His daughter Zindzi put this hope plainly in an address to white students at the University of the Witwatersrand: "The call for Mandela's release," she declared, "is merely to say there is an alternative to the inevitable bloodbath."[17]

The ANC had also received a somewhat paradoxical boost as a result of Soweto and its aftermath. The savage suppression of the revolt had propelled many young activists into jail where they came into contact with ANC members. Mandela, in his autobiography tells of the shock felt by the older prisoners at the influx of these defiant youths at Robben Island in 1976, and of his own attempts to come to terms with the black

[15] Cited in E. S. Reddy, "Free Nelson Mandela," July 1988 (available on the ANC's internet site, www.anc.org.za/ancdocs/history/campaigns/prisoner.html).
[16] Security Council Resolution 473 of 13 June 1980, and General Assembly Resolution 35/206 of 16 December 1980.
[17] Cited in Meredith, *Nelson Mandela*, pp. 342–343.

consciousness ideas they brought with them.[18] There was inevitably competition between the various political organizations represented in prison to win the allegiance of the undisciplined newcomers, and from this lengthy, sometimes violent, contest the ANC emerged largely triumphant. Meanwhile, some 14,000 other youths fleeing into exile were funneled by ANC groups into *Umkhonto* bases in Mozambique and some of them onto training in East Germany or the USSR. Tambo's well-developed external ANC organization here came into its own. The young runaways, eager to gain military training in order to strike back at their oppressors, went naturally to this existing organization but had to pay the price of subjection to the discipline of the ANC and acceptance of its nonracialist principles.

The Freedom Charter that enshrined these principles had fallen into relative desuetude with the decline in the ANC's fortunes after 1960, and Tambo was anxious to reinstate it as the guiding light of the renewed struggle. The name Mandela, according to Tambo, proved an important aid in this. Reviewing his promotional efforts in his 1981 party address, he noted that the launching of the Free Mandela Campaign had been "enormously timely and appropriate," adding that the people of South Africa, in their support of the latter, had spoken "with a unity rarely known and strikingly non-racial."[19] The moral capital of "Comrade Mandela," effective across so many constituencies and parties, was thus of enormous help to the ANC in its struggle to reassert its leadership and ideology. But the very fact that Mandela was so widely and comprehensively acknowledged had the effect of separating him somewhat from his ANC roots. His moral capital was no longer clearly mediated by the organization to which he belonged but rather had become his own peculiar property. Mandela was acutely aware of this tension, but was determined to exploit his new status as carefully as he might.

The conjoined causes of Mandela and the ANC were considerably advanced after 1983, the year that then President P.W. Botha promulgated a new constitution. This provided for two additional representative chambers for coloreds and Indians respectively, but nothing for blacks. Constitutional reform was accompanied by a set of reform Bills setting up black municipal councils through which township blacks were supposed to run their own affairs, while new regulations granted urban status only to those who had jobs and "approved" accommodation. The intention of these measures was to sever the common interests of blacks and other

[18] Mandela, *Long Walk to Freedom*, pp. 421–424.
[19] O. R. Tambo, "Extend and Defend Our Revolutionary Gains!", Statement, 8 January 1981 (www.anc.org.za/ancdocs/history/jan8-81.html).

racial groups, as well as of urban and country blacks, a divide-and-rule strategy that provoked a massive, sustained and wholly unanticipated popular reaction. About 600 anti-apartheid groups formed an umbrella organization called the United Democratic Front (UDF). The UDF acted as a popular front, conducting hugely successful mass rallies and demonstrations across the country. It also identified itself with the Free-dom Charter of 1955 and so, as Allister Sparks notes, "by an association that evaded legal restrictions, brought the ANC back into the center of the political arena."[20]

Between 1984 and 1988, protest also took the form of well-organized township violence, mostly directed at the new councils and their "collab-orator" occupants. The ANC-in-exile exhorted militant comrades to conduct a "people's war" that would "make the townships ungovern-able." Thus began a cycle of protest rally leading to violence and deaths, which in turn led to funerals that themselves turned into protest rallies and so on. At each stage of this cycle the flag of the ANC could be seen prominently displayed alongside that of the UDF. The persistent calls for the release of Mandela were now invariably accompanied by the demand for the unbanning of the ANC so that negotiations might commence for a fully democratic constitution.

Rhetoric/symbolism: the living symbol

Mandela in Robben Island had by this time become the stuff of legend, the tempo of glorification continually increasing rather than abating. In all parts of the world, honors were bestowed on him *in absentia* – human rights prizes from various organizations, the freedom of a dozen cities, honorary degrees from universities, the dedication of streets, buildings and institutions to him and Winnie. The name Mandela had become familiar to people around the globe, much less for what he had done than for what he had adventitiously become: the representative detainee of the apartheid regime, the exemplary martyr for his cause. There were other prisoners, other leaders, as long confined, as enduring, but it was Man-dela who had come to symbolize their sacrifice and their suffering. By the time of his release he had been in prison for over 27 years. Article after article dwelt with sympathetic horror on the sacrifice implied by the sheer length of this incarceration, on the unimaginable pain of separation from a loved spouse, from children now hardly known, from friends and normal life, from a political calling that in other circumstances might have produced a great statesman. The longer Mandela sat, or toiled, or what-

---

[20] Sparks, *The Mind of South Africa*, pp. 332–333.

ever it was that people conceived of him as doing in prison – the longer he *endured* – the greater grew the world's admiration and the more powerful a symbol he became for the hope of a new South Africa. And when the great transition was at last achieved and the elections of 1994 won, black voters would say that Mandela was the main reason they had voted for the ANC. Why? Because "he went to prison for us."[21]

The moral capital that any adherent to a dissident cause gains through persecution was thus hugely amplified in Mandela by virtue of his role as living symbol. The place of imprisonment – Robben Island – became itself intimately attached to the symbol. The prison and the sacrifice it represented formed the central element in a story that could stand for the story of all black South Africans – one of prolonged bondage, suffering, endurance and, ultimately, of liberation. The ANC explicitly made the identification in 1988 when it called for an international observance of Mandela's seventieth birthday. "His life," it said, "symbolises our people's burning desire for freedom; his imprisonment is the imprisonment of the whole South African nation; the fight for his unconditional release, and that of all political prisoners and detainees, is the glorious fight against injustice, racial bigotry, and man's inhumanity to man."[22]

By the time of his release, the symbol had, in fact, largely eclipsed the man. About the latter the world knew little. Since no photographs were permitted or had been taken since the start of his imprisonment, Mandela was hardly more than a name that rang well in a popular protest song. (In his biography, Mandela says he was told that many London youngsters thought his Christian name was Free.[23]) E.S. Reddy, writing at the time, claimed that "Nelson Mandela had so inspired millions of people around the world that they spontaneously found means to honour him and thereby declare solidarity with the cause of freedom to which he had dedicated his life."[24] But the words of a Mandela biographer ring more accurately: "Millions of people who supported the campaign [to release Mandela] had little precise idea of who he was. Virtually nothing had been heard of him for fifteen years. But the tide of hostility towards apartheid was now running strong, making him the most famous prisoner in the world."[25] If he avoided the category of the wholly mythical it was largely by virtue of his conjugal attachment to the all-too-visible Winnie, whose abundant reality seemed to argue some sort of actuality for his own corporeal, if mysteriously isolated, existence.

Mandela himself perfectly understood that his huge store of moral

[21] Meredith, *Nelson Mandela*, p. 518.
[22] *ANC Struggle Update*, June/July 1988 (www.anc.org.za/ancdocs/history/or).
[23] Mandela, *Long Walk to Freedom*, p. 440.
[24] Reddy, "Free Nelson Mandela."   [25] Meredith, *Nelson Mandela*, p. 343.

capital had the character of a windfall, and never failed to emphasize the distinction between "the man and the myth." Nevertheless, that which had accumulated to the myth had to be borne by the man, and how well it was borne would depend on the man himself. And if the mantle of moral greatness fell somewhat serendipitously on the shoulders of Nelson Mandela, it was also true that the garment fit him remarkably well. His prison experience had helped prepare him for its assumption. It was true that he had entirely adapted to life on Robben Island – where no tomorrow could be expected different from today, wisdom and survival seemed to dictate relinquishment of hope. Yet he had been head of the "High Organ," or high command, of ANC inmates, and his autobiography contains small, telling revelations of his preoccupation with the things that top leadership entails. And the personal lessons taken in prison, the character self-created in the light of them, were peculiarly adapted to the symbolic role that a dangerously turbulent South Africa demanded. It was a role that emphasized tolerance, a magnanimous spirit, a willingness to look constructively forward rather than vindictively backward.

Mandela's embodiment of these qualities was (in his own words) a triumph of "brains over blood." The headstrong, passionate man he had been in his youth, uncompromising in argument and intolerant of opposition, had not disappeared but had been strictly disciplined over the years by a dispassionate, lawyerly mind that calculated what could realistically be achieved and what was necessary to achieve it. The toughness of mind, the strength of will, and the patience required to tame strong emotions were the same qualities he would need to oversee the birth of a new nation without recourse to civil war. The tragedy of Bosnia, Mandela said, was a result of the fact that people there had thought with their blood and not their brains. Where Slobodan Milosevic chose consciously to inflame Serbian sentiment against other nationalities for the sake of a Greater Serbia, Mandela consciously chose to calm bellicose spirits and to encourage unity. His role was to act as a stable center that could hold in orbit all the disparate, conflicting and potentially explosive forces at play in a highly volatile situation. Political rival Neville Alexander, who spent fifteen years on Robben Island with Mandela, commented:

Mandela had this quality of being able to keep people together. It didn't matter whether you were PAC or ANC or what, we all tended to congregate around him. Even his critics – and he had them – deferred to him in the end of the day as a moral leader. He still has that quality. Without him I can't visualize how the transition would have gone.[26]

In 1978, convinced that events were moving towards inevitable free-

26 Cited in Anthony Lewis, "The Mandela Behind the Saint," *New York Times Magazine*, 23 March 1997, pp. 42–43 and 45.

dom, Mandela became concerned to keep in touch with current developments and thinking so that when he walked out of prison it would not be as "a political fossil from an age long past." His moral elevation had given him the chance at the leadership role but could not guarantee him against contemporary irrelevance when the living symbol encountered brutal political reality. According to Mandela'a own account, President de Klerk was, after Mandela's release in 1990, banking precisely on the hope that he *would* prove an incapable fossil. The government, he writes, was in no hurry to begin negotiations after the euphoric moment of his release, wanting "to allow time for me to fall on my face and show that the former prisoner hailed as a savior was a highly fallible man who had lost touch with the present situation."[27]

But Mandela was an intensely political man with a keen sense of power and its uses, conscious of both the opportunities and dangers his unprecedented stock of moral capital presented. In his first speech after his release, he told the people he stood before them not as a prophet but as their humble servant, pledging the remaining years of his life to their cause. He wanted to make clear, he later wrote, "that I was not a messiah, but an ordinary man who had become a leader because of extraordinary circumstances." But his task was delicate and somewhat contradictory. He wanted to "demythify" Mandela in order to restrain unrealistic expectations even as he prepared to exploit the political opportunities mythification had made possible. And his first political imperative – if he were to ensure that a negotiated end to apartheid be pursued with himself central to the process – was to secure the leadership of the party. But this required reassuring the party of his absolute allegiance and submission to its collective discipline even as he planned to bend it to his own direction.

In that same first speech, Mandela strongly affirmed that he was "a loyal and disciplined member of the African National Congress," an affirmation he would insistently repeat right up to the time of his resignation from the presidency of the party seven years later (when he would also insist, as usual, that his legendary self had been solely a political creation of the ANC, or rather of the "Tripartite Alliance" of ANC, union movement and Communist Party).[28] If the speech was stiff and disappointing to many observers who had been expecting something more inspirational,[29] it was because it was aimed more at the ANC and its

[27] See Mandela, *Long Walk to Freedom*, pp. 428, 436, 437 and 503.
[28] The Tripartite Alliance was formed between the Congress of South African Trade Unions (COSATU), the South African Congress Party (SACP) and the ANC in 1990, after the political parties were unbanned. The ANC has always been acknowledged as its political leader. "Address by Nelson Mandela to the Closing Session of the 50th National Conference of the ANC."
[29] See David Ottaway, *Chained Together: Mandela, de Klerk and the Struggle to Remake South Africa* (New York, Time Books, 1993), p. 21.

executive committee than at the assembled throng.[30] It may have seemed to the world at large, and to many black South Africans, that Mandela was the unquestioned leader of his party and his people (this, after all, had been the case that had for years been made for his release), but the matter was far from clear within his own party. In fact, party activists were prone caustically to assert that, however convenient Mandela had proved as a rallying symbol, he was after all just an ordinary ANC member. Cyril Ramaphosa, a young and able trade union organizer with broader leadership potential, said explicitly that Mandela should not expect just to walk out of prison and take over.[31] To him, as to many of the younger generation who had for years conducted the internal political struggle through the United Democratic Front and the union movement, the real authority of a man so utterly out of touch with modern South Africa and its political situation had to be seriously in doubt.

But the fear among his own people went far beyond doubts about his capability or his claim to rank. Whatever moral capital Mandela had accumulated in the world at large, among significant portions of his party he was suffering a serious deficit. He was in fact widely suspected by revolutionary comrades of being that most reviled of figures, a "sell-out," one who had "gone soft" on the regime. And the serious question mark that hung over his head was precisely the result of his exploitation, while in prison, of the opportunity for independent action that his unique status had given him.

Political action: second period

In Pollsmoor Prison (to which he, Sisulu and others had been transferred in 1982), Mandela had realized that his new moral status gave the authorities an incentive to deal with him, if only in the hope of driving a wedge between himself and the external party. He had no intention of allowing that to happen but was determined to initiate independent talks with the government.[32] Among prison colleagues, he had long been arguing against the party's express policy of nonnegotiation, but this had opened a serious rift between himself and communist hardliner, Govan Mbeki,[33] who was outraged at Mandela's "moderation." Mandela was therefore secretive now about pursuing meetings with government officials (via the

---

[30] It had been written in cooperation with other ANC leaders; Mandela, *Long Walk to Freedom*, pp. 493–494.

[31] Cited in Meredith, *Nelson Mandela*, p. 446.

[32] In December 1988, after a bout of tuberculosis, he had been transferred again to a comfortable cottage in Victor Verster prison, near Paarl – a "gilded cage," as he termed it. See Mandela, *Long Walk to Freedom*, pp. 476–477.

[33] Father of Thabo Mbeki, Mandela's successor as President of South Africa.

prison authorities). Botha's government was also obdurate about negotiation although the failure of the tricameral parliament had confirmed the practical impossibility of genuine "separation" of white from other races, while pressures of economic downturn, trade sanctions and international politics all tended in one direction. Botha felt caught between the necessity for radical change and the impossibility of it (given his assumption that surrendering white supremacy, so long and bitterly held, invited white annihilation). Mandela, however, was convinced that, to avoid bloody conflict, negotiations should begin sooner rather than later, particularly when it was clear to him that military victory by the black majority remained "an impossible dream." His own initiatives were designed to break the deadlock between parties he regarded as equally intransigent in their shared view of discussion as a sign of weakness. In a most interesting passage of his autobiography, he reveals:

> I chose to tell no one of what I was about to do. Not my colleagues upstairs or those in Lusaka. The ANC is a collective, but the government had made collectivity in this case impossible. I did not have the security or the time to discuss these issues with my organization. I knew that my colleagues upstairs would condemn my proposal, and that would kill my initiative even before it was born. There are times when a leader must move out ahead of his flock, go off in a new direction, confident that he is leading his people the right way.[34]

But talks were slow to get going and often frustrated. Nevertheless, a secret committee was eventually formed that included Dr. Niel Barnard, the head of the National Intelligence Service, and it met weekly with Mandela after May 1988. As news of these meetings leaked out, Mandela sought to reassure anxious colleagues that he was discussing only the possibility of a meeting between the government and the National Executive Committee (NEC) of the ANC, which Tambo and the committee retrospectively approved. In fact, however, the talks centered on the armed struggle, the link with communists and the fate of whites under majority rule.[35]

Though Mandela had broken the ice and met Botha personally, his talks bore little positive fruit until the accession to power of F.W. de Klerk in August 1989. De Klerk, noting the failure of Botha's increasing reliance on security and taking a lesson from the fate of Ian Smith in Rhodesia, had concluded that there was no alternative to negotiations. Moreover, he had accepted the advice of numerous world leaders that no accommodation

---

[34] Mandela, *Long Walk to Freedom*, pp. 458–459.
[35] For the reactions of his fellow prisoners, see Mandela, *Long Walk to Freedom*, p. 466. In fact, some of the external ANC were coming to the same conclusions as Mandela, and an exceedingly complicated series of secret talks was taking place between ANC people and representatives of the Afrikaners; see Sparks, *Tomorrow is Another Country*, pp. 72–79.

could be reached without Mandela and the ANC. Nevertheless, his own and his cabinet's hope was that the ANC would prove so poorly organized for peace that it would fall apart, allowing the government to forge a dominant alliance with conservative black leaders like Buthelezi. Hoping to disorient Mandela and his party by seizing "the moral high ground," de Klerk stunned the nation on 2 February 1990 by effectively ending apartheid. He unbanned all liberation organizations (including the Communist Party), abolished media restrictions, suspended capital punishment, repealed apartheid laws, and outlined aims for a new democratic constitution and a universal franchise. He saved his grandest gesture till last – the unconditional release of Nelson Mandela, who, he declared, could play an important part in negotiations toward a peaceful settlement.

Mandela was fully prepared to play such a part but was well aware of the suspicions he had aroused by his independent action, not just in the ANC but among leaders of the UDF who felt he had violated their cardinal rule – not to act without the mandate of the people.[36] Appeasement was difficult, moreover, when a mass press conference the day after his release demonstrated the *de facto* independent leadership role he had acquired. (The weight of acquired authority was evident in his very person, according to one old friend.)[37] Deflecting questions about what he had suffered in prison to stress what he had learned – the futility of hatred and bitterness – he sought to reassure white people about the critical role that ANC policy assured them in a new, nonracial South Africa. He wanted them to see "that I loved even my enemies while I hated the system that turned us against one another."[38] The cause of nonracial democracy was morally right and just, he said, and it was this fact, more than the inner strength of any individual, that had sustained and fortified him and his comrades during years of imprisonment. The conference delighted observers who felt they were seeing the real Mandela for the first time.

His triumphant tour of Africa and the world in the months following his release demonstrated clearly what a remarkable asset he had become to his organization (though he upset the Americans by expressing admiration for Fidel Castro and Colonel Gaddhafi, and excusing them of human rights abuses). The fact that the world *had* assumed that Mandela would be the leader to undertake the task of transition could not easily be ignored at home. But it would take a long time for Mandela to translate his moral capital into effective authority. One political factor played to his

---

[36] See Sparks, *Tomorrow is Another Country*, p. 61.
[37] Hilda Bernstein, cited in Meredith, *Nelson Mandela*, p. 409.
[38] Mandela, *Long Walk to Freedom*, p. 495.

advantage: the National Executive Committee of the ANC-in-exile was still dominated by the "old guard," men much less opposed to his assumption of authority than the generation of leaders that had arisen within the country itself. He had one crucial opponent on this committee, Chris Hani, who had been calling for an intensification of the armed struggle. Hani was a hardline communist guerrilla commander, hugely popular with millions of black youths and with a consequent ability to influence and control the party's more wildly militant elements. At a conference in Lusaka, Mandela won him over. The NEC elected Mandela secretary-general, a position that made him (in the absence of Tambo, who had suffered a stroke) the *de facto* if not *de jure* leader of the party.[39]

But the task of governing the party while pursuing unpopular talks with the government was intensely difficult. Mandela recognized that the exiled ANC leadership was as out of touch with realities in South Africa as himself. A way had to be found to accommodate the experienced leaders of other organizations like the UDF and the Congress of South African Trade Unions (COSATU) over which the ANC had theoretical political ascendancy.[40] This meant reconstructing the ANC itself. Its secretive, authoritarian mode of operation, adapted to existence as an underground guerilla organization, was deeply resented and resisted by the internally democratic and loosely federated UDF groups. Mandela, though he saw his leadership role as that of unifier and conciliator, was himself reportedly happier making independent, autocratic decisions with minimal questioning and consultation. Nevertheless, he saw that the ANC's clandestine habits had to be discarded if it was to meet the changed circumstances and unify the forces of opposition under its effective leadership.[41] In particular, the party and its allies had to be solidly united behind a policy of negotiation with the government, something that could only be assured if clear gains were forthcoming without too much having been given away.

When "talks about talks" preliminary to actual negotiations dragged on for over a year, the prospects for this began to look dim. Though Mandela was elected president of the ANC without opposition at its first conference in July 1991, there was, as he sadly noted, no praise and much angry criticism of himself and the entire old guard. He managed to win a continuing commitment to the talks but had not the authority to prevent the election (wildly popular with other delegates) of Cyril Ramaphosa as

[39] See Mandela, *Long Walk to Freedom*, p. 500.
[40] The UDF and COSATU formed an alliance in 1989 called the Mass Democratic Movement to coordinate a nationwide defiance campaign.
[41] Mandela, *Long Walk to Freedom*, pp. 516–517.

secretary-general.[42] The most frequent criticism was of Mandela's high-handedness in excluding ANC members from the negotiating process. He admitted some neglect but pleaded that the delicacy of the talks meant there was no alternative to proceeding with a certain, necessary confidentiality. This only fueled suspicion that he had gone soft on the government and was closer to de Klerk than to his own people, a suspicion reinforced by the lack of clear gains from his strategy. Mandela was unable to assert authority over revolutionary elements still thirsting for action while progress remained so slow.

Part of the problem was that de Klerk too was under constant pressure, both from his own party and from breakaway parties on his extreme right, to show results from the reform process that did not sell out white interests. His position was substantially eased, however, when the gamble of a referendum on the reform process in March 1992 resulted in a solid yes vote. The real continuing problem thereafter was with de Klerk himself and his forlorn hope that Mandela's ANC might prove a paper tiger. He failed to see that his best chance for a peaceful settlement lay in a central alliance between Mandela and de Klerk holding against the extremes on either side, and that the success of Mandela's leadership was thus in his own interest. Mandela could credibly represent the whole opposition movement, thus providing a single figure with whom meaningful negotiations could be conducted. It was to the regime's benefit, too, that Mandela, despite his avowed socialism and despite *Umkhonto we Sizwe*, was an essentially *moderate* figure. His nonracialist stance, his democratic commitments and his clear lack of vengefulness made it possible for the regime to contemplate a deal which might make the transfer of power to black leadership a less than disastrous outcome for whites.

But the white president would not relinquish his dream of a constitutional agreement formed by a more congenial alliance with conservative African groups – homeland leaders, and Indian and colored organizations. A lingering hope for the Buthelezi connection in particular was at the heart of many of the most severe impediments to progress between 1990 and 1993. It mired the National Party in what Mandela came to call a "double agenda" – talks with the ANC, on the one hand, support for the murderers of ANC people (namely Buthelezi's Zulu Inkatha movement) on the other. For, as much as the government might harp on about the ANC's "terrorism," the real and increasing violence in the country was of the so-called black-on-black variety in Natal and in the immigrant-worker hostels on the Reef of the Witwatersrand. Tensions between rural

[42] Ramaphosa, as well as a potential leadership rival, was an adamant critic of Winnie Mandela and her Mandela United Football Club.

immigrant workers and black township dwellers were politically exploited
by Buthelezi and his Inkatha movement who feared losing political control of KwaZulu-Natal to the ANC.[43]

The escalating cycle of murder by axe-wielding Inkatha supporters and
retaliation by ANC members under the command of bloody-minded,
Stalinist ANC official Harry Gwala turned into a territorial war that
threatened to derail the whole transition process. Here Mandela's incomplete authority over the party cost the nation dearly. His initial instinct
upon his release had been to trust in his powers of persuasion and
conciliation and meet immediately with Buthelezi, but stern opposition
from Gwala and other NEC members had prevented him. The result was
that Buthelezi, feeling snubbed, became more recalcitrant than ever, and
later meetings and agreements brought no improvement. Mandela's own
attempts to end the violence by exerting his moral authority at mass
meetings also proved an utter failure. The spiraling violence was made
even worse by the inaction of the government's enforcement agencies
who were suspected of, and later proved to be, aiding and abetting
Inkatha and funding its organizations. But if Inkathagate, as it was
inevitably called, embarrassed both Buthelezi and de Klerk, it also called
into question Mandela's judgment in trusting the white president and
repeatedly affirming belief in his integrity.

Mandela came personally to despise de Klerk while never doubting his
continuing need for him.[44] It took de Klerk much longer to accept his
need for Mandela. With the establishment of the Convention for a
Democratic South Africa (CODESA) on 20 December 1991, however,
the ex-prisoner began to assert himself psychologically over the Afrikaner
leader. The time would come when Mandela would be able to demand
terms of de Klerk that would once have been inconceivable – the release
of three ANC prisoners condemned to death for murder – and demand
them with a brutal intransigence that startled even so forceful a negotiator
as Cyril Ramaphosa. Mandela's hand, however, had by then been
strengthened within his own organization after a series of harrowing
events.

A second deadlocked session of CODESA had resulted in an ANC
walkout and a party decision to pressure the government with a program
of "rolling mass action" beginning on 16 June 1992.[45] Simultaneously,
there occurred a shocking massacre by Inkatha hostel dwellers of forty-
five men, women and children in a small town in the Vaal Triangle,

---

[43] This violence had complex causes. See Mahmood Mamdani, *Citizen and Subject: Contemporary Africa and the Legacy of Colonialism* (Kampala, Fountain, 1996), chapter 7.
[44] See Meredith, *Nelson Mandela*, p. 499; and Mandela, *A Long Walk to Freedom*, p. 533.
[45] The sixteenth anniversary of the start of the Soweto uprising.

bringing the usual accusations of police collusion. Two days later police killed three people during a protest against the massacre. These events combined to give the upper hand in the ANC to senior officials who believed in insurrection and forcible seizure as the only sure paths to power. Their strategy ended in disaster in September when one of them, Ronnie Kasrils, led 70,000 marchers to Bisho, the capital of the Ciskei homeland, to overthrow the collaborationist government of Brigadier Oupa Gqozo. The Ciskei army opened fire and killed 28 marchers. In the chastened mood that followed, Mandela called off the mass action, severely dressed down Kasrils and made conciliatory moves toward de Klerk. De Klerk reciprocated. A resulting summit meeting concluded with a signed Record of Understanding between Mandela and de Klerk that finally locked the government into dealing with the ANC, ending all hope of the Buthelezi option. Like it or not, de Klerk's partnership with Mandela now formed the vital center that would hold against all spoiling elements in the outer circle, from Eugene Terre'Blanche of the neo-Nazi Afrikaner Weerstandbeweging (AWB) to the furiously sidelined Buthelezi himself, and to still disgruntled elements within the ANC.[46]

Continuing distrust of Mandela among his own militants meant that it was difficult for him to suggest compromises he thought necessary to give positive impetus to the talks. He had to rely on the intervention of Joe Slovo, a white communist and co-founder of *Umkhonto* with impeccable revolutionary credentials. The principal sticking point over the long course of negotiation had been the constitutional question of simple majority rule, insisted on by the ANC, versus a system of checks and balances desired by the government to ensure blacks could not govern without white agreement. Slovo now suggested "shock therapy" for the ANC, recommending that, rather than go immediately for outright power, the party accept a "sunset clause" in the constitution that would entrench power-sharing in a government of national unity for a fixed period. He also suggested offering regional guarantees, amnesty for security officials and the honoring of contracts of civil servants (almost exclusively white, of course). Despite the outrage of the hardliners, this compromise was supported by Mandela and eventually approved by the National Executive Committee after an acrimonious debate. It provided the basis for fruitful negotiations.

Ensuing bilateral meetings between government and ANC produced, by February 1993, a basis for discussion at a new multiparty negotiating conference scheduled for April. The general inclusiveness of significant

[46] Including Winnie Mandela; see Meredith, *Nelson Mandela*, pp. 480–481.

parties at this congress promised well, but in the midst of it there occurred an event that, in the unstable political state of the nation, threatened to undo all that had been accomplished and cause a civil war. This was the assassination of Chris Hani by a member of the AWB, with surrounding circumstances that, as they emerged, pointed to a right-wing conspiracy.

It was a crisis that revealed where the leadership of the emergent nation actually lay. As ANC officials made appeal after appeal for calm, de Klerk and his government were hardly to be seen. Mandela went on television to address the nation with the words: "With all the authority at my command, I appeal to all our people to remain calm and to honor the memory of Chris Hani by remaining a disciplined force for peace." A week of mass protest was announced to try to channel and contain the anger of the black population. On the eve of a planned day of mourning, Mandela once again appealed via radio and television for calm, making pointed use of the fact that it had been a white Afrikaner woman who had risked her life to identify the assassin and bring him to justice. It was a time, he said, for all South Africans to stand together to achieve the goal for which Hani had given his life, and a time to exhibit the sort of discipline upon which Hani had always insisted. His plea was heeded by the mass of black South Africans, whose feelings of outrage were, save for a few excesses, intensely but peacefully expressed. The government, as a consequence, was moved to agree to a firm date for the elections that would establish a new assembly in which power would be shared for a period of five years.[47] No other event, as Meredith notes, had "revealed so clearly to the white community how important Mandela was to their future security." When it came to the point of elections, whites would not vote for him, but they would accept a government of which he was the leader.[48]

Conclusion

Politics, as we have noted, is about ends, and Mandela had finally achieved the goal he had so long sought. He was inevitably the star turn in the election campaign of April 1994, greeted by cheering crowds everywhere as the man who had brought them freedom at last.[49] The ANC swept to victory in the new national assembly and Madiba was inevitably elected president. On assuming office, he raised his stock of moral capital even further by announcing a firm intention to retire at the end of his term

[47] See Mandela, "Opening Address by President Nelson Mandela to the 49th Conference of the African National Congress," 17 December 1994 (www.anc.org.za/ancdocs/history/mandela/1997/sp941217 at p. 7).
[48] Meredith, *Nelson Mandela*, pp. 484 and 498.   [49] See *ibid.*, p. 500.

in 1999 (which he duly did, an almost unprecedented relinquishment of power by a black African leader).[50]

Mandela's story reveals the extraordinary potential for the generation of moral capital in dissident politics where the whole world, as it were, takes sides. It also illustrates how such capital, attributed to a single individual, can become virtually an independent force that presents new political opportunities as well as new political problems. Prior to his imprisonment, Mandela's relationship with the cause he served was conventionally mediated by the party he believed to be the best vehicle for pursuing that cause. The moral capital he gained in prison, on the other hand, was accumulated by virtue of his designation as *the* imprisoned leader of black South Africa. It became in effect a personal resource of the man himself, largely independent of the ANC. Unlike de Gaulle, however, Mandela had no wish to use this capital to elevate himself above parties. He realized that his new moral status gave him room for independent maneuver, but he was also convinced, through a combination of realistic calculation and steadfast loyalty (a key virtue), that the party was an essential vehicle for negotiating with the Afrikaner government and, after the transition, for fighting an election. He therefore had to establish his effective authority within the party, difficult after such long isolation, while at the same time using his capital to forward the negotiating process even against party wishes, thus courting the condemnation of colleagues and jeopardizing his own internal authority. That he succeeded in holding it all together during the long, traumatic years of negotiation was a tribute to the political skill he brought to the exploitation of his extraordinary moral capital.

After the elections, this capital remained the glue that held the new republic together while the settlement stabilized and the country attempted to set itself on the road to renewed and equitable development. With the enormous economic difficulties the nation faced, with the madly skewed pattern of development and underdevelopment that was the legacy of apartheid, with the anger and indignation aroused by decades of enmity still to be assuaged, and with the hopes of his own constituency raised unrealistically high, there was of course only so much even Mandela could do. At home he tirelessly deployed his rhetoric and his gift for symbolic action to foster the unity he desired, while the ANC government over which he presided tried to get to grips with the fact of being now in control of State power rather than its victim. Abroad, Mandela took an independent foreign policy stance sometimes described

---

[50] Eleanor Sisulu (personal communication) insists on the significance of this promise among South Africans, black and white.

as "universalist," a very ambitious one for a relatively small nation.[51] He would claim on the occasion of President Clinton's visit in 1998 that it was his "moral authority" that allowed him a policy truly independent of the world's only superpower. His vision was of a new and fairer world order between North and South, East and West, and of his own responsibilities, as leader of a new South Africa, in helping to further it. He laid aside his socialism, arguing that, with the onset of globalization, the whole world was searching for a better life "without the imprisonment of dogma."[52]

Mandela's moral status remained secure, though he was often criticized. His foreign policy stance was loudly condemned;[53] his administration was at times accused of incompetence, lack of accountability and minor corruption (Bishop Tutu raised ANC ire with his critical observation that the government had stopped the gravy train only long enough to climb aboard). His government was criticized for failing to secure anticipated levels of economic investment, for doing too little to advance black education, housing and employment, for encouraging a widening income gap between a new black elite and the impoverished masses, and for failing to tackle continuing problems of police reform and endemic violence. Even the saintly Archbishop Tutu's Truth and Reconciliation Commission, intended by Mandela to heal the wounds of a savage past and encourage unity, was often condemned by whites as a witch hunt and by blacks as a denial of justice. The crescendo of criticism grew so loud in the organs of the still largely white-owned media that Mandela at one stage attacked them for using a privileged position, inherited from apartheid, to promote a "counter-revolutionary" agenda under the guise of press freedom.

Nevertheless, Madiba seemed personally immune from harsher criticism. When British commentator Brian Walden debunked Mandela's moral credentials in a BBC television show, one of the president's most outspoken critics in parliament, Tony Leon, merely noted that Mandela's moral stature was not in doubt, even if his recent political judgments might be. In the UK and elsewhere the reaction to Walden's critique was one of outrage – questions of propriety were raised in the House of

---

[51] See Greg Mills, "Bridges Across the South Atlantic: A Comparative Perspective on South Africa's and Brazil's Foreign Policies," in S. Pinheiro Guimarães (ed.), *South Africa and Brazil: Risks and Opportunities in the Turmoil of Globalisation* (Brazil, IPRI, 1996), p. 117.

[52] Mandela, "Closing Session of the 50th National Conference of the ANC."

[53] See, e.g., Joseph Diescho, *The Limits of Foreign Policy Making in South Africa* (Pretoria, Unisa Press, 1996).

Commons.[54] In an unheroic age, Mandela was a true hero, and the world did not want him subjected to the processes of cynical depreciation that politicians commonly suffer. He was after all more than a common politician. He was a moral phenomenon.

[54] See Ruaridh Nicoli, "Walden Dismisses 'Feckless' Mandela," *Guardian*, 3 February 1998, p. 11.

6   Aung San Suu Kyi: her father's daughter

> If they ever assassinate me, make sure you really make capital out
> of it.   Aung San Suu Kyi to party colleagues

Though the story of Aung San Suu Kyi (pronounced Awng Sahn Su
Chee) is interwoven deeply with that of modern Burma,[1] it was chance or
perhaps destiny that found her present at the most critical hour of its
recent history. Normally resident in the UK with her English husband
and two sons, she had returned to the country of her birth to care for her
terminally ailing mother, Khin Kyi, and was therefore on hand when the
country erupted into full-scale revolt in August 1988.

Trouble had begun the year before when an unpopular decision by
President Ne Win had provoked strong student protest.[2] It was a spark
that, in the combustible conditions of Burmese society, produced an
eventual conflagration. After a quarter-century of authoritarian misrule
by Ne Win and his Burma Socialist Programme Party (BSPP), it had
become abundantly clear that the "Burmese road to socialism" down
which the ageing dictator had been taking the country since 1962,[3] and for
the sake of which he had effectively isolated the country from the international community, led nowhere but to economic ruin.[4] In 1987, Burma
had been forced to apply for the status of Least Developed Country to
gain relief from its burden of foreign debt. For a potentially rich nation
that had once been Asia's leading rice exporter, this was a cause of deep
shame and frustration.

---

[1] Renamed Myanmar by the military regime. This chapter follows the recommendation of
various human rights organizations and the practice of the leadership of Suu Kyi's
National League for Democracy in using the old names.
[2] See Bertil Lintner, *Outrage: Burma's Struggle for Democracy* (London and Bangkok, White
Lotus, 1990), pp. 67–68.
[3] When he had led a military coup against the elected government of U Nu. See Robert
Taylor, *The State in Burma* (Honolulu, University of Hawaii Press, 1987); Lintner,
Outrage, chapter 2.
[4] See Josef Silverstein, *Burma: Military Rule and the Politics of Stagnation* (Ithaca, Cornell
University Press, 1977).

Ne Win and his party had lost their last shred of public credibility, but retained control of the armed forces and of Burma's dreaded secret police, the DDSI.[5] Power was maintained as it had always been, through repression. The brutal and deadly force dealt out to the street marchers of 1988 was the military's traditional response to protest. This time, however, the shootings, arrests, tortures and rapes failed to intimidate an angry populace. People merely grew more incensed, and larger and larger sections of the population began to join the demonstrations. On 8 August 1988 – the day that became notorious as 8-8-88 – a general strike began in Rangoon[6] and spread quickly to the countryside. Millions took to the streets, marching beneath photographs of Suu Kyi's father, Aung San, the martyred hero of Burmese independence. They demanded democracy, human rights, an end to the socialist economic system and the resignation of the BSPP government. The army replied with bullets, and over the next few days some unknown thousands of protesters were massacred.

Aung San Suu Kyi, tending her mother in hospital and an agonized witness to the developing crisis, was increasingly pressed by pro-democracy leaders to lend her illustrious name to the cause. After the massacres of 8 August the pressure intensified, and on 15 August Suu Kyi signaled her first entry into political life with an open letter to the acting head of state. The letter lamented the "situation of ugliness" in Burma and proposed the formation of a People's Consultative Committee to act as a mediator between government and students. Then, on 26 August, Daw Aung San Suu Kyi[7] made her first public appearance before the famous Shwe Dagon Pagoda in Rangoon. A crowd of half a million curious and excited people gathered to hear the daughter of Aung San speak below a huge portrait of her father. They heard her declare her devotion to her country, and to its democratic cause. She concluded:

The present crisis is the concern of the entire nation. I could not, as my father's daughter, remain indifferent to all that was going on. This national crisis could, in fact, be called the second struggle for independence.[8]

The speech was rapturously received. Suu Kyi had publicly committed herself to Burma's "second struggle" and taken her first step on a rapid climb to the effective leadership of the democratic forces.

The path would be difficult and dangerous. A few weeks later, the hard-pressed military cast aside all pretence at civilian government and

[5] The Directorate of the Defense Services Intelligence.
[6] Renamed Yangon by the military regime.
[7] "Daw" is an honorific which means simply "Lady," or perhaps "Madame."
[8] Cited in Lintner, *Outrage*, pp. 115–116.

established rule through a junta, the State Law and Order Restoration Council (SLORC), behind which the hand of Ne Win was, as ever, plainly evident. SLORC (later to transmute into the State Peace and Development Council) was to become the great and infamous antagonist of Suu Kyi and her party, the National League for Democracy. There would be long years marked by hardship and peril, by intense campaigning followed by the isolation of long incarceration, by the triumph of an overwhelming election victory followed by the dashed hopes of power disallowed. But Suu Kyi's commitment proved full and final. Though the moment of her entry into Burmese politics may have been contingently unforeseen, there was a sense in which she had been long prepared for the destiny that, potentially, awaited her in Burma and for the leading role that would be hers should she ever, deliberately and consciously, open her arms to embrace it.

In studying Mandela, it was necessary to examine the question of political action in two separate parts – before and after his acclamation as living symbol. In Suu Kyi's case, it will be the *symbolic* sources of her moral capital that are doubly treated. Because Suu Kyi began her political career as an invested symbol, I must look first at the nature and manner of her inheritance from her father. I will then examine her *cause, action* and *example* before returning to her use of *rhetoric/symbolism*, not just within Burma but on the wider world stage where the memory of her father played no role at all.

One of the interesting things about the moral capital bequeathed by the original Aung San was that it played across a constituency that incorporated virtually the whole of Burma. It included even the army (the *Tatmadaw*) that Aung San had founded but which became his daughter's main antagonist. This curious, shared connection between the opposing parties gave Suu Kyi considerable personal protection. It also presented political options that she was, however, reluctant to take for fear of the consequences. Suu Kyi's *cause* – that of a unified, democratic Burma – was also part of her inheritance though she significantly adapted it to current political conditions. Her *action* in the service of this cause led to the triumph of her party in the elections of 1990, a victory that gave her political legitimacy and, because denied by the junta, turned into an enduring source of moral capital both at home and abroad. The question of *example* is of interest in Suu Kyi's case because of the persistent and egregious attacks made upon her character by a military junta hoping to discredit her in the eyes of her followers. Her insistence on the democratic character of her party and on its strict adherence to a policy of non-violence were also important in this category. I will examine all these factors before returning to the question of Suu Kyi's deployment of her *rhetorical/symbolic* resources for the sake of a goal that, at the time of writing, has yet to be achieved.

Symbolic sources: the inheritance of moral capital

We all, no doubt, enter the world bearing some freight of moral respect or disrespect that is unearned and undeserved. It is a moral heritage either to be lived up to or lived down, a judgment of ourselves based not on whatever, individually, we may happen to be but on where, socially speaking, we came from. In Suu Kyi's case the phenomenon occurred at a national level. Relatively unknown as an individual and totally inexperienced politically, she became, in the traumatic circumstances of 1988, a figure around whom the disparate forces of opposition could rapidly congeal. The immediacy of her effect on Burmese politics was altogether due to her inherited moral capital. Though she professed discomfort at her elevation ("I do not like to be thought of as anything more than an ordinary person"),[9] it was never given to a daughter of hero-patriot-martyr Aung San to be ordinary in Burma even if she were, in her own person, unexceptional.[10]

Suu Kyi's rise conformed, in many respects, to the common pattern for women leaders in this still heavily male-dominated part of the world. In almost every modern case – Benazir Bhutto in Pakistan, Corazon Aquino in the Philippines, Indira Gandhi in India, both Sirimavo Bandaranaike and Chandrika Kumaratunga in Sri Lanka, Sheikh Hasina Wazed in Bangladesh, Megawati Sukarnoputri in Indonesia – the mantle of leadership has descended from famous and respected fathers or husbands, many of whom have been either assassinated or executed. As the symbolic representatives of relatives memorialized in the public mind as great benefactors or defenders, such women become living vessels of the hopes and aspirations of masses of people.

The significance to Burma of Suu Kyi's father, Aung San, is something like that of George Washington for the United States, or even greater.[11] He was a student hero of the Burmese nationalist movement known as the

---

[9] Michele Manceaux, "Fearless Aung San Suu Kyi," *Marie Claire Magazine*, May 1996, p. 53. Also "Aung San Suu Kyi: Interviewed after Release," July 1995 (Free Burma internet page, sunsite.unc.edu./freeburma/assk/assk3-1e.html).

[10] See Kanbawza Win, *Daw Aung San Suu Kyi, the Nobel Laureate* (Bangkok, CDDSK, 1992), p. 70.

[11] See Roger Mathews' introduction to Aung San Suu Kyi's biography of her father, *Aung San of Burma* (Edinburgh, Kiscadale Publications, 1991), p. vii. See also Edward Klein, "The Lady Triumphs," *Vanity Fair*, October 1995, pp. 120–144.

thakins[12] centered on the University of Rangoon during the 1930s, and in 1939 helped form the Communist Party of Burma with himself as general secretary. In 1940 he fled the country to escape arrest and landed in China where he was recruited by a Japanese agent. In Japan, he assembled a group that became famous in Burma as the Thirty Comrades, trained by the Japanese to form the core of the Burma Independence Army (BIA) that Aung San commanded, and that collaborated with Japan to force the British out of Burma in 1942. A year later, Aung San was appointed Minister of Defense in the puppet regime installed by the Japanese, though by this time he was apparently more resentful of Japanese domination than he had been of the British. He helped create a new resistance movement, the Anti-Fascist People's Freedom League (AFPFL), that, in collaboration with the Western allies, rose against the Japanese in 1945.[13] Aung San had used the Japanese occupation to build a strong army under his direct control which he kept intact and threatened to use if the British, now reinstalled in Burma, refused to relinquish their colonial dominion. But Clement Attlee's post-war Labour government proved amenable to Burmese desires, and Aung San traveled to London to negotiate the country's independence, finally granted in 1947. Before it was formally inaugurated, however, he was assassinated along with most of his cabinet by a jealous political rival. His daughter, Suu Kyi, was then just two years old.

Aung San already stood unrivaled in the people's affections, and his martyrdom at the age of thirty-two enshrined him forever in the public memory. He became an icon for Burma and for the Burmese defense forces, the *Tatmadaw*, that he had founded. The date of his death – Martyrs' Day – became a day of national observance ever after, even through the years of military rule. Aung San, while he lived, had been determined to accommodate all the ethnic nationalities of Burma within a unified democratic state[14] and he had turned his considerable conciliatory abilities to that end. Memory of this transformed him into an enduring symbol of what might have been in modern Burma but was not. The

[12] *Thakin*, meaning "master," was normally applied to the British colonizers but ironically adopted by nationalists. See Frank M. Trager, *Burma: From Kingdom to Republic: A Historical and Political Analysis* (New York, Praeger, 1966), pp. 44–45. See also Htin Aung, *A History of Burma* (New York, Columbia University Press, 1967), pp. 283–285; Lintner, *Outrage*, pp. 16–17.

[13] See Daniel Chirot, *Modern Tyrants* (Princeton University Press, 1994), p. 324, for an assessment of the Japanese influence on and significance for the Burmese independence movement.

[14] There are somewhere round 100 languages spoken in Burma. The dominant 68 percent of the present population of 43,500,000 is Bama/Burman who are of Chinese-Tibetan extraction. See *The SBS World Guide* (4th edn., Melbourne, Reed Reference Australia, 1995), p. 91.

socialist democracy he left to the prime ministership of his comrade, U Nu, was beset by intractable problems from the beginning: communist insurgency; armed insurrection by the ethnic minorities – Shans, Mons, Karens, Kachins and others; even an incursion by Nationalist Chinese troops.[15] Economic problems were exacerbated by a Cold War policy that was strictly neutralist and "go-it-alone," discouraging foreign investment.[16] An incorrigibly stagnant economy eventually caused discontent and fragmentation in U Nu's ruling party, setting the scene for the 1962 coup led by Ne Win,[17] head of the army and another former comrade of Aung San.

U Nu was a decent and respected figure who could find no solutions to Burma's chronic problems, and it is an open question whether Aung San would have done better. It is quite probable that death saved his reputation from the erosion that failure would have caused it. Aung San's ideology – a Burmese mixture of Buddhism, Marxism and democratic thought forged during the anti-colonial period – was indistinguishable from that shared by all the old guard of the nationalist movement, and it is unlikely that his economic policies would have differed much from those of U Nu. Ne Win, significantly, claimed he had moved against U Nu because he considered the latter to have betrayed Aung San's vision of a united, socialist Burma, a vision the dictator himself tried to realize through his "Burmese road to socialism."

But the leadership of an independent Burma was a test that Aung San never had to meet, and the sorry trajectory of Burmese history thus served only to sanctify his memory the more. He left a legacy of love, respect and disappointed hope that his family members might at some time draw upon should they choose to do so. Senior leaders of the pro-democracy movement of the 1980s were quite aware of the value of this inheritance and keen to harness it. They had approached Suu Kyi's brother, Aung San Oo, hoping he would leave his private life in California to lead the struggle, but he declined.[18] Suu Kyi, despite the relative disadvantage of being a woman, proved more truly her father's child. Her complete lack of experience in politics, Burmese or any other, was no barrier and probably even an

---

[15] See Htin Aung, "Postscript," in *A History of Burma*, p. 309*ff.*

[16] Also, the only real business class Burma had, the Indian Chettiars, had fled during and after the war to escape reprisals. On the Chettiars, see J. S. Furnivall, *Colonial Policy and Practice: A Comparative Study of Burma and Netherlands India* (New York, New York University Press, 1948), pp. 109–116 and 196–197.

[17] On Ne Win's relation to Aung San, see Aung San Suu Kyi, "Whoever Shoots Me," *Time*, 14 October 1989. But see Maung Maung, *Burma and General Ne Win* (New York, Asia Publishing House, 1969). For a brief account of Ne Win's journey from "national savior to military dictator" after 1962, see Chirot, *Modern Tyrants*, pp. 326–339.

[18] See Kanbawza Win, *Daw Aung San Suu Kyi*, pp. 74–75; and Lintner, *Outrage*, p. 108.

advantage, for it meant an absence of the political taint carried by many of the other opposition leaders, most of whom had served under Ne Win.

Of course, stainlessness combined with her father's moral capital might have made Suu Kyi a figurehead for the democracy movement and nothing more, and it was possible that inexperience might translate into stumbling naivete. The huge crowds that turned out to see the daughter of Aung San in the days of 1988–89 came largely from curiosity. Undoubtedly, a glimmer of hope was inevitably aroused by the very name, but whether that glimmer could be transformed into a beacon depended on Suu Kyi herself. To truly realize her inheritance, she had to show that she was something *more* than her father's daughter – or rather that she was her father's daughter in more than mere consanguinity. It helped that she bore a striking physical resemblance to him, and it was claimed by those who had known the first Aung San that she had a similarly direct manner of talking, similar personality and sense of humor, and the same gift of inspiring trust in those who made her acquaintance. It was frequently said that she was "like a reincarnation of Aung San." To many Burmese it came to seem, once she had effectively captured their imagination, a matter of destiny: at a time of national crisis, an Aung San had once again arisen to bring salvation.

It was a destiny whose possibility Suu Kyi had long foreseen. Though her life before 1988 had been private and scholarly, she had, according to husband Michael Aris, always been acutely conscious of her Burmese heritage and of the burden of potential responsibility that it carried. She had steeped herself in her father's and her nation's history, deeply identified with both, and written a short biography of the first Aung San (whose name she had deliberately added to her own – Burmese do not pass down family names). Aris reports that, throughout their marriage, she warned him repeatedly that she might some day be called upon to serve her country, appealing for his support should that day ever come.[19] She had mentally prepared herself for the assumption of her father's legacy. She would make his moral capital her own and mobilize it on behalf of the cause for which he had lived and died, a free and democratic Burma.

Cause: Burmese democracy

In late 1995, after her release from house arrest, Suu Kyi went on an informal pilgrimage to Thamanya, the residence of a Buddhist holy man. Afterwards she wrote:

[19] "Introduction," in Aung San Suu Kyi, *Freedom from Fear and Other Writings* (M. Aris, ed., New York, Penguin, 1991), p. xvii.

How fine it would be if such a spirit of service were to spread across the land. Some have questioned the appropriateness of talking about such matters as *metta* (loving kindness) and *thissa* (truth) in the political context. But politics is about people and what we had seen in Thamanya proved that love and truth can move people more strongly than any form of coercion.[20]

The passage gives a flavor of Suu Kyi's political philosophy, clearly expressed elsewhere in her essays, interviews and articles. Well versed in Burma's political, social and religious history and also in Western political theory, she attempted, in the spirit of Gandhi, to synthesize Eastern (specifically Buddhist) and Western traditions. Her thinking thus carried a more explicitly spiritual resonance than usually found in Western democratic discourse.

The cause Suu Kyi inherited from her father was not simply adopted, but adapted and modernized. She accepted the commitments to democracy and to a unified Burma but explicitly distanced herself from his socialistic economic policies. Her National League for Democracy expressed a firm commitment to growth pursued through a market economy, increased foreign investment, improved tourism and a tax system that ensured the profitability of private enterprise. Implicitly rejecting the "Chinese road" to capitalist development, she insisted that the institution of democratic government and the rule of law was the only way to achieve the trust and security that secure economic development requires.[21] Only thus, too, she argued, could the equitable distribution of the benefits of development be ensured. To the junta's argument that economic development must precede and lay the foundations for democracy, Suu Kyi replied that, on the contrary, democracy was an essential ground for successful and sustainable economic development.

As to the means by which the transition to democracy was to be pursued, Suu Kyi, unlike Mandela, adhered profoundly to Gandhi's doctrine of nonviolent political action, accepting it as politically applicable to the Burmese situation. She was horrified by the violence of 1988, whether committed by soldiers or citizens, and feared its resurgence. Though at times she noted the Buddhist abhorrence to violence in principle, her main claim was that violence was counter-productive in the fight for democracy, that the potential consequences of unleashing it were too terrible to contemplate. In a statement that mirrored Mandela's views, she referred to the example of Yugoslavia as a country that thought

[20] Aung San Suu Kyi, "Thamanya: A Place of Peace and Kindness," *Mainichi Daily News*, 17 December 1995.
[21] See Aung San Suu Kyi, "The Key to a Successful Open Market Economy: A Note on Economic Policy," *Mainichi Daily News*, 5 February 1996. Also BBC interview, "Burmese to Burma," 30 January 1996, BK0202025096, 1345 GMT.

it could resolve its problems by fighting, and contrasted its fate with that of South Africa that chose the path of dialogue. The stress on dialogue was a constant. She noted that, even when the way of violence was chosen, the final settlement inevitably came down to talking and bargaining. Over and over she argued that problems and conflicts are best addressed by the parties talking things out in order to build trust, to foster understanding and to create an equality of participation on questions affecting the nation. Her oft-repeated offer to the generals, and her consistent response to the question of the conflicts among Burmans and ethnic minorities was – dialogue. For her, the value of dialogue was intimately connected to that of democratic government. She argued:

This is one of the reasons why dialogue is so important, because we want to get people into the habit of talking over the problem rather than fighting it out. If you have a problem, if you have something about which you disagree, the best thing to do is to sit down and talk about it. It is no use shooting each other . . . It would kill both of you but it is not the way to solve the problem. That is why democracy is important. Democracy is not just the will of the people . . . It is [also] about resolving problems through political means and not through violent means.[22]

In a region where "Western notions" of human rights and democracy have been frequently rejected as no part of Asian traditions (a constant refrain of the junta's), Suu Kyi was vehement in her defense of them.[23] If democracy was a good thing then it was a good thing everywhere and should be welcomed – must every nation reinvent the wheel, or television? Democracy, at any rate, was not in the least alien to Burma's social traditions, she argued, finding in Burma's history a long tradition of self-government and independence at village level.[24]

If democracy – necessary for both economic development and the resolution of conflict – was the goal, and nonviolent political action the means chosen, then certain values needed to be stressed and encouraged in the day-to-day struggle. One of these was patience. Suu Kyi always said that she was not in a hurry, that what she achieved must be of lasting value, and that democracy would not come easily or quickly. But perhaps the most important value, and one she constantly reiterated in her public addresses, was the need for discipline in both personal and political conduct. This was a value stressed by Gandhi too, but it was one that already resonated deeply in Burma by virtue of that country's Buddhist

[22] "Aung San Suu Kyi: Interviewed after Release." Note that the transcripts of these interviews, which were transmitted through ASIA TV satellite and monitored in Bangkok, are rendered in extremely poor English. I have therefore made minor amendments to preserve the clearly intended sense.

[23] Aung San Suu Kyi, "In Quest of Democracy," in Aris, Freedom from Fear, p. 167.

[24] There was some truth to this. See Furnivall, Colonial Policy and Practice, pp. 16–17.

traditions. It was on the latter that Suu Kyi drew to explain her idea of discipline as a response to fear.

To live under an authoritarian regime is to live with constant fear. To fear, Suu Kyi said, is natural, but to act despite one's fear requires discipline. To act in a useful rather than a reckless way – which is to say nonviolently – also requires discipline. Just as Gandhi had pointed to the passivity and acquiescence of Indians as the real barrier to political change, Suu Kyi pointed to fear as the element that Burmese people must overcome if they were to win progress. *Bhaya-gati* in Burma's Buddhist tradition is corruption through fear, and for Suu Kyi it was the worst form of corruption. "It is not power that corrupts, but fear," she wrote.[25] Fear warps reason and conscience. The freedom that counts in the end is precisely freedom from this corrupting, crippling fear. It permits one to do what one knows to be right, whatever the dangers and costs. In an interview after her release, Suu Kyi commented that she never felt unfree during her arrest precisely because she had *chosen* this path, for her the only right one. She said:

I think to be free is to be able to do what you think is right, and in that sense, I felt very free – even under house arrest. Because it was my choice. I knew that I could leave any time. I just had to say "I'm not going to do politics any more." But it was my choice to be involved in the democracy movement. So I felt perfectly free.[26]

This is a moral conception of freedom very different, of course, from the liberal version of freedom as an absence of restraint. Her argument that democracy was not alien to Burma's social history was echoed in her claim that neither was it alien to its religious (specifically Buddhist) values. In fact, she believed the latter offered a salutary complement and corrective to the materialist values of the West. She regarded the formal institutions and procedures of democracy as necessary but insufficient for a healthy society, positing deeper moral and spiritual aims drawn, in her case, from Burmese traditions. Though clearly not an anti-materialist as Gandhi was, she insisted that a revolution that aimed *merely* at changing policies and institutions for the sake of material improvement would not achieve genuine success. What was required was a "revolution of the spirit" that committed one to a life of constant struggle.

Without a revolution of the spirit, the forces which produce the iniquities of the old order would continue to be operative, posing a constant threat to the process of reform and regeneration. It is not enough merely to call for freedom, democracy and human rights. There has to be a united determination to persevere in the

---

[25] "Freedom from Fear," in Aris, *Freedom from Fear*, p. 180.
[26] Claudia Dreifus, "The Passion of Suu Kyi," *Interview* (New York, Seven Stories Press, 1997), p. 37.

struggle, to make sacrifices in the name of enduring truths, to resist the corrupting influences of desire, ill will, ignorance and fear.[27]

These, in essence, were the values that Suu Kyi sought to encourage in her Burmese audiences and that became an essential part of her political persona, as much an aspect of her identity as the fact of her parentage. It was an attempt at moral as well as political leadership, or rather at political leadership that fused spiritual, moral and material values in Gandhian fashion.

Political action: triumph and repression

To this clearly articulated cause and to this political philosophy, Suu Kyi committed her life and devoted all her energies after 1988. Her journey from political novice to seasoned campaigner was a matter of only a few months, and her exertions helped secure a resounding victory for her National League for Democracy (the NLD) in the 1990 elections.

This multiparty election was the fulfillment of a promise that the BSPP government had made in September 1988 in a last attempt to cool the revolutionary situation confronting it. But it was a concession that merely provoked insistent demands from Suu Kyi and other leaders for an immediate setting up of an interim government to ensure the elections were fair. The military responded with a so-called coup that established the rule of SLORC.[28] "Order," of the totalitarian kind, was quickly restored through a renewal of savage repression, and the most violent turbulence of 1988 subsided. Nevertheless, SLORC unexpectedly confirmed the commitment to elections, calculating that opposition groups would be too fragmented and divided among themselves to mount an effective challenge to the military-backed party, now reorganized as the National Unity Party (NUP). Burmese history, marked by interminable conflicts among a plethora of groups, gave good warrant for this expectation. Natural fragmentation was, moreover, reinforced by the peculiar provisions of SLORC's own "Political Parties Registration Law." This entitled registered parties to the privilege of four telephone lines and 70 gallons of petrol a week at a low official price, with the result that the number of political parties soon soared to over 200. A united opposition in such circumstances seemed highly improbable. The junta had not, however, reckoned on the National League for Democracy and its new general secretary, Suu Kyi.

The NLD was created by Suu Kyi and two of her venerable fellow

---

[27] "Freedom from Fear," in Aris, *Freedom from Fear*, p. 183.
[28] See Mya Maung, *Totalitarianism in Burma: Prospects for Economic Development* (New York, Paragon House, 1992), pp. 64–65.

leaders, Tin Oo and Aung Gyi, to be an inclusive organizational vehicle that would give Suu Kyi's attractive power political effect. Its first essential task was therefore the unification of the disparate forces of opposition. Asked later why she had chosen the moment for intervention that she had, Suu Kyi replied that it had been at a time of upheaval when the people of Burma had decided they wanted change. "There were a group of us," she said, "who were trying to make sure that tremendous outpouring of energy was channeled in a positive direction, in a positive way."[29] She herself was to be the essential conduit. In Burma, the identification of a common foe had created strong impulses and incentives toward the establishment of a united front among normally bitter antagonists, but the realization of effective unity depended on overcoming existing ethnic, religious and political divisions liable to be destructively exploited by a ruthless opponent.[30] Suu Kyi, because of the universal respect in which her father was held, was the point around which a coherent political force could form. (Zoë Schramm-Evans, traveling in Burma in 1996, spoke to students in Mandalay arguing inconclusively about whether the nation had voted in 1988 *for* Suu Kyi or *against* the junta.[31] The missed point was that Suu Kyi's involvement gave people something singular to vote for *in order to* vote effectively against the junta.)

To establish the NLD, Suu Kyi undertook a grueling electoral campaign across Burma, a country where travel is at the best of times extremely difficult and often hazardous. Wherever she went, and despite official intimidation, tens of thousands of people turned out to see and hear the daughter of Aung San. The NLD soon became by far the dominant party of opposition, a fact that SLORC honored in its customary way – by arresting and torturing its leaders and members. On 20 July 1989, Suu Kyi was placed under house arrest according to martial law. As a detainee, she was disqualified from standing in the elections held in May 1990, but the unexpectedly overwhelming victory of the NLD and parties allied to it was everywhere interpreted as a triumph for herself. The party won 392 of the 485 parliamentary seats (81 percent) while the SLORC-backed NUP won only 10 (2 percent). SLORC refused to honor the election result, merely issuing vague promises to step down after holding a new constitutional convention at an unspecified date, proceeding in the meantime to imprison whatever leaders of the opposition remained at large. Many elected members fled to Karen territory where they eventually set up a parallel government, the National Coalition Government of

[29] "Late Night Live," ABC Radio National, Australia, 6 June 1996.
[30] See Lintner, *Outrage*, pp. 79–82.
[31] Zoë Schramm-Evans, *Dark Ruby: Travels in a Troubled Land* (London, Pandora, 1997), pp. 138–139.

the Union of Burma (NCGUB), with a cousin of Suu Kyi's, Dr. Sein Win, as prime minister.

In 1991, SLORC sought to deprive the still-detained Suu Kyi of the institutional authority that attached to her leadership of her party by terminating her membership of the NLD. It issued a regulation prohibiting political parties from having members who were charged with offenses by the state. The NLD was forced to expel Suu Kyi, Tin Oo and Kyi Maung in order to retain its legal status. The party continued under the formal leadership of Aung Shwe, a former military leader whose history went back to the days of the Burma Independence Army. After Suu Kyi's release in July 1995, the NLD tried to reinstate her as general secretary, and Tin Oo and Kyi Maung as vice chairmen, only to be told that the appointments were illegal without the approval of an "election commission" composed of SLORC members. Nevertheless, the party continued to regard her as its leader and rejected talks with the junta when they refused to recognize her as such. To all intents and purposes, Suu Kyi *was* the NLD, and the junta's efforts to deny the fact were hopeless from the start.

The contrast with Mandela's relationship with his party is worth noting here. Mandela and the ANC always insisted that the ANC had "made" Mandela (that is, the "myth of Mandela") for its own purposes, or, as I would say, that the party was the ultimate source of his extraordinary moral capital. But as we saw, despite its usefulness, Mandela's capital created tensions within the party to which he was theoretically subservient and threw up obstacles to his effective leadership. The NLD, on the other hand, was created precisely as a channel for Suu Kyi and her inherited capital, and the party's legitimacy was thus to a large extent a reflection of her personal legitimacy. She might, of course, have become a mere figurehead leader controlled by *eminences grises* of the party, but Suu Kyi had too decisive and determined a character for that. Even the most hagiographic accounts of her reveal the steel beneath the delicate exterior, as well as a ready temper and a sharp will not easily dominated.[32] Suu Kyi was party leader in fact as well as form from the beginning. This is not to say that there were no tensions or divisions within the party, but these were not sustained by an inherent conflict between the rational-legal authority of a preexisting party structure and the inherited authority of Suu Kyi. In fact, Suu Kyi's major problem was to make the party something more than a ramshackle coalition of groups assembled round her name, to build a securely functioning and enduring party structure out of disparate elements under the very difficult conditions created by a crudely obstructionist government.

[32] See, for example, Ang Chin Geok, *Aung San Suu Kyi: Towards a New Freedom* (New York, Prentice Hall, 1998).

The junta, for its part, would have preferred an NLD more independent from Suu Kyi herself. Its curious dance of policy with respect to her in the period following her release revealed that it simply did not know what to do with her. In their more hysterical moods, the generals expressed the heartfelt desire to crush and annihilate her and her party, but the fact of her famous name made them unwilling or unable to act ruthlessly on this impulse. In calmer moods they knew they had somehow to accommodate the NLD, but wanted to accommodate it without Suu Kyi, believing, it seems, that they were unlikely to get from her concessions on the army's role in any new constitutional arrangement. The State-controlled press, while resolutely denying that she could be her party's leader, simultaneously argued that "Suu Kyi's prominence dwarfs her party in importance."[33] She also had the support of the Burmese students unions,[34] and even the ethnic resistance organizations acknowledged her and supported her in her struggle (though they rejected nonviolence as a way for themselves and were wary of her, as a Burman, with regard to ethnic policies).

The junta's inability either to eliminate or to accommodate Suu Kyi produced an extended political stand-off. Through the long years of stalemate, continuing suppression and intimidation, the NLD was sustained by the fact of its 1990 election victory. However much SLORC regretted its decision to allow the election (generally agreed to be remarkably free and fair), it could not undo the results once they had been broadcast. It was aware, too, that the NLD and its allies had triumphed even in military cantonments.[35] It had inadvertently handed the NLD the moral and political legitimacy of a sweeping popular mandate, and then aroused worldwide outrage by preventing the party from fulfilling it. Whatever assertions of national necessity the junta might thereafter advance on its own behalf, it had been permanently disbarred from claiming to represent the popular will. Suu Kyi was henceforward the head of a party improperly denied office, the virtual leader-in-waiting of her nation. The moral capital she thus gained could now be effectively deployed on the world stage to bring international pressure to bear.

Moral capital by example

With her concern to give her cause a clear articulation and to impart its values to her following, Suu Kyi elected to be a transformational leader.

---

[33] U Than Maung, "When Will the Snake Charming End?," *KYEMON*, 19 May 1996 (translated by the Foreign Broadcast Information Service, and reprinted in *Burma Debate*, May/June 1996).

[34] The All Burma Students' Democratic Front and the All Burma Students' League.

[35] Bertil Lintner, *Aung San Suu Kyi: Burma's Unfinished Renaissance* (Centre of Southeast Asia Studies Working Paper No. 64, Melbourne, Monash University, 1990), p. 25.

For this kind of leadership to be effective, the character of the teacher must of course be all-of-a-piece with the teaching. There were in fact a number of areas where effective example was important to the defense or maintenance of Suu Kyi's moral capital. The first was with regard to the authenticity of her connection to her Burmese constituency; the second was the connected but distinct question of her moral character and motives; the third was her ability to practice what she preached with respect to her doctrine of fearlessness; the fourth concerned the commitment to democratic procedures and democratic inclusiveness; and the fifth related to effective practice of the commitment to nonviolent opposition. Finally, as in the case of other dissident politicians, unchosen but exemplary sacrifice in the form of imprisonment gave a huge boost to Suu Kyi's moral capital among a worldwide constituency.

One sure measure of the importance of Suu Kyi's moral capital was the desperate persistence with which SLORC attempted to undermine it by detaching her from the constituency that she claimed to represent – that is, from Burma itself. Through its media organs and via the dissemination of malicious rumor, the junta attacked her as an *arriviste* and opportunist who used her father's good name for the sake of her own egoistic ambition. For all her rhetoric, it said, she cared nothing for Burma and was not even truly Burmese but rather a corrupted Westerner. It was an issue on which Suu Kyi was potentially vulnerable. Though she had retained her Burmese citizenship and visited the country regularly, sending her sons to Buddhist monasteries in Burma as novices, prior to 1988 she had lived a largely expatriate life.[36] Her Western education, her English husband and children, provided a ready target, and she was concerned to scotch the criticism right at the start, in her very first speech at the Shwe Dagon Pagoda:

A number of people are saying that since I have spent so much time abroad and am married to a foreigner I could not be familiar with the ramifications of this country's politics. I wish to speak from this platform very frankly and openly to the people. It is true that I lived abroad. It is also true that I am married to a foreigner. These facts have never interfered and will never interfere with or lessen my love and devotion for my country by any measure or degree.[37]

---

[36] At the time of Ne Win's coup in 1962 she had been a seventeen-year-old schoolgirl living in India with her mother, who was then Burma's ambassador to that country. She attended the University of New Delhi, went on to Oxford to do a BA degree in politics, philosophy and economics, and later worked for two years at the General Secretariat of the United Nations in New York. In 1972, she married British Tibetologist, Michael Aris, with whom she lived for a while in Bhutan and by whom she had two children. During the 1980s she spent time as a visiting scholar in both Japan and India, and was, in 1988, resident in Britain.

[37] Cited in Kanbawza Win, *Daw Aung San Suu Kyi*, p. 72.

Her success in the nine months of speech-making that followed suggested that people accepted her Burmese credentials, though the junta, alarmed by the rapid burgeoning of her following, pressed the "foreigner" charge ever more desperately. Throughout her imprisonment and even after it, the government spread ever more unlikely tales: her husband was not only English but also Jewish; or Muslim; or she had not one husband but four.[38]

Suu Kyi's behavior and habitual demeanor usually proved an effective antidote to such nonsense. To her followers she seemed quintessentially Burmese, for she maintained the grace and modesty of manner proper to an aristocratic Burmese lady and was scrupulous about showing the necessary deference and sensitivity where custom decreed. (From very early on, she was universally known among Burmese simply as "the Lady"; Ne Win, on the other hand – when he was not "Number One" – was generally referred to as "the Old Man.") Her devotion to the Buddhist faith was also important, particularly to ethnic Burmans, in a land where Buddhism has always played a central role in state and society.[39] She spoke faultless Burman and drew frequent favorable comment for her fondness for the traditional wraparound *lungyi* that she habitually wore. Her appearance and conduct, in short, continually supported her claim to be a true daughter of Burma. Such Western influences as she had absorbed, moreover, could be interpreted as a needed modernizing force in a Burma impatient for democratic change.

The junta fared little better with its attempt to portray her as a selfish, power-hungry opportunist intent on deceiving the Burmese people with high-sounding rhetoric. Suu Kyi herself professed to dislike power politics and political maneuvering and to have no intrinsic desire for political office or power. Her sudden commitment to Burmese politics was, she claimed, an act of moral necessity, and of fidelity to her father's memory – she could not fail her country in its hour of need once the opportunity to help had presented itself.[40] Since the Burmese people had had long experience in discounting practically everything their government told them, most preferred to believe in Suu Kyi's sincerity and integrity rather than accept the junta's word. In addition, her frank and fearless truth-telling style of address (so like her father's, it was said) tended to inspire trust. The contest between her and her discreditors was, in fact, a rather uneven one, for Suu Kyi's sallies were sharp and ironical. The junta's slanders, by comparison, were usually too crude and clumsy to be be-

---

[38] Dreifus, "The Passion of Suu Kyi," *Interview*, p. 48.
[39] See Furnivall, *Colonial Policy and Practice*, pp. 12–13.
[40] See Klein, "The Lady Triumphs," p. 122; also C. Fink, interview for BurmaNet, 18 July 1995 (sunsite.unc.edu/freeburma/assk/assk3-1d.html).

lieved save by indoctrinated youngsters. (She was memorably described in one article as "The England-returnee miss, who, after living in England humbly for 28 years, showed herself in Myanmar in a saucy manner.")[41] According to Suu Kyi, the junta's relentless personal attacks had exactly the opposite effect to the one intended: "Before the 1990 elections we used to say, 'Every time one of them opens their mouths, the votes come pouring down on our side'."[42]

Nor was there much doubt about her capacity to live up to her own doctrines of fearlessness and dedication. She sacrificed family life, risked her own life, suffered hunger and health problems but never publicly wavered in her commitment to the struggle. Before her arrest she campaigned under threat of violence, confronted gun-pointing soldiers, spoke out against government crimes, and openly accused Ne Win himself at a time when merely to speak his name aloud in Burma was considered shocking and dangerous. She accepted her long house arrest with patience and fortitude, establishing a strict routine for coping, and practicing her favorite virtue, discipline.[43] To the junta's disappointment, she would not go away, even when it offered to release her from arrest so she could leave Burma with her husband and children "on humanitarian grounds." Knowing that she would never be allowed back, she refused, and in 1999 her husband died of cancer in England having seen her only briefly during the intervening years.

It must be noted, without deprecating Suu Kyi's courage, that the status of her father and also of her mother afforded her more protection than was available to the ordinary Burmese dissident. As a young woman working at the United Nations in New York, she was once told by a Burmese representative, to whom she had expressed criticisms of Ne Win's government, that "she had the courage of her connections as well as of her convictions."[44] Her inherited moral capital not only provided her with political opportunity but, in Burmese circumstances, with a considerable measure of protection. The generals, for all they hated her as a persistent thorn in their side, never quite dared to harm her physically, for she was a living representative of the icon of their own armed forces. Suu Kyi admitted, too, that it is easier having a foreign husband and children who live in England: the junta could not threaten her through her family as it did other of her colleagues. She paid tribute to the sacrifices of ordinary people whose names are unknown but who possess a "courage

[41] U Than Maung, "When will the Snake Charming End?"
[42] Dreifus, "The Passion of Suu Kyi," *Interview*, p. 50.
[43] For an account of her confinement, see Alan Clements, *The Voice of Hope: Aung San Suu Kyi in Conversation with Alan Clements* (Harmondsworth, Penguin, 1997).
[44] Ma Than E, "A Flowering of the Spirit: Memories of Suu and Her Family," in Aris, *Freedom from Fear*, p. 259.

that dares without recognition, without the protection of media attention . . . a courage that humbles and inspires and reaffirms our faith in humanity."[45] Yet her own indomitability and fearlessness inspired confidence and instilled courage among the democratic forces of Burma. When she was isolated under house arrest the voices of democratic dissidence within Burma were muted, almost silent; when she began to speak out after her release, a chorus of dissent rose once more. The license she took was quickly seized by others.

Exemplary conduct was also important in the field of internal democratic politics. Despite her position in her party, Suu Kyi attempted to be scrupulously correct about acting as the elected leader of a democratic party representing, and subject to, the popular will. She appeared to have a conscious strategy of behaving as though she and the NLD were operating in a democratic political arena rather than under the rule of a military junta. Her idea seemed to be to get the Burmese used to working democratically *before* the transition to power in the hope of institutionally containing the instability that ethnic and ideological quarreling was sure to cause when and if the junta collapsed. Suu Kyi regarded this constructive side of her enterprise as distinguishing her own "political" stance from what she regarded as Gandhi's purely "oppositional" one.[46] She always warned that democracy would not come easily or quickly to Burma, and the long delay, she said, had certain advantages for a fragmented nation with not much useful experience of democratic governance. She was careful to invite members of the various ethnic communities into her party and her confidence, and always to consult and form alliances. It was an attempt to build, from a position of dissidence, habits of trust and cooperation that would secure the foundations of the future democratic state.

Despite her insistence on democratic procedure, the NLD was firmly stamped with Suu Kyi's own imprint, in particular in its adoption of a strategy of nonviolence, indeed of nonconfrontation. In the circumstances of 1988, this had been a difficult point to carry. Fighting back with makeshift weapons against overwhelming firepower was a matter of pride, especially among the young, and the anger of the populace had been so inflamed that soldiers, DDSI men and informers unlucky enough to be captured were very often beheaded in the streets to the cheers of onlookers. Though Suu Kyi regularly sent her people to intervene and to try

---

[45] "Letter from Burma" (No. 48), *Mainichi Daily News*, 10 November 1996. For the fate of Leon Nichols, Honorary Secretary-General to Denmark and friend and supporter of Suu Kyi, who died in Insein prison, see eyewitness testimony by Moe Aye, "The Last Days of Mr. Leon Nichols," *Burma Debate* 5(1) (Winter, 1998).

[46] "Late Night Live" interview, ABC Radio National, Australia.

to prevent such occurrences, they were not always successful.[47] Suu Kyi was convinced, nevertheless, that the Gandhian "moral ju-jitsu" of non-violent action was not only morally appropriate but also politically necessary in Burma. Her strategy was to apply constant pressure on the regime, but pressure always tempered with caution. The genie of violence had to be kept in the bottle, for she considered the loss of life that had occurred previously tragic and useless. In July 1989, just prior to her arrest, she had called off a march previously announced for Martyrs' Day – the annual memorial for her father and his slaughtered cabinet – because SLORC's menacing mobilization threatened another bloodbath.

Part of her concern was to avoid alienating the army as an organization, one she honored, she said, for her father's sake (she always took pains to distinguish between the army and those members of it who had usurped political power). She would make no attempt to cause a split within the armed forces, though this was always a plausible option given her support among military personnel and the power of her father's name.[48] She feared that the result would be a destructive and uncontrollable civil war rather than the bloodless "people power" triumph that Cory Aquino had enjoyed in the Philippines because of a similarly divided military.

But the insistence on nonviolence required that the democratic opposition demonstrate discipline. Within the party, this could be partially exerted by issuing rules against participation in the street lynchings and ordering the expulsion of members who failed to observe them. Wider acceptance, however, depended on Suu Kyi's being able to convince people, through repeated argument, of the political wisdom of the non-violent path. She had, in other words, to convert her moral capital into effective moral authority. Her first demonstrated success was at the funeral of her mother who died on 27 December 1988. Given Khin Kyi's status as Aung San's widow, this was inevitably something of a State affair, and both the military and the people had feared that the emotion generated would lead to renewed protest and violence. Yet though hundreds of thousands of people marched in the funeral procession on 2 January 1989 to show faith with the democratic cause and with fallen comrades, the event passed peacefully. NLD workers had been charged with the responsibility of guarding security and maintaining order, and a student leader admonished the vast crowd to behave with self-control and dignity. Bertil Lintner regarded this display of discipline as a sign of the growing maturity of the opposition, and argued that Khin Kyi's funeral marked something of a watershed in post-coup politics.[49]

Finally, with regard to example, we must note the exemplary sacrifice

[47] Lintner, *Outrage*, pp. 121–122.
[48] See Kanbawza Win, *Daw Aung San Suu Kyi*, p. 95.   [49] Lintner, *Outrage*, p. 171.

that is almost a necessary badge of acceptability among dissident politicians – unjust imprisonment. Suu Kyi's arrest and incarceration (albeit in the relative safety of her own home) raised her stock of moral capital to unprecedented levels, both internationally and at home. She remained under house arrest for six years, becoming, in the process, a detainee of global fame. Far from neutralizing her influence, detention enlarged its scope by making her a constant occasion for international criticism of, and pressure on, the junta. Suu Kyi detained was Suu Kyi martyred and thus the object of intensified media attention. She was declared a prisoner of conscience by Amnesty International and awarded a series of human rights prizes *in absentia*, including the Nobel Peace Prize of 1991. (It was a point of great pride to fellow Burmese that she was the first of their nation ever to obtain a Nobel Prize.) Her face became familiar everywhere, a potent symbol for use by activists and organizations around the globe trying to raise awareness of the plight of Burma. She became, indeed, *the* face of democratic Burma.

Rhetoric/symbolism

The relationship between the accumulation and the mobilization of moral capital is always highly dialectical. A word or act provokes respect, respect commands attention, and if attention is rewarded with further words or acts that amplify respect and awaken trust, the possibility of influence or advantage is born. And as with other forms of capital, a realized stock, soundly invested, reaps returns themselves available for reinvestment, creating a virtuous cycle of enlargement. When Suu Kyi stepped, literally, onto the political stage in Rangoon in 1988, she had only the inherited capital of her father to commend her to the crowd and command its provisional respect. Turning that capital into a politically usable stock by dint of her own gifts, virtues and commitment was the task immediately facing her. Her simple but compelling oratory proved a crucial means for accomplishing it. In a still predominantly peasant country like Burma, direct communication with people is essential, and Suu Kyi proved to have a gift for making emotional contact. Her speeches were short and to the point, and people responded eagerly to her lucidity and directness.[50] Her capacity to convert crowds of people into admirers and supporters set in motion a swift cycle of accumulation that swept her rapidly into the leadership, symbolical and actual, of the nation.

With respect to its symbolic aspects, there was a dramatic piquancy in the very image of her leadership that swelled the coffers of her moral

---

[50] Karen Swenson, "Battle of Wills in Myanmar," *New Leader*, 3–17 June 1997, p. 8.

capital. She was the delicate but indomitable Beauty to SLORC's clumsy Beast, the heroic underdog confronting a powerful and ruthless opponent whose long-time acronym (SLORC) seemed deliberately chosen to emphasize its stupidity and beastliness. Suu Kyi's physical appearance, enhanced by the trademark flowers in the hair, projected a persona of combined strength and fragility that had charm not just for Burmese people but for the wider world. She had always understood the vital importance of international pressure and had reached the world via innumerable interviews – to press, radio and television – whenever access to the media was not wholly restricted. A natural interviewee, she was periodically in heavy demand (the world's attention could never stay focused on Burma the way it did on South Africa), a fact that helped her become the definitive voice and face of the democratic cause of Burma. Her name and image became the central motifs on which the network of expatriate Burmese dissidents could pin their campaigns.

Though Suu Kyi thus made effective use of her own symbolic status to bring international pressure to bear (she gave that pressure most of the credit for securing her release in 1995), her own characteristic view was that symbols are all very well but do not get any work done.[51] What she most wanted to be was an effective political leader, a task that included but was not confined to the creation of an effective political organization. She sought to be a genuinely transformational leader, which is to say an effective teacher. She had, as we have seen, values and virtues to preach as well as cautions concerning the road taken toward democracy, and she sought to impart them at every opportunity. In the six months prior to her arrest, the mood of the meetings she addressed changed. Rather than political rallies filled with slogans and chanting, they became quiet, educative affairs, with Suu Kyi expounding the meaning of democracy and her strategy for achieving it, particularly with regard to the continuing need for discipline, while people listened quietly and asked thoughtful questions. In 1996, writing of those early campaigns, she outlined her communicative-consultative-educative leadership strategy:

In building up the NLD our chief concern was to establish a close, mutually beneficial relationship with the general public. We listened to the voice of the people that our policies might be in harmony with their legitimate needs and aspirations. We discussed with them the problems of our country and explained why, in spite of its inevitable flaws, we considered democracy to be better than other political systems. Most important of all, we sought to make them understand why we believed that political change was best achieved through nonviolent means.[52]

[51] "Aung San Suu Kyi: Interviewed after Release," Free Burma internet page.
[52] Letter to the *Mainichi Daily News*, 17 June 1996.

After her release from house arrest she conducted weekend sessions of this kind over the back fence of her house in University Avenue, Rangoon, meetings that sometimes blocked the street and became internationally famous thanks to the presence of the world press.

The junta, for its part, was eternally busy trying to counteract Suu Kyi's influence. In addition to its attempts to suppress her voice and to sideline and vilify her, it pursued more positive strategies aimed at reestablishing the foundations of its legitimacy and power. These were: the establishment of a national convention for the writing of the new Constitution, rigged (needless to say) to secure an Indonesian-style arrangement of permanent military involvement in government; the creation of a rival to the NLD in a mass organization called the Union Solidarity and Development Association (USDA), an attempt "to recreate civil society in its own manner while suppressing alternative possibilities"[53] (among other things, USDA was used to assemble mass rallies in support of the government and to mobilize youths for destructive attacks on the opposition, including in late 1996 on a motorcade in which Suu Kyi herself was traveling); the reequipping of Burma's armed forces (by China) to crush the ethnic independence movements; and foreign investment-led economic development.

The junta had some success in its campaign to "annihilate all insurgent movements," though its international image was hardly improved by repeated incidents of rape, murder and forced labor of the ethnic populations during the various offensives. It also had some early success in encouraging economic development through which it hoped to give citizens a self-interested stake in the *status quo* and thus still the voices of protest. Here again, however, some of its methods of development became the object of severe criticism, particularly its conscription of people into "voluntary" labor gangs for road construction and other infrastructural projects, including the cleaning up of areas for the sake of tourism. Its main push was to gain more foreign investment and to attract more tourists bearing much-needed hard currency. While SLORC issued invitations, offered deals and built hotels, Suu Kyi pleaded with nations and corporations not to invest and not to visit Burma until democracy and the rule of law were installed.

Investment in Burma therefore became a global political issue, and a test of Suu Kyi's capacity to mobilize international opinion on behalf of the democratic cause. Her success was not, of course, complete, but it was significant. The new tourist hotels stayed largely empty, at least in part because of Suu Kyi's pleas to boycott SLORC's "Visit Myanmar

[53] David Steinberg, "The Union Solidarity and Development Association," *Burma Debate* 4(1) (January/February 1997), p. 3.

Year 1996/97." Success in discouraging the investment of large private companies was mixed, though Suu Kyi and Burmese activists worldwide gained some notable victories. The regime remained hard-pressed by the policies of Western democracies, most of which had cut all but humanitarian aid to Burma after the detention of Suu Kyi and the failure to honor the election results. The United States, one of the most consistent critics of the SLORC regime, kept up pressure for political reform by blocking all funding from the International Monetary Fund and the World Bank and, in 1997, imposing sanctions on all new investment in Burma. (It was this last decision that reportedly led directly to the attack on Suu Kyi noted above. USDA youth argued that Washington had been swayed by "falsehoods spread by Aung San Suu Kyi.")[54] On the other hand, the ASEAN group of nations, Burma's closest trading partners, resisted pressure from the West and took a softer line, arguing for a policy of "constructive engagement" rather than one of ostracism, admitting "Myanmar" to membership of the organization in 1997. This strategy was crippled, however, by the Asian currency crisis of late 1997 followed by the fall of Suharto and the democratic attack on the role of the Indonesian military.

A facelift in November 1997, when SLORC was dissolved and a nineteen-member State Peace and Development Council (SPDC) established in its place, did nothing to revive the junta's sagging fortunes and or to improve its dismal image.[55] By 2000, despite (or because of) the best efforts of the generals, economic salvation appeared nowhere on the near horizon, and the junta appeared to be surviving through its connections to the illicit drug and jade trades.[56] In April 2000, in a videotaped message smuggled from Burma for presentation to the UN Human Rights Commission in Geneva, Suu Kyi claimed Burma was becoming a two-class country divided between the military and everyone else, and appealed to the international community to reflect on recent events in East Timor to "learn to help when help is needed, and not only when help is too late."[57]

Part of Suu Kyi's case rested on the appalling state of the Burmese economy and the consequent suffering of the people, but for a number of commentators some of the responsibility for this state of affairs lay with Suu Kyi's own insistence on sanctions and the diplomatic isolation of the junta. Japanese business consultant, Ohmae Kenichi, pointed an accusing finger at the United States who, he said, had made Suu Kyi the Joan of

[54] Voice of America News Report, 4 May 1997.
[55] Ron Corben, "Burma's Generals Shuffle the Deckchairs," *Australian*, 17 November 1997, p. 6.
[56] See Louis Kaar, "Waiting for Windfalls Won't Help Creditors," *Burma Debate* 4(2) (March/June 1997), p. 23.
[57] Bangkok, Associated Press Report, 5 April 2000.

Arc of Myanmar for its own democratic propaganda purposes, turning her into a burden on her developing country. Australian Greg Sheridan argued that, because of her imprisonment and the denial of her democratic victory, Suu Kyi had been given a power of moral veto over Western policy toward Burma with disastrous economic and social results.[58] Of course, the effectiveness or counter-productiveness of sanctions, and in general the causal connection between development and liberalization, are perennial themes of debate. Certainly, Suu Kyi always took a very hard line on the matter. Whether or not one finds the results of her stance deplorable or admirable, one must admit the international effectiveness of her mobilization of moral capital.

Conclusion

Suu Kyi always deprecated the tendencies of admirers to portray her as a secular saint, but she was well aware that the peculiar esteem in which she was held was the key to her political influence and to the strategies available to her. At the time of writing, her political odyssey is yet unfinished and her future still in doubt. Should she survive and the military come to the point of real negotiation and compromise, it may feel itself fortunate to have Suu Kyi to deal with. The junta must realize, in spite of all its attempts to demean and vilify her, that she is, like Mandela, an essentially moderate leader, unlikely to seek vengeance or reprisal once the tables of power are turned. She has, moreover, consistently avowed respect for the army (if not for its present leadership) and for its role as defender of the nation, and has refused to try to divide it against itself to gain political advantage. It has some reason therefore to trust her, and its leaders have learned to respect her, however grudgingly. The name of Aung San, which still carries great moral force within the *Tatmadaw*, may once again prove its value in such negotiations. The pain and loss of face attached to any compromises conceded may be ameliorated if the shade of the first Aung San, manifest in his daughter, can be represented as demanding them.

The question will then turn to the future leadership role she might play. Asked once about this, she replied: "I don't think it is for me to say I want to be like this or I want to be like that or even that I want to be leader. It is for the people to decide."[59] This is probably tantamount to a declaration

---

[58] Ohmae Kenichi, "1997: A Year of Transition," *Asiaweek Special Collectors' Edition*, December 1997, p. 5; "Mrs Suu Kyi is becoming a burden for developing Myanmar," *SAPIO*, 12 November 1997; and Greg Sheridan, *Asian Values, Western Dreams* (St. Leonards, NSW, Allen & Unwin, 1999).

[59] "Aung San Suu Kyi: Interviewed after Release," p. 5.

of readiness for political office in a democratic Burma. A new democratic state of Burma will undoubtedly need her as its solid center if it is not once again to be rapidly sundered by the forces of economic challenge, military reordering, political rivalry and ethnic conflict. There is no one else who commands such universal respect and at least provisional confidence across the whole spectrum of Burmese life. As in South Africa, there will inevitably be an explosion of hopes, expectations, demands and fears. An elected government will have to contain expectations without destroying hope, and to satisfy or reject demands while calming fears. It will face three very difficult tasks: setting a ruined economy on a sound developmental path; satisfying the demands and fears of the ethnic nationalities; and recreating the military as servant rather than master of the people. There will more than ever be a need, as Suu Kyi herself has warned, for those virtues of discipline and patience upon which she has always insisted. There will be use for a leader who in her person embodies those values, and who inspires the trust and faith of so many.[60] As in Mandela's case, Suu Kyi's moral capital, boosted one presumes by the victory itself, should continue to be a vital sustaining and stabilizing force.

[60] See Josef Silverstein, "Aung San Suu Kyi: Is She Burma's Woman of Destiny?" in Aris, *Freedom from Fear*, especially pp. 278–282.

PART IV

Moral capital and the
American presidency

In his 1997 State of the Union address, Bill Clinton, a "New Democrat" presiding over the final demise of the post-war liberal consensus, deployed traditional American frontier rhetoric to defend a reconceived role for the modern State. Having embraced schemes of welfare reform and balanced budgets traditionally championed by Republicans, Clinton was attempting to redress the Democratic balance by articulating more clearly his promised "third way," that fabled middle road between the big government, tax-and-spend policies of liberals and the "leaner, meaner" government dreams of conservatives. The new frontier, Clinton said, was an environment of changed demographic, political and economic conditions, of new threats and opportunities in a globalizing world, of new constraints on government. The correct response was neither small government nor big government, but an efficient, adaptive government that would have to be reduced in some domains but enlarged in others, including social areas traditionally beloved by Democrats.

The day after this address, I introduced it for discussion to a group of Yale undergraduates in a class on frontier ideologies. When I asked what they had made of it (all had watched it on television) the response was blank surprise. They had made nothing of it. "It was just *him* talking," said one. "When *he* speaks," said another, "I see his lips move and hear the sounds but it doesn't *mean* anything." I was curious. Clinton was an able speaker and his State of the Union speeches had, in the past, always produced a jump in his Harris poll approval rating, temporarily hauling him out of whatever scandal-dug hole he was currently in. Moreover, I had expected these typically engaged Yale students to pay closer than average attention. But the problem was respect, or lack of it. "You can't take anything that man says seriously," said one student, confirming the truth of Aristotle's dictum that the "proof" furnished by rhetorical speech depends, in the first instance, on a judgment of the moral character of the speaker. It was impossible for Clinton to persuade this particular audience either by an emotional appeal to culturally available myths or by the strength of the argument itself.[1] Moral judgment had turned his words into mere noise.

I recall this incident because it points to the enduring enigma of the Clinton presidency. Despite the failure of moral respect, despite the political and ideological "adjustments" (Willie's slickness), despite the large policy failures and the political, financial and sexual scandals, despite the sheer embarrassment of Monica Lewinsky and the impeachment trial – despite all this, his record in government was by no means a disaster. He survived two terms against the odds, beating back a severe Republican challenge in the first with considerable political adroitness. Though many media commentators opined that Clinton's scandals had so damaged his "moral authority" that he would be ineffectual at home and abroad, this proved not to be the case. In his second term he achieved some notable foreign policy successes, while at home he presided over a burgeoning economy that seemed to have entered an era of perpetual, inflationless growth. He managed, even as impeachment loomed, to maintain consistently high public approval ratings – for his governing if not his morals. At his worst moment, when forced to admit publicly that he had lied about his "inappropriate" relationship with Lewinsky, his rating faltered a moment then soared to its highest point, confounding pundits. What was going on? And how was it possible for a president with, as it seemed, no moral capital worth mentioning to govern America more or less effectively for eight years?

I will argue in what follows that it was not true that Clinton, whatever his personal problems, altogether lacked moral capital. More significantly, though, I want to argue that the moral questions raised by the Clinton presidency cannot be understood independently of the modern history of the office he occupied. The history of the presidency in the latter half of the twentieth century is, I will argue, a moral history of contemporary America itself.

The institution of the presidency is a particularly suitable candidate for this kind of instructive examination both because of its inherent moral significance and because of the crisis of legitimacy it has undergone in modern times. The presidency occupies a pivotal position within the governmental structure of the United States, having become not just the locus of national executive power and prestige, but the focal point of the moral capital invested and embodied in both the political system and the nation at large. As a result, perceived moral damage to the office – a

---

[1] Power to move an audience emotionally and strength of argument are the other two important factors noted by Aristotle. See *Rhetoric* 1356a, *Aristotle* (J. H. Freese trans., London, William Heinemann, 1926), vol. 22, p. 5.

draining of its moral capital – affects more than just the presidency and its occupants: it affects the entire governmental system and the nation it is supposed to serve.

The dramatic decline in public trust in American government generally over the last thirty years has been widely noted. Alan Brinkley expressed it thus:

The bonds that link our leaders and our political system with the larger public – the bonds of at least minimal respect and confidence that are essential to the stability and effectiveness of a democratic state – are badly frayed. An almost palpable cynicism has penetrated our public belief, a cynicism that seems to be felt at almost every level of society. There is a widespread popular belief that no one in politics is to be trusted, that nothing government attempts works . . . We are experiencing a crisis of political leadership and legitimacy.[2]

This popular view has been extensively confirmed by political scientists who observe a long-term decline in trust of government since the mid-1960s.[3] Various explanations have been advanced for this phenomenon – poor performance by governments, dissatisfaction with policies and outcomes, government deficits and economic downturn – but the one thing that has clearly emerged is that political trust is most strongly a function of presidential approval. This is understandable given that the president is usually seen as, and is portrayed by the media as being, the central actor of American government.[4] It has been argued, therefore, that the behavior and character of successive incumbents (whatever their party, ideology or policies) must be a causal factor in the general decline of trust.

If, however, distrust were related only to the character, policies and

[2] Alan Brinkley, "What's Wrong with American Political Leadership," *Wilson Quarterly* 18(2) (Spring 1994), pp. 47–48.

[3] See, for example, Arthur H. Miller, "Political Issues and Trust in Government," *American Political Science Review* 68 (September 1974), pp. 951–972; Jack Citrin, "Comment: The Political Relevance of Trust in Government," *American Political Science Review* 68 (September 1974), pp. 973–988; Steven J. Rosenstone and Mark Hansen, *Mobilization, Participation and Democracy in America* (New York, Macmillan, 1993); Stephen C. Craig, *The Malevolent Leaders: Popular Discontent in America* (Boulder, CO, Westview, 1993); Stephen C. Craig (ed.), *Broken Contract: Changing Relations Between Americans and Their Government* (Boulder, CO, Westview, 1996); John R. Hibbing and Elizabeth Thiess-Morse, *Congress as Public Enemy: Public Attitudes Toward American Political Institutions* (New York, Cambridge University Press, 1995); Joseph Nye, Philip Zelikow and David King, *Why People Don't Trust Government* (Cambridge, MA, Harvard Universtity Press, 1997); Arthur H. Miller and Ola Listaug, "Government Performance and Political Trust," in Pippa Norris (ed.), *Global Support for Democratic Government* (Oxford, Oxford University Press, 1999).

[4] Jack Citrin and Donald Philip Green, "Presidential Leadership and the Resurgence of Trust in Government," *British Journal of Political Science* 16 (October 1986), pp. 431–453; Donald R. Kinder and Susan Fiske, "Presidents in the Public Mind," in Margaret G. Hermann (ed.), *Handbook of Political Psychology* (San Francisco, Josey-Bass, 1989), pp. 193–218.

performance of a particular president or presidents, the situation would be potentially remediable by a change of incumbent. But if, as appears to be the case, distrust is a function of a decline in "diffuse support" – support for the regime and its goals and values rather than for specific performance – then the question of the legitimacy of the regime itself is raised.[5] Evidence has been offered of a reciprocal effect here: dissatisfaction with political leaders engenders distrust and ingrained distrust in turn causes failing support that can powerfully damage the president's standing thus making effective government much more difficult.[6] Such political science findings seem to support the observation of Lloyd Cutler, who acted for both Jimmy Carter and Clinton as White House counsel (a post, note, intended to protect the office of the presidency, not the interests of the incumbent). Cutler believed that "the tragic bottom line was that the public no longer trusted the presidency. It wasn't just the person in the office. It wasn't just politicians or public figures. It was the presidency itself."[7] If this was so then it may be that Bill Clinton's problems were not all Bill Clinton's fault. It is possible that in his troubled occupancy of the White House we hear the reverberating echoes of the trials – sometimes the agonies – of the American presidency and of the nation itself since 1963.

I will not, therefore, be pursuing a detailed analysis of the Clinton presidency in this section but taking the more circuitous historical route of examining the office itself, particularly since the time of John F. Kennedy. I will be less focused on particular individuals than in the previous case studies and more on the relation of individuals to the office they hold. My general aim is to examine the reciprocal effects of the actions of incumbents on the moral capital that attaches to a respected office, and the repercussions of these effects throughout the political system. This, I will argue, is by no means a simple story of flawed or misguided men betraying their sacred duties and thus squandering and sapping the moral capital inherent in the institution with which they have been entrusted.

Before commencing, I must note that I will *not* be attempting to tackle the voluminous theoretical literature on the American presidency or to take part in some of the ongoing debates about how it ought to be studied. Many different approaches have been adopted on this, but one can

[5] David Easton, *A Systems Analysis of Political Life* (New York, Wiley, 1965).
[6] Marc J. Hetherington, "The Political Relevance of Political Trust," *American Political Science Review* 92(4) (December 1998), pp. 791–808, at p. 799.
[7] Quoted from Bob Woodward, *Shadow: Five Presidents and the Legacy of Watergate* (New York, Simon & Schuster, 1999), p. 271.

discern two broadly opposed tendencies: first, an institutional perspective that looks at the developing powers of, and political and constitutional constraints on, the office in its relations with the other institutions of government – Congress, the judiciary and the permanent governmental bureaucracy; secondly, an examination of the presidency in terms of the character and leadership of the men who have successively occupied the post. This might be regarded as a matter of emphasis, since institutional studies can only proceed through analysis of actual presidencies, and leadership studies can scarcely ignore the political and institutional contexts in which leadership is exercised, but it is at heart a question of causal primacy. To put it oversimply, the question is whether the nature and development of the office, and the actions of its occupants, are determined by the historical-institutional context or, alternatively, by the character and leadership of the persons who occupy it.[8]

My own view, which I will not defend at length here, is that it is artificial to separate these perspectives too strictly, and that whether an individual has the capacity to choose in such a way as to shape or reshape an office must itself be, at least in part, a question of institutional structure. Where extensive discretionary decision-making authority is invested in an office, it is difficult to conceive that the quality of the decisions made, the strength with which they are defended and the determination, adaptiveness and perhaps guile with which they are carried through have no dependency on individual character. Of course, extensive decision-making authority may be combined with a lack of power to alter the scope of that authority and thus the nature of the office itself. Nevertheless, it seems reasonable to surmise that the greater the discretionary authority, the greater is likely to be the reciprocal effect of office and incumbent. Where a constitution permits significant power to reside in a single individual, as in the presidency, the character and ideology of incumbents may become important determinants of the evolution of the institution itself, for there are invariably ambiguities and lacunae in the structure of designated authority that may be exploited by a strong-minded and politically adroit office-holder, though success will of course also depend on the strength and opposition of countervailing institutions and on contingent political factors. Prevailing political circumstances may be

[8] On character, see Erwin C. Hargrove, *The President as Leader: Appealing to the Better Angels of Our Nature* (Lawrence, University Press of Kansas, 1998); Robert Shogan, *The Double Edged Sword: How Character Makes and Ruins Presidents, from Washington to Clinton* (Boulder, CO, Westview Press, 1998). On institutionalism, see Fred I. Greenstein (ed.), *Leadership in the Modern Presidency* (Harvard, Harvard University Press, 1988); Terry Moe, "Presidents, Institutions and Theory," in George Edwards, John H. Kessel and Bert A. Rockman (eds.), *Researching the Presidency: Vital Questions, New Approaches* (Pittsburgh, University of Pittsburgh Press, 1993).

such as to frustrate an office-holder's most determined attempts at re-definition of policy settings or institutional power, or they may, on the contrary, encourage general acquiescence in even far-reaching changes.[9]

The interpretation of the moral history of America that I pursue in the following chapters does assume a reciprocal moral effect between office and incumbent, but is less concerned with the character of individual presidents than with the historical, political and institutional preconceptions and constraints that led, in post-war conditions, to a crisis in the regime. The most significant institutional constraint – the president's lack of authority over the legislature – plays an important part in this story, but I assume that this oft-noted feature of the office (which has produced the double image of the presidents as at once excessively strong and excessively weak) is relatively uncontroversial.

Finally, I must note that it may seem, in the ensuing interpretation, that I speak less often about moral capital than about American pride and virtue. This is because the presumed unity of these two were at the heart of what I call the essential American myth upon which a great deal of the American moral capital was founded. The fracturing of this myth post-Kennedy produced a debilitating loss of institutional moral capital (particularly of that residing in the presidency) but also of that national moral capital upon which Lincoln had once relied to ensure the forebearance of European nations during the Civil War. Indeed, it threatened to destroy the fund of capital on which the national *morale* was founded, undermining the self-faith of ordinary Americans and causing anger, disillusionment, guilt and confusion and causing a deep wound that a series of American presidents attempted, in different ways, to heal.

---

[9] See Stephen Skowronek's idea of "political time" and regime type, *The Politics Presidents Make* (Cambridge, MA, Belknap, 1993); and the revised edition, *The Politics Presidents Make: Leadership from John Adams to Bill Clinton* (Cambridge, MA, Belknap, 1997). Also his "Henry Jones Ford on the Development of American Institutions," *PS Political Science & Politics* 32(2) (June 1999), pp. 233–234. For deterministic readings of Skowronek, see Peri E. Arnold, "Determinism and Contingency in Skowronek's Political Time," *Polity* 37 (1995), pp. 497–508; Donald R. Brand, "Republicanism and the Vigorous Executive: A Review Essay," *Political Science Quarterly* 109 (1994–95), pp. 901–902; and Douglas J. Hoekstra's exchange with Skowronek in *Presidential Studies Quarterly* 29(3) (September 1999): Hoekstra, "The Politics of Politics: Skowronek and Presidential Research" (pp. 657–671); Skowronek, "Theory and History, Structure and Agency" (pp. 672–681); Hoekstra, "Comments on Theory and History, Structure and Agency" (pp. 682–684).

7 Kennedy and American virtue

> *Mythology*, n.: The body of a primitive people's beliefs concerning its
> origin, early history, heroes, deities and so forth, as distinct from the true
> accounts which it invents later.   Ambrose Bierce, *The Devil's Dictionary*

Reflecting on the legacy of Vietnam in April 2000, twenty-five years after
the fall of Saigon, Henry Kissinger wrote:

> one of the most important casualties of the Vietnam tragedy was the tradition of
> American "exceptionalism." The once near-universal faith in the uniqueness of
> our values – and their relevance round the world – gave way to intense divisions
> over the validity of those values and the lengths we should go to promote and
> defend them. And those schisms have had a profound impact on the conduct of
> American foreign policy ever since.[1]

Kissinger claims that protest against the war rapidly turned into doubt
about "American exceptionalism," and soon into the conviction that the
"ultimate cause of the crisis was not errors in judgment but moral rot at
the core of American life." Far from desiring an American victory in the
war, the protesters sought an American defeat as "a desirable national
catharsis." A demoralized establishment, faced with radicals who "knew
no limits" in their violent critique, found itself unable to vindicate the
values on which American post-war policy had been based.

The implication of Kissinger's argument is that the unity of faith then
lost was never recovered. He claims that one legacy of the conflict was a
deeply divided national leadership permanently uneasy with American
power and its uses. Even at the start of a new century, people broadly of
the left-wing (for example, the Clinton administration) tended to view the
Cold War as a misunderstanding, almost an American invention. "They
recoil before the concept of the national interest and distrust the use of
power unless it can be presented as in the service of some 'unselfish' cause
– that is to say, as reflecting no specific American interest." On the
right-wing, on the other hand, disciples of Ronald Reagan sought to
replace the old communist enemy with some external danger that would

[1] Henry Kissinger, "Legacy of Defeat," *Courier-Mail*, 29 April 2000, p. 26.

provide a focus around which foreign policy may be organized. "Vietnam," wrote Kissinger, "bequeathed a new generation divided into two camps – one in search of riskless applications of our values, another in an erratic quest for a focal point for our national strategy." Implied rather than stated here is the view that a proper understanding of the Vietnamese conflict would help heal the "schism" in American politics and permit the emergence of a more realistic outlook that would form the basis of a new consensus on foreign policy. Kissinger concludes that: "A balanced judgment on Vietnam remains our challenge – not as a question of historical justice towards individual presidents but of historical truth about a national tragedy."

Kissinger gestures in this article toward an important explanation of what happened to America and American leadership in the latter half of the twentieth century. His argument is, however, drastically underdeveloped. There is a tone of regret, even of lingering resentment, over those radical protesters who observed no limits in their rejection of establishment values, but no accounting for the virulence of their reaction. Nor is an explanation offered as to why the establishment should have been so demoralized as to fail utterly to defend its own post-war values. Kissinger rightly asserts the Cold War to be something more than an American invention but offers no analysis of the way that the values embodied in "American exceptionalism" were both subsumed in and distorted by the grim logic generated by Cold War fears. The persistently bifurcated attitude of national leaders after Vietnam is correctly attributed to confusions over morality and power, but the precise nature of the division and its fundamental causes are not explored.

What is clear is that Kissinger wants to see Vietnam reinterpreted, not so much as an American error and far less an American crime, but as a national "tragedy." This is a descriptor that carries intimations of an impersonal fate over which the actors involved have little control and for which, consequently, they have diminished responsibility. Kissinger, of course, was a major player in the "tragedy" (he was head of the National Security Committee and then Secretary of State under Presidents Nixon and Ford) and may have particular reasons for wishing to see the war thus depersonalized. Nevertheless, he is right to want an account that does not simply attribute Vietnam to the actions and misdeeds of particular presidents and their advisers, but examines the wider context of American values and attitudes in which those actions occurred. In the next four chapters I want to pursue such an explanation.

Kissinger's thumbnail version of American exceptionalism specifies the "uniqueness" of American values and the presumption of their relevance to the whole world. It is more accurate, however, to speak of the proclaimed uniqueness of Americans themselves as the exemplary bearers of universal values. Though United States history has been punctuated by episodes of messianic zeal and imperial domination, the most fundamental view of the nation's self-conceived historic "mission" has been to act as an example to humanity of what ordinary people in circumstances of freedom and self-government can achieve. America best served its mission, in other words, not by paternalistically or imperialistically imposing its values on others but simply by being itself and thus revealing to the world the true worth of those values. In his recantatory memoirs, Robert McNamara, defense secretary under both Presidents Kennedy and Johnson and chief architect of the policy of containment in Indo-China, claimed that the humbling lesson America had learnt in Vietnam was that it had no God-given right to shape other nations in its own image as it might choose.[2] The presumption of this right was, in American terms, already aberrant. It was an error that the nation had long been drawn into by consciousness of its own power and belief in its own virtue, a combination that grew critical in the dangerously competitive circumstances of the Cold War.

George Herring, one of the earliest historians of the Vietnam war, wrote (in a manner foreshadowing Kissinger's analysis) that one of its chief casualties was that "pervasive optimism" that was part of the American character.[3] I will argue that the reason American optimism was such a conspicuous casualty was that it was founded on a confidence in American capacity and power that was mythologically linked to a belief in American innocence and virtue. American power was seen as a felicitous by-product of the peculiar American virtue, and American virtue was believed in turn to be a guarantee of the beneficent use of American power. This presumptively indissoluble conjunction of virtue and power – existentially experienced by Americans as a harmonious combination of innocence and pride – was the core of what I here term the central American myth. The myth was sundered by events including and following the death of John F. Kennedy, and successive presidents struggled to reassemble it. Vietnam was the great catalyst, but it was not the only factor involved and itself requires explanation within the general trajectory of post-war American politics.

The most secure single locus of the American myth, the institution most responsible for tending its sacred flame, was the office of the

[2] Robert S. McNamara, *In Retrospect: The Tragedy and Lessons of Vietnam* (New York, Times Books, 1995), p. 13.
[3] George Herring, "The Wrong Kind of Loyalty: McNamara's Apology for Vietnam," *Foreign Affairs* 74(3) (1995), pp. 154–158. Herring's history is *America's Longest War: The United States and Vietnam, 1950–1975* (New York, Wiley, 1979).

presidency. Because of this, it was inevitable that the presidency, or rather presidents, would be key players in the drama that saw the fracturing of the myth, and indeed would be held by many to be responsible for the damage caused. Undoubtedly the actions of successive presidents severely affected the moral capital of the office itself, but understanding both why these actions were taken and why the damage was so extensive requires an understanding of the nature and problems of the presidential office in its relation to the whole of government and to the American people at large. It also requires an appreciation of the American response to the challenge of the Cold War, and the way in which Cold War domestic politics trapped successive administrations, both Democratic and Republican, into accepting a rigidified version of the American myth that would prove destructive of itself, divisive of the nation, and damaging to the national moral capital.

The presidency and the national moral capital

One of the principal problems consciously addressed by the founders of the United States of America was that of maintaining a stable balance between efficiency and accountability in government. They desired an effective executive but, having fought a revolutionary war against British "tyranny," were fearful of creating a home-grown American "czar." Many of them thought it possible to establish a government of virtuous and disinterested men but were alive to the corrupting effects of power and concerned to design their institutions so that temptation and opportunity were minimized. They therefore debated the merits of a plural executive or of an ancillary Council of State that might forestall presidential tyranny, but were afraid such institutional courses would cause executive paralysis.[4] In the end, confidence was placed in George Washington to put a singular presidency on the right track, his moral reputation being such that he could be trusted to give the office the necessary weight to found its legitimacy without setting himself up as dictator. Washington established the essential shape of the presidency and set the moral tone of the office, becoming himself a moral standard for succeeding generations of Americans, the very embodiment of national republican virtue.

Apart from Washington and his exemplary precedent, it was hoped that a separation of power between executive, legislature and judiciary, and its division between federal government and the States, would provide the necessary checks and balances to prevent the accumulation of tyrannical power in *any* branch of government or in any legislative majority. But

[4] See the discussion in Arthur M. Schlesinger, Jr., *The Imperial Presidency* (London, Andre Deutsch, 1974), pp. 382–386.

separation led inevitably to contestation between Congress and the presidency over control of the national agenda (with the Supreme Court – guardian and interpreter of the Constitution – playing an adjunct and variable role capable in some circumstances of turning into limited political leadership).[5] The advantage between Congress and the presidency shifted back and forth, with one or other in the ascendancy for often long periods. The trend for most of the twentieth century, particularly since the time of Franklin D. Roosevelt, is usually said to have been toward the presidency and away from Congress, though the reality is much more complex than a simple pendulum image suggests (especially given the complexity of Congress and the increasing fragmentation of authority within it). Though presidents assumed ever greater powers in modern times, they did so very unevenly. Nevertheless, as the power and visibility of the presidency grew, its symbolical role as the heart of American government grew also. The president came to represent in his person the virtue, power and promise of the whole American democracy.

The nationally representative function of the chief executive seemed a natural consequence of the fact that, in a federal system, the presidency was the only location in which national authority could be securely embodied. It was the only office that could consistently defend truly national interests as well as intervene to protect the rights of citizens endangered by powerful local interests. With increasing democratization in the nineteenth century, the presidency also became more strongly associated with the popular as well as the national interest. The development of the convention system of nomination and changes in the Electoral College turned the election of president and vice-president into a popular poll. Congressmen, elected to look after the concerns and interests of particular constituencies and States, inevitably spoke (save in exceptional circumstances) with discordant voices, but the president could claim a national mandate that allowed him to assert a univocal national leadership in the interest of all American people. This unique position made the presidency, as Teddy Roosevelt said, "a bully pulpit" if the incumbent were inclined to use it – and presidents in the twentieth century were increasingly so inclined.

According to scholars of the "rhetorical presidency" school, the growing use of the presidential podium to garner policy support among the public altered the very nature of the presidency. Its moral tone changed from one of high republicanism toward a more democratic mode. While presidents in the nineteenth century were expected (as we saw in the

---

[5] On the constitutional foundations of the presidential–Congressional relationship and its evolution, see Robert J. Spitzer, *President and Congress: Executive Hegemony at the Crossroads of Government* (Philadelphia, Temple University Press, 1993).

chapter on Lincoln) to adopt an aloof and dignified style of governing that avoided any hint of demagoguery, the rhetorical presidents of the twentieth century have, allegedly, ushered in a much more plebiscitary form of democratic governance.[6] Franklin Roosevelt's "fireside chats," broadcast on radio, set an important precedent here. By assuming a new intimacy with the people, by teaching a new public philosophy and persuading Americans to accept programs like social security, Roosevelt showed that it was possible to nurture and mold public opinion through intelligent use of modern media. By the same means he hoped also to strengthen the hand of the executive against Congress.[7] Subsequent presidents became ever more reliant on this form of plebiscitary leadership, partly perhaps because the decline of political parties in post-war America produced a need for alternative means of political mobilization. One effect, according to some scholars, was the increased "personalization" of the presidency, a process that got a sharp boost from John F. Kennedy's use of television as a means of image projection in the 1960s.[8]

Arthur Schlesinger has claimed, however, that the presidency was "a personalized office from the start, both for political reasons – the interests of the President – and psychological reasons – the emotional needs of the people."[9] But, however one reads the history, the outcome is the same: national hopes and expectations have tended to become intensely focused on the presidency which has consequently had to carry a disproportionate part of the moral weight of the entire governmental system. The necessity for national leadership, the democratically representative nature of the presidency, the increasingly direct communication between president and people accompanied by greater personalization of the office – all these combined to give the presidency a unique and pivotal role. It also gave it a unique responsibility, not just for the effective wielding of power but for the maintenance of public faith in American government. The president represented the American people at home and he represented America to the world, and he must of course represent both at their best.

[6] See Jeffrey K. Tulis, *The Rhetorical Presidency* (Princeton University Press, 1987); Murray Edelman, *Constructing the Political Spectacle* (Chicago, Chicago University Press, 1988); George C. Edwards III, *The Public Presidency: The Pursuit of Popular Support* (New York, St. Martin's Press, 1983); Samuel Kernell, *Going Public: New Strategies of Presidential Leadership* (Washington, DC, CQ Press, 1986); Richard J. Ellis (ed.), *Speaking to the People: The Rhetorical Presidency in Historical Perspective* (Amherst, University of Massachusetts Press, 1998).

[7] And also against the political parties, according to Sidney M. Milkis, "Franklin D. Roosevelt, Progressivism, and the Limits of Popular Leadership," in Ellis, *Speaking to the People*, pp. 184–209.

[8] Theodore J. Lowi, *The Personal President: Power Invested, Promise Unfulfilled* (Ithaca, Cornell University Press, 1985).

[9] This is from a revised edition of *The Imperial Presidency* (Boston, Houghton Mifflin, 1989), p. 428.

He must represent the people in accordance with that virtuous image of themselves and their nation they had so long and so publicly cherished, that they had indeed idealized, apotheosized and transmitted to the wider world in their finest works of popular art. The pilgrims' "shining light on the hill"; the "land of the free, sweet home of liberty" promised by revolutionary principles, guaranteed by constitutional laws crafted by the founding fathers and painfully and resoundingly reconfirmed by Lincoln; the brave new world of sturdy individual enterprise and self-government whose economic success and power were not so much selfish ends as a manifestation of the fruits of virtuous independence and thus an example to all humankind; the priority of the popular will in domestic politics and the projection of disinterested generosity and goodwill toward foreign nations – all this the presidential incumbent was perforce required to shoulder and maintain amidst the normal messy, banal, sometimes sordid realities of daily government and politics.

If the weight of moral capital with which the office was thus imbued constituted something of a burden on the incumbent as he pursued everyday political ends, it was also often a boon. Any important office in a respectably legitimized governmental system carries, I have argued, a certain quantum of moral capital that is transmitted to an incumbent merely by the fact of their incumbency (at least until such time as they may show themselves deeply unworthy of it). This moral capital is something over and above the respect and prestige that accompanies the assumption of power. Where an office is presumed to exist for a good purpose in a good system – and *a fortiori* where it has become symbolically representative of that system – its moral capital inevitably cloaks the office-holder in a mantle that signifies moral standing and commands (sometimes exaggerated) moral respect. This mantle can afford the wearer serious protection even when their actual actions, judged coldly, invite condemnation or censure (as even Independent Counsel Kenneth Starr accepted in the midst of his determined pursuit of Bill Clinton).[10]

The problem for any office, but particularly for exalted ones like that of the presidency, is how to guarantee a match between the moral capital of the office and the moral worthiness of the office-holder. Schlesinger wrote with respect to this that: "In giving great power to Presidents, Americans declared their faith in the winnowing processes of politics."[11] Electoral Colleges and party conventions were presumed to eliminate aspirants who rejected constitutional restraints and the republican ethos. Presidents might be more or less worthy, more or less competent, occasionally

[10] See Bob Woodward, *Shadow: Five Presidents and the Legacy of Watergate* (New York, Simon & Schuster, 1999), pp. 286 and 436.
[11] Schlesinger, *The Imperial Presidency*, p. 378.

even corrupt, but by and large the system produced leaders who were faithful to their trust. Theodore White went further and argued that the "crowning myth" of the presidency was:

that the people, in their shared wisdom, would be able to choose the best man to lead them. From this came the derivative myth – that the Presidency, the supreme office, would make noble any man who held its responsibility. The office would burn the dross from his character; his duties would, by their very weight, make him a superior man, fit to sustain the burden of law, wise and enduring enough to resist the clash of all selfish interests.[12]

What made automatic moral respect for the incumbent something more than a gratuitous endowment was, on this view, the anticipated transformation wrought by the honorable weight of the office itself. The records of remarkable presidents of various origins and experience – Washington, Lincoln, Wilson, the Roosevelts – lent substance to the myth, while even stupid, hypocritical and limited men chose to honor it in their public attitudes. It thus held up pretty well for almost two centuries – until the advent, says White, of Richard Nixon.

Yet, despite this concentration of political prestige and moral grandeur in a single office, presidents have never had an easy time negotiating the contradictory expectations with which the American people encumber them. Thomas Cronin and Michael Genovese[13] provide an extensive list of what they call the "paradoxes of the presidency": Americans are suspicious of centralized power but want a strong president; they want a common person, one of themselves, but with heroic qualities; they desire a decent, moral leader who is nonetheless capable of Machiavellian guile; they prefer a nonpolitical president who must be a political master to gain and hold office; they want a visionary leader but one who will keep in step with public opinion; they want a president powerfully active on the nation's behalf who must nevertheless be institutionally and legally restrained. As *The Economist* once put it, Americans want to be led, but they do not want to be led too much.[14]

Yet Tocqueville long ago drew the general case from the American example, arguing that modern people "want to be led and they want to remain free. As they cannot destroy either one of these contradictory propensities, they strive to satisfy them both at once [through democratic government]."[15] The paradoxes listed are in fact common in greater or

[12] Theodore H. White, *Breach of Faith: The Fall of Richard Nixon* (New York, Atheneum Press, 1975), pp. 323–324.
[13] Thomas E. Cronin and Michael A. Genovese, *The Paradoxes of the American Presidency* (New York, Oxford University Press, 1998).
[14] "Leadership, and the Lack of It," *Economist* 348(8084), 5 September 1998, p. 27.
[15] Alexis de Tocqueville, *Democracy in America* (Ware, Herts, Wordsworth Classics, 1998) vol. II, Book 4, chapter 5, p. 359.

lesser degree to all democracies. Democratic leadership is, in consequence, always peculiarly difficult. Rare is the leader who can meet all of
its contradictory demands which was why Walt Whitman called Lincoln,
who came closer than most, a "democratic genius." It is also why Lincoln
became the president to whom most succeeding presidents looked as the
example to be followed, the challenge to be met, and the standard to be
achieved if they were to leave a comparable mark on the republic.

The peculiar acuteness with which these paradoxes are experienced by
American presidents, however, is largely the result of the answer provided
by the authors of the Constitution to the problem of how to harmonize
governmental efficiency and effectiveness with democratic accountability
and constraint. Opposing a singular, authoritative executive to a radically
separate legislature led to the real, central paradox of the United States
presidency: a combination of great power and great weakness. The inherent weakness of the presidency was the theme of Richard Neustadt's
ground-breaking work in 1960 and was much explored thereafter.[16] Lack
of control of the legislature such as prime ministers in parliamentary
systems enjoy and a corresponding lack of party discipline, made presidential command of the political agenda crucially and continuously dependent on an ability to "handle" Congress – a Congress which has not
only votes to disburse but, by constitutional grant, power over governmental expenditure. The notable exception was in foreign affairs where
the executive most successfully established its prerogatives, generally
with congressional complaisance, by asserting control in matters of war
and security. As American economic and military power grew, therefore,
there arose the anomaly of a political leader who could cut an impressive
figure on the world stage while having difficulty delivering on his policy
promises at home. As Geoffrey Hodgson put it: "Never has any one office
had so much power as the President of the United States possesses. Never
has so powerful a leader been so impotent to do what he wants to do, what
he is pledged to do, what he is expected to do, and what he knows he must
do."[17]

Hodgson spoke of the "false promise" of the modern presidency, while
others speak of the "expectations gap."[18] If presidents were inevitably

[16]   Richard E. Neustadt, *Presidential Power and the Modern Presidents* (New York, John Wiley
& Sons, 1990) (first published in 1960 as *Presidential Power: The Politics of Leadership*). See
also Thomas Frank (ed.), *The Tethered Presidency* (New York University Press, 1981);
Harold Barger, *The Impossible Presidency* (Glenview, IL, Scott Foresman and Co., 1984);
William Grover, *The President as Prisoner* (New York, SUNY Press, 1989); Aaron Wil-
davsky, *The Beleaguered Presidency* (New Brunswick, NJ, Transaction, 1991); Gary L.
Rose, *The American Presidency Under Siege* (Albany, SUNY Press, 1997).

[17]   Geoffrey Hodgson, *All Things to All Men: The False Promise of the Modern American
Presidency* (London, Weidenfeld and Nicolson, 1980), p. 13.

[18]   Bruce Buchanan, *The Presidential Experience: What the Office Does to the Man* (Englewood

saddled with an institutional incapacity to fulfill increasingly exaggerated expectations, then promises could never adequately be kept and faith in the office must grow strained in the long run. What is the good of holding the most resounding democratic mandate for a policy of clear national importance if a fractious and undisciplined Congress, prey to the lobbying of powerful opposed interests, can with impunity cut a presidential legislative initiative to shreds? Certainly, all presidents, including those regarded as the most successful, have suffered mortally from the frustrating lack of effective controls on the giant ship of state. The result has been the oft-remarked tendency, even of presidents who come to power stressing domestic reform, to turn at length to the field of foreign affairs where their actions can be made to count. The traditional executive domination of foreign policy was, indeed, a prime factor in the moral history I will relate. Just as serious, however, was a perennial temptation to circumvent political, legal and constitutional restraints that obstruct actions a president deems necessary for national security or national welfare, often under a cloak of secrecy or deception. Taking paths of doubtful constitutionality produces political conflict, while taking paths of illegality produces (if detected) anger and disillusionment. In striving to fulfill the trust placed in them, presidents can be tempted to exceed the limits of their authority and in the process undermine trust in general. This is certainly part of the story for Lyndon Johnson, who acted extraconstitutionally, and for Richard Nixon, who acted both extraconstitutionally and illegally.

Yet the frustrations of institutionally hamstrung presidents do not by themselves explain the conditions under which some might be tempted to circumvent the constraints of the office in such a manner as to threaten the legitimacy of the office itself. Nor can public disillusionment in the presidency be reductively explained by the actions, however reprehensible, of one or more presidents. Consider what might happen to the moral capital of an office when the standards expected of its occupant are betrayed as Nixon, most notoriously, betrayed them. The tarnishment of the individual may well be expected to affect the office itself. It might therefore be argued that the revelations of Nixon's criminal actions in the Watergate affair resulted in a loss of moral capital that proved not only politically fatal for himself but seriously injurious to the office he held (the underlying thesis of Bob Woodward's book, *Shadow*).

Cliffs, NJ, Prentice-Hall, 1978); Thomas E. Cronin, *The State of the Presidency* (Boston, Little, Brown and Co., 1980); Theodore J. Lowi, *The Personal President: Power Invested, Promise Unfulfilled* (Ithaca, Cornell University Press, 1985). See also chapters 1–3 in Richard W. Waterman (ed.), *The Presidency Reconsidered* (Itasca, IL, F. E. Peacock, 1993), pp. 1–68.

Yet, if an office is sufficiently robust and the system sufficiently well supported, singular stains can surely be washed away by a new incumbent of upright character – this was precisely the promise Nixon made on succeeding Johnson, and the hope placed in Gerald Ford when he assumed the presidency after Nixon. The presidency had in the past survived the odd bad apple – Warren Harding, for example – without significant damage. Though it is conceivable that an unending series of corrupt or otherwise reprehensible occupants might bring an office into enduring disrepute, this does not accurately describe what happened to the American presidency.

Gail Sheehy, speaking of the "credibility gap" that Lyndon Johnson opened up in American political life, argued that "that legacy, the start of a long-term mistrust of the president that would profoundly influence the nation's history, can be laid directly at the door of one man's character."[19] I will argue to the contrary that, although the legacies of Johnson and Nixon were indeed difficult for succeeding presidents to overcome, the trials of the presidential office were not solely traceable to their particular characters nor to the characters and actions of their successors. Given the unique moral and political responsibility of the office, it was inevitable that the presidency should be in the spotlight taking much of the heat. But the "crisis of legitimacy" that is often said to have afflicted the presidency in the latter part of the century was a crisis of which Johnson and Nixon were, in important ways, as much symptoms as causes. Also implicated were the entire government and its various agencies, and beyond them American society and the American people themselves, and the myth to which they had held for so long. The crisis was, to put it rather grandly, a crisis of the American soul – or at least of some of America's fondest illusions about itself and its own innocence. And the damage was not just to the moral capital of the presidency, but to the moral capital of the nation itself.

Kennedy and American virtue

It has been said that American innocence is perennial: regularly lost and just as regularly regained. Whatever hard knocks historical experience has delivered to the American psyche, faith in the essential goodness of America and Americans has somehow survived – until recently. At the dawn of a new millennium, Al Gore in his campaign for the Democratic primaries invoked the traditional appeal to the myth of peculiar innocence, claiming that Americans "are still the most decent people on earth

[19] Gail Sheehy, *Character: America's Search for Leadership* (New York, William Morrow and Co., 1988), p. 17.

and are actually growing in service and selflessness."[20] But the tone of invocation was now considerably chastened. Americans, said Gore, were decent *despite* suffering "cultural soul sickness" (a reference to the disturbing spate of school shootings of the 1990s). Something had happened to America's self-belief in the latter half of the twentieth century that made such traditional rhetoric fall bleakly on the ear.

The reason that American innocence has been so often renewed is that it is a consequence of America's belief in its peculiar virtue, the central component of the dominant national myth of a triumphant individualism in an ever-virginal continent. Though the United States at over two centuries of age is one of the oldest of modern States, it is always in American imagination the new frontier where decent, industrious, commercially minded individuals may make and remake themselves at will, unencumbered by the confining categories of the ancient world and uninfected by its corruptions. In its historical formation this individualist, libertarian, expansionist ideology incorporated a shift of religious sentiment from an acceptance of original sin to a belief in what Garry Wills has called "original sinlessness."[21] According to the former doctrine, brought over from the Old World by the Pilgrims, human beings were fallen creatures to whom paradise on earth was eternally lost and who therefore must admit their sin and sincerely repent. But in America Adam and Eve were reborn in a new Eden where individual enterprise and the free market could create conditions of earthly paradise. Optimism displaced pessimism about the human condition, belief in innocence replaced consciousness of sin, and happiness was promised in this life for those willing to exert their energies and exercise their pragmatic abilities in an abundant land.

It was a version of the myth of progress that had produced the Enlightenment and fueled European development and expansion, transfigured in America into a national myth. Indeed it was important that the myth – what could be termed "the dream of America" – was at least as much the product of the European imagination as of the American. To enlightened thinkers on the continent, to would-be democrats, constitutionalists and libertarians of the Old Regime, post-revolutionary America with its enthusiasm for State and national constitution-writing seemed like a fulfillment of Enlightenment political thought and a promise of future progress. America seemed to realize the myth of the social contract. It proved that free men with inalienable rights could in solemn

---

[20] Cited in Cameron Forbes, "Vote for Them, for God's Sake," *Australian*, 20 December 1999, p. 11.
[21] Garry Wills, *Reagan's America: Innocents at Home* (New York, Doubleday, 1987), chapter 41.

deliberation devise virtuous institutions in which authority was delegated and limited, that they could govern according to a rigorous principle of equality before the law, and that they could uphold freedoms of press, religion, assembly and freedom from arbitrary arrest by officials.[22] After the French revolution, with a growing historical consciousness in America of the nation's place and significance in the progressive history of the world, the American myth began to take definitive shape at home.[23]

This was the version of the myth that gave pride of place to *example* as the prime generator of American moral capital. As America grew in might, however, this exemplary role came to be rivaled by the role of actor for good in the world through the use of American power. In time, those who argued the conservative, purely exemplary view of American exceptionalism became a minority. (In the argument with Woodrow Wilson in 1919 over entry to the League of Nations, those who thought America should concentrate on domestic affairs, letting "the example of a successful America win international influence and authority for the nation," were among the few true "isolationists" left in foreign policy.)[24] It was, in general, taken for granted that American power represented no real threat to American exemplary virtue. In government, virtue and power were taken to be reconciled by the genius of the founding fathers who had wisely ensured that the temptations of power for fallible individuals were institutionally resisted. American government itself thus both evidenced and guaranteed American virtue.

The enlargement of American power proceeded, of course, from accumulation of wealth, a growing population, and continental and industrial expansion, but all this too was conceived as a consequence of virtue. It was the natural outcome of the pursuit of a good and prosperous life by a free, independent, democratic people possessed of a certain practical and inventive genius. In America's case, great wealth and power gave occasion for a virtuous people to demonstrate goodwill and disinterested generosity rather than the selfish aggrandizement so typical of European States. The myth assumed a most un-Machiavellian marriage of power and morality in which the partners seldom if ever conflicted. If power inevitably brought status and influence in the world, what State could be

[22] A still useful book is Werner Stark, *America, Ideal and Reality: The United States of 1776 in Contemporary European Philosophy* (London, K. Paul, Trench, Trubner, 1947). See also D. Echevarria, *Mirage in the West: A History of the French Image of American Society to 1815* (Princeton University Press, 1957); Gordon S. Wood, *The Creation of the American Republic* (Chapel Hill, University of North Carolina Press, 1969); R. H. Gabriel, *The Course of American Democratic Thought* (3rd edn., New York, Greenwood, 1986).

[23] See Joyce Appleby, Lynn Hunt and Margaret Jacob, *Telling the Truth About History* (New York, Norton, 1995).

[24] William Appleman Williams, *The Tragedy of American Diplomacy* (2nd revised and enlarged edn., New York, Delta, 1978), p. 111.

said to have a more benign record in its use than America? Though power might always in theory be used for evil ends, American power could not, for American ends were almost by definition good. Power had been innocently gained and would be innocently used. It was only natural that pride should accompany consciousness of such power, and perhaps Americans were sometimes wont to express their pride in too naively boisterous a manner. It was natural too that some Americans should want to assert the nation's power abroad, though American virtue ensured that this assertion would have beneficial consequences for the world. Any arrogance was offset by American innocence, any pride disarmed by virtue and well-meaningness.

Yet there were a number of significant tensions, even contradictions, within America's self-conceived exemplary combination of power and virtue which would prove recurringly problematic for its relations with the rest of the world. Freedom was a universal value, but in America it became identified with free enterprise rather than with the freedom to choose ways of life that might differ from the American, or forms of economic organization that might be either pre-capitalist or anti-capitalist. From the time of the Jacksonian Democracy in the 1820s, the conviction had steadily deepened of an intrinsic connection between democracy and a regime of private property and capitalist enterprise. Capitalism was, of course, by its nature expansionist, but the identification of freedom and free enterprise made American expansion a matter, as Jackson said, of extending the area of freedom on earth. It came to be argued, indeed, that the continuing health of American democracy was radically tied to the need for permanent expansion, whether of the imperialist nineteenth-century kind or of the somewhat less blatant economic variety. In the first half of the twentieth century, economic expansion was pursued via an "open door" foreign policy that saw American power consolidated behind a program to secure ever-increasing markets and sources of raw material for American enterprise. America came to assert domination in China, Africa, Cuba and Latin America through what Appleman Williams called an "informal imperialism."[25]

American expansion took place under early and late doctrines of "Manifest Destiny," the former justifying continental expansion and the latter expansion overseas.[26] If there was a religious as well as secular tone to such doctrines, it was no doubt because it seemed plain to Americans that God was on their side. An element of religious "chosenness" also underpinned the nation's wholehearted adoption of the racial assumptions that served to justify nineteenth-century European expansion

[25] Williams, *The Tragedy of American Diplomacy*, p. 47. On the Open Door Policy generally, see *ibid.*, chapters 1 and 2.

[26] A. K. Weinberg, *Manifest Destiny* (Baltimore, Johns Hopkins Press, 1935).

generally. Americans accepted as preordained the sweeping aside of "inferior" peoples, or their domination and "civilization" by members of the white race of whom there could be no better representatives on earth than the virtuous Americans. The ruling assumption was that what was good for America was good for the world, that doing right for America was simultaneously to do right for the world. This assumed coincidence – or identity – of values and interests made it impossible for Americans to separate self-interest from the universal good. Foreigners who resented American domination or desired different ways of life were presumed to reveal either their backwardness or their lack of real freedom to choose and thus their ripeness for American education and reform.

It became difficult for Americans to appreciate or understand criticisms of their foreign policy. Appleman Williams argued that this policy was always guided by three ideas: a generous humanitarian impulse to help others; a principle of self-determination for people individually and nationally; and a feeling "that other people cannot *really* solve their problems and improve their lives unless they go about it in the same way as the United States."[27] The third of these was, of course, quite incompatible with the second. American power, combined with Americans' perception of themselves as uniquely virtuous bearers of universal values, thus easily produced a mentality which saw lesser peoples as rightly dominated for their own good.

Yet the myth of the unique American amalgamation of power and virtue continued to hold solid sway among both elites and populace. Significantly, it inspired and was triumphantly reaffirmed in a popular culture that America largely invented and then exported to the rest of the world – music, books and, above all, movies. "I have discovered my theme," said the great Irish-American director John Ford in 1938 after making *Stagecoach*, "and my theme is America." It was a sentimentalized, hugely appealing America where men were men and women were worthy of them; it was an America where even a rugged outlaw was good at heart, his lawlessness more a symptom of the restless freedom and yearning for betterment that defined the American male than a sign of innate evil – for all his wildness he would be sure to choose right in the end. Of course there were bad guys in America against whom a hero had to pit his strength and virtue (often they were Indians malignantly standing in the way of human progress). The quintessential American was not, of course, the villain but the good guy who always overcame his evil adversary in the last reel. Abroad, all Americans were good guys, bringing a fresh, egalitarian spirit, a cocky confidence, a natural goodwill and material succor to a

[27] Williams, *The Tragedy of American Diplomacy*, p. 13.

surprised and grateful world. So ingrained was this self-image, and so well packaged – even, on occasion, so true – that many non-Americans grew up believing in it as sincerely as did the natives.

The enduring charm of the American myth enabled its individualistic component to survive the contrary evidence of an anti-individualist society powered by the gigantic forces of industrial capitalism in the late nineteenth century. It survived even the Great Depression of the 1930s – though it was touch and go in a world offering fascism and communism as polar solutions to this crisis of capitalism. Once a resurgent post-war capitalism began delivering increasing material benefits to all, convictions of individualism, equality of opportunity and social mobility quickly recovered from the doubts raised by industrialization and depression (when people are relatively well off and expecting better they may comfortably indulge fantasies of rugged, go-it-alone individuality). The shaking of popular belief in American innocence and virtue that occurred in the latter half of the century was, however, a more serious matter from which it was much harder to recover.

Exactly when the first mild tremors were felt is a matter for speculation, though a reasonable guess would be some time in the 1950s. Rebellion against a materialist, conformist culture had always characterized certain fringe elements in American society, but in the 1950s rebellion became for the first time a leitmotif of a newly well-heeled, increasingly independent class of youth (and was promptly turned, of course, into a commodity for sale to the ostensible rebels). The 1950s primed the youth revolt of the 1960s and gave birth to its favored mode of expression, rock and roll. In the interim, though, there occurred a dramatic flowering of the more zealous spirit of American virtue nurtured largely by the black civil rights movement which helped set many Northern youths on a more positive path.

With an inactive President Eisenhower in the White House and Congressional action on civil rights blocked by a powerful conservative bloc of Southern Democrats and right-wing Republicans, the burden of American institutional virtue had, in this matter, been assumed by a crusading Supreme Court. Southern rednecks were intransigent, of course, even when presented with legal directives, but then that was the South, still in many respects unreconstructed since the Civil War. The South was the hard rock against which the societal bearers of American virtue – the nonviolent movement of Southern blacks led by Martin Luther King and the Northern "freedom riders" who put themselves at hazard to support them – bravely beat until it crumbled. As the 1950s shaded into the 1960s, the times seemed really to be a'changing. America entered a brief era energized by folk anthems and fueled by considerable belief (at least among the vocal and educated young) in the power of goodness to transform a wicked world.

President John F. Kennedy, at his advent, symbolized this youthful spirit, a symbolization massively assisted by a glamorous first lady who would rapidly become the object of public fascination and adulation. Most importantly, Kennedy symbolized the feeling of hope and change that was abroad. Indeed his New Frontier rhetoric both fed upon and encouraged it, demanding service rather than promising services. It made a connection between this spirit and the American myth of eternal re-birth, of the brave young country always there to be newly rediscovered. Kennedy had the ability, as one writer put it, "to catch and thus define within his own political persona the transient spirit of the age."[28] Accord-ing to one of the foremost of his intellectual cheer-squad, he reestablished the Republic as the first generation of its leaders had seen it.[29] American rebirth would, in this case, have global implications, for Kennedy's inaug-ural promise was to "pay any price, bear any burden, meet any hardship, support any friend, oppose any foe, to ensure the survival and success of liberty." One of his earliest acts was to establish a Peace Corps which encouraged young Americans to contribute their time and skills to "the great common task" of bringing a decent way of life to peoples round the globe. As his term of office proceeded, it appeared that he and his brother Robert, as Attorney-General, were serious about tackling not just civil rights but that other enduring blemish on the face of American virtue, organized crime. It became possible to believe once again in the moral leadership role of the presidency.

Though Kennedy had in fact always been what Americans called "moderate" on civil rights, in his campaign and during his presidency he associated himself explicitly with the cause. In June 1963 he mobilized the Alabama National Guard to secure the admittance of two black students to the University of Alabama, declaring that the nation faced a "moral crisis" over the denial of rights to black citizens. Later that month he called for extensive civil rights legislation, which was inevitably obstruc-ted by the conservative coalition of right-wing Republicans and Southern Democrats in Congress that formed the major roadblock to all liberal legislation in America. It might not have succeeded at all had not Ken-nedy's successor, Lyndon B. Johnson, mobilized the mass of moral capital generated by Kennedy's assassination to push through the Civil Rights Act of 1964 (and an astonishing array of other measures tackling

---

[28] Jon Roper, "Richard Nixon's Political Hinterland: The Shadows of JFK and Charles de Gaulle," *Presidential Studies Quarterly* 28(2) (Spring 1998), pp. 422–435, at p. 423.

[29] Arthur M. Schlesinger, Jr., *A Thousand Days: John F. Kennedy in the White House* (New York, Houghton Mifflin, 1965).

long-standing social and economic problems that laid the foundations of his Great Society program). Kennedy's ghost could preside over this remarkable political achievement because of his symbolic identification with the forces of moral renewal and regenerative action at home.

This identification was part of the reason that his death formed a watershed moment in the American loss of faith in the national moral capital, but there was more. Kennedy, through his status as Cold War hero, was a veritable and attractive embodiment of American virtue not just at home but also on the world stage. It was significant that his inaugural address had been given over entirely to foreign affairs, emphasizing the leadership burden that Americans must bear in the long struggle against the common enemies of humanity: tyranny, poverty, disease and war. But in the post-war context, tyranny was synonymous with communism, and aid to underdeveloped nations was usually part of a competitive struggle with Soviet-backed forces for the hearts and minds of poor nations, an attempt to prevent revolutions of the type that had succeeded in Cuba under Fidel Castro. As for war, that had become a highly problematic matter, and so, consequently, had become the defense of American virtue.

America had emerged from World War II with its faith in its own goodness reaffirmed by the defeat of fascism in Germany and Japan. But when its wartime ally, the Soviet Union under Josef Stalin, reverted to form and became America's greatest threat, belief in American goodness (as opposed to communist evil) became virtually compulsory. American virtue in a world characterized by hostile ideological bifurcation assumed cosmic significance – the true good of free humanity against the utter evil of communist tyranny. Virtue became fatally tied to a dogmatic, politically inflexible anti-communism.

There was no doubt that the United States had little choice but to assume the leadership of the anti-communist world; it was not only the most powerful country on earth but also the only major industrial-capitalist nation left standing after the war. Necessity as well as generosity demanded that it deploy its economic and military might to help rebuild the economies of its allies and to defend the liberties that communists, dreaming of world domination, would expunge. But stern resolution gave way to something like hysterical panic in 1947 when Russia revealed its development of atomic weaponry, and again in 1949 when China fell to communism. These events profoundly shocked Americans, for they seemed to reveal just how dangerous and determined was an enemy hitherto assumed to be relatively weak. The alleged "loss" of China, which Republicans blamed on Democratic President Truman and "traitorous" Democrats in general, had particularly serious long-range political consequences. By crippling the Truman presidency and providing the impetus for Senator McCarthy's communist witch-hunt, it sent a grim warning to future Democratic presidents tempted to palter with communism abroad. Democrats as much as conservative Republicans became locked into a rigid foreign policy stance that precluded subtle and informed analysis of local political conditions in far-flung countries and foreclosed on suitably graduated responses.[30] The political contest became absolutized as one between the forces of good, under American leadership, and the forces of what Ronald Reagan would one day call "the Evil Empire." It was a mortal contest in which American leaders could not afford to falter or show weakness. If fear and vigilance had some unfortunate side-effects at home, most notably the McCarthyism that embittered domestic politics for a generation, this was surely a forgivable aberration in view of the larger picture. There could be no doubt where real evil was located in the world.

Yet mutual possession by America and the Soviet Union of growing arsenals of nuclear missiles ensured that it was an evil that could not be directly confronted except with the gravest danger to oneself and to all life on earth. If evil could not be destroyed in its lair, however, it might be contained there and stopped from spreading. America was determined that there would be no more Chinas. It was worth a bitter, costly war to keep communism north of the 39th parallel in Korea. It was necessary to support friendly regimes, even corrupt ones, in South-East Asia or Latin America to prevent their fall to insurgents self-identified as communists. To surrender at even one point would be to strengthen and encourage an enemy – perceived as singular and monolithic – who was ready to take advantage of any weakness to topple province after province (the logic of the famous "domino theory" that guided American foreign policy in this period). At stake in a nuclear world was American "credibility," the country's ability to use its great power for its defense and the achievement of its global goals, and to credibility attached not only national security but national pride and national honor.[31] The mortal contest would thus be conducted by proxy in small, underdeveloped nations all over the world whose very poverty made them ripe for communist takeover.

In this cosmic struggle, the charismatic Kennedy became, by virtue of words and deeds, the iconic type of the heroic Cold Warrior. It hardly mattered that his stirring rhetoric was often somewhat divorced from

---

[30] Michael H. Hunt has emphasized the influence here of the popular 1958 book, *The Ugly American* by William J. Lederer and Eugene Burdick. See his *Lyndon Johnson's War: America's Cold War Crusade in Vietnam, 1945–1968* (New York, Hill and Wang, 1996), chapter 1.

[31] On the development of the "doctrine of credibility," see Jonathon Schell, *The Time of Illusion* (New York, Knopf, 1975).

political reality; America's leadership of the "Free World" and his own telegenic appeal combined to make him the ideal representative not just of Americans but of non-communist peoples everywhere. Ironically, Kennedy had hoped as president to defuse nuclear tensions by establishing better relations with the allegedly mortal foe – his vow to combat the scourge of war itself virtually required such an aim. But his own action and rhetoric stimulated the natural assertiveness of the highly competitive Soviet Premier Nikita Khruschev. There was tension in Europe over Berlin, where the communists threw up a Wall to divide East physically from West ("*Ich bin ein Berliner,*" Kennedy grandly and implausibly cried on his way to a Moscow summit), and crisis in Cuba, on America's very doorstep, where Castro had allied himself firmly with the Soviets. The discovery of Soviet missiles in Cuba produced a critical face-off between a Russian fleet attempting to deliver nuclear warheads to arm them and an American fleet ordered by Kennedy to stop them. In this nuclear version of *High Noon*, Khrushchev "blinked" and withdrew, and the world gave a huge collective sigh of relief. Behind the scenes, however, implicit deals had been done. The stakes were too high for either side to eschew horse-trading, but American domestic politics demanded that there be no (visible) compromise with evil.[32]

It was, in the public's eye at any rate, Kennedy's finest hour, and it put an heroic stamp on his Cold War leadership. It was true that by late 1963 Kennedy's administration, deadlocked by a conservative Congress, was looking decidedly moribund and failing to live up to its initial promise, but his assassination in November changed the mood instantly. His death was immediately translated into the death of the moral hero. He had aroused the admiration and hope of the world, he had stood for liberal social reform at home and freedom abroad, and he had had the stomach to take the world to the very brink in defiance of evil. His murder was thus a tragic and deeply shocking event, and it presaged the cracking of the American dream of peculiar innocence.

[32] See James G. Blight and David A. Welsh, *On the Brink: Americans and Soviets Reexamine the Cuban Missile Crisis* (New York, Hill and Wang, 1989).

8   Crisis

Wicked people bring a like quality to their positions of honor, and stain
them with their infection.   Boethius, *The Consolation of Philosophy*

The legacy of John Fitzgerald Kennedy has been the subject of massive
scholarship and disagreement, but in this chapter I want to draw attention
to three principal parts of it that played central, and interconnected, roles
in the American loss of moral capital: one was the symbolic legacy of
continuity and connection with the martyred president; the second was
the legacy of the assassination itself and the general suspicion it aroused;
and the third was the political legacy of reform at home combined with
anti-communist action abroad, most crucially in Vietnam.

The symbolic legacy

One aspect of the symbolic legacy was the astonishingly enduring hope
for a rebirth of that shining moment of Camelot in the person of another
Kennedy, a hope that, though dwindling, was not wholly extinguished
until the death of JFK Jr. in a plane crash in 1999. (It was a hope that
showed once again the potential transmissibility of certain forms of moral
capital to *bona fide* inheritors.) But the symbolic legacy also affected
Kennedy's successors and their views of the possible role and purposes of
the presidency itself. Assassination had inevitably enlarged Kennedy's
heroic status to semi-mythical proportions, and in its dramatic aftermath
his immediate successor, Lyndon B. Johnson, felt it expedient to bolster
and legitimize his authority by emphasizing continuity with the Kennedy
administration (though his own relationship with Kennedy had been
abysmal). He not only adopted and extended its social and foreign
policies and the conflicts inherent within them, but retained key Kennedy
advisers like McGeorge Bundy, Dean Rusk and Robert McNamara with
ultimately disastrous consequences.[1] Nixon, in his turn, was obsessed

---

[1] See Moya Ann Ball, "The Phantom in the Oval Office: The John F. Kennedy Assassination's Symbolic Impact on Lyndon B. Johnson, His Key Advisers, and the Vietnam

with the image of presidential leadership that his old rival for the presidency had bequeathed, craving the adulation given to Kennedy and desperate to be seen as at least the equal of Kennedy in terms of heroic leadership.[2] Virtually every president (or presidential aspirant) thereafter felt constrained to respond in some fashion to the dominating image of Kennedy. Democrats in particular sought to rekindle the presidential fire that Kennedy had lit, or at least to associate themselves with his myth through their speeches, appearance or programs.[3]

The assassination legacy

The irony of the symbolic legacy was that it was itself deeply implicated in the progressive disheartening of America. An important element in this was the legacy of the political assassination itself which set an unhappy modern precedent for other attempts, successful in the cases of Martin Luther King and Robert Kennedy, unsuccessful in the case of Ronald Reagan. It produced a climate where democratic leaders needed a virtual praetorian guard to ensure security and where a Colin Powell, who could well have been the nation's first black president, was reportedly dissuaded from running because of his family's fear for his life. Worse, it contributed to a general sense that something was deeply wrong with America. ("I used to love my country," a young Divinity student said to me after the death of Bobby Kennedy, "but now I hate it. We kill all our best people.") It was a feeling heightened by the miasma of suspicion that eventually arose around the Kennedy killing and also that of King. There is no need to rehearse the endless speculations, theories and "proofs" adduced in articles, books and movies that began to flow after 1967,[4] nor to consider their credibility or lack of it. The point is that the dissatisfaction with the single-assassin account became, in both cases,

Decision-Making Process," *Presidential Studies Quarterly* 24(1) (1994), pp. 105–119; also Ball, *Vietnam-on-the-Potomac* (New York, Praeger, 1992).

[2] For an account of the relationship between Nixon and Kennedy see Christopher Matthews, *Nixon and Kennedy: The Rivalry that Shaped Cold War America* (New York, Simon & Schuster, 1996). See also Jon Roper, "Richard Nixon's Political Hinterland: The Shadows of JFK and Charles de Gaulle," *Presidential Studies Quarterly* 28(2) (Spring 1998), pp. 422–435.

[3] See Paul R. Henggeler, *The Kennedy Persuasion: American Presidential Politics Since JFK* (Chicago, I. R. Dee, 1995) (expanded version of his 1991 book, *In His Steps: Lyndon Johnson and the Kennedy Mystique*).

[4] The flood was started with the controversy surrounding William Manchester's *Death of a President* (Harper & Row, 1967). Jim Garrison's *On the Trail of the Assassins: My Investigation and Prosecution of the Murder of President Kennedy* (New York, Sheridan Square Press, 1988), turned by Oliver Stone into the movie *JFK* in 1991, was the most commercially successful of the assassination plot books, but there are more than 300 others listed by the John F. Kennedy Library in Boston.

widespread and enduring, and that people became increasingly willing to entertain the thought that dark and complex forces might be at work within their government.[5] Improbable (but conceivable) alliances of Cuban exiles, communist agents, the Mafia, the CIA and even Vice-President Johnson were alleged to have generated devilish plots and murders. The long-range psychological effect of the conspiracy theories was to create the fear that a terrible gulf existed between the external actions of American politics – the schoolbook accounts of how democratic government worked – and the way it really operated. Beneath the surface there appeared to be a play of secret and sinister forces beyond the power of the democracy to control. Congressional investigations would reveal in 1975–76 that US intelligence agencies were indeed guilty of many abuses at home and abroad, thus lending credence to this fear. It would soon become a cliché of fictional thrillers and movies that the bad guys would turn out in the end to be a rogue agency of the government itself. In such an atmosphere, the traditional repositories of public trust became increasingly suspect.

These developments played a part in undermining the symbolic legacy of Kennedy, for the revelations of a gap between public image and internal reality went right to the top. The literature on the president himself up until 1970 had been mostly commemorative and laudatory, dominated by keepers of the flame like Schlesinger and Theodore Sorensen (the latter was Kennedy's speech-writer, who said of the Kennedy legacy that it could be no more summed up in a book "than a Mozart concerto can be summed up by . . . black notes on white score paper").[6] The release of the first Kennedy papers in 1969 in the midst of the Vietnam maelstrom inaugurated a substantial revisionist historiography. A different and disillusioning picture of the hero began to emerge. He was: a virtual invalid kept going by injections of corticosteroids and amphetamines; an obsessive womanizer incapable of emotional connection with women; a man with Mafia connections, whose election in 1960 had been bought with the help of gangsters; a man as fatally seduced by seedy underworld glamor as by the glitter of the Hollywood stars he befriended and bedded; a man who condoned and perhaps ordered assassination attempts of leaders in Cuba, South Vietnam, the Congo and the Dominican Republic; a man who had put the world at hazard by himself bringing on the Cuban missile crisis through his obsession with overthrowing Castro; and a man who, far from pushing civil rights, had incurred the permanent contempt of Martin Luther King for his dilatori-

[5] An exception was Gerald Posner's *Case Closed* (New York, Random House, 1993), the only book to argue that Oswald was the lone assassin.
[6] Theodore C. Sorensen, *The Kennedy Legacy* (New York, Macmillan, 1969), p. 18.

ness and cowardice in confronting the Dixiecrats.[7] Part of Nixon's fascination with Kennedy, it turns out, lay in the latter's ability to get away with dirty tricks while maintaining a pristine image, and much of Nixon's bitterness was the differential treatment he felt he received for his own similar, and perhaps lesser, crimes.[8]

The sullying of the Kennedy myth was general. Robert was implicated with his brother in most of the above allegations, but the entire Kennedy clan was variously impugned. The patriarchal father, Joseph, was an ex-Nazi sympathizer, political briber and all-round bastard who, among other things, goaded his sons to compete in sexual conquests. Edward, next-in-line for the succession after Bobby, was undone by the womanizing learnt at his father's knee when an accident connected with a sexual liaison at Chappaquiddick effectively ruined his chance ever to be president. America's love affair with widow-heroine Jackie ended abruptly when she married Greek billionaire Aristotle Onassis, and disenchantment was deepened by stories of compulsive spending that strained even that plutocrat's pocket and patience. Seldom has the disparity between beautiful facade and sordid interior been so dramatically exposed as in the case of the Kennedys. Given the attendant disillusionment, it was perhaps not to be expected that faith in the nation's "best and brightest" would ever again be so readily and innocently invested. But there were larger forces involved in this disillusionment that multiplied the effect.

The legacy of reform at home: anti-communism abroad

The obsessive chipping at the Kennedy shrine began in, and was significantly stimulated by, a national atmosphere radically different from that which Kennedy himself had inhaled. It was the era of Johnson, Nixon and the trauma of Vietnam, of the clash of a "counter-culture" with the shocked, confused, resistant core of conservative America. And this era too was part of the Kennedy legacy, or more accurately of that Cold War

[7] Just a few of the books making such allegations/revelations are: Thomas Reeves, *A Question of Character: A Life of John F. Kennedy* (London, Bloomsbury, 1991); Richard Reeves, *President Kennedy* (New York, Simon & Schuster, 1993); Seymour Hersh, *The Dark Side of Camelot* (New York, HarperCollins, 1998); Thomas G. Paterson (ed.), *Kennedy's Quest for Victory: American Foreign Policy, 1961–1963* (New York, Oxford University Press, 1989); Aleksand Fursenko and Timothy Naftali, *"One Hell of a Gamble": Khrushchev, Castro and Kennedy* (New York, Murray, 1997); Ernest May and Philip Zelikow (eds.), *The Kennedy Tapes: Inside the White House During the Cuban Missile Crisis* (Harvard University Press, 1997); Taylor Branch, *Pillar of Fire: America in the King Years* (New York, Simon & Schuster, 1998).

[8] According to Henry Kissinger, Nixon spent hours every week ruminating on the ruthless tactics and gimmicks he believed had made the Kennedys so formidable; *The Years of Upheaval* (Boston, Little, Brown, 1982), p. 1182.

legacy transmitted through and symbolically embodied in Kennedy. During Johnson's term the threat from the Soviets appeared to be receding and the Chinese–Soviet split made the enemy seem less monolithic. But old patterns of thought persisted, and Washington remained deeply concerned about communist China and its support for revolutionary movements worldwide. A new containment policy now settled on China and its clients in South-East Asia. America had maintained a low-level involvement in South-East Asia since 1950, but JFK had increased American military support (in the shape of some 16,000 "advisers") to Laos and South Vietnam to prop up regimes under threat from nationalist insurgents backed by China. Kennedy-philes would later argue that their hero would never have committed America to a major war in Vietnam, and it was true that he was unhappy about involvement there. Nevertheless, Lyndon Johnson, responding to the ongoing weakness and failure of South Vietnamese regimes, was continuing and furthering a process already begun by Kennedy.

Johnson, the big Texan, was at least as macho a Cold Warrior as his predecessor and much more determined to get his "fellas" out into the jungles of Vietnam to "whip hell out of some communists." He wanted to prevent the Chinese and "the fellas in the Kremlin" from thinking Americans were "yellow and don't mean what we say."[9] But Johnson merely wanted to win the war as rapidly and decisively as possible so he could concentrate on his domestic program. He was in truth no happier than Kennedy about the Vietnamese entanglement, and was presciently warned in 1964 of the likely consequences of escalation by his own Under-Secretary of State, George Ball. The White House tapes revealed, many years later, that even as he drove relentlessly on with the military build-up in Vietnam, Johnson thought that country "the biggest damn mess" he ever saw and not worth fighting for.[10] However, he had surrounded himself with Kennedy men resolutely committed to their master's course, and there was always Robert Kennedy, the man LBJ feared most, waiting in the Democratic wings should Johnson stumble. Most important, though, was the memory of Truman, China and McCarthyism, which haunted Johnson as it had haunted Kennedy. What would Congress and the country do to a president who showed himself "soft on communism"? Johnson could not afford to "lose" Vietnam to the mortal enemy as Truman had "lost" China. The rigidified American virtue identified with anti-communism thus led the nation into a decade of

[9] Cited in Michael H. Hunt, *Lyndon Johnson's War: America's Cold War Crusade in Vietnam, 1945–1968* (New York, Hill and Wang, 1996), p. 79.
[10] Michael Beschloss (ed.), *Taking Charge: The Johnson White House Tapes* (New York, Simon & Schuster, 1997). Reported in *New York Times*, 18 March 1997, p. 12.

destructive and futile warfare that would induce a loss of faith in American virtue and provoke something like a revolution at home.

Johnson failed to take his courage in his hands and withdraw because he dreamed of domestic glory through the expansion of Kennedy's reform program. Johnson's Great Society project was made feasible by his landslide victory in the 1964 elections which had also greatly strengthened the liberal Democratic contingent in the House of Representatives, but he knew it would be destroyed in the political furore that Republicans would foment if he abandoned Vietnam. The terrible irony for Johnson was that the necessary price of his domestic program was commitment in Vietnam, while the escalating cost and distraction of the war inevitably crippled that program which fizzled after the first astonishing burst of achievement in 1964–65. He might have solved the problem by doing as the Pentagon urged and asking Congress for a tax increase in 1966, thus covering the costs of both war and reform, but here the inherent weakness of the presidency came into play. Johnson had spent a large part of the previous year and a vast amount of political capital persuading Congress to grant a tax *cut*, and he had not the heart to recommence the enervating process of seeking a reversal – and probably could not have got the votes if he had.[11] Unable to relinquish either his Great Society or the war, he pursued inflationary spending that would have dire economic consequences in the 1970s, while feeling compelled to hide the full truth of the situation from the public and from Congress.

It was also lack of presidential power – the power to declare war without Congressional approval – that led Johnson to use deception to achieve escalation of American military commitment in Vietnam. The device he employed (used only moderately by previous presidents) involved seeking a "blank check" from Congress for the contingent use of force in an area where American interests had been threatened by a local disturbance. In 1964, an "incident" of North Vietnamese aggression in the Tonkin Gulf provided the pretext, and on the strength of it Johnson gained nearly unanimous Congressional approval for whatever action he deemed necessary. He used the Tonkin Gulf resolution to pursue, not the limited action Congress had envisaged, but what was in effect an undeclared war. Resentment at this trickery when it was finally revealed fed into growing antiwar sentiment, stimulating moves by Congress to assert some of the constitutional prerogatives in foreign policy it had hitherto largely ceded to the executive. Thus the actions of the so-called Imperial Presidency

[11] Geoffrey Hodgson, *All Things to All Men: The False Promise of the Modern American Presidency* (London, Weidenfeld and Nicolson, 1980), p. 48. See also Richard E. Neustadt, *Presidential Power and the Modern Presidents: The Politics of Leadership from Roosevelt to Reagan* (New York, Free Press, 1990), pp. 210–211.

provoked a Congressional reaction aimed at curtailing presidential powers in the only arena that imperial powers could be displayed, foreign affairs.

Johnson's deceptions did not cease with this initial piece of trickery. In an effort to protect his domestic objectives, he went on for as long as he could concealing from both the legislature and the public the real extent and cost of America's deepening military involvement during 1964–65. Likewise, he systematically obscured the infuriating failure of South Vietnamese governments, enmeshed in their own internecine conflicts, to establish a viable nation capable of standing on its own feet and fighting its own fights. Secrecy no doubt came naturally to LBJ, but concealment and deception were also an integral part of Cold War mentality and its obsession with espionage. Former presidents, not least Kennedy, had been just as cavalier as Johnson about deceiving Congress when it suited them, and he, as former Democratic Senate majority leader, knew better than most the capacity of Congress to frustrate presidential action. But in the bitter atmosphere created by Vietnam, deceptive executive conduct created strong congressional antipathy and suspicion that would lead, in Nixon's time, to attempts to monitor more closely the secret activities of the executive and its intelligence agencies.

Johnson's strategy of deception bought him short-term political maneuverability at the price of long-term erosion of public and Congressional confidence. Not all his considerable cunning, blustering and bullying could in the end conceal the fact that America was hopelessly stuck in the quicksands of Vietnam. In the end his presidency would sink in the quagmire, but the cost was not only Johnson's. According to Brian VanDeMark, Johnson's strategy of concealment:

tarnished the presidency and damaged popular faith in American government for more than a decade . . . LBJ's decision, however human, tragically undermined the reciprocal faith between President and public indispensable to effective governance in a democracy. Just as tragically, it fostered a pattern of presidential behavior which led his successor, Richard Nixon, to eventual ruin amid even greater popular alienation.[12]

To this I would enter the caveats that Nixon's model was Kennedy as much as Johnson, and that the American loss of faith cannot be explained simply by reference to Johnson's and Nixon's concealments and crimes, causally important though these were. The dereliction of a successive pair of delinquent incumbents should not, I have argued, necessarily seriously

[12] Brian VanDeMark, *Into the Quagmire: Lyndon Johnson and the Escalation of the Vietnam War* (New York, Oxford University Press, 1988), p. 217. See also Doris Kearns, *Lyndon Johnson and the American Dream* (New York, Alfred A. Knopf, 1976); and Robert A. Caro, *The Years of Lyndon Johnson* (2 vols., New York, Knopf, 1982–84).

affect the moral capital of the office itself unless larger forces are at work, as indeed they were here. The sullying of the Kennedy myth and the general suspicion raised about government and its agencies were an important part of the larger disillusioning process, and so was, connectedly but distinctly, the profound impact of the war itself on the American conscience.

Vietnam

In February 2000, William Cohen became the first US defense secretary to visit Vietnam since the Nixon era. A month later, on the twenty-fifth anniversary of the war's end, television channels, magazines and newspapers all over America ran reflective pieces of a generally reconciliatory tone. According to teachers, the war had become forgotten history for most students, while Richard Haas of the Brookings Institution noted that there were few attempts now to understand the lessons of Vietnam.[13] It seemed that the American people had finally laid to rest the ghosts of the most divisive and traumatizing conflict that America had suffered since the Civil War. Indeed the moral effects of Vietnam were arguably much deeper and more scarring than those of the nineteenth-century conflict which, for all its tragedy and suffering, was at least ennobled by the sacred causes of Union and liberty. The Civil War could in good faith be commemorated in triumph as well as sorrow (if we exclude the feelings of an embittered and defeated South). The Vietnam memorial wall in Washington, visited by tens of thousands of people each year, was by way of contrast a site of grief, painful regret and still-lingering confusion and anger.

Part of the lasting injury was, understandably, to American pride. George Ball had warned LBJ in July 1965 that a long protracted war would expose US weakness, but Johnson had worried about the loss of national credibility if he failed to honor commitments to South Vietnam. Ball had responded: "The worse blow would be that the mightiest power in the world is unable to defeat guerillas."[14] And so it happened: the richest, most powerful nation the world has ever seen was humbled in Vietnam by a backward but tenacious peasant people, the North Vietnamese, and their southern guerilla allies, the Viet Cong.

Vietnam revealed how far American pride had turned into outright arrogance on the part of both military and political elites. For too long these elites persisted in the optimistic belief that American power must

[13] Martin Kettle, "25 Years On, the US Lays Vietnam War to Rest," *The Age* (reprinted from *Guardian*), 28 April 2000, p. 12.
[14] Box 1, Meeting Notes File, Johnson Papers, cited in Hunt, *Lyndon Johnson's War*, p. 103.

necessarily prevail in the end. As the war continued, dispatches from the front and from policy-makers in Washington declared repeatedly that the corner had at last been turned, the end was in sight. Victory was forever at hand and forever postponed, but the tone of optimism remained; "pacified" villages and regions were exhibited and the infamous body count adduced to demonstrate the enemy's superior and unsustainable losses and hence its ultimate, inevitable defeat. This continual prevarication eventually engendered mistrust at home as the returning body bags mounted. Defenders of the war (most notably Commanding General Westmoreland) liked to say after the event that Vietnam, the first television war, was lost by media which portrayed even American–South Vietnamese victories (for instance, the 1968 Tet offensive) as defeats. In fact the bulk of the media dutifully purveyed the official line on the conflict for several years, adopting a more critical tone only after public sentiment at home began to turn significantly against the war in 1967.

Americans eventually became divided on the war, sometimes within themselves. (Bob Hope could get a massive, ironic cheer from troops in Vietnam with the line: "I've come over here to assure you guys that the country is 50 percent behind you.") Whether or not one thought United States involvement wise or necessary, the fact that it *was* involved meant national pride was irrevocably at stake. Many argued, therefore, that superior firepower should be backed with the necessary will and confidence to finish the job. But confidence was severely dented in Vietnam, and the inability to attain a victory meant inevitable injury to the national pride. Humiliation is hard to bear even when it is salutary, as McNamara would later claim it was in Vietnam. The damage done to US pride would have long-range effects that were inextricably bound up with long-term moral effects of the conflict. Such moral effects went well beyond regret for the sin of overweening arrogance.

Being bloodied and frustrated by a pygmy nation was an offense to pride, but why was the giant pounding at the pygmy in the first place? Because the pygmy was not really a pygmy but just one extended tentacle of a vast and monstrous foe licking malignantly at a small, independent and relatively weak nation that the leader of the Free World was obliged to defend. American virtue (as transfigured in rigid anti-communism) was engaged here as much as American pride and power. Except that South Vietnam with its corrupt, feuding, incompetent leaders was a poor excuse for an innocent victim, and the indigenous struggle was as much a national one with local historical roots as an instance of creeping global communist menace. Had South Vietnam been capable of establishing itself as a genuine and viable State with widespread popular support it might all have been different, but it was not. The result was that American pride and American virtue were not only independently injured in Vietnam, but severed from one another with damaging results.

The political failure of successive South Vietnamese regimes meant that loyalty was always uncertain at best among the local population. It became famously difficult for American troops and their allies to distinguish innocent friend from deadly foe, to tell Charlie from a peasant girl in black pyjamas who might, after all, be the same person. The trouble with communists was that they did not necessarily sport badges or share a particular skin color. The safest bet for frightened soldiers in a dangerous situation where everyone looked much the same seemed to be a general presumption of enmity. Where discrimination between friend and enemy was so difficult, violence itself tended to become indiscriminate. Though there was much talk of winning hearts and minds in South Vietnam, coercion often seemed the surer route. The remark of one senior American commander engaged in "resettling" peasants to deny the sanctuary of their villages to the Viet Cong – "Grab 'em by the balls and their hearts and minds will follow" – was perhaps less the expression of a callously cynical military mind than a reflection of the general frustration and moral confusion that reigned on the ground. In Vietnam, American anti-communism shaded into American racism: a slope was a slope and a gook was a gook. Friend or enemy, they were all the responsible for American boys dying miserable deaths in paddies, villages and jungles thousands of miles from home. It was an atmosphere in which massacres like that at My Lai – merely the most publicized of American atrocities – were almost bound to happen. (Significantly, when cameraman Ronald Haeberle, present at the massacre, showed his harrowing photographs to civic organizations in Cleveland, people refused to believe it. "They said Americans wouldn't do this," he noted.)[15]

War, we may safely assume, is always brutalizing, obscene and liable to atrocities, redeemed, if at all, only by necessity and a cause believed to be worth killing and dying for. But as more and more troops and materiel were committed to Vietnam, apparently to little effect, the necessity and high moral purpose of the war were increasingly questioned and doubted. The words of a popular song – "One, two, three/What are we fighting for?" – summed up the gathering mood. As the conviction grew among many that the war was wrong, American carpet bombing, napalming, strafing and the incidents of all the "dirty little war stories"[16] that

[15] Cited in Tom Engelhardt, *The End of Victory Culture: Cold War America and the Disillusioning of a Generation* (New York, Basic Books, 1995), p. 219. Note that Engelhardt's central theme in this book parallels my own, though he pursues the disillusioning process through an examination of the mythology of what he calls the "American war story," largely using an analysis of cultural materials like books, films and television shows.

[16] The phrase is Michael Herr's from *Dispatches* (London, Picador, 1978).

circulated back home began to appear radically unredeemed and un-redeemable. And in this lay the real moral shock and the long-term moral effect of Vietnam for America. Americans, as well as being on the winning side, were supposed by definition to be on the *right* side. They were the good guys – tough, of course, but good. This was the disillusionment that veteran-against-the-war Ron Kovic pointed to when he began his book, *Born on the Fourth of July*, with the assertion that John Wayne had cost him his legs.[17] The image of the tough-but-decent, heroically dutiful sergeant storming the beaches of Iwo Jima in a just and necessary cause, there to meet a sad but ennobling death, was belied or betrayed in Vietnam (and Wayne's own Vietnam film, *The Green Berets*, that attempted to impose the traditional image of American virtue on the conflict, merely looked laughably anachronistic).

At home, the developing counter-culture of students, hippies, dropouts and potheads focused much of its moral energy on the "crime" of Vietnam. Part of the stimulus for its general rejection of inherited mores was the shock of discovery that peculiar American virtue and innocence were after all only a myth, that in Vietnam Americans could be the bad guys. A wave of sudden cynicism swept the culture. "Violence," it was discovered "was as American as apple pie." The West, that prime repository of the mythology of American virtue, was reinterpreted. Far from being the glorious settlement by heroic and virtuous individuals of a virgin land, it was a savage dispossession of the native peoples wrought by violence and massacre – My Lai, it seemed, was nothing new. American racism was general and ineradicable according to the new radical black movements that, to President Johnson's bafflement and dismay, seemed to bite the hand that fed them their civil rights. If some of these movements turned to violence, then it was justified as a response to an "establishment" that was wreaking unjustified violence on a massive scale abroad ("LBJ! LBJ! How many kids have you killed today?"), that felt no compunction about using it at home on citizens taking to the streets in protest. The virulence and anger of the antiwar protests revealed the depth of betrayal and disappointment felt by youth reared on the American myth, who had imbibed the rhetoric and believed the promise of the Kennedy years. Symbolic burnings of flags and draft-cards, and visits to Hanoi by dissenting celebrities, seemed to declare that a noisy segment of the American population had become positively anti-American. Yet it was surely no accident that the love-and-peaceniks with their fantasy of an innocent, anti-materialist, apolitical Eden, realizable if we all tuned in

[17] Ron Kovic, *Born on the Fourth of July* (New York, McGraw-Hill, 1976).

and dropped out, were indulging a different but no less naive version of the American myth. They discarded patriotism because that is what the preservation of virtue seemed to require. They broke with government and national institutions, particularly the presidency, because they believed them to be forces of violence and oppression, thus antithetical to virtue.

There was, of course, a generational issue here that went well beyond the moral crisis of Vietnam, for the sixties divided the generations – parents and children, old and young – on more value issues and at more points than perhaps any era before or since. But by 1968 attitudes to the war had become more than one of mere generational difference, for the numbers of "doves" (people against the war) as opposed to "hawks" from all strata and ages of society had steadily increased. The strength and savagery of the official response to this burgeoning movement, most notoriously displayed at the Chicago Democratic Convention of that year, revealed the hurt and bafflement of heartland America at the apparently unpatriotic rejection of everything it held dear and sacred. A key slogan for this America, voiced by the more reactively combative of its representatives, was the venerable cry of English patriots, "My country, right or wrong!" Yet, in American terms, this was already an admission of defeat, for it accepted the severance of virtue and patriotic pride and thus the shattering of the essential myth.

The clash on the streets, in universities and in homes, between the forces of the establishment and those of the counter-culture (to put the division crudely) was the visible manifestation of this bifurcation. On the one side was a virtue that insisted on challenging an evil policy even at the cost of impugning patriotic pride; on the other a fundamental patriotism that upheld loyalty to country even at the expense of virtue. If patriotic pride had its way, America would not accept military defeat, its first ever, at the hands of a midget nation, but would enlarge its military response (not excluding nuclear weapons, insisted the most hawkish of hawks) until the war was decisively won. If the war had been a "mistake" from the start, well so be it; pride at least would be served. If, on the other hand, virtuous refusal to continue in an evil course held sway and America withdrew with the outcome of the war still in doubt, then virtue would have been purchased at the cost of national pride. This was the dilemma: in Vietnam, Americans found a war where America could not be what its ideology claimed it must be, both victorious and virtuous. Part of the legacy of Vietnam, then, was simple damage to pride, but the essential moral legacy was the radical severing of pride and virtue and the problem of how to put them back together again.

The Nixon–Kissinger "solution"

This was Richard Nixon's central problem when he won election in 1968 promising to end the war and restore "unity." He did not believe the war could be won, but nor did he believe that it was politically possible to tell the American people that it was lost. His solution therefore was to perpetrate a great lie: America could have both victory and virtue by enabling the South Vietnamese to win their own war. The strategy was to scale down American ground troops (thus drastically cutting American casualties) and to rapidly "Vietnamize" the war through intensive training of Army of the Republic of Vietnam (ARVN) soldiers. The process of withdrawal would acknowledge and correct the mistake of having gotten involved in the first place, while Vietnamization would discharge the duties inevitably incurred to an ally who had, whatever the rights and wrongs of the matter, become an American dependant.

Given the condition of South Vietnam, there was in fact scant likelihood that it would be able to hold out against the North for long once America withdrew completely. The final pull-out would inevitably constitute a betrayal of the South (for, in terms of virtue, this had truly become a no-win situation for the United States). Nixon and his Secretary of State, Kissinger, nevertheless determinedly pursued the fiction for four years because they needed a plausible scenario to provide a semblance of respectability to their withdrawal. They mendaciously assured the American people that the war was being won at the same time as, to maintain American "credibility" in the face of a withdrawal,[18] they extended it into Cambodia and Laos and intensified the bombing, trying to force the North into serious negotiations about a ceasefire, borders and other arrangements. Tellingly, when Nixon's Democratic opponent in the 1972 election, George McGovern, presented a scheme for ending the war that was identically but honestly the one that Nixon would soon negotiate, Nixon labeled it a "peace with surrender."[19] When the settlement was at last agreed in January 1973 – on condition of complete US withdrawal and release of all POWs – Nixon declared it, on the contrary, a "peace with honor." Fighting in Vietnam, of course, scarcely paused. The South's cause was finally, irrevocably doomed when the United States drastically cut its continuing military aid in August 1974, causing ARVN morale to plummet instantly. In 1975 the country was overrun. The last remaining Americans ignominiously

[18] Schell pronounced this strategy "one of the purest applications of the American doctrine of credibility"; *The Time of Illusion*, p. 307.
[19] See Kathleen Hall Jamieson, *Packaging the Presidency: A History and Criticism of Presidential Campaign Advertising* (3rd edn., New York, Oxford University Press, 1996), p. 315.

evacuated Saigon in helicopters while hordes of their erstwhile friends and allies scrambled, mostly hopelessly, to be among them. In these closing scenes of the long drama, American "honor" appeared hollow indeed.

In the White House, it was now President Ford (along with the lingering Kissinger) who watched in an agony of shame. For by then Nixon had suffered his own downfall, the cause of which is usually summed up in the word "Watergate." There was, however, much more to it than the detection of Nixon's "plumbers" burgling and wiretapping Democratic National Committee headquarters and the revelation of the subsequent cover-up of the president's own involvement. In the Watergate affair, all the political chickens set running in the years since Kennedy's assassination returned to roost, and they returned to the White House.

It was during Nixon's tenure that post-war America's moral-ideological firmament really began to crack, as formerly stalwart ideologues began to take a more sophisticated view of an altered reality. Nixon, a Republican politician who had founded his career on efficient and zealous anti-communism, who had dreamed of surpassing Kennedy as the nation's leading Cold Warrior, this same Nixon pursued as president a policy of détente with the allegedly implacable enemy. Under Kissinger's influence, he laid aside the notion of the mortal conflict and the too-expensive doctrine of containment and embraced a nineteenth-century *realpolitik* vision of a balance of power that could ensure peaceful co-existence. In 1972, in his greatest foreign relations coup, Nixon visited China and opened the way to normalization of relations between that country and the US. He also opened strategic arms limitation talks with the Soviets, visited Moscow, addressed the Russian people on television, and signed trade, science and cultural agreements.

These were laudable initiatives in a nuclear world, but their rationale reduced the ideological, winner-takes-all contest for global domination to mere rivalry between powerful States which, however different their creeds, shared common problems and interests precisely *as* States, including interests in a stable environment. And if co-existence with the old rival was possible, even necessary, then the last shred of the original justification for involvement in Vietnam – the implacable anti-communism of which Nixon had been so vocal and effective an exponent – dissolved. Nixon, paradoxically, was committed to fighting communism in a tiny South-East Asian country while simultaneously extending the hand of friendship to the great rival centers of world communism. Yet the war went on, and it went on too long. The problem with Nixon's construction of a plausible scenario for honorable withdrawal was that the weakness of the Saigon regime and the tenacity of the one in Hanoi made it a very extended process, leaving ample space for continuing opposition by the press, congressmen, college students and black and white radical groups. The incursion of American and South Vietnamese forces into Cambodia and Laos brought criticism for widening the war. The Cambodian incursion in particular sparked massive antiwar rallies and seemingly endless campus clashes with authorities, in one of which, at Kent State in 1970, four students were shot and killed, provoking national revulsion and further unrest.

It was highly significant that Nixon regarded all this criticism as akin to disloyalty, and responded to it vindictively with illicit covert operations against innumerable persons categorized as threats to national security. It was a reaction that seemed to suggest where Nixon stood in relation to the question of national pride versus national virtue: if people protesting against what they sincerely believed to be an immoral national policy were to be branded "disloyal," then pride appeared to outrank virtue. But this was not how Nixon saw it. For him the virtue that had once attached to anti-communism was now transferred to his grand plan for peace through power-balance and ideological co-existence, a shift largely applauded by the public. Yet, while he was busy trying to make the world a safer place for Americans, elements in the nation seemed intent on tearing the country apart from within. Protests, sometimes violent, by the war's opponents and by black radicals threatened, in Nixon's view, the very stability and existence of the Republic, making the protesters virtual traitors.

Nixon appealed to and tried to mobilize the "silent majority" of Americans that he claimed disagreed with the vocal minority, but this strategy merely highlighted and reinforced the deep division that had opened up in society. It was a division that even in Nixon's terms was one between those who put loyalty to their country first and those who did not, the latter pursuing instead a misguided and destructive moral imperative to stop the war unconditionally. It was a strategy that reproduced the dilemma of faith in the American myth without solving it. Nixon felt that the rightness of his global strategy made the virtue of the administration unquestionable, justifying the great lie which offered the illusion of victory and of virtue as a political solution to the now anomalous situation in Vietnam. The trouble with this was that, whether in illusion or in reality, the great lie was incapable of satisfying, far less re-uniting, *either* of the terms of the pride–virtue equation. There was precious little virtue to be found in the long continuance of a war for which no good ideological justification or national interest could any longer be advanced; and precious little pride to be gained in dropping more bombs than had been dropped in all of World War II on a small, backward country that remained, in spite of that, defiantly belligerent.

In the presidential election of 1972, Nixon rested his campaign on his presidential dignity, on his undoubted status as a statesman promoting world peace, and on conservative domestic policies that were widely approved. The imminent end of American involvement in the war had induced a relative calm in the exhausted nation which enabled him to present himself, too, as the restorer of national normality and presidential legitimacy. He won a huge victory over perceivedly ultraliberal McGovern (though without "coat-tails," the Democrats gaining majorities in both houses). Beneath the surface of apparently restored normality, however, the rot of the Nixon presidency was already well advanced. A paranoid culture of secrecy and suspicion had long reigned in the White House, mirroring the worst aspects of Nixon's complex character and reinforced by the closed, hierarchical organization of a White House staff dominated by men deficient in political, not to say moral, sensibility. Yet this culture was also a manifestation of the syndrome that had afflicted previous presidencies, namely, an approach to foreign policy that instinctively resorted to deceit. Nixon was to pay an even dearer price for it than Johnson. His great lie had necessitated further lies to Congress and the people – about the extent of the bombing in Vietnam, about Laos and Cambodia, and about the weakness of South Vietnam. Constrained to maintain the web of deception about matters abroad and faced with virulent opposition at home, the administration grew obsessed with secrecy, believing itself beleaguered by enemies of doubtful loyalty who would scupper its grand strategy unless forestalled.[20] Indicative of the climate in the Oval Office was Nixon's never implemented "Huston plan," which envisaged the formation of a kind of secret political police force. His "plumbers' unit," an incompetent team of shady special investigators set up to stop foreign policy leaks, was also used to find material to discredit people identified as opponents. It was working on behalf of the Committee to Re-elect the President when it broke into the Watergate building and started the chain of events that led to Nixon's ultimate disgrace and resignation.

The hurt that Nixon caused the presidency involved a heavy irony, for no president had a more exalted, not to say exaggerated, conception of the respect that should be accorded the office *per se*. He wanted to augment the power of that office so that it matched his conception of its prestige – to convert, in Schlesinger's words, the imperial presidency abroad into the revolutionary presidency at home by asserting an expanded presidential prerogative against Congress.[21] In other words, he

[20] Schlesinger, *The Imperial Presidency*, pp. 380–338, conveys the surreal White House atmosphere.
[21] Congress resented many other things, not least Nixon's frequent assertion of "executive

attempted not only to reunite the sundered elements of the American myth but also to correct one of the factors that had been responsible for the original damage: presidential weakness. But Nixon's attempts to shift the constitutional balance of authority toward the presidency only strengthened congressional resolve to clip the imperial wings, and also meant that sympathy for the president was thin on the ground when charges of illegality were added to those of unconstitutionality. Since Nixon (and his sometime Vice-President Spiro Agnew) had also bitterly attacked the press and tried by fair means and foul to curtail its powers, the scent of blood in Watergate was pursued by some of its representatives with more zeal than might otherwise have been the case – with well-known consequences. Watergate effectively gave birth to that combative and intrusive press that has been the plague of politicians ever since.

It was notable that almost all of Nixon's attempts to extend the presidential prerogative were justified on grounds of "national security." The fact that national security often came down to protecting the president by concealing his more dubious activities was perhaps less indicative of an instinct for petty chicanery than of Nixon's surreal identification of his presidency with the last defensive stronghold of American virtue. The problem with the silent majority was precisely that it *was* silent, leaving the task of defense to the only person that could speak politically for all the American people – the *real* American people of the conservative heartland. The Republic that Nixon represented in his person was in danger, and only he could reliably defend it against its enemies in the colleges and the streets (where they shouted at him), in the Congress (where they obstructed him), in the permanent government in Washington (whose habitués had never accepted him), and even in his own cabinet and staff (where members sometimes showed too delicate and scrupulous a sensibility for the hard task at hand). Defense of the great cause justified, for Nixon, that deviousness and ruthlessness whose practice he had so much admired in the Kennedys. Yet, when the means he had used were brought to light, the American public on whose behalf he had allegedly employed them failed to understand (and Nixon always felt himself the most misunderstood of men). The people refused to see the larger picture and were simply dismayed because there was a crook in the White House. Their trust in the president, in the presidency itself, plummeted.

privilege" and his use of the power of "impoundment" of funds voted by Congress for policy programs not to his liking, the exercise, in effect, of a veto on Congress' constitutional use of the money power.

Conclusion

Theodore White claimed that Nixon's breach of faith had "destroyed the myth that binds America together," the myth that "somewhere in American life there is at least one man who stands for law, the President." Of the president's three main duties, he says – as chief executive, as policy-maker and as High Priest – the one that Nixon forgot or failed to recognize was his priestly function as custodian of the faith.[22] My argument is rather that the central myth was of the essential and compatible union of American power and virtue, and that a deep fissure had already opened up in that before Nixon came to office. His attempt both to heal the rift and to preserve intact its two elements, at least in appearance, failed; and his misguided reactions to the results of that failure led to numerous breaches of faith which, when revealed, were indeed deeply disillusioning to Americans, increasing their distrust of the presidency. The flaws in Nixon's character undoubtedly played a crucial role, but the larger context in which those flaws were fatally revealed was America's ideological response to the Cold War and the actions of previous presidents in the light of it. The pivotal moral, political and symbolical role of the presidency made it the natural focus of the crisis of faith and confidence that was played out in American life during this period, but the crisis involved much more than just a loss of the moral capital of the presidency or of individual presidents. At stake was the moral capital of the nation itself insofar as this informed the nation's sense of its own rightness and founded its morale.

Nixon's sins and his fall were not the prime causes of the loss of this capital, merely the things that put a definite seal upon it. Nixon inherited a dilemma he could not solve, and which in fact he deepened in trying to solve. His successors faced the difficult task of trying to solve the same dilemma without the benefit of the automatic trust that Americans traditionally accorded their new presidents.

---

[22] Theodore H. White, *Breach of Faith: The Fall of Richard Nixon* (New York, Atheneum Press, 1975), pp. 322 and 338–339.

9 Aftermath

There is only one nation in the world which is capable of true leadership among the community of nations, and that is the United States of America. Jimmy Carter

Nixon was deeply conscious of the centrality of the presidency, not just as a functioning part of the American political system but as the symbolic heart of that system and of the nation itself. He banked on the extraordinary respect normally accorded the office to see him through the "horrors" that began to unfold after April 1973 – the revelations of lies, cover-ups, abuses of power, illegalities, corruption and sheer mean-spiritedness. But Nixon's actions and deceits, like those of Johnson before him, had squandered much of that inherent respect. They had fallen victim of the fact that presidential prestige and the expectations placed on presidents are inadequately matched by presidential power, and succumbed to the omnipresent temptation to circumvent or overcome the legal and constitutional obstacles to action – by deceit, by assertion of novel prerogatives and by illegalities. Faced with difficult and often contradictory political imperatives, they put at hazard the office's moral capital and set in motion events that fractured not just trust in the presidency, but an essential article of American self-faith.

The legacy they left succeeding presidents was, therefore, a complex and unhappy one. As well as all the common difficulties of government and economy that administrations must manage, Nixon's successors had to cope with the problem of national healing. This involved three issues. The first was the issue of trust in government in general, and of the president in particular, and how to restore it; the second was the issue of declining American power and the problem of pride associated with it; and the third, inevitably intertwined with the second, was the loss of innocence and the restoration of American virtue. I will deal with each in turn before examining the different solutions offered by Carter and Reagan.

The problem of trust

The problem of trust manifested itself in many different ways in the years after Nixon. On the legal front, the Watergate experience eventually produced in 1978 an initiative that was to trouble all presidents thereafter. This was, in effect, an act of legislative mistrust that provided for the appointment of independent counsels to investigate illegal actions alleged against presidents. Independent counselors were given a staggeringly wide remit in terms of resources, time, investigative leeway, and powers of subpoena. Once a counsel was appointed to look into a particular allegation of wrongdoing, he or she could choose to follow any other line of inquiry that might arise in the course of it, however far afield. The result was that presidents, their cabinets, their staffs, even their wives and acquaintances became subject to perpetual and multiple independent counsel investigations that dragged on unconscionably, often for years after a presidency had ended.[1] This was an external check that presidents were constrained publicly to welcome or tolerate as a guarantee of probity, however much they hated the often painful intrusion and distraction from the main job of governing that constant probing entailed. Their own political task, however, was to establish some positive reasons for the reinstatement of public trust. Note that this was in reality a two-way democratic problem, for instilling public trust meant in part learning to trust the public; the loss of trust had in large part, and most acutely in Nixon's case, arisen from administrative distrust of what the public's reaction might be if it were told the bitter truth.

Thanks to revisionists, conspiracy theorists and Congressional investigations, public mistrust post-Nixon extended to the whole of executive government and its agencies. But the first priority must be to get things right at the top. This was why the nation breathed a sigh of relief when Vice-President Gerald Ford took office after Nixon, having narrowly avoided impeachment, went into premature retirement. Ford was truly an accidental president, a man of no previous ambition and in no way outstanding either politically or intellectually, but universally agreed to be fundamentally decent and honest. After a brace of presidents who were too-clever-by-half these were precisely the qualities the nation seemed to need. And Ford's presidency did bring to presidential politics a state of dull normalcy far removed from the excitement, controversy and scandal that had marked it since 1961, for which Americans had cause to be grateful. Yet he himself is best remembered for a single act which

---

[1] This is the central subject of Bob Woodward's *Shadow: Five Presidents and the Legacy of Watergate* (New York, Simon & Schuster, 1999).

destroyed his chance of being elected in his own right – his rapid granting of a pardon to Richard Nixon for any crimes he may have committed while president.[2] Ford had begun his presidency with the words "our long national nightmare is over," and the pardon, he said, was granted "to heal the wounds throughout the United States." Public reaction gave the lie to both these statements. There were howls of outrage and accusations of a deal having been struck (a presidency in return for a pardon). Ford seems in fact to have been motivated by a stubborn sense of loyalty to a man he admired,[3] but the sudden act smacked of favor, of top politicians looking after their own, particularly since so many of Nixon's underlings were left to face the ordeal of trial and imprisonment.

A Harris poll in 1976, the year of Carter's election and Ford's defeat, found that only 11 percent of respondents felt "great confidence" in the executive branch as compared to 41 percent in 1966.[4] Trust was something that all candidates had now to address in one way or another. One response was the populist absurdity of running for the highest political office in the land on anti-political rhetoric; if candidates could not convincingly deny they were politicians, they could at least assert their uncontamination by the corrupt politics of federal government, their status as Washington outsiders. It was a line that Reagan managed to run through nearly the whole eight years of his presidency. In 1999, even Al Gore, a beltway insider *par excellence*, felt impelled to establish his campaign headquarters in Nashville to suggest symbolic distance from the distrusted capital. It was Carter, as a new Democrat from the new South with only gubernatorial experience in Georgia as political baggage, who pioneered this line. Vietnam and Watergate had altered what James MacGregor Burns called the "structure of opportunity" of American politics, making outsiderdom an attractive and possible path to power.

Carter also went further than most in stressing his personal honesty and trustworthiness. In professing his lack of selfish interest in seeking power, he drew heavily on the American myth of virtue and innocence, saying that he wanted only what everyone wanted, "to have our nation once again with a government as good and honest and decent and truthful and fair and competent and idealistic and compassionate, and as filled with love as are the American people." He also made a promise absurd for any politician, however personally honest, to make: he promised never to lie to the people, never to make a misleading statement and never to betray

---

[2] See Richard Reeves, *A Ford, Not a Lincoln: The Decline of American Political Leadership* (London, Hutchinson, 1976), pp. 97–101.

[3] See Woodward, *Shadow*, pp. 3–38.

[4] Cited in John Dumbrell, *The Carter Presidency: A Re-evaluation* (Manchester, Manchester University Press, 1995), p. 22.

their trust. If he ever lied, he said, they could take him out of the White House.[5] Understandable as this might have been with the specter of Watergate hovering still so near and given Carter's genuine conviction of his own born-again purity, it was nevertheless a dangerous tactic. Promises of exceptional probity raise either exaggerated hopes or exaggerated cynicism, but they inevitably raise levels of scrutiny while lowering tolerance of discovered slips. Carter's campaign promises gave him an early lead in the polls, but this evaporated at the end because of accusations of temporizing on major issues, a worrying "fuzziness" on policy. This form of deceit is a political necessity in democratic politics where candidates, to gain power, must appeal across many constituencies while offending none, but it is bound to be more harshly judged as a reflection of individual character where a candidate has promised exceptional honesty and frankness. In the White House, Carter's moral reputation largely recovered (he was the nearest thing to a saint the White House ever had, according to one of his speech-writers),[6] though his loyal defense of his friend Bert Lance, director of the Office of Budget and Management, accused of financial improprieties back in Georgia, caused a severe drop in his approval rating in 1977. The dramatic decline in Carter's standing, however, had causes other than perceived venality or deceit, as we shall see later.

Subsequent presidents suffered much more than Carter from a gap between ethical commitment and actual performance. In the case of Reagan, the so-called "teflon" president to whom no scandal would stick, his popular presidency closed under the pall of the Iran–Contra scandal. This followed disclosure of the secret breach of a firm presidential commitment – no deals with terrorists – and the linked, secret pursuit of a Congressionally disapproved policy in Nicaragua. The deceit of Congress and people was reminiscent of the deceits of previous presidencies. Coral Bell comments, however, that "if Mr. Reagan had not so zealously talked a high moral line, especially about dealings with terrorists, there would have been much less shock to US opinion in the disclosure of the actual dealings."[7] Reagan's successor, George Bush, was also touched by Iran–Contra ("What did Bush know?"), but the thing that really ethically hobbled his presidency was his famous broken campaign promise of no new taxes ("Read my lips!"). Bill Clinton, in his turn, came to power

[5] Betty Glad, *Jimmy Carter in Search of the Great White House* (New York, W. W. Norton & Co., 1980), pp. 354–355.
[6] Hendrik Hertzberg, "Jimmy Carter 1977–1981," in R. A. Wilson (ed.), *Character Above All* (New York, Simon & Schuster, 1995).
[7] Coral Bell, *The Reagan Paradox: American Foreign Policy in the 1980s* (London, Edward Elgar, 1989), p. 137, and see especially pp. 138–139: "As someone said, it was like a John Wayne movie in which the hero ends up selling guns to the Indians."

promising the most ethical administration the country had ever seen, with predictable results. The extraordinary events of Clinton's presidency, however, appeared to shift the trust question to another dimension, with his approval ratings apparently revealing a novel distinction between job performance and personal moral trustworthiness – of which more later.

The problem of trust and politicians is, of course, perennial and universal (which is what makes the statement "Trust me, I'm a politician" a joke in itself). But in America this ordinary problem had acquired broader ramifications because of the pivotal role of the presidency and the part that presidents had played in undermining the American myth. At issue was not just what people thought of the moral quality of their leaders but what they thought of America itself and of themselves as Americans. Each new presidential incumbent had to negotiate provisional public mistrust rather then enjoy provisional trust while not only tackling the outstanding domestic issues of the day but at the same time bearing the responsibility of solving the deeper problem of American confusion over national self-faith and self-confidence. The latter, I have said, was a question of the decline of American power and the damage to pride associated with it, inseparable in America from the question of American virtue and its fate.

The problem of power and virtue

There was more to the decline of American power than failure in Vietnam, which was merely where hubris got its most corruscating comeuppance. Important too was the loss of absolute economic dominance that was a natural result of America's own policies (sound for both economic and Cold War political reasons) of helping rebuild, via American credit and trade policies, the shattered wartime economies of future rivals. In the 1970s the problems of the almighty dollar – that monetary symbol and conveyor of American supremacy – were a consequence of West German and Japanese development exacerbated by inflationary spending on Vietnam. The dollar's decline, along with the oil-price shocks induced by OPEC (the oil-producers' cartel), signaled the end of the post-war boom and of the liberal consensus based on it (funding social reform and the expectations of labor through economic growth). It was the start of a huge international economic readjustment toward a complex multipolar world in which the United States would be, at most, only *primus inter pares*.

There were also deeply annoying political injuries to American pride in addition to that suffered in Vietnam. For one thing, the benign intentions of American aid and involvement in poor countries were increasingly questioned in the 1960s and 1970s. Soviet–American competition in

third-world countries had led to American support for right-wing dictatorial regimes with nothing to recommend them but anti-communism;
often these client regimes appeared to function mostly to suppress their
own populations in the interests of the large American extractive and
primary industries that dominated the local economy. Even poor democratic countries felt themselves victims of this American economic imperialism, and in the United Nations General Assembly, where poor
nations formed a majority, they had a forum in which to express their
disgruntlement. The endless critiques and anti-American resolutions
angered the United States and engendered official hostility toward the
organization itself, and a withholding of dues. Meanwhile, in the Middle
East, American material and moral underwriting of the existence of Israel
evoked a differently motivated and more virulent anti-Americanism in
Arab countries. This, combined in some places with the familiar complaints of economic and cultural imperialism, fed into a developing
Islamic backlash against modernization. Religious solidarity planted the
seeds of anti-Americanism in even the most forward-looking of Islamic
nations.

All this was largely extraneous to the communist–anti-communist conflict, and ran hurtfully contrary to America's traditional view of its own
virtue and its beneficent use of power. It was baffling for Americans to
have their good intentions internationally arraigned. It came to seem that
anything bad that happened anywhere in the world would be blamed
somehow on America, which therefore deserved whatever punishment
and insult that governments, terrorists and protesters might mete out.
(The puzzled defensiveness this evoked in Americans was nicely caught in
the Billy Joel song that chanted a list of the world's trouble-spots followed
by the refrain: "We didn't start the fire / Though we didn't light it, we've
been trying to fight it.") Had it not been for Vietnam (and the subsequent
tragedy of Cambodia/Kampuchea in which American actions played an
invidious causal role), this weight of critique and hostility might have
been more easily borne. The trouble with Vietnam was that, there,
America (or at least a significant part of it) had condemned *itself*, found
itself guilty of real sin. Vietnam catalyzed America's self-doubt and rad-
icalized its self-critique, making it more vulnerably receptive to external
criticism than it otherwise might have been. It also left a residue of vocal
domestic dissidents of the likes of Noam Chomsky, always willing to
believe the worst about America and American intentions.

Such consciousness of sin may evoke, either in individual or collective
life, one of two responses: honest soul-searching and acceptance of
guilt accompanied by a resolve to reform; or simple denial.[8] The first
requires humility and a determination to find honest grounds for the

reestablishment of self-esteem; the second produces resentment combined with a blustering self-assertion whose shallowness betrays the underlying, unresolved doubt and loss of innocent self-belief. America after Vietnam hovered uncertainly between these alternatives. In the political realm, Jimmy Carter tried to take something resembling the first course, but the failure of his presidency was also the failure of his redemptive strategy. This left the way open for Ronald Reagan to apply the second option, with at least superficial success.

The Carter solution

Carter had a remarkably clear sense of the loss of trust and the severing of power and virtue that Vietnam and Watergate had caused and thus of the damage done to the moral capital of America. His aim was nothing less than to forge a new unity between power and virtue within a revitalized myth, one that humbly and realistically admitted the limits of American power in an increasingly multipolar world. Instead of an ideologically bifurcated world, Carter envisioned a "global community" the relations of whose members were to be guided by moral responsibilities encoded in international law. For America's part, Carter rejected the rigidified virtue of Cold War anti-communism as no longer appropriate to a changing reality, and repudiated also the *realpolitik* of Nixon and Kissinger as lacking moral foundations, substituting instead a foreign policy doctrine of human rights. In making this shift, Carter retained the characteristic belief in America's difference from other nations, namely that possession of a unique virtue which had been sadly compromised by an erroneous identification with false doctrines.[9] But to return to its true, traditional mission, government must maintain the standards of ethics and honesty that the American people allegedly observed in their private lives. Speaking of the difficulty of supporting human rights throughout the world he said:

It requires a balancing of tough realism on the one hand, and idealism on the other. Of our understanding of the world as it is, and as it ought to be. The question, I think, is whether in recent years we have ignored those moral values that have always distinguished the United States of America from other countries.[10]

---

[8] Some may like to add a third based on the old joke about Catholics: guilt and confession followed by an absolution that leaves one free to go out and sin again. This was never an option for America whose cultural heart, despite its heterogeneity, remains resolutely Protestant.

[9] See Glad, *Jimmy Carter*, pp. 316 and 347.

[10] Cited in Dumbrell, *The Carter Presidency*, p. 2.

Human rights had the appearance of an unideological, almost apolitical, doctrine, one as applicable to Latin American dictators as to communist tyrants. Under it, America would not again fall into the sin of hypocrisy, betraying its own ideals by supporting unfree regimes for the sake of anti-communism. Its foreign policy would be all of a piece and morally based, devoid of the contradictions which were the ultimate grounds of dissensus at home. The application of American power and influence on behalf of human rights would give American foreign policy that virtue which the American myth had always claimed for it, would in effect *realize* the myth, making America what it was always supposed to have been and obviating the need for lies and deception. The doctrine was to be applied at home as well, where Carter saw the role of government as defending and promoting a "common good" (reducible to the good of individuals as the bearers of rights that guaranteed their dignity, welfare and equality) against the encroachments and secret machinations of divisive special interests.[11] He was also sensitive to the fact that preaching human rights abroad while ignoring their denial at home (a subject that his own ambassador to the United Nations, Andrew Young, was uncomfortably to raise with reference to continuing poverty in America) would give substance to renewed charges of American hypocrisy.

If this was a reordering that might heal the nation's moral wounds, what kind of leadership did it demand? Carter, a voracious reader who clearly knew his imperial presidency literature, proposed a strong presidency that could combat destructive special interests but one that was not isolated from the people by walls of undemocratic grandeur and secrecy. It was to be a "shirt-sleeves" presidency, in which the spurious reverence and concealment of the Johnson–Nixon years would be replaced by informality and openness to public scrutiny and public input. Thus the human rights policy would, by reintegrating American power and American virtue, provide the basis for national consensus, while an open presidency vigorous on behalf of the people would form the grounds for reestablishing democratic trust.

Garry Wills, contrasting the appeal of Reagan's optimism with Carter's emphasis on limits, remarked that voters found Carter lacking in the higher confidence in man, in America. "He talked of limits and self-denial, of tendencies toward aggression even in a 'saved' nation like America. He believed in original sin."[12] On this view, Carter in effect repudiated the American myth by reintroducing the Pilgrims' belief in

---

[11] See Dumbrell, *The Carter Presidency*, chapter 3, p. 20. For Carter's own view of the dangers of special interests, see his *Why Not the Best?* (Eastbourne, Kingsway, 1977), p. 104.

[12] Garry Wills, *Reagan's America: Innocents at Home* (New York, Doubleday, 1987), p. 385.

fallen humanity. It was true that "the age of limits" was one of his central themes, and that he felt part of the task of a leader was honestly to persuade people of the need to adjust to these limits, even preaching that Americans were themselves the "enemy" in failing to conserve energy. But in his populist rhetoric Carter usually laid sin specifically at the door of governments that had let down a still virtuous people. "The people of this country are inherently unselfish, open, honest, decent, competent and compassionate," he claimed. "Our government should be the same, in all its actions and attitudes."[13] Americans deserved a government both moral enough and competent enough to be worthy of them (the theme of his famous "crisis of confidence" speech in the midst of his 1979 setbacks). This was flattery of the people which ignored one of the bitterest lessons of Vietnam: not that a virtuous people could be betrayed by its government (though the rot may have started there), but that Americans were as capable of being bad as any other people in the world. Carter did not repudiate the myth of American virtue and the American mission, but rather tried to restore and reconstruct it in the aftermath of that recent fall from grace.

I have claimed that, at its foundation, the American myth did not conceive of the United States as a proselytizing nation actively seeking converts abroad, but as an exemplary one that revealed to a naturally curious world what independent, free, competently self-governing humanity could be and do. Americans accomplished their mission best just by being themselves. The claim by members of the Carter administration that the success of liberal democracy was a sufficient retort to the challenge of communism was perfectly consonant with this and reflected Carter's own views.[14] A possible objection to such a stance, however, was that it might give ideological support to an isolationism that would abrogate the responsibilities and engagements that inevitably come with power. Morally, this would be hardly more acceptable than the aberrant proselytization that had degenerated into the disastrous attempt to impose America's will on other nations. Carter attempted to carve a responsible middle road between these two paths. To do this he had to combine three imperatives that were bound to be in constant tension: the maintenance of America's modest exemplary role; the steadfast defense of its own legitimate interests; and the acceptance and fulfillment of its ineluctable responsibilities as a great power in an increasingly complicated world.

Despite good intentions Carter's single-term presidency was widely

[13] Glad, *Jimmy Carter*, p. 316.
[14] See Erwin C. Hargrove, *Jimmy Carter as President* (Baton Rouge, Louisiana State University Press, 1988), p. 168.

seen as a dismal failure and mercilessly attacked as such by the Republican administration that followed. This is not the place to dissect in detail
all that went wrong,[15] but I must outline some points salient to my thesis.

Carter had come to power promising "compassion and competence,"
and while perhaps being given credit for the former, he was widely seen as
an incompetent manager. His strategy of honesty was intended in part to
make Americans face up to the limits to American economic and political
power, but an economy emerging from recession declined on his watch
into a state of stagflation (inflation combined with growing unemployment) to be further rocked by the cessation of Iranian oil after the
revolution there. As for the human rights doctrine, this did achieve a
measure of consensus in the first two years of his term and was generally
approved by the public, but there were many problems in instituting it as
a moral basis for the conduct of foreign relations. The difficulty of
operationalizing an imprecise concept meant that administrative practice,
instead of striking a balance between tough realism and idealism, was in
constant danger of falling into either naivete or cynicism. It was, anyway,
far from easy for Carter's Human Rights Bureau to force the institutional-
ization of the human rights agenda onto powerful career bureaucracies
firmly wedded to older imperatives and long-standing clients. There were
also technical and conceptual problems which multiplied the difficulties:
how, for example, was America to obtain reliable data on the human
rights record of various nations; how was it to rank them even if it could;
and should it take account of the very different social, economic and
historical conditions of countries in so doing, or was the concept universal
and absolute?[16] Further, though Carter never intended that national
security should be compromised by human rights considerations (as
Reagan would later charge it had been), what trade-off on human rights
should be deemed acceptable for, say, an American naval base in the
Philippines? How far should criticism of the Soviet Union's policy on
political prisoners be pushed while America was simultaneously seeking
agreement with the Soviets on limiting strategic arms?

Nor was it easy to disentangle the United States from relationships
formed in the previous era or to reestablish them on a fresh basis, as
Carter's acute difficulties with the brutal Somoza regime in Nicaragua
and with that of the Shah of Iran (both under domestic revolutionary
pressure) dramatically illustrated. There was, too, the problem of the

---

[15] Stephen Skowronek, *The Politics Presidents Make* (Cambridge, MA, Belknap, 1993), pp.
361–406, characterizes him as a "late regime affiliate," in other words a president at the
tail-end of the liberal consensus who recognized that the old solutions no longer worked,
but were in fact now part of the problem.
[16] See Dumbrell, *The Carter Presidency*, pp. 179–180. Also A. Glenn Mower, *Human Rights
and American Foreign Policy* (New York, Greenwood, 1987), chapter 2.

point at which human rights abuses made it justifiable or imperative that the United States intervene in a country. Since such an option clearly did not apply to countries like Russia (with whom Carter, until Afghanistan, continued his predecessors' policy of détente) or China (with whom Carter established full diplomatic relations), but only to those over which the United States had traditionally exercised hegemonic power, the Carter regime was inevitably exposed to charges of moral inconsistency. Where such hegemonic power existed, however, the question of whether or not to intervene could hardly be avoided, yet any exercise of power was bound to be criticized as the old American imperialism dressed up in a bright new moral suit. These, of course, are difficulties that still dog attempts to take account of human rights in American foreign policy considerations, and those of other countries as well; the fact that they are still nevertheless very much on the agenda is in part due to the persistence with which Carter promulgated his doctrine.

Carter's vision came seriously undone after 1978. The trouble was that the world remained ideologically divided. Its competitive logic continued to drive an arms race that was difficult to control effectively, and which therefore continued to create anxiety in people living under the shadow of nuclear holocaust. This anxiety was exacerbated by the USSR's increasingly imperialistic assertion in Africa and the Middle East, a sharp reminder that Cold War rivalry was not a figment of overheated Republican imaginations. The Russian invasion of Afghanistan in 1979 triggered a panic among government and intelligence circles in Washington who interpreted it as an attempt to gain control of the Persian Gulf, a region where America's vital interests were engaged. Carter's hope for a global community was lost, and in response he promulgated a new foreign policy doctrine that promised to defend American interests wherever and whenever they were threatened, and by any means necessary, including military force. This was a retreat to Cold War confrontation and containment, except that the chance of a direct confrontation between the principals became more terrifyingly real. The Carter administration moved from a stance of nuclear deterrence, grounded in the unthinkability of a nuclear exchange, to embrace the possibility of a "limited" nuclear engagement winnable by the United States.[17]

The difficulties of conducting a moral foreign policy in such a divided world were dramatically demonstrated in Iran, where Islamic fundamentalists took control of a successful revolution (1979 was truly Carter's *annus horribilis*). America had installed the Pahlavi dynasty in Iran in 1953, and continued to support and arm it, despite its dismal record on human rights, because Iran was an oil-rich nation of strategic importance

---

[17]   See Cyrus Vance, *Hard Choices* (New York, Simon and Schuster, 1983), p. 394; Zbigniew Brzezinski, *Power and Principle* (London, Wiedenfeld and Nicolson, 1983), pp. 459–460.

both to Middle Eastern politics and, more importantly, as a bulwark against communism in the region (the US maintained large military bases in Iran). Carter maintained US support for the same reasons, buoyed by an understanding that the Shah was moving rapidly in a liberalizing direction. But Carter strained both credibility and political commonsense when, on a visit to Tehran in New Year 1978, he toasted the Shah as an "enlightened monarch." His complaisance deeply disappointed the Iranian opposition (who had greeted Carter's election and his human rights policy with optimistic hope) and called down the wrath of the Ayatollah Khomeini who condemned him as a hypocrite. The consequent hostility of the successful revolutionaries produced the Iranian hostage crisis that was to play such an important part in Carter's election defeat in 1980.

The public mood during the desultory campaigns of that year was a mix of depression and anxiety. Reagan attacked Carter for endangering America by his softness on communism and by undermining American intelligence through his CIA accountability reforms. Reagan himself, however, aroused anxiety rather than confidence with his Cold War saber-rattling. He won the election less because people leaned toward him than because they leaned away from Carter whose approval ratings dropped to below that of Nixon's at his resignation.

The reasons for the public disenchantment are telling. Carter had stressed morality and virtue more than power. His emphasis on the limits of American power and wealth had called for a sense of humility more than pride; but at the end of his term what Americans seemed to be feeling most was baffled pride. Polls revealed that the American public felt "bullied by OPEC, humiliated by the Ayatollah Khomeini, tricked by Castro, out-traded by Japan and out-gunned by the Russians."[18] Castro had, in many people's opinion, used Carter's human rights doctrine to force the government to admit large numbers of Cuban refugees. Americans were still held hostage in Iran (an airborne attempt to save them having gone embarrassingly and tragically wrong) and the Ayatollah had labeled America "the Great Satan." The American economy seemed to grow ever weaker as its rivals grew stronger. Carter's own shift to containment had alerted the public on the arms race issue, and the perceptions were that America had fallen significantly behind the Soviet Union during his tenure.[19] A New York Times post-election poll showed 77 percent of people expected the new president to "see to it the US is respected by other nations."[20]

[18] Daniel Yankelovich and Larry Kaagan, "Assertive America," Foreign Affairs 59 (1981), pp. 696–713, at p. 696.
[19] See Hargrove, Jimmy Carter as President, p. 191.
[20] Cited in Dumbrell, The Carter Presidency, p. 203.

Carter's attempt to reconcile American power and American virtue had failed, and was no doubt premature in a world still divided into opposing blocs.[21] Certainly, Kissinger dismissed it as "romantic," while the neo-conservative Jeanne Kirkpatrick, significantly, faulted it as a conception of the national interest in which US power was "at best irrelevant." Most notable and most ironic was the retrospective judgment of Reagan's Secretary of State George Schultz, who called it a "cop out," a way of "making us feel better."[22] It was true that Carter wanted Americans to feel better about themselves, their government and their country; but he believed they could only feel better in the knowledge that their government was doing right, and could only feel justified pride if they knew that American power was being rightfully disposed. He had taken the straight and narrow path as a good Christian should, but had stumbled on its difficult surface; it was left to Ronald Reagan, the ultimate "feel-good" president, to take the broader and easier route.

The Reagan solution

Erwin Hargrove argued that Carter was too much the rational technocrat and too little the politician in his approach to difficult problems, and that he failed to understand the importance of (and certainly failed to engage) popular emotion in politics.[23] His successor, if he understood little else, at least understood this. His sobriquet "the great communicator" was granted on the strength of his uncanny ability to plug into the emotional sockets of the American public, an ability that brought him a second term in 1984. As to what the great communicator actually communicated, the answer lies less in the outlines of the simple, unvarying conservative political faith that he preached than in just that emotional reassurance that he conveyed to the American people. It did not matter that he was as corny as those old Hollywood movies that he had once played in and that he loved and tirelessly quoted (indeed most of Reagan's knowledge of history and politics seemed to be derived from old movies), for he understood the deep strain of corniness in the American heart and consciously appealed to it. Reagan knew how to play a scene in a way that set America's emotional chords vibrating. His brave, self-deprecatory

---

[21] See Jerel A. Rosati, "Jimmy Carter, a Man Before His Time? The Emergence and Collapse of the First Post-Cold War Presidency," *Presidential Studies Quarterly* 23(3) (Summer 1993), pp. 459–476.

[22] All these citations come from Dumbrell, *The Carter Presidency*, p. 192.

[23] Hargrove, *Jimmy Carter as President*, pp. 174–175; Hargrove, "The Carter Presidency in Historical Perspective," in H. B. Rosenbaum and A. Urgrunskey (eds.), *The Presidency and Domestic Politics of Jimmy Carter* (Westport, CT, Greenwood Press, 1994), pp. 17–28, at p. 27.

quips following his wounding at the hands of a would-be-assassin could have been scripted in Hollywood forty years previously, and were perfectly, no doubt instinctively, judged to weld him once-and-for-all to the nation's heart with bonds of sentimental love.

For many intellectual observers, study of the Reagan phenomenon is rather akin to the study of an inexplicable natural event, a search for purely causal explanations rather than the divination of the movements of an active mind and character working on the world. When they search for the man beneath the public persona, they seem to find just the practiced actor moving rather mechanically from scene to scene.[24] Thus when intellectuals play at that old favorite game of ranking past presidents, Reagan tends to be placed at the low end of "average." There are exceptions to this view, especially among conservative intellectuals.[25] The historian Forrest McDonald puts Reagan up there with Washington, Jefferson, Lincoln and Teddy Roosevelt, and for a revealing reason: "He made the country feel good about itself. He had the supreme confidence in the American people and in himself. He played the role of leader so well."[26]

Reagan's buoyant optimism, based more it seems on a cinematic dream of America than on any judgment of reality, was what America in the 1980s seemed to want to see in their leader and to feel in themselves. His simple, indeed simplistic, solutions to problems of the economy (less taxes, less spending, less regulation) and government (less government), whatever their actual policy effects, their successes or failures, were equaled in importance by the emotional message conveyed: there is nothing seriously wrong with America or Americans; America is just fine. Michael Reagan, the president's son, later said that his father's great achievement was to bring the Republican Party "back from the black hole of Watergate," to give people reason to believe in the GOP once more.[27] If he did, it was by virtually denying, in his failure to acknowledge it, that Watergate had ever happened. America, Reagan implied, was the great nation it had always been. In his second Inaugural Address, Reagan summoned the old American myth via the spirits of Valley Forge, of Lincoln, of the Alamo, of the settler pushing west with an echoing song:

---

[24] Gail Sheehy, *Character: America's Search for Leadership* (New York, William Morrow and Co., 1988), pp. 282–286.

[25] See, e.g., Dinesh D'Souza who in retrospect is struck by how much he underestimated Reagan as statesman and leader; *Ronald Reagan: How an Extraordinary Man Became an Extraordinary Leader* (New York, Free Press, 1997).

[26] Quoted in Stephen Goode, "The Reagan Legacy," *Insight on the News* 13(39) (27 October 1997), pp. 10–13, at p. 10.

[27] *Ibid.*, p. 11.

It is the American sound. It is hopeful, big-hearted, idealistic, daring, decent, and fair. That's our heritage; that is our song. We sing it still . . . [We are] one people under God, dedicated to the dream of freedom that He has placed in the human heart, called upon to pass that dream on to a waiting and hopeful world.[28]

The comforting subliminal message in his bland, avuncular assurances was that America was still the best country in the world and ordinary Americans the best people. In fact, he said, they were heroes. They would prove it if allowed to get on with their individual lives unencumbered by government taxes that robbed them of the fruits of their labors and by government regulations that stifled their enterprise.

Unencumbered, too, by the residue of unnecessary guilt left by the 1960s and 1970s, that guilt that Jimmy Carter had so needlessly and fruitlessly dwelt upon in his *mea culpa* style of politics. Americans, Reagan seemed to say, had nothing with which to reproach themselves. Their involvement in Vietnam had been justified on anti-communist grounds, and it had merely been confusion wrought by unrepresentative (un-American) radicals that had made it seem otherwise. It was time to cast aside weakening self-doubt and self-recrimination, for there was a moral crusade yet to be won against the "Evil Empire" of Soviet communism and only America could lead it. Americans could and would "walk tall" in the world once more, and indeed must do so for the sake of liberty. They would be once again like the John Wayne of the old western movies, strong and decent, tough but fair, honestly self-reliant (and rather impatient of those who would not help themselves), ready to stand up to, and teach a rough lesson to, anyone who insulted their dignity and honor or threatened their liberty.

Reagan's version of the American myth simply reasserted the archaic unity of virtue and power while retaining the post-war link between virtue and anti-communism. The only difference was that the latter was supplemented now by an anti-terrorism which always threatened to shade into anti-Muslimism or anti-Arabism (for it followed that, since America was good, anyone who hated or opposed America was by definition evil). Reagan's solution to the problem of the severance of power and virtue was tacitly to deny that it had happened, that there was a problem at all. It was not a matter of proof and argument but of assertion and attitude. All that was needed was an act of optimistic will, a touch of Norman Vincent Peale, and the nation would be reborn to its own true self.

Abroad, America would walk tall and pursue a strategy of "peace through strength," unafraid to strike back when it was threatened or when freedom needed defending. In this spirit Reagan invaded the

---

[28] President Reagan's Second Inaugural Address, 21 January 1985, available on the Reagan Information Interchange (reagan.com/plate.main/ronald/speeches/rrspeechoe.html).

Caribbean island of Grenada (allegedly to protect Americans trapped in a Marxist coup there, and also to prevent another Cuba), shot down Libyan aircraft and bombed Libya itself (hatching ground of terrorism). These actions, whatever political justifications could be offered for them, were highly symbolic. Their true forerunner was President Ford's massive military operation to rescue thirty-nine Americans captured in the Cambodian *Mayaguez* incident, the intention of which was to show, post-Vietnam, that America was not a helpless giant prey to insult and injury from every midget with a grudge – that it could still kick ass when necessary. The immense surge of popular enthusiasm that both Ford's and Reagan's adventures elicited revealed how acute was the American sense of injured pride. And yet these actions could do little more than give pride a transient boost, partly because they were so small when measured on the scale of Vietnam (though smallness – and this revealed the element of cowardice hidden in the Reagan solution – was undoubtedly part of their attraction given the fear of extended and uncontrollable entanglements that Vietnam had bequeathed).

Their impact on pride was also frequently muffled by the world's refusal to conform to the neat formulae of American action movies. Some days after the *Mayaguez* incident, for example, it was revealed that more men had died in the action than had been rescued. The Grenada invasion had been immediately preceded by the death by suicide bombing of 241 American servicemen in Lebanon, a country whose labyrinthine politics and cross-cutting enmities revealed the impotence and vulnerability of even a Great Power in a complicated world. Moreover, the compensation for this tragedy provided by the successful Grenada operation was rather dampened by revelations of the desperate bungling and lack of preparedness of the invading forces, and by the puzzlement of "rescued" Americans who claimed never to have been in danger. Still, these were only sideshows to the main event, which was the ongoing contest with the old enemy. Walking tall with respect to the Russians meant substantially beefing up defense spending, while gaining peace through strength meant deploying intermediate-range missiles in Europe and changing the mode in the arms race by the Strategic Defense Initiative (SDI) (Star Wars, so-called); SDI envisaged the neutralization of Soviet missiles and therefore the possibility of a nuclear-proof United States (and a frighteningly vulnerable Soviet Union).

Conclusion

It is sometimes said that Reagan's greatest limitation – his simple, unintellectual right-wing creed and the set of policies flowing from it – was also his greatest strength, for his lack of doubt lent him a steadiness and certainty that instilled confidence. With respect to the Cold War, however, his greatest asset turned out to be how easily his alleged intransigence melted before the personal charm of Mikhail Gorbachev. The reforming Soviet leader was such a good sort of fellow and apparently so trustworthy that Reagan, on his own initiative, struck a deal with him, agreeing to a ban on all nuclear weapons – to the horror of his advisers and cabinet. Reagan was no doubt fortunate to be in power as the Soviet Union approached its surprisingly sudden demise. It is debatable whether his own SDI project had contributed to it by straining Soviet responsive capabilities beyond their limit or whether it was just a case of inexorable collapse from within; but it was perhaps as well that he was president and not some harder-headed leader whose suspicious reactions might have counter-productively forestalled the changes underway in Russia. Reagan, at any rate, reaped the political benefit. He was given credit, too, for the fact that, whether due to his "Reaganomics" or not, the curse of stagflation gave way during his tenure to the boom of the 1980s (the "greed is good" decade).

The drama and slow agony of the Iran–Contra affair undoubtedly sullied Reagan's administration, though the president continued to the end to assert plausible deniability with respect to deals with terrorists or knowledge of the connection with the Contras in Nicaragua. Even if accepted, these denials, combined with numerous stories of the president's failing mental powers, tended to paint a picture of a nation with no one at the helm, an image reinforced by revelations of the extent of the internecine conflicts that raged within the administration. Despite Iran–Contra, despite a severe budget blow-out, despite the stock market shock of 1987, Reagan managed to leave office with high approval ratings, buoyed up it seemed by the genuine affection he had inspired in many Americans. But the Iran–Contra hearings that dragged on long after he had left office aroused grave suspicion about the honesty of the outsider who had represented himself as the upholder of traditional American values, the restorer of American pride, and a renewed sense of disillusionment and betrayal seeped through the electorate.[29]

As to the central dilemma of pride and virtue, Reagan's bland assurances had temporarily soothed it without solving it, a fact that would be dramatically demonstrated during the office of his successor, his own Vice-President George Bush.

[29] Sheehy, *Character*, pp. 299–300.

10   Denouement

The truth is rarely pure, and never simple.

Oscar Wilde, *The Importance of Being Earnest*

Reagan's popularity was such that George Bush, a man of small political profile and experience, had little choice but to run on the promise of continuity with the great communicator (though upon election he proceeded, as steadily as he could, to distance himself from his predecessor). The dominant public sentiment in 1988 seemed no longer one of injured national pride, but fear of recession and unemployment,[1] and in the end it would be Bush's perceived inability to handle the economy that would cost him a second term. Continuity meant, for Bush, reaping some of the economic problems sewn but not ripened in the Reagan years, the budget deficit in particular. A Democrat-dominated Congress did not ease his task, and he was saddled with his own campaign promise of "no new taxes."[2] Continuity also meant that Bush's own central commitments remained something of a mystery. Earnest and hard-working rather than inspiring, he seemed to have no clearly articulated moral purpose, no vision of America, to which to harness his undoubted political ambition and, consequently, he was often accused of "wimpish" indecisiveness.

This was part of the reason that Bush's apparently brilliant foreign policy successes failed to translate into votes at home. The larger story was that the Bush presidency marked the definite end of the era that had produced America's moral crisis. With the collapse of the communist governments of Eastern Europe and the fragmentation of the Soviet Union itself, the old enemy simply disappeared, and with it the consolidating effects that enmity had had, not only on America but on all the nations of the First World. So much of the internal and international political structures of these nations had been premised, blatantly or

---

[1] See Michael Duffy and Dan Goodgame, *Marching in Place: The Status Quo Presidency of George Bush* (New York, Simon & Schuster, 1992), pp. 18–19.

[2] Bush had the lowest success rate with Congress of any post-war president; see Charles O. Jones, *The Presidency in a Separated System* (Washington, DC, Brookings Institution, 1994), pp. 114–115.

subtly, on the presumption of Cold War opposition that its disappearance was bound to have profound, often unanticipated, effects. America now stood alone as the world's only superpower in a swiftly changing world, and the question was what, if any, sort of leadership it was going to give that world.

Bush and American leadership

The complexity of the problems facing post-Cold War presidents, starting with Bush, can be seen by comparing them with the previous era. Given that foreign strategy must always involve some calculation of power, interests and responsibilities (with particular actions, omissions or interventions usually based on an estimate of likely consequences), it is apparent that Cold War containment, whatever its shortcomings, had at least the advantage of radically simplifying policy problems by fusing interests and responsibilities: America's interest in defending itself and the West from communism was identical with its responsibility for doing so, and the necessary application of its power was the guarantee of both. Moreover, this outlook settled policy on a global basis, for there was no corner of the world where ideological competition might not activate the strategic imperative. But absent a rival superpower to be contained or balanced, it became unclear whether America's interests were involved at all in many of the world's trouble spots or what responsibilities it should accept even if immediate interests were lacking. The proximity of places like Haiti and Cuba meant that problems there had immediate relevance to America, while historical and/or cultural alliances inevitably engaged the US in North Korea, Taiwan, Ireland and Israel. A policy of mini-containment persisted with nations identified as "rogue" – Libya, Cuba, Iran and later Iraq – and in the Caucasus countries of the former Soviet Union there were important new oil interests to be safeguarded. But what of Bosnia, Rwanda, Somalia, Serbia/Kosovo and East Timor? Against humanitarian responsibilities, a president had to balance his responsibility to an electorate that showed small enthusiasm for sacrificing American lives where American interests were not directly involved. America was not willing to be, no doubt could not be, the world's policeman.

Yet Americans could not simply turn inwardly isolationist once the larger threat of nuclear rivalry had disappeared, for the United States was now locked deeply and irreversibly into the world politico-economic system. Moreover, its economic and military dominance automatically gave it a leadership role that it would have to fulfill, albeit under conditions that made leadership more difficult than formerly. The developed nations of the West that had relied on America's aid, trade and nuclear umbrella – while often simultaneously resenting the preponderant and occasionally overbearing influence their dependency gave that nation – were now in the process of establishing different kinds of relationship both with the United States and with one another. American power though still preponderant was less hegemonic. Old allies became much more recalcitrant about doing America's bidding while still, nevertheless, expecting America to show traditional leadership. Presidents had necessarily to devise more subtle, complex, flexible (and indeed tactful) responses to cope with the demands for leadership that their power still inevitably invoked.

Bush, who in his career had been an ambassador to the United Nations, head liaison officer to communist China, and director of the CIA, was something of a practiced expert in such relationships. Strategically, however, he had no definite program to offer. "Vision" was not his thing, as he said, and his foreign policy tended to be conducted as elite diplomacy on a pragmatic problem-by-problem basis.[3] Given the splintering effect of the Eastern bloc's collapse, and the inevitable uncertainty about how the now scattered pieces of the jigsaw might be reordered, this was perhaps a prudent way of proceeding.[4] Yet Bush, though not given to Reaganite flights of rhetorical fancy, shared with the former president certain gut ideological instincts about America's superpower status and the need to counter with a firm hand aggressive acts against American interests. America would not be kicked around on Bush's watch any more than on Reagan's. Bush even finished some unfinished business of the Reagan administration when, in December 1989, he ordered troops into Panama to take down the troublesome drug-trafficking General and local strong-man Manuel Noriega. This, however, proved to be little more than a dress-rehearsal for the much larger show in the Arabian Gulf, the most dramatic episode of Bush's term of office and the most significant for the moral history being traced here.

Catharsis: the Gulf War

The Gulf War of 1990–91 was truly Bush's war. It was he who made the decision to resist Iraqi leader Saddam Hussein with military force if diplomacy failed, he who began the deployment of American troops in

---

[3] His style was described as "patrician pragmatism" by Cecil V. Crabb and Kevin V. Mulcahy in "The Elitist Presidency: George Bush and the Management of Operation Desert Storm," in Richard W. Waterman (ed.), *The Presidency Reconsidered* (Itasca, IL, F. E. Peacock, 1993), pp. 275–330, at p. 281. Bush himself and his national security adviser Brent Scowcroft used the term "practical intelligence"; George Bush and Brent Scowcroft, *A World Transformed* (New York, Knopf, 1998), p. 35.

[4] See David Mervin, *George Bush and the Guardianship Presidency* (New York, St. Martin's Press, 1996); Charles Tiefer, *The Semi-Sovereign Presidency: The Bush Administration's Strategy for Governing Without Congress* (Boulder, CO, Westview, 1994).

the Gulf five days after Saddam's invasion of tiny, oil-rich Kuwait, he who put and held together the disparate international coalition that supported and helped fight the war, he who oversaw it strategically, and he who terminated it when he judged his mandate fulfilled (there was little "wimp factor" in evidence during this crisis). At home, his decisive action revealed that the supposedly defunct imperial presidency was anything but, and that the presidential prerogative in matters of foreign policy still held. Bush (remembering the Johnson–Nixon years) made a conscious effort to consult with Congressmen and gain formal Congressional approval, receiving in the process some criticism from Congress (mostly tactical rather than principled). Yet the crisis showed that Congress, however much it might frustrate Bush on the domestic front, was still not a reliably independent source of foreign policy. Over the Gulf, it virtually acquiesced in traditional fashion to the president's firm lead.

Whatever its intrinsic motives, the Gulf War was also effectively the last act of the drama that had begun decades earlier. It is impossible to understand its course outside of the context of American post-war history and, in particular, of the defining experience of Vietnam.[5] Vietnam had taught, for one thing, the importance of international backing for American actions, and Bush performed a remarkable and sustained feat of personal diplomacy to build a United Nations coalition that provided moral, financial and military support. The most important lesson, though, was the need to gain and keep American public support, and here again Bush succeeded astonishingly well. The question of popular support dominated the conduct of the war. Bush assured the people that the mistakes of Vietnam would not be repeated. Once the deadline he had set for Iraqi withdrawal had passed and all diplomatic initiatives had failed,[6] "Operation Desert Storm" commanded by General Norman Schwarzkopf proceeded in such a way as maximally to avoid allied casualties – a long aerial bombardment using every type of modern ordnance to soften resistance followed by a determined and swiftly victorious allied push. Estimates placed Iraqi casualties at around 100,000 against a total of 188 Americans, only 79 of them in combat. Schwarzkopf expressed sincere fatherly concern about preserving his soldiers' lives, but underlying this concern was the general belief that popular support would crumble if too many troops came home in body bags. The press (to its intense annoyance) was also tightly controlled as it had not been in Vietnam, so that the news could not be "distorted" in the way the establishment believed it had been in the previous war.

[5] See Crabb and Mulcahy, "The Elitist Presidency," p. 282.
[6] For why Bush had to have the war once committed, see Bob Woodward, Shadow: Five Presidents and the Legacy of Watergate (New York, Simon & Schuster, 1999), pp. 184–188.

It was a stunning victory for the allies, for Schwarzkopf, and for Bush. In the general euphoria, Bush forgot himself and started talking in semi-visionary terms about a New World Order (naturally under American leadership). In the joy and relief of the moment, the victory appeared to have performed in actuality the healing of American pride and virtue that Reagan had performed only in make-believe. Bush himself exclaimed "by God, we've kicked the Vietnam syndrome once and for all." The American reaction demonstrated how deep the papered-over wounds of the past still went. The lengthy title of a piece by Stanley Cloud in *Time* magazine said it all: "Exorcising an old demon: a stunning military triumph gives Americans something to cheer about – and shatters Vietnam's legacy of self-doubt and divisiveness." The pain of the Vietnam memories, said Cloud, had somehow only increased with the years, but the victory of US-led forces in the Gulf had defeated the virulent old ghosts: "Self-doubt, fear of power, divisiveness, a fundamental uncertainty about America's purposes in the world." America had demonstrated that is was not only powerful, "but credibly so." American servicemen were no longer baby-killers who had to "slink home" in shame, but heroes who would return to ticker-tape celebrations. An American marine in the Gulf took an old flag, given him by a dying comrade in Vietnam, and laid it before the gates of the Kuwaiti embassy: "a circle had been completed, a chapter closed." What had made it all work was a combination of "the rightness of the cause and the swiftness of the victory."[7] Pride and virtue, in other words, power and goodness, had at last been restored and reunited.

Once the initial euphoria had subsided, however, things did not seem quite so clear-cut. At the root of the problem were the reasons given for embarking on military involvement in the first place. Bush, in keeping with the Carter doctrine, had initially asserted the danger to American strategic and economic interests represented by an expansionist Iraq whose next target looked set to be Saudi Arabia with its massive oil reserves. (One curiosity about this was that the main strategic interest was tied to Cold War rivalry, yet the United Nations coalition had been obtainable only because of the US' much improved relationship with Moscow.) Moreover, if America did not take up the challenge it was certain that no one else would, having neither the power nor the will to do so. Immediate public reaction, however, indicated an unwillingness to risk a large-scale war for the sake, as it seemed, of oil. Bush therefore promptly fell back on a simple story of an evil dictator with ambitions to dominate the whole Gulf region, one who had cruelly invaded a small and

[7] *Time* 137(10) (11 March 1991), pp. 52–53.

innocent neighbor to the accompaniment of rape, murder and pillage. Bush went into uncharacteristic rhetorical overdrive. Saddam was likened to Hitler – mad, bad and cunning, a megalomaniacal bully who understood only the argument of force and whom it was dangerous policy to appease. Public opinion swung firmly behind the president. The story worked because Saddam was clearly a thoroughly bad lot (though no more of one, perhaps, than some other leaders in the region), and he had undeniably broken the cardinal rule of international law by invading another country. Nor could opposition to him be interpreted as anti-Arab, for Bush had brought on side several Arab allies, obtaining even Syria's acquiescence.

There were, however, difficulties with Bush's simplistic moral scenario that honest reporters soon began to point out. Saddam had, until recently, been an American ally, and large amounts of his sophisticated weaponry and training had been provided by, among others, America itself. This aid had been given, despite Iraq's clear threat to Israel, in order to assist Saddam in his long and fruitless war against neighboring Iran, itself utterly demonized in American eyes by the hostage crisis and the virulent anti-Americanism of its clerical leadership. This former complicity with the enemy mattered less, though, than the aftermath of the victory. The Iraqi leader had been portrayed in such fiendish terms by Bush that it seemed expulsion from Kuwait would not be enough; only his fall would bring long-term peace to the Gulf and relief to Saddam's own people. Yet Bush had ordered the allied forces (which Schwarzkopf was keen to push on to Baghdad) to halt at the border of Kuwait. Bush correctly pointed out that expulsion, not invasion, was all the allied forces had been legally sanctioned to perform, and he was bitter about the "sniping, carping, bitching, [and] predictable editorial complaints" that followed.[8] He had, however, brought the criticism on himself – his moral tale of goodies versus the big baddy hardly squared with such belated legalistic propriety. It was as though the allies of World War II, having pushed Hitler back behind the German border, considered their job done and called off the war. Worse, Bush had gone so far as to call for an uprising against Saddam within Iraq with an at least implicit promise of American support. This turned out not to be forthcoming when the Shi-ite population of the South and the Kurdish population of the North duly obliged with rebellion. Saddam proceeded to use the remnants of his still powerful army to put down the uprisings with his usual ruthlessness (this American betrayal was one of the central themes of a popular movie, *Three Kings*, a decade later). It took some time for the realization to sink in

---

[8] A Bush diary entry quoted by Woodward, *Shadow*, p. 188.

to the public mind that Saddam was not going to be toppled, perhaps for a long time, perhaps ever. For months afterwards Americans watched as Kurdish refugees huddled in the northern mountains of Iraq under the tardy shield of American air power.

Apart from legality, there were any number of *realpolitik* reasons that could have been adduced for non-intervention in Iraq: the prospect of long-term American entanglement; the difficulty of setting up a friendly regime with popular support; the consequent probability of accusations of new imperialism and offense to other Arab nations; the risk of creating a power vacuum that would enlarge the influence of Iran; the connection of Southern Shi-ites with Iran (a Shi-ite Islamic nation); and the connection of rebel Kurds with Kurds demanding independence in Turkey, America's ally. Bush, however, could not publicly adduce any of them. They did not fit easily with his simple tale of good versus evil and evil defeated. Bush had been caught by the American mythology, by the need for American power to be seen to be used only for clearly and cleanly virtuous ends, a need made more sharply acute by the wounding betrayal of the myth in Vietnam. An action deemed necessary to defend American interests was impossible without public support, but a plain assertion of even justified American interests was judged insufficient to secure that support. Bush therefore had recourse to a fabrication, not quite a lie but not at all the whole complicated truth; and the ultimate consequence was not quite the annihilation of a triumph but its muddying with a further dose of disillusionment.

Bush had reportedly been convinced of the need for prompt military intervention by British Prime Minister Margaret Thatcher, who had herself acted decisively over the Argentinian invasion of the Falkland Islands in 1982. Bush could hardly have been unconscious of the fact that British success in that conflict had propelled her, hitherto one of the most unpopular of prime ministers, to a landslide election victory in 1983 and continuing power thereafter. But, whatever the rights and wrongs of that war, it had been conclusive: Thatcher had achieved precisely what she had said she was going to do. Bush had stuck to the letter of his mandate but not to the spirit of his rhetoric, and the resulting lack of a satisfactory conclusion to the drama he had constructed rubbed the shine from his achievement. Americans would be reminded of the unfinished nature of the conflict in 1994 when Bill Clinton redeployed troops to a newly threatened Kuwait, and again in 1996 when he bombed Iraq to force it to comply with weapons inspection agreements. Those who were paying attention would also have heard how continuing international sanctions caused suffering, not to the wicked regime itself but to ordinary Iraqi men, women and children, and perhaps have wondered at the moral complexities involved in taking an active stand against evil.

Bush's ending was not the clean and happy one that his story demanded, and his splendid victory soon began to taste of ashes. His ratings, sky high in the immediate aftermath, began to decline steadily, eventually to drop drastically when problems of the budget, the economy and the tax hike set in with a vengeance. Reagan had managed to raise taxes several times and still maintain his anti-tax image but Reagan had had a reserve fund of trust that Bush did not – Reagan might lose some battles (politics was like that), but no one doubted his life-long commitment to tax reduction. Though Bush mouthed the Reagan rhetoric, in him it sounded thin and unconvincing, and in fact his conservative credentials were always rather suspect among Republicans. He seemed lacking in firm prejudices, never mind principles. Though he had a reputation for personal integrity, this, unsupported by the moral capital that accrues from long and visible public adherence to a cause, proved very vulnerable when he broke his pledge by signing the largest single tax increase in US history to that date.[9]

There was therefore little enthusiasm for his reelection in 1992, a year in which America was troubled at home by murderous riots in Los Angeles. Polls showed that Americans were by now only marginally concerned with foreign affairs, Bush's special field, and Democratic nominee Bill Clinton endeavored to capitalize on this preoccupation (his motto for the campaign being, famously, "the economy, stupid"). But Clinton had a huge question of character already hovering over his youthfully grey head, and was forced repeatedly to combat charges that he was not a man to be trusted with the presidency any more than pledge-breaker Bush. Indeed, trust was a major and dispiriting theme of the presidential race. Third candidate Ross Perot's entire campaign was built on distrust of the Washington establishment to which Bush belonged. The nation appeared to be suffering a deeper sense of disillusion with its political system than ever before. An American Viewpoint survey in March asked 1,000 voters whether they agreed with the statement that "The entire political system is broken. It is run by insiders who do not listen to working people and are incapable of solving our problems." Seventy-three percent agreed.[10] Uninspired by the regular party candidates, the electorate flirted with outsiders – Paul Tsongas, Pat Buchanan, Jerry Brown, most of all Perot – as if longing for the traditional hero on horseback who would ride into Washington and clean the varmints out.

[9] See Richard Brookhiser, "The Leadership Thing," *Time*, 136(5) (30 July 1990), p. 72.
[10] Cited in Martin Walker in *Clinton, the President They Deserve* (London, Vintage, 1997), p. 140.

Finding no wholly convincing champion, however, they gave the prize to Clinton by default. In a three-way contest, he gained power with a mere 43 percent of the vote on a 56 percent turnout.

Clinton in a changing world

Clinton was exceptionally well cast for dramatizing the historical residue of disillusionment affecting the presidency. He was, after all, an authentic product of the same history that had bequeathed him a damaged institution and a distrustful nation. The appropriateness of his matching to the nation's first office at the end of the twentieth century may have been ironic but was nonetheless genuine. Each was a distinctive progeny of post-war America. Clinton was a beneficiary of the educational opportunities opened up by post-war prosperity and social reform that gave ordinary but clever and ambitious boys a ladder up which to climb. Unlike the presidents before him, his boyhood had been spent under the shadow, not of World War II, but of the Cold War with its threat of nuclear holocaust. He had been inspired by the myth of Kennedy's Camelot and had shaken the sainted president's hand (which reportedly transmitted the divine spark of political ambition). As a white, Southern youth he had supported civil rights and would benefit from the emergence of a new, revitalized South. He had, like many others, been seared by the war in Vietnam and had, also like many others, opposed it (dodged it, so it would be claimed). He had been part of the 1960s generation, and partaken of (though not inhaled) its values and attitudes – Clinton would never be radically "anti-establishment," but the 1960s mélange of high if woolly ideals, disparate interests, empathetic engagements, and narcissistic self-absorption, self-indulgence and casual sexuality comported perfectly with a character in which personal indiscipline, vaulting ambition and the desire to do good in the world could never be wholly disentangled. In 1972 he had helped in the management of Democratic candidate George McGovern's Texas campaign. In 1973 he had been offered a post on the House Judiciary Committee investigating the possible impeachment of Richard Nixon over Watergate, but had passed the job on to the girlfriend he had met in his law classes at Yale, Hillary Rodham, who thus became one of the first to learn of the "smoking gun" contained in the Nixon tapes. When Clinton married it was not to a traditional housewife-doormat but to this same Hillary Rodham, a strong, highly intelligent career woman with values, opinions and ambitions of her own. And Clinton, the ultimate young achiever of his generation, had taken the outsider's route to Washington opened up by Watergate, using the springboard of several terms as governor of Arkansas to gain the highest office in the land at the age of forty-eight. He was the first baby-boomer president, and the first to be elected in the post-Cold War era to face a world in which the old fearful certainties had been replaced by puzzling complexity, unpredictability and rapid change. Clinton's struggles with the presidential crown were thus, in Prince Hal's words, "the quarrel of a true inheritor."

What did the nation expect of this new president of whose character – as marital cheat, alleged draft-dodger and pathological fibber – it already knew some of the worst? It hoped for sound economic management and improvement, of course, and given that Clinton was the first Democratic president for twelve years, it anticipated (with loathing or joy, depending on party affiliation) the reversal of many Republican policies. But what were its expectations with regard to the malaise whose course I have been tracing here? Since 1963 the national soul had been shocked and appalled, sundered and conflicted, dismayed and indignant, challenged and disappointed, comforted and coddled, exulted and disquieted – and each of these consecutive states had been in large measure induced by presidential actions and attitudes.

In 1993 the dominant national mood seemed one of generalized uncertainty. The Gulf War had undoubtedly been a cathartic experience, and the relief of that national venting could not be annuled by the messy non-ending that inevitably tempered the sense of triumph. This may help explain why, during Clinton's two terms of office, there were comparatively few signs of either national self-recrimination or macho posturing. There was some chastened reflection on the state of the national virtue occasioned by shocking events such as the Oklahoma bombing and the shootings by school-age children of their fellows, but concern about national pride seemed to have been replaced by more mundane anxieties over things like jobs, incomes, crime and health care. Curiously enough the relative decline of America, so long a source of anxiety, was reversed during the Clinton era. As the former Soviet Union wallowed in a political and economic quagmire, as Japan and a reunified Germany grappled with severe economic difficulties, as the former Asian "tigers" struggled in the wake of a financial collapse, America forged ahead with nearly full employment, low inflation and strong growth. Yet the knowledge that it was now the world's sole superpower aroused little exultation, and no renascent missionary or imperialist zeal to intervene willy-nilly in the affairs of other nations. The world had changed too much, was changing every day, and many of the ordinary anxieties of Americans related to fears about the contours and consequences of those changes. Despite the Gulf War, a remnant of the "Vietnam syndrome" still affected citizens, Congressmen and the military (most notably in the case of sometime Chairman of the

Joint Chiefs of Staff General Colin Powell). It was expressed in a reluctance to commit American forces to uncertain adventures short of some clear and overwhelming American interest, a reluctance reinforced by the grim experience of American troops involved in a UN "peace-keeping" operation in Somalia (an engagement Clinton had inherited from the Bush administration).

Aside from caution about military engagements, however, Americans were simply unsure about what to do with their power in the post-Cold War world. With communism now a nullity, the post-war identification of American virtue with anti-communism had dissolved forever, and perhaps Americans would never again be so unquestioningly sure as they had once been of their peculiar virtue. Yet power, when possessed, cannot be ignored, and the question of the policy that should guide its use had to be answered.

Bush's professional piecemeal pragmatism, however apparently prudent in the circumstances, had in fact left Clinton with a series of disparate and extremely troubling engagements which caught him off-guard, getting his foreign policy off to a very bad start.[11] Yet Clinton, the president self-dedicated to domestic problems, would try to forge the foundations of a new strategic consensus on American foreign policy, one attuned both to the uses and preservation of American power, and to its beneficent use in an increasingly interdependent world. Though Clinton was inclined to talk the brave traditional talk of the new frontier and eternal renewal, his solution to the problem of American power and virtue was not an especially heroic one. It was rather one scaled and adapted to the perceived reality of the changed global landscape and to the historical legacy he had received.[12]

It could be argued that what was required of America in a changed world was that it be neither crusader, missionary nor hegemon, but a good, leading international citizen that accepted its wider economic, political and moral responsibilities and tried (consonant with its own interests and defense) to fulfill them in accord with its capacities. This would in fact be a reasonable characterization of the view of foreign policy at which Clinton eventually arrived. His administration's poor early efforts – the result of his team's inexperience and his own inattention – had led to accusations that Clinton did not understand the uses of American power. Such charges, combined with such domestic disasters

[11] William Hyland, *Clinton's World: Remaking American Foreign Policy* (New York, Praeger, 1999).
[12] For which he is castigated rather unfairly by James MacGregor Burns and Georgia J. Sorenson, *Dead Center: Clinton–Gore Leadership and the Perils of Moderation* (New York, Charles Scribner's, 1999).

as the resounding failure of his key health care policy and the furore over admitting gays in the military, helped produce in 1994 the historic mid-term triumph of Newt Gingrich's Republicans that ended forty years of Democratic dominance of Congress. Yet the Republican success turned out, paradoxically, to be the political making of Clinton. Among other things, it helped him lay the foundations of a new foreign policy consensus.

Clinton's main opposition hitherto had been the liberal Democrats in Congress who had resisted his attempt to drag the party toward the center (in other words, rightwards) where he was convinced it needed to be. The Republicans were much more inclined than the Democrats to pass Clinton measures that were hard on crime, that rewarded the working rather than the indigent poor, that cut spending and balanced budgets, and that ended welfare "as we know it." They were also more generally in sympathy with a liberalization of world trade, a policy that would be at the immediate expense of American labor. Domestic and foreign policy were here deeply interconnected: domestic policy aimed at allowing America to meet the challenge of the global economy while international policy aimed at positioning America so as to be able to direct it. Clinton's fiscal conservatism and his domestic focus on education, individual effort and increased productivity tried to ensure the former; the latter was to be achieved by locking America into free-trading arrangements with each of the emergent regional blocs – Europe, the Americas and Asia. Ideally, this transformation of the geo-politics of the Cold War into "geo-economics" would not only prolong American influence into the twenty-first century, but prevent potentially destructive protectionism among the blocs and help to ease the entry of a rapidly developing China into the international system.

America's economic strength and leadership were thus to be used to facilitate global development through improvements to trade (via, for example, NAFTA and APEC, through crisis aid to Mexico and the Asian economies, and by getting China admitted to the World Trade Organization). Continuing commitments to human rights were, of course, as problematic for this strategy as they had been for Carter's, particularly in the case of China. Even so, as the twentieth century drew to a close the world seemed to be edging uncertainly toward a Carterish doctrine in which human rights occasionally gave legitimate grounds for intervention in other nations. Clinton would sometimes combine inherited caution with calculated military and diplomatic action to enforce moral and international law upon outlaw nations and human rights violators (in Bosnia, Iraq, Kosovo and East Timor). The United States shouldered other moral responsibilities too (apart from guiding peaceful world development), playing an eminent diplomatic role as honest peace-broker in places like Israel or Ireland. Indeed, during Clinton's time it came to seem that no significant political problem in the world could be solved in the absence of a member of the American administration, a sign not just of American power but of a level of restored international trust in the good offices of the presidency.

The relative freedom of foreign policy from the symbolic issues of American pride and virtue that had colored it so highly for thirty years was an undoubted blessing. The real symbolic danger after Monica Lewinsky and the impeachment hearings was (on the assumption that personal redemption is as hazardous a motive in the conduct of foreign relations as national redemption) that Clinton would, as he privately indicated, attempt to redeem himself and his historical legacy by exaggerated efforts. Yet the American people appeared reasonably satisfied on the whole with his performance on the world stage. Certainly there was not the least doubt that the foreign policy prerogative remained with the executive or that Americans still looked largely to the president to demonstrate appropriate international leadership. And Clinton, for all his humiliations and even in the very midst of them, could be trusted to put on a bold face as the leader of the most powerful nation on earth.

By and large, moreover, he seemed in his actions to stand for both America's legitimate interests and the general right. Americans under Clinton avoided empty triumphalism and had little of which they need feel ashamed in their international relations. The pundits who predicted that Clinton's moral authority abroad would be fatally compromised underestimated the need that foreign leaders had to deal with and associate themselves with the legitimate representative of the United States whoever he may be. There was division among foreign commentators, just as there was among Americans, as to the relationship or lack of it between private and public morality, and as to whether Clinton's lies were to be dismissed as the culpable but understandable concealment of sexual folly or condemned as illegalities deserving of censure or dismissal. But these were matters for American domestic decision. Clinton in the meantime, though personally embarrassed, never became an embarrassment to his counterparts abroad who showed little inclination to be affected by his domestic troubles.

Clinton and moral capital

Yet this is to be reminded that, whatever Clinton's achievements were, they were overshadowed for much of his presidency by the series of scandals that all but engulfed him. If one judged only by the media coverage at its height one might well have thought there was little else but scandal to the Clinton presidency. In his second term, the press scented presidential blood as it had with Nixon and consequently anticipated his fall, at least in the public estimation if not from office. When the fall failed to occur quite as expected there was a scrabble to understand what was going on. Approval ratings of Clinton's (sexual) morality declined markedly, but his job approval ratings went in the reverse direction, climbing from around 50 percent at the start of 1998 to around 70 percent at the height of the Lewinsky impeachment affair. According to one political scientist, this result showed that political substance – peace, prosperity and moderate centrist policies – was more important than appearances in American politics, and that "the public is, within broad limits, functionally indifferent to presidential character."[13] Arthur H. Miller noted that this was an important hypothesis to examine, because "the normative implication . . . is that Americans will follow immoral leaders as long as they provide economic prosperity."[14]

Miller's more nuanced analysis of the data revealed that only among independents, and not among Republicans or Democrats, did individual assessments of the national economy have any statistical impact on Clinton's rating. Among the general public, the strongest indicator of attitude was the perception of Clinton as a strong, caring and compassionate leader, while among self-identified Republicans the dominant indicator was evaluation of his "immorality." The latter link was especially strong among far right-wing Republicans upon whom, certainly, the admitted strength of the economy had no discernible impact. Perception of excessive partisanship was the key factor in the whole affair, with both independents and Democrats overwhelmingly reacting to the Starr investigation and the Congressional impeachment process as unfair and partisan. This is what caused Clinton's approval rating to rise a little at each new attack. The public, according to Miller, understood what the media apparently did not, that character is multidimensional and sexual morality only one aspect of it. The empirical evidence, he writes, "demonstrates that the public is very capable of differentiating how they evaluate the various aspects of character."[15] It was also undoubtedly important that Clinton's lies and cover-ups had themselves no partisan motives, but

---

[13] John R. Zaller, "Monica Lewinsky's Contribution to Political Science," *PS Political Science & Politics*, 31(2) (June 1998), pp. 182–189, at p. 188.

[14] Arthur H. Miller, "Sex, Politics, and Public Opinion: What Political Scientists Really Learned from the Clinton–Lewinsky Scandal," *PS Political Science & Politics*, 32(4) (December 1999), pp. 721–729, at p. 725. Note that such a view (and indeed the way polls are often constructed) ignores the fact that managing the economy is a central feature of good leadership and of legitimate public expectation. To divorce economic factors from broadly "moral" factors in this manner is always rather simplistic.

[15] Miller, "Sex, Politics, and Public Opinion," p. 723.

were about protecting personal affairs – sordid, no doubt, but hardly sinister.[16]

The huge irony of the Clinton presidency was the role the Republicans played in sustaining him, which they did in two ways: by legislatively supporting measures that liberal Democrats opposed; and by providing him at the same time with an opposition against which he could take a moral stand. The dominant impulse in the Republican Party was provided by a religiously oriented core that stood for extreme economic-libertarianism and highly moralistic social policies. This core hated Clinton with an almost irrational passion even as he promoted measures that its leadership basically approved. Indeed, Clinton's successful co-optation of Republican policies may have intensified their loathing. Their disagreements with Clinton (for example, over balancing the budget) were often about timing and details rather than fundamentals, but their detestation of Clinton (who was always portrayed by them as radically leftist)[17] caused them to push small differences to political extremes. Given that Clinton's centrist-globalizing policy carried the danger of alienating large sections of traditional Democratic voters – for example, labor organizations and welfare recipients – the virulent opposition of the Republicans was a Godsend for rallying the troops. Compared to the Republican zealots who, Clinton claimed, would destroy Medicare for the elderly and Medicaid for the poor, the president appeared sensibly and compassionately moderate. Clinton, by a kind of moral jiu-jitsu, skillfully used this contrast at the major turning point in his first term, when in late 1995 he vetoed a series of budget Bills that represented, he alleged, extreme attacks on the New Deal heritage. He thus forced a partial shutdown of government that the public then blamed on the Republicans.

It was not Clinton's skill at political maneuver, however, that produced the same effect during the Lewinsky impeachment affair. Though Hillary talked of a "right-wing conspiracy," there was general circumspection within the administration about accusing Kenneth Starr of partisanship, knowing that an attack on a judge-appointed independent counsel could easily backfire.[18] The tactic was hardly needed, however, for the hardcore Republicans persistently and pig-headedly wrongfooted themselves, They took a politically suicidal stance in the face of overwhelming evidence that the non-Republican public, though dismayed by Clinton's

---

[16] James P. Pfiffner, "Sexual Probity and Presidential Character," *Presidential Studies Quarterly* 28(4) (Fall 1998), pp. 881–887, at p. 886.

[17] Gingrich described the Clintons as "counter-culture McGoverniks"; cited in Martin Walker, *Clinton*, p. 329.

[18] See Woodward, *Shadow*, pp. 266ff.

philandering and lying, did not want impeachment to proceed. The Republicans chose to exalt America's republican rule-of-law heritage above its democratic tradition of popular sovereignty, arguing the principle that presidents must not be seen to be above the law, and that even relatively minor infringements by those in high office had to be relentlessly prosecuted. But this high moral ground was interpreted by non-Republicans as a partisan redoubt constructed to support a spitefully vindictive assault on a president whose major sin was less perjury or obstruction of justice than that of being Bill Clinton, a man who failed dismally to conform with the conservative Republican's narrow version of morality.[19] Clinton thus gained moral capital despite himself, as a victim of partisanship that had apparently gone beyond the bounds of fairness or even sense. He would survive so well that, by the time of his stirring State of the Union address in January 2000, Vice-President Gore – who had begun his own presidential campaign under the virtual banner "I am not Bill Clinton" – had become a little less cautious about associating himself with the Clinton legacy. Indeed, had he had the courage to affirm the link wholeheartedly the presidency would probably have been his.

Conclusion

The really telling moment in the whole Clinton affair was the one in which his job approval ratings, after he had publicly confessed to lying about Lewinsky, momentarily dipped before recovering and ascending once more. The public was taken aback, distressed and disappointed. Many of them had been willing to believe (perhaps willed themselves to believe) the president when he had assured them in ringing tones that there was no truth in the stories of a sexual liaison. One could almost sense the nation taking stock, deciding what it thought important and what not in all this.

Yet it had in a sense been in preparation for that moment for decades. Had anyone among the astonishingly complaisant press of 1963 decided to go public with the truth about John F. Kennedy, there is little doubt that the revelations would have shattered not only the beautiful image of Kennedy and his family but also his presidency. But 1998 was not 1963. The nation had been treated to a steady diet of revelations about each of its presidents and about a host of subsidiary players since then. It had discovered that it had been repeatedly lied to and deceived by its leaders, treated contemptuously by some of them, and in the process it had learnt to lodge distrust where once it had laid its dearest political faith. It had

---

[19] For the after-effects of this and of the "intellectual exhaustion" of die-hard conservative Republicans, see Sean Wilentz, "Bankruptcy and Zeal: The Republican Dialectic," *Dissent* 46(3) (Summer 1999) (www.dissentmagazine.or/archive/su99/wilentz.html).

been frequently disappointed and dismayed and some of the disappointments had gone very deep, to the heart of the political system, to the heart of America itself, even to the souls of individual Americans. Clinton came at the tail end of a process that had provoked national self-questioning and self-doubt on a grand scale, that had produced alternately frustrated hopes of redemption and longings for false comfort and reassurance, that had caused international events to be dangerously freighted with exaggerated symbolical significance. The country had been lied to again, disappointed again, by Bill Clinton, but in the light of past deceits and disappointments this seemed very small beer, and personal not political. The nation decided to be realistic, to accept a leader flawed in human terms but one who, in other important respects, appeared to have striven to fulfill his obligations conscientiously, in politics the first and foremost ground for the attribution of moral capital. Whether one agreed or disagreed with his domestic policy program, whether one understood or cared about his foreign policy agenda, Clinton had at least given the country no cause for soul-searching anguish and doubt – embarrassment, yes, but let those without sin cast stones on this account.

The excess of moral capital invested in the presidency had been in part a reflection of the American myth of peculiar virtue and eternal innocence, of the American propensity to want its heroes and its heroic leaders to be idealized versions of themselves – good through and through – and the relentless probing of the modern media should perhaps be seen as a perverse symptom of longing for, rather than a denial of this hope. But the fact that no character could survive current levels of scrutiny wholly untarnished must be taken to show the unrealistic nature of the hope. In that case, the public acceptance of Clinton might be interpreted as a new dawn of realism, part of a general acceptance that Americans are as flawed as any other human beings and that their presidents are, after all, only human. Indeed, public admission of flaws and past sins (expressed with suitable regret) became part of the campaign strategy of John McCain in 2000, running dramatically if ultimately unsuccessfully in (by now traditional) outsider mode for the Republican nomination. Publicly rattling all the skeletons up-front was both a means of forestalling criticism and a signal of honesty, and McCain, with his prisoner of war experience, had sufficient proof of character to balance the admitted faults. But revealing the flaws also emphasized the ordinary humanity of the candidate – no saint, no Caesar, but a truly democratic candidate, genuinely representative of the nation's flawed but still decent people (and, by his suffering in captivity, representative of the bitter national experience related here).[20]

[20] The McCain candidacy provided an interesting coda to the saga related here, in that he was someone who at last managed to squeeze some moral capital from the Vietnam war and put it to political use. As the prosecutor of a war who had become its victim, yet who

After Clinton, then, Americans may be disposed to expect less of their leaders provided they receive enough from them. If so, then what might on the surface have seemed the nadir of the American presidency in the twentieth century, the seedy, squalid, rather sad depths beyond which it could sink no further, may prove on closer inspection to be something more complicated. Clinton, who came to the job with a distinct lack of personal moral capital (indeed with a moral deficit), who found himself handicapped by a morally diminished institution, by an intrusive press, by constant legal harassment that was the legacy of the sins of past presidents, and who was further tripped by his own profligate nature, nevertheless built a store of genuine moral capital, partly on the basis of a politically foolish and vindictive opposition and partly on a record of faithful service. It was not an heroic level of moral capital but it was sufficient to govern effectively in unheroic times. There is no doubt, of course, that it would all have been blown away, sound economy or not, if the endless investigations had turned up any hard evidence of a "smoking gun" in one of the more serious scandals. There remains a level of moral capital below which no incumbent can safely drop and hope to survive. When serious offenses are charged but unproven, the majority of the public appears to operate on the principle of the presumption of innocence, or at least of benefit of the doubt, thus providing a reserve of moral credit sufficient to ensure continuance in government. In the Lewinsky affair, the public was forced to decide exactly what it did or did not consider an offense serious enough to withdraw that credit.

What though had been the impact of the Clinton presidency on the moral standing of the office itself? McCain, in one of his television ads, placed George Bush Jr. in direct line with Clinton by asking the public: "Do you really want another politician in the White House that America can't trust?" Yet it is a curious and significant fact that indicators showed that trust in the presidency between 1994 and the end of 1998 (toward the peak of the impeachment affair) actually rose for affiliates of all parties, including the Republicans. The index did not reach positive figures, it is true, but nevertheless it rose.[21] Clinton did not restore the presidency to its preeminent place as the main repository of the national moral capital; certainly, he was not much of a role model except in a negative sense for the nation's children, and indeed his juvenile antics must be regarded as having sullied the office in this respect. They left, as the *Economist* said, "a sense of unsettling discrepancy between the gravity of the office and the man who holds it."[22] Yet Clinton seems to have inflicted no great perma-

came through with self, courage, pride and integrity more or less intact, he embodied both America's sin and proof of its redemption.
[21] See Miller, "Sex, Politics, and Public Opinion," p. 728.

nent damage on the office and even to have done some good. Part of the reason was that few of the moral issues raised by the Clinton tenure were those that had so deeply hurt the presidency during the previous decades and drained it of much of its moral capital. Indeed with respect to issues of national virtue and pride as these are figured in the world at large, Clinton performed creditably enough.

There may, of course, be other reasons than those I have been pursuing why the presidency has lost status in a changing world (disenchantment with central governments is not a phenomenon confined to the United States). Yet for all the changes afoot, the presidency will continue to be a vital, pivotal office in the American system and must, by virtue of its unique role, continue to carry the largest portion of both the leadership, the prestige and the moral weight of the nation. Americans will inevitably have a strong interest, not just in whether governments are capable of delivering the domestic prosperity and social justice citizens seek, but in whether they utilize, dispose and preserve American power in ways consonant with the moral self-respect of the nation. They will inevitably still look above all to the presidency for the accomplishment of these things. Whether the exaggerated awe and respect with which presidents were once commonly regarded will ever be revived is another question. In 1974, Arthur Schlesinger argued that this tendency had anyway gone too far in American life and that institutional solutions were needed to "dispel the spurious reverence that had come to envelop the office."[23] Schlesinger has perhaps got his wish. After Nixon, reverence was much less evident; after the degrading if more trivial antics of Clinton it might be socially impossible to regenerate.

Post scriptum

The election of George W. Bush occurred after the above had been written. In the speculation about the direction the younger Bush's conservative foreign relations team was likely to take, it was generally conceded that Clinton's geo-economic policies would be continued but with a more cautious approach to non-economic foreign entanglements. What was notable was the slogan that Condaleeza Rice coined to express the approach of the new administration: "humility and strength." Awkward and anomalous though it sounded, it was clearly intended to encompass

---

[22] *Economist* (editorial), 330(7844) (8 January 1994), pp. 18–19. See also David Marsland, "Morality, Legality and Democratic Leadership," *Society* 36(3) (March–April 1999), pp. 47–52.

[23] Arthur M. Schlesinger, Jr., *The Imperial Presidency* (London, Andre Deutsch, 1974), p. 392.

both terms of the power–virtue equation that has been the subject of my argument. What it will mean in practice is difficult to say, though the suspicion is raised that the United States has yet to come to some final, consensual view of the problem of the responsible deployment of American power.

Epilogue

This book has been about those continuous judgments that people make which give rise in the political realm to what I have called moral capital – the credit accorded to individuals or institutions that helps support them in their political existence and enables them to perform intended functions and purposes. My underlying assumption has been the ubiquity and effect of moral judgment in politics, as in all of life.

As social creatures dependent upon each other for everything, from the most basic requirements of survival to the higher requirements of a life worth living, we have a necessary and perennial interest in mutually judging one another. We judge constantly, instinctively and variously according to whatever aspect of others we are, in the moment, concerned to assess; we judge lazily and habitually or acutely and urgently depending on circumstances or on individual predilection. At the lowest level, the boundless realm of gossip betrays our abiding interest in even the minutiae of the conduct and character of others. At higher levels, where interest is more materially engaged, the assessments we make are infinitely and variously consequential. We appraise the intentions, sincerity, trustworthiness, capabilities and deeds of those whose actions may impinge directly or indirectly on us or on our own, or which may have a bearing on purposes we desire to see advanced. And we judge not just individuals but the institutions in which the collective powers of social humanity are organized for either good or ill, which may promise much but deliver little, whose operation may either oppress or enable us, or both at once. Our judgments may change over time, reflecting our particular experience and our particular capacities, often our innate temperaments. We may develop attitudes of trust, loyalty, love, hate, skepticism, cynicism, belief, devotion, hope, disillusionment, resentment, sometimes all of these in confusion. But judge we must and judge we do, until at last we close our eyes and can judge no more.

The implication of this is that all our choices, actions or attitudes may at any time be subject to moral appraisal, and may evoke reactions of approval or disapproval, condemnation or complaisance, respect or contempt, acquiescence or resistance. Because all we do and say, and every attitude we adopt, has effects in a shared world, others always have a potential interest, not only in morally appraising but also in trying to shape us and our choices, and we likewise in appraising and shaping both them and ourselves. Nor are our relationships immune, for they are always normatively defined and justified (if only implicitly) and thus forever vulnerable to revisionist critique. No set of human actions, attitudes or relations can be considered unproblematically non-moral in the sense of being beyond the possibility of moral challenge. Though ordinary acts may seem entirely neutral, this is an illusion. Washing the dishes, for example, may also be: fulfilling a proper responsibility; being unfairly put upon by a partner now slouched in front of the TV; mindlessly conforming to suspect bourgeois values of cleanliness; or heedlessly pouring damaging detergents into the ecosystem. There is no place one can go, not even to the kitchen sink, where one can be beyond the reach of the moral question. There is no *inherently* "private" realm in morality any more than there is in politics, for presumed "natural" or "normal" actions, attitudes and relations can always be moralized and thus politicized.

We may be but dimly aware of the deep moral grooves within which our habitual actions and relations flow until the judgments of others create impediments to their smooth course. Then it becomes clear that our whole lives are lived within a profoundly normative environment, and that moral norms form a distinctive and ubiquitous substrate. Indeed, we live in an era where moral challenges to established ways of thinking and behaving are so frequent and so cumulative, in which the possibility of achieving some cozy *status quo* are so diminished, that one might think the ubiquity of the moral stratum self-evident. Moral discomfort seems to have become a permanent condition. The eye of the other is always upon us. Our innocence is frequently and unexpectedly affronted, arraigned and brought before the court of moral opinion. What once we unthinkingly regarded as lacking moral connotation has proved to be deeply implicated in matters of justice, and innocence lost can never be regained. We suffer offense to our sense of our own *rightness*. Justifications are demanded for things we thought scarcely needed justification, and arguments required where we thought none necessary. We must respond, defend, deny, reconstruct and try to move to a more self-conscious plane where moral comfort (which is all we miss of innocence) may be recovered. If we fail, our whole life may fall seriously out of kilter with our moral sensibility. Our discomfort becomes anxiety and anxiety seeks resolution, one way or another. If anxiety turns to anger, we may seek resolution by force or violence: "Analyze this!"

Force is the response of the totalitarian who fears the perpetual human propensity to judge in ways that cannot, in principle, be totally controlled. The totalitarian in fact seeks not to control judgment but to annihilate it, since free consent is as much an obstacle to total domination as free opposition. The aim of totalitarian education, according to Hannah Arendt, "has never been to instill convictions but to destroy the capacity to form any."[1] If totalitarians cannot utterly annihilate judgment, they can at least extinguish its power to have real effect. They have proved that this can be accomplished, at least partially. People can be de-moralized, de-humanized, their judgments and actions, their very lives and deaths made not to count, their capacities undermined. It can be done, but it requires fanatical ideological intent and incredible power of ruthless organization. To realize the necessary conditions for totalitarian government, the real world must be replaced by a fantasy world in which human beings act, but no longer humanly. And to succeed at all, totalitarianism must, by definition, succeed completely, it must destroy the power of independent judgment entirely and universally. The very extravagance of the aim reveals its insanity, and in the act of conceiving it totalitarians pay tribute to the reality, ubiquity and significance of the human capacity for judgment.

Despite the ubiquity of moral judgment, however, and despite the fact that most public debate and comment on politics is couched in deeply moralized language, many practitioners in the discipline of political science have tended either to discount or to ignore it. When they *do* approach the subject of ethics or morality in politics, it is often with an apology. Robert Jackson, for instance, commences an essay on the "situational ethics" of statecraft with the following observation:

Anyone who writes on the ethics of statecraft immediately meets with skepticism on the part of those international relations scholars who see only a contradiction in that expression. For them the conduct of foreign or military policy is governed by self-interest or expediency and not by morality; it is an instrumental and not a normative subject: power politics.[2]

Jackson goes on to argue that such excessively "realist" positions fail to capture something true about international statecraft, namely, that its practice occurs within a complex normative environment, marked by ambiguity and uncertainty, which demands *responsible* action of national leaders. In other words, State leaders can be, and often are, held legally

---

[1] Hannah Arendt, *The Origins of Totalitarianism* (London, Andre Deutsch, 1973), pp. 451 and 468.
[2] Robert H. Jackson, "The Situational Ethics of Statecraft," in Cathal J. Nolan (ed.), *Ethics and Statecraft: The Moral Dimension of International Affairs* (Westport, CT, Praeger, 1996), p. 21.

and morally accountable for their choices, choices which may occasionally require an assertion of moral character and a display of virtues other than instrumental efficiency in the pursuit of national self-interest.

The skepticism to which Jackson refers can be encountered over the whole domain of political science. This goes much further than the exercise of a healthy skepticism about politicians. When a politician plays the ethics card to undermine an opponent, or has it played against him- or herself in turn, analysts are rightly skeptical. Indeed, provisional skepticism about the professed motives of politicians is merely a matter of sound policy. "When a politician starts talking morality, I put my hand on my wallet," said Mark Twain. But in political science, healthy skepticism has congealed into what I have called an entrenched *methodological cynicism*.[3] This has at its core the belief that human action is best explained by presuming only the most narrowly self-interested of motivations, all references by agents to moral factors and motivations being implicitly regarded as indicative of bad faith or of wishful thinking.

Such a presumption has, in fact, a long history in modern political thought. Montaigne complained of it in the sixteenth-century Italian historian Guicciardini, who always attributed action to:

some vicious motive or to the hope of gain. It is impossible to imagine that among the infinite number of actions on which he passes judgment, not a single one was inspired by motives of reason. Corruption can never have affected men so universally that someone did not escape infection.[4]

The rise of science, with its materialist and mechanistic accounts of the natural world, undoubtedly encouraged this tendency. Western social and political theory has been deeply influenced at all its stages by the contemporaneous development of modern science. Its understanding (or usually misunderstanding) of the latter has varied from era to era, but the temptation to assimilate human behavior to the deterministic universe allegedly revealed by science (or, in the case of Kant, to try to make room for it) has been perennial. Hobbes, with his adaptation of Galileo's "resolutive-compositive" method to the explanation of political life, brilliantly set the pattern of this ambition right at the start of our modern era.

Hobbes, of course, was providing a *justification* for political power as a necessary protection of interests, whereas political science offers *explanations* of political phenomena in terms of interests and the mobilization of

---

[3] See Rogers M. Smith, "Still Blowing in the Wind: The American Quest for a Democratic, Scientific Political Science," *Daedalus* 126(1) (Winter 1997), pp. 253–287; also Rogers M. Smith, "Science, Non-science and Politics," in T. J. Mcdonald (ed.), *The Historic Turn in the Human Sciences* (Ann Arbor, University of Michigan Press, 1996), pp. 119–159.

[4] Michel de Montaigne, "On Books," in *Essays* (J. M. Cohen trans., Harmondsworth, Penguin, 1971), p. 172.

resources for their defense and furtherance. The more readily determinable interests are, the easier explanation will be, and the temptation is therefore to interpret them as narrowly as possible. Given the success of natural science, it is hardly surprising that a new discipline calling itself, in emulation, political science should be so often tempted down this reductionist pathway in search of the *real, causal wellspring of human behavior,* nor that it should so often come up with an account of narrow self-interest virtually indistinguishable from moral selfishness. Predictivity and generalizability, the presumed hallmarks of the scientific enterprise, seemed to depend on keeping the causes of human action as simple and as singular as possible.

To which we might reply, paraphrasing Aristotle, that we should accept whatever degree of predictivity and generalizability the object of study will permit. If the human world does not, because of its normative complexity, lend itself to explanation in terms of reductive universal laws then that is simply a fact that political science must accommodate. At any rate, the effect of the scientistic tendency is to leave the moral with much the same dependent status as that attributed to it by Karl Marx, that self-proclaimed "realist" of the nineteenth century.[5] Politics becomes simply power in motion, and morality a deceitful garment cloaking all the naked, selfish interests that power serves.

It would be absurd, of course, to claim that power and interests are *not* centrally at issue in politics. The political analyst with no nose for the scent of power in defense of interest is in the wrong profession. But, in the practice of politics, as opposed to the study of them, the interests defined and defended are, as I have said, always claimed to be *justified* and *legitimate* interests, and a great deal of political action revolves precisely round the moral demand that these be adequately and justly addressed. However mundane or exalted such interests may be, when they are perceived to be ignored, slighted or overridden they arouse deep feelings of injustice among both the offended and their sympathetic champions. This is to say that the central discourse of practical politics is, at base, a moral discourse, a fact which helps to account for the passion, sometimes unto death, with which political positions are defended.

Yet a hardened realist may admit all this and still say that, when push comes to shove, political outcomes are explained neither by superior moral argumentation nor by moral action, but simply by the preponderance of political power or superior force. That the victors inevitably sanctify their gains in the language of moral right merely proves the point,

[5] See my "The End of Morality? Theory, Practice and the 'Realistic Outlook' of Karl Marx," *NOMOS XXXVII: Theory and Practice* (New York University Press, 1995), pp. 403–439.

for the moral cloak may be necessary even if deceitful. Or it may be just that we dislike the sensation of moral discomfort, and have a fortunate genius for persuading ourselves, whatever our circumstances, of the rightness of our cause. Given the well-chronicled fallibility of human beings, the realist's argument cannot be lightly dismissed. Nor can we deny the recalcitrance of human social structures and institutions, and of the vested interests embedded in them, to reform along lines allegedly dictated by moral reason.

But the traditional divide between "realists" and "idealists" in political thought can be grossly exaggerated. "Was there ever a realist so pure," asks Otto Pflanze, "as to be untouched by ethico-ideological concerns? And is not the opposite question also valid: was there ever an idealist unconcerned about power and its uses?"[6] If it is hopelessly utopian to expect too much of morality in politics, to discount it altogether as a significantly operative force is to give too much away too easily. This, at least, has been the presumption informing this book. My case is that the methodological cynics (and lay cynics, too, for that matter, whose attitude is more an expression of moral disappointment than anything else) overlook the real and complex causal roles that moral factors and attitudes play in the pursuit and defense of power and interests. Nor are these roles wholly explicable as either hypocrisy or self-deceit. There is an inevitable and ineradicable moral dimension to life, political life included, which is neither ineffable nor epiphenomenal, but which, on the contrary, has significant, and highly variable, causal effect.

Insofar as factors of moral judgment come significantly into play in any set of events, to that extent will any explanation which omits them be deficient. In this work I have applied the concept of moral capital to a variety of political situations to try to demonstrate the truth of this, and to show that any account of politics that, *a priori*, leaves out the moral dimension does not wholly deserve the appellation "realist."

---

[6] Otto Pflanze, "Realism and Idealism in Historical Perspective: Otto von Bismarck," in Nolan, *Ethics and Statecraft*, p. 39.

Bibliography

Appleby, J., Hunt, L. and Jacob, M., *Telling the Truth About History*, New York: Norton, 1995

Arendt, H., *The Origins of Totalitarianism*, London: André Deutsch, 1986

Aristotle, *Aristotle*, translated by J. H. Freese, London: William Heinemann, 1926

Arnold, P. E., "Determinism and Contingency in Skowronek's Political Time," *Polity* 37 (1995), pp. 497–508

Asplund, R. (ed.), *Human Capital Formation in an Economic Perspective*, Helsinki: Physica-Verlag, 1994

Aung San Suu Kyi, *Aung San of Burma*, Edinburgh: Kiscadale Publications, 1991
  Freedom from Fear and Other Writings, edited by Aris, M., New York: Penguin, 1991

Aye, M., "The Last Days of Mr. Leon Nichols," *Burma Debate* 5(1) (Winter 1998)

Ball, M. A., "The Phantom in the Oval Office: The John F. Kennedy Assassination's Symbolic Impact on Lyndon B. Johnson, His Key Advisers, and the Vietnam Decision-Making Process," *Presidential Studies Quarterly* 24(1) (1994), pp. 105–119
  Vietnam-on-the-Potomac, New York: Praeger, 1992

Barger, H., *The Impossible Presidency*, Glenview, IL: Scott Foresman and Co., 1984

Basler, R. P., Pratt, M. D. and Dunlap, L. A. (eds.), *The Collected Works of Abraham Lincoln*, New Brunswick, NJ: Rutgers University Press, 1953–55

Bass, B., *Performance Beyond Expectations*, New York: Free Press, 1985

Becker, G., *Human Capital*, New York: National Bureau of Economic Research, 1975

Bell, C., *The Reagan Paradox: American Foreign Policy in the 1980s*, London: Edward Elgar, 1989

Benjamin, M., *Splitting the Difference: Compromise and Integrity in Ethics and Politics*, Lawrence, KS: University Press of Kansas, 1990

Beschloss, M. (ed.), *Taking Charge: The Johnson White House Tapes*, New York: Simon & Schuster, 1997

Blight, J. G. and Welsh, D. A., *On the Brink: Americans and Soviets Reexamine the Cuban Missile Crisis*, New York: Hill and Wang, 1989

Branch, T., *Pillar of Fire: America in the King Years*, New York: Simon & Schuster, 1998

Brand, D. R., "Republicanism and the Vigorous Executive: A Review Essay,"

Political Science Quarterly 109 (1994–95), pp. 901–902

Brinkley, A., "What's Wrong with American Political Leadership," *Wilson Quarterly* 18(2) (Spring 1994), pp. 47–48

Bromberger, M. and Bromberger, S., *Les 13 Complots du 13 Mai*, Paris: Fayard, 1969

Brookhiser, R., "A Man on Horseback," *Atlantic Monthly* (January 1996), pp. 51–64

Bryman, A., *Charisma and Leadership in Organizations*, London: Sage, 1992

Brzezinski, Z., *Power and Principle*, London: Wiedenfeld and Nicolson, 1983

Buchanan, B., *The Presidential Experience: What the Office Does to the Man*, Englewood Cliffs, NJ: Prentice-Hall, 1978

Burns, J. McGregor, *Leadership*, New York: Harper Colophon, 1978

Burns, J. M. and Sorenson, G. J., *Dead Center: Clinton–Gore Leadership and the Perils of Moderation*, New York: Charles Scribner's, 1999

Burt, R., "The Social Structure of Competition," in Nohria, N. and Eccles, R. G. (eds.), *Networks and Organizations: Structure, Form and Action*, Boston: Harvard Business School Press, 1992, pp. 57–91

Bush, G. and Scowcroft, B., *A World Transformed*, New York: Knopf, 1998

Canovan, M., "Trust the People! Populism and the Two Faces of Democracy," *Political Studies* 47 (1999), pp. 2–16

Caro, R. A., *The Years of Lyndon Johnson*, 2 vols., New York: Knopf, 1982–84

Carter, J., *Why Not the Best?*, Eastbourne: Kingsway, 1977

Cate, C., *André Malraux*, London: Hutchinson, 1995

Chin Geok, A., *Aung San Suu Kyi: Towards a New Freedom*, New York: Prentice-Hall, 1998

Chirot, D., *Modern Tyrants*, Princeton University Press, 1994

Citrin, J., "Comment: The Political Relevance of Trust in Government," *American Political Science Review* 68 (September 1974), pp. 973–988

Citrin, J. and Green, D. P., "Presidential Leadership and the Resurgence of Trust in Government," *British Journal of Political Science* 16 (October 1986), pp. 431–453

Clements, A., *The Voice of Hope: Aung San Suu Kyi in Conversation with Alan Clements*, Harmondsworth: Penguin, 1997

Coleridge, S. T., *Introductory Address, Addresses to the People*, London: no publisher named, 1938

Conger, J., *Learning to Lead*, San Francisco: Jossey-Bass, 1992

Crabb, C. V. and Mulcahy, K. V., "The Elitist Presidency: George Bush and the Management of Operation Desert Storm," in Waterman, R. W. (ed.), *The Presidency Reconsidered*, Itasca, IL: F. E. Peacock, 1993

Craig, S. C., *The Malevolent Leaders: Popular Discontent in America*, Boulder, CO: Westview, 1993

(ed.), *Broken Contract: Changing Relations Between Americans and Their Government*, Boulder, CO: Westview, 1996

Crawley, A., *De Gaulle: A Biography*, London: Collins, 1969

Cronin, T. E., *The State of the Presidency*, Boston: Little, Brown and Co., 1980

Cronin, T. E. and Genovese, M. A., *The Paradoxes of the American Presidency*, New York: Oxford University Press, 1998

Crozier, B., *De Gaulle*, New York: Charles Scribner's Sons, 1973

D'Souza, D., *Ronald Reagan: How an Extraordinary Man Became an Extraordinary Leader*, New York: Free Press, 1997

De Gaulle, C., *Major Addresses, Statements and Press Conferences of General Charles de Gaulle, May 19, 1958–January 31, 1964*, New York: French Embassy Press and Information Division, 1965

The Army of the Future, London: Hutchinson, 1940

The Complete War Memoirs of Charles de Gaulle, New York: Simon & Schuster, 1967

The Edge of the Sword, London: Faber and Faber, 1960

De Montaigne, M., "On Books," in *Essays*, translated by J. M. Cohen, Harmondsworth: Penguin, 1971

De Tocqueville, A., *Democracy in America*, Ware, Herts: Wordsworth Classics, 1998

Diescho, J., *The Limits of Foreign Policy Making in South Africa*, Pretoria: Unisa Press, 1996

Donald, D., "Getting Right with Lincoln," *Atlantic Unbound* (originally 1956, online version 1999, www.theatlantic.com/issues/99sep/9909lincoln2.htm)

Lincoln, London: Pimlico, 1996

Lincoln Reconsidered, New York: Knopf, 1959

Dreifus, C., "The Passion of Suu Kyi," *Interview*, New York: Seven Stories Press, 1997

Duffy, M. and Goodgame, D., *Marching in Place: The Status Quo Presidency of George Bush*, New York: Simon & Schuster, 1992

Dumbrell, J., *The Carter Presidency: A Re-evaluation*, Manchester: Manchester University Press, 1995

Easton, D., *A Systems Analysis of Political Life*, New York: Wiley, 1965

Echevarria, D., *Mirage in the West: A History of the French Image of American Society to 1815*, Princeton: Princeton University Press, 1957

Edelman, M., *Constructing the Political Spectacle*, Chicago: Chicago University Press, 1988

Edwards, G. C., *The Public Presidency: The Pursuit of Popular Support*, New York: St. Martin's Press, 1983

Eisenhower, D. D., *Crusade in Europe*, Garden City, NY: Doubleday, 1948

Ellis, R. J. (ed.), *Speaking to the People: The Rhetorical Presidency in Historical Perspective*, Amherst: University of Massachusetts Press, 1998

Engelhardt, T., *The End of Victory Culture: Cold War America and the Disillusioning of a Generation*, New York: Basic Books, 1995

Fehrenbacher, D. E. (ed.), *Abraham Lincoln: A Documentary Portrait Through His Speeches and Writings*, Stanford University Press, 1964

Fiedler, F., *A Theory of Leadership Effectiveness*, New York: McGraw-Hill, 1967

Foucault, M., "Truth and Power," in Rabinow, P. (ed.), *The Foucault Reader*, Harmondsworth: Penguin, 1984, pp. 51–75

Frank, T. (ed.), *The Tethered Presidency*, New York: New York University Press, 1981

Fried, A., *Muffled Echoes: Oliver North and the Politics of Public Opinion*, New York: Columbia University Press, 1997

Fukuyama, F., *The End of History and the Last Man*, London: Hamish Hamilton, 1992

Furnivall, J. S., *Colonial Policy and Practice: A Comparative Study of Burma and Netherlands India*, New York: New York University Press, 1948

Fursenko, A. and Naftali, T., *"One Hell of a Gamble"*: *Khrushchev, Castro and Kennedy*, New York: Murray, 1997

Gabriel, R. H., *The Course of American Democratic Thought*, 3rd edn., New York: Greenwood, 1986

Galante, P., *The General*, London: Leslie Frewin, 1969

Gardner, J. W., *On Leadership*, New York: The Free Press, 1990

Garrison, J., *On the Trail of the Assassins: My Investigation and Prosecution of the Murder of President Kennedy*, New York: Sheridan Square Press, 1988

Glad, B., *Jimmy Carter in Search of the Great White House*, New York: W. W. Norton & Co., 1980

Goldhagen, D. J., *Hitler's Willing Executioners: Ordinary Germans and the Holocaust*, New York: Knopf, 1996

Greenstein, F. I. (ed.), *Leadership in the Modern Presidency*, Harvard: Harvard University Press, 1988

Grover, W., *The President as Prisoner*, New York: SUNY Press, 1989

Hargrove, E. C., *Jimmy Carter as President*, Baton Rouge: Louisiana State University Press, 1988

"The Carter Presidency in Historical Perspective," in Rosenbaum, H. B. and Urgrunskey, A. (eds.), *The Presidency and Domestic Politics of Jimmy Carter*, Westport, CT: Greenwood Press, 1994

The President as Leader: Appealing to the Better Angels of Our Nature, Lawrence: University of Kansas, 1998

Harper, R. S., *Lincoln and the Press*, New York: McGraw-Hill, 1951

Havel, V., *Disturbing the Peace*, New York: Knopf, 1990

Helliwell, J. F., *Economic Growth and Social Capital in Asia: Working Papers*, Cambridge MA: National Bureau of Economic Research, 1996

Helliwell, J. F. and Putnam, R. D., "Social Capital and Economic Growth in Italy," *Eastern Economic Journal* 21(3) (1995), pp. 295–307

Henggeler, P. R., *The Kennedy Persuasion: American Presidential Politics Since JFK*, Chicago: I. R. Dee, 1995 (expanded version of his 1991 book, *In His Steps: Lyndon Johnson and the Kennedy Mystique*)

Herr, M., *Dispatches*, London: Picador, 1978

Herring, H., *America's Longest War: The United States and Vietnam, 1950–1975*, New York: Wiley, 1979

"The Wrong Kind of Loyalty: McNamara's Apology for Vietnam," *Foreign Affairs* 74(3) (1995), pp. 154–158

Hersh, S., *The Dark Side of Camelot*, New York: HarperCollins, 1998

Hertzberg, H., "Jimmy Carter 1977–1981," in Wilson, R. A. (ed.), *Character Above All*, New York: Simon & Schuster, 1995

Hetherington, "The Political Relevance of Political Trust," *American Political Science Review* 92(4) (December 1998), pp. 791–808

Hibbing, J. R. and Thiess-Morse, E., *Congress as Public Enemy: Public Attitudes Toward American Political Institutions*, New York: Cambridge University

Press, 1995

Hodgson, G., *All Things to All Men: The False Promise of the Modern American Presidency*, London: Weidenfeld and Nicolson, 1980

Hoekstra, D. J., "Comments on Theory and History, Structure and Agency," *Presidential Studies Quarterly* 29(3) (September 1999), pp. 682–684

"The Politics of Politics: Skowronek and Presidential Research," *Presidential Studies Quarterly* 29(3) (September 1999), 657–671

Hoffman, S. and Hoffman, I., "The Will to Grandeur: de Gaulle as Political Artist," in D. A. Rustow (ed.), *Philosophers and Kings: Studies in Leadership*, New York: George Braziller, 1970

Htin Aung, *History of Burma*, New York: Columbia University Press, 1967

Hunt, M. H., *Lyndon Johnson's War: America's Cold War Crusade in Vietnam, 1945–1968*, New York: Hill and Wang, 1996

Hyland, W., *Clinton's World: Remaking American Foreign Policy*, New York: Praeger, 1999

Iyer, R. N., *The Moral and Political Thought of Mahatma Gandhi*, New York: Oxford University Press, 1973

Jackson, R. H., "The Situational Ethics of Statecraft," in Nolan, C. J. (ed.), *Ethics and Statecraft: The Moral Dimension of International Affairs*, Westport, CT: Praeger, 1996, pp. 21–36

Jamieson, K. H., *Packaging the Presidency: A History and Criticism of Presidential Campaign Advertising*, 3rd edn., New York: Oxford University Press, 1996

Jones, C. O., *The Presidency in a Separated System*, Washington, DC: Brookings Institution, 1994

Jones, H., *Union in Peril: The Crisis over British Intervention in the Civil War*, Chapel Hill: University of North Carolina Press, 1992

Kane, J., "The End of Morality? Theory, Practice, and the 'Realistic Outlook' of Karl Marx," *NOMOS XXXVII: Theory and Practice*, New York University Press, 1995, pp. 403–439

Kant, I., *Perpetual Peace: A Philosophical Essay*, M. Campbell Smith trans., London: Dent, 1915

Kearns, D., *Lyndon Johnson and the American Dream*, New York: Alfred A. Knopf, 1976

Kernell, S., *Going Public: New Strategies of Presidential Leadership*, Washington, DC: CQ Press, 1986

Kinder, D. R. and Fiske, S., "Presidents in the Public Mind," in Hermann, M. G. (ed.), *Handbook of Political Psychology*, San Francisco: Jossey-Bass, 1989, pp. 193–218

Kissinger, H., *The Years of Upheaval*, Boston: Little, Brown, 1982

Kovic, R., *Born on the Fourth of July*, New York: McGraw-Hill, 1976

Likert, R., *Human Organization*, New York: McGraw-Hill, 1967

Lintner, B., *Aung San Suu Kyi: Burma's Unfinished Renaissance*, Centre of Southeast Asia Studies Working Paper No. 64, Melbourne: Monash University, 1990

Outrage: Burma's Struggle for Democracy, London and Bangkok: White Lotus, 1990

Lowi, T. J., *The Personal President: Power Invested, Promise Unfulfilled*, Ithaca:

Cornell University Press, 1985

Machiavelli, N., *The Discourses*, Harmondsworth: Pelican, 1970

MacKinnon, C. A., *Toward a Feminist Theory of the State*, Cambridge, MA: Harvard University Press, 1989

Malraux, A., *Fallen Oaks: Conversations with de Gaulle*, London: Hamish Hamilton, 1972

Mamdani, M., *Citizen and Subject: Contemporary Africa and the Legacy of Colonialism*, Kampala: Fountain, 1996

Manchester, W., *Death of a President*, Harper & Row, 1967

Mandela, N., *Long Walk to Freedom*, Boston: Little, Brown & Co., 1994

The Struggle is My Life, South Africa: Mayibuye Books, 1994

Mandela, W., *Part of My Soul*, edited by Anne Benjamin and adapted by Mary Benson, Harmondsworth: Penguin, 1985

Marsden, P. V. and Lin, N. (eds.), *Social Structure and Network Analysis*, Beverly Hills: Sage, 1982

Marsland, D., "Morality, Legality and Democratic Leadership," *Society* 36(3) (March–April 1999), pp. 47–52

Matthews, C., *Nixon and Kennedy: The Rivalry that Shaped Cold War America*, New York: Simon & Schuster, 1996

Maung, M., *Burma and General Ne Win*, New York: Asia Publishing House, 1969

Totalitarianism in Burma: Prospects for Economic Development, New York: Paragon House, 1992

Mauriac, C., *The Other de Gaulle: Diaries 1944–1954*, Moura Budberg trans., London: Angus & Robertson, 1973

May, E. and Zelikow, P. (eds.), *The Kennedy Tapes: Inside the White House During the Cuban Missile Crisis*, Harvard University Press, 1997

McNamara, R. S., *In Retrospect: The Tragedy and Lessons of Vietnam*, New York: Times Books, 1995

McPherson, J. M., "A Passive President?," *Atlantic Monthly* (November 1995), www.theatlantic.com/issues/95nov/lincoln/lincoln.htm

Mehta, P. B., "Pluralism after Liberalism?," *Critical Review* 11 (1997), pp. 503–518

Meredith, M., *Nelson Mandela: A Biography*, London: Hamish Hamilton, 1997

Mervin, D., *George Bush and the Guardianship Presidency*, New York: St. Martin's Press, 1996

Milkis, S. M., "Franklin D. Roosevelt, Progressivism, and the Limits of Popular Leadership," in Ellis, R. J. (ed.), *Speaking to the People: The Rhetorical Presidency in Historical Perspective*, Amherst: University of Massachusetts Press, 1998, pp. 184–209

Miller, A. H., "Political Issues and Trust in Government," *American Political Science Review* 68 (September 1974), pp. 951–972

"Sex, Politics, and Public Opinion: What Political Scientists Really Learned from the Clinton–Lewinsky Scandal," *PS Political Science & Politics* 32(4) (December 1999), pp. 721–729

Miller, W. L., "Lincoln's Second Inaugural: The Zenith of Statecraft," *Center Magazine* 13 (1980), pp. 53–64

Mitgang, H. (ed.), *Lincoln as They Saw Him*, New York: Collier Books, 1962

Moe, T., "Presidents, Institutions and Theory," in Edwards, G., Kessel, J. H. and Rockman, B. A. (eds.), *Researching the Presidency: Vital Questions, New Approaches*, Pittsburgh: University of Pittsburgh Press, 1993

Mower, A. G., *Human Rights and American Foreign Policy*, New York: Greenwood, 1987

Neely, M. E., Jr., *The Last Best Hope of Earth: Abraham Lincoln and the Promise of America*, Cambridge, MA: Harvard University Press, 1995

Neustadt, R. E., *Presidential Power and the Modern Presidents: The Politics of Leadership from Roosevelt to Reagan*, New York: Free Press, 1990

Nevins, A., *The Statesmanship of the Civil War*, New York: Collier, 1962

Nye, J., Zelikow, P. and King, D., *Why People Don't Trust Government*, Cambridge, MA: Harvard University Press, 1997

Oakeshott, M., *On Human Conduct*, Oxford: Clarendon Press, 1975
  The Politics of Faith and the Politics of Scepticism, New Haven: Yale University Press, 1996

Ottaway, D., *Chained Together: Mandela, de Klerk and the Struggle to Remake South Africa*, New York: Time Books, 1993

Paludan, P. S., *A Covenant with Death: The Constitution, Law, and Equality in the Civil War Era*, Urbana: University of Illinois Press, 1975
  "A People's Contest": The Union and Civil War 1861–1865, New York: Harper & Row, 1988

Paterson, T. G. (ed.), *Kennedy's Quest for Victory: American Foreign Policy, 1961– 1963*, New York: Oxford University Press, 1989

Pfiffner, J. P., "Sexual Probity and Presidential Character," *Presidential Studies Quarterly* 28(4) (Fall 1998), pp. 881–887

Pflanze, O., "Realism and Idealism in Historical Perspective: Otto von Bismarck," in Nolan, C. J. (ed.), *Ethics and Statecraft: The Moral Dimension of International Affairs*, Westport, CT: Praeger, 1996, pp. 39–56

Pickles, D., *The Fifth French Republic*, London: Methuen, 1962

Posner, G., *Case Closed*, New York: Random House, 1993

Putnam, R., "Tuning In, Tuning Out: The Strange Disappearance of Social Capital in America," 1995 Ithiel de Sola Pool Lecture to the American Political Science Association, *PS: Political Science and Politics* 28(4) (December 1995), pp. 664–683

Putnam, Robert D. (with Leonardi, Robert and Nanetti, Raffaella Y.), *Making Democracy Work: Civic Traditions in Modern Italy*, Princeton: Princeton University Press, 1993

Reeves, R., *A Ford, Not a Lincoln: The Decline of American Political Leadership*, London: Hutchinson, 1976
  President Kennedy, New York: Simon & Schuster, 1993

Reeves, T., *A Question of Character: A Life of John F. Kennedy*, London: Bloomsbury, 1991

Riker, W. H., *The Art of Political Manipulation*, New Haven: Yale University Press, 1986

Roe, M. (ed.), *Speeches and Letters of Abraham Lincoln, 1832–1865*, London: J. M. Dent & Sons, 1907

Roper, J., "Richard Nixon's Political Hinterland: The Shadows of JFK and

Charles de Gaulle," *Presidential Studies Quarterly* 28(2) (Spring 1998), pp. 422–435

Rosati, J. A., "Jimmy Carter, a Man Before His Time? The Emergence and Collapse of the First Post-Cold War Presidency," *Presidential Studies Quarterly* 23(3) (Summer 1993), pp. 459–476

Rose, G. L., *The American Presidency Under Siege*, Albany: SUNY Press, 1997

Rosenstone, S. J. and Hansen, M., *Mobilization, Participation and Democracy in America*, New York: Macmillan, 1993

Rousseau, J.-J., *The Social Contract*, Harmondsworth: Penguin, 1968

Schell, J., *The Time of Illusion*, New York: Knopf, 1975

Schlesinger, A. M., Jr., *A Thousand Days: John F. Kennedy in the White House*, New York: Houghton Mifflin, 1965

The Imperial Presidency, London: Andre Deutsch, 1974 and 1989

Schoenbrun, D., *The Three Lives of De Gaulle*, London: Hamish Hamilton, 1966

Schramm-Evans, Z., *Dark Ruby: Travels in a Troubled Land*, London: Pandora, 1997

Sheehy, G., *Character: America's Search for Leadership*, New York: William Morrow and Co., 1988

Sheridan, G., *Asian Values, Western Dreams*, St. Leonards, NSW: Allen & Unwin, 1999

Shogan, R., *The Double Edged Sword: How Character Makes and Ruins Presidents, from Washington to Clinton*, Boulder, CO: Westview Press, 1998

Silverstein, J., *Burma: Military Rule and the Politics of Stagnation*, Ithaca: Cornell University Press, 1977

Skowronek, S., "Henry Jones Ford on the Development of American Institutions," *PS Political Science & Politics* 32(2) (June 1999), pp. 233–234

The Politics Presidents Make, Cambridge, MA: Belknap, 1993

The Politics Presidents Make: Leadership from John Adams to Bill Clinton, Cambridge, MA: Belknap, 1997

"Theory and History, Structure and Agency," *Presidential Studies Quarterly* 29(3) (September 1999), pp. 672–681

Smith, R. M., "Still Blowing in the Wind: The American Quest for a Democratic, Scientific Political Science," *Daedalus* 126(1) (Winter 1997), pp. 253–287

Sorensen, T. C., *The Kennedy Legacy*, New York: Macmillan, 1969

Sparks, A., *The Mind of South Africa*, Ballantine Books: New York, 1990

Tomorrow is Another Country, Cape Town: Struik, 1994

Spitzer, R. J., *President and Congress: Executive Hegemony at the Crossroads of Government*, Philadelphia: Temple University Press, 1993

Stam, A., *Win, Lose or Draw: Domestic Politics and the Crucible of War*, Ann Arbor: University of Michigan Press, 1996

Stark, W., *America, Ideal and Reality: The United States of 1776 in Contemporary European Philosophy*, London: K. Paul, Trench, Trubner, 1947

Stewart, T. A., *Intellectual Capital: The New Wealth of Organizations*, London: Nicholas Brealey, 1997

Stogdill, S., *Handbook of Leadership*, New York: Free Press, 1974

Strauss, L., *Liberalism Ancient and Modern*, New York: Basic Books, 1968

Susser, B., *The Grammar of Modern Ideology*, London: Routledge, 1988

Taylor, R., *The State in Burma*, Honolulu: University of Hawaii Press, 1987

Tiefer, C., *The Semi-Sovereign Presidency: The Bush Administration's Strategy for Governing without Congress*, Boulder, CO: Westview, 1994

Tournoux, J.-R., *Secrets d'Etat*, Paris: Plon, 1960

Trager, F. M., *Burma: From Kingdom to Republic: A Historical and Political Analysis*, New York: Praeger, 1966

Trollope, A., *North America*, New York: Alfred A. Knopf, 1951

Tulis, J. K., *The Rhetorical Presidency*, Princeton University Press, 1987

Vance, C., *Hard Choices*, New York: Simon & Schuster, 1983

VanDeMark, B., *Into the Quagmire: Lyndon Johnson and the Escalation of the Vietnam War*, New York: Oxford University Press, 1988

Viansson-Ponté, P., *Histoire de la République Gaullienne*, Paris: Fayard, 1970

Walker, M., *Clinton, The President They Deserve*, London: Vintage, 1997

Waterman, R. W. (ed.), *The Presidency Reconsidered*, Itasca, IL: F. E. Peacock, 1993

Weber, M., *Economy and Society*, New York: Bedminster Press, 1968 (originally published 1922)

"Science as a Vocation," in Gerth, H. H. and Mills, C. W. (eds.), *From Max Weber*, London: Routledge, 1970

Weinberg, A. K., *Manifest Destiny*, Baltimore: Johns Hopkins Press, 1935

Werth, A., *De Gaulle, A Political Biography*, New York, Simon & Schuster, 1965

France: 1940–1955, New York: Henry Holt, 1956

The de Gaulle Revolution, London: Robert Hale, 1960

White, R. and Lippitt, R., *Autocracy and Democracy: An Experimental Inquiry*, New York: Harper, 1960

White, T. H., *Breach of Faith: The Fall of Richard Nixon*, New York: Atheneum Press, 1975

Wildavsky, A., *The Beleaguered Presidency*, New Brunswick, NJ: Transaction, 1991

Williams, B., "Realism and Moralism in Political Theory," paper delivered to Law Society, Yale University, May 1997

Williams, W. A., *The Tragedy of American Diplomacy*, 2nd revised and enlarged edition, New York: Delta, 1978

Wills, G., "Lincoln's Greatest Speech?", *Atlantic Monthly* (September 1999) www.theatlantic.com/cgi-bin/o/issues/99sep/9909lincoln.htm

Reagan's America: Innocents at Home, New York: Doubleday, 1987

Win, K., *Daw Aung San Suu Kyi, the Nobel Laureate*, Bangkok: CDDSK, 1992

Wood, G. S., *The Creation of the American Republic*, Chapel Hill: University of North Carolina Press, 1969

Woodward, B., *Shadow: Five Presidents and the Legacy of Watergate*, New York: Simon & Schuster, 1999

Wright, J. S., *Lincoln and the Politics of Slavery*, Reno: University of Nevada Press, 1970

Yankelovich, D. and Kaagan, L., "Assertive America," *Foreign Affairs* 59 (1981), pp. 696–713

Zaller, J. R., "Monica Lewinsky's Contribution to Political Science," *PS Political Science & Politics* 31(2) (June 1998), pp. 182–189

Index

Adams, Gerry, 33
African National Congress (ANC), 115,
  118–145, 159,
  in exile, 121, 129, 131, 132
  National Executive Committee (NEC)
    of, 124, 137, 139, 141
  radical elements within, 123, 136, 139,
    140, 141–142
  complex relations with Mandela of, 119,
    120, 124, 129, 135–142
  resurgence of, 130–132
Agnew, Spiro, 216
Alexander, Neville, 134
American presidency, 3, 37, 43, 175–179,
    183–190, 200–201, 218, 250–253
  and Congress, 184–185, 188–189,
    205–206
  and containment policy, 182, 198, 204,
    213, 228, 229, 236
  control of US foreign policy by, 188–189,
    190, 205–206, 238, 247
  crisis of legitimacy in, 175, 190
  effects of McCarthyism on, 198,
    204–205
  "false promise" of, 188
  institutional moral capital of, 3, 41, 43,
    175–176, 177, 179, 183–187, 190, 217,
    251–253
  and the office of Independent Counsel,
    219
  "paradoxes" of, 187–188
  "personalization" of, 185
  popular representative function of, 184
  power and, 175, 180, 182, 183–184,
    186–188
  and the problem of trust, 176–177,
    219–222, 225, 242
  in the structure of American
    government, 183–184
  study of, 177–179
  weakness of, 188–189, 205, 216
  worthiness of the incumbent of, 186–187

Ang Chin Geok, 159n
Appleby, J., 192n
Appleman Williams, W., 192n, 193–194
Aquino, President Corazon, 32, 150, 165
Arendt, Hannah, 14n, 22nn, 256
Arnold, P.E., 179n,
Aris, M., 153, 155n, 156n, 157n, 163n,
    171n
Aristotle, 57, 174, 175n, 258
Asplund, R., 6n
Attlee, Prime Minister Clement, 151
Aung Gyi, 158
Aung San of Burma, 148, 149, 150–3, 170
  foundation of the Burmese Army
    (*Tatmadaw*) by, 151
  moral capital bequeathed by, 150,
    152–153, 163, 170
Aung San Oo, 152
Aung San Suu Kyi, 31, 42, 114–117,
    147–171
  Buddhism of, 154–156, 162
  character of, 159, 161–164
  compared to Mandela, 116–117, 154,
    159
  and democracy, 154–157, 164
  and the elections of 1990, 149, 158–159
  Gandhi's influence on, 154–157
  incarceration of, 158, 166
  leadership abilities of, 159
  likeness to her father of, 153
  moral capital of, 149–150, 153, 160, 161,
    165–167, 171
  and the National League for Democracy
    (NLD), 149, 157–160, 164, 165, 167
  political cause of, 154–157
  political policies of, 154, 164–165,
    168–169
  relationship to Burmese Army
    (*Tatmadaw*) of, 116, 149
  rhetorical ability of, 166–167
  symbolic status of, 162, 167
Aung Shwe, 159